A History of Spain and Portugal (1)

ALSO BY STANLEY G. PAYNE

Falange: A History of Spanish Fascism (1961)
Politics and the Military in Modern Spain (1967)
Franco's Spain (1967)
The Spanish Revolution (1970)

Stanley G. Payne

A HISTORY OF
Spain and Portugal

IN TWO VOLUMES (1)

The University of Wisconsin Press

Published 1973
The University of Wisconsin Press
Box 1379, Madison, Wisconsin 53701

The University of Wisconsin Press, Ltd.
70 Great Russell St., London

First printing

Printed in the United States of America
For LC CIP information see the colophon

ISBN 0-299-06270-8

For my son Michael

Contents

4)   Castile-León in the Era of the Great Reconquest   55

5)   The Rise of Aragón-Catalonia   85

6)   The Emergence of Portugal   113

7)   Medieval Hispanic Catholicism   131

8)   Castile and Aragón in the Late Middle Ages   141

Illustrations

Sixteenth-century galleons

Felipe II, by Sánchez Coello (El Prado)

Felipe IV

Carlos II, by Juan Carreño de Miranda (Hispanic Society, New York)

The Infante D. Henrique. Detail of the polyptic by Nuno Gonçalves

Vasco da Gama. Portrait in the collection of the Sociedade da Geografia

Afonso de Albuquerque, Viceroy of the Indies

Royal cloister in the great monastery at Batalha, in Manueline style

Manueline exterior of the Mosteiro dos Jerónimos, Lisbon

Sebastião

Maps

A physiographic map of the Iberian Peninsula will be found on the last two facing pages of the insert of illustrations

Tables

Genealogical Charts and Lists of Rulers

Preface

This work has been prepared in an attempt to meet the need for a reasonably full and up-to-date comprehensive history of Spain and Portugal. It has been conceived both for use as a textbook in courses on Spanish history and as an interpretive account for other readers. It is based on the most recent scholarly literature in the field, and brief bibliographies for each chapter are appended. This account deals with political and institutional history and with social and economic history, but does not attempt to treat literary and art history in any detail, for these are the only aspects of Hispanic affairs that are intensively studied outside the peninsula, while it is to remedy deficiencies in the treatment of the ordinary areas of Spanish and Portuguese history that the work was undertaken. Similarly, it does not deal in detail with the rise of the Spanish and Portuguese empires overseas, about which there is an abundant literature, particularly with regard to Spanish America.

I want especially to thank four people for their assistance: C. Julian Bishko, dean of Spanish historical studies in the United States, who read the first three-fifths of the manuscript with great care and saved me from many mistakes; Juan J. Linz, who has done so much to stimulate contemporary Spanish political and social studies and has greatly influenced my thinking about recent Spanish history; Thomas Glick, who read the entire manuscript and offered some important new insights; and my wife Julia, who made many suggestions about the preparation of the manuscript and assisted in a multitude of ways. Though they have not been able to rescue my work from all its shortcomings—for which of course I bear responsibility—I am extremely grateful to them.

Stanley G. Payne

Madison, Wisconsin
July 1972

A History of Spain and Portugal (1)

1

Ancient Hispania

The Hispanic peninsula lies at the extreme southwestern tip of Europe, in the direction of Africa and the outer Atlantic. It is partially separated from the rest of Europe by the Pyrenees and forms a geographic stepping stone between that continent and Africa. Despite its unique location, the peninsula does not form a fully unified geographic entity, for it is divided by steep internal mountain ranges and in some regions by virtual deserts. It is second only to Switzerland as the highest area in western Europe, the land rising rapidly from the narrow coastal lowlands to hill country. Save for the green belts that comprise the northern and northwestern fringes, it is a predominantly dry area, in most parts of which the rainfall scarcely exceeds fifteen inches a year. Though the peninsula contains mineral deposits of value, its soil has always been poor compared with that of most of western Europe. According to a classic categorization made in 1891, only 10 percent of the surface of the peninsula is genuinely fertile. Approximately 45 percent is moderately arable. Another 35 percent can be used for any sort of productive purpose only with difficulty, and 10 percent is totally useless.

Most formal histories of Spain devote considerable space to the peninsula's prehistory. During the past century some attention has been given to archaeology, and even more to hypothetical definitions of the various ethnic groups that inhabited the region before the

Roman conquest. A great deal of this remains speculation, for the
data unearthed by archaeological study in Spain is still rather scant,
and the origins, culture, and duration of pre-Roman ethnic groups are
for the most part poorly defined.

During the first millennium B.C. the peninsula was inhabited by a
complex variety of peoples, most of them organized into tribal
groups. There has been much controversy over the ethnic and geographic origins of the ancient inhabitants. In the early twentieth
century the "African" thesis was in vogue, postulating that the ancient Hispanic tribes were mainly the descendents of white migrants
from northwest Africa. More recent interpretations, however, have
stressed immigration and cultural influences from southern Europe
and the eastern Mediterranean. Conclusive proof for any single unified interpretation is lacking, but the weight of evidence now favors
the "Europeanist" interpretation. At any rate, in ancient times the
peoples of the peninsula were not radically distinct from but possessed many of the cultural characteristics of the population of other
parts of southern Europe and the Mediterranean littoral. The largest
single ethnic element were the Iberian tribes that moved into the
peninsula at some point during the second millennium B.C.—whether
from north Africa or southern Europe—and spread out over a broad
area. The first clearly definable group of immigrants from central or
northern Europe was a sizable wave of Celtic migrants who entered
the peninsula during the eighth and ninth centuries B.C.

It appears that the main ethnic and genetic components of the
historic Hispanic peoples were already present before the Roman
conquest, and that the great majority of subsequent "Spaniards" (or
"Portuguese") were descendents of the original highly diversified
ethnic stocks established in the pre-Roman period. Though the peninsula has been subject to invasion and very light immigration throughout its history, population movement at any time since the Roman
conquest was not heavy enough to alter the genetic or phenotypical
composition of the inhabitants significantly. The Romans described
members of most of the Hispanic tribes as rather short, dark-haired,
white-skinned, and physically agile, if not particularly muscular—
characteristics which would seem to describe modern as well as
ancient inhabitants of the peninsula.

Hispania, the name given by the Romans to the peninsula, was a
strictly geographic label without specific cultural or political connota-
tion. The peninsula had always been divided into geographic and
ethno-cultural regions which differed greatly from each other. The
most advanced of the ancient Hispanic communities was the kingdom of Tartessos in the south, covering roughly the modern region of
western Andalusia. When first encountered by Greek traders, Tartes-

sian society was centered in a number of fairly large cities and had a well-developed economy based on agriculture, cattle-raising, fishing, commerce, and mining. Its technology was comparatively sophisticated, as evidenced in its mining, shipbuilding, irrigation, and ox-drawn plows. The society was highly stratified, dominated by warrior and priestly castes and a small class of large landholders and wealthy merchants. Much of its land cultivation and cattle production was undertaken on the large estates owned by the upper classes, and the bulk of the population were peasants with few rights. In general, Tartessos was not greatly dissimilar to other relatively advanced urbanized societies of the Mediterranean. It was governed by a despotic monarchy legitimized by divine myth and thaumaturgy. The Tartessian state reached its maximum strength in the late seventh and early sixth centuries B.C., dominating the southern part of the peninsula and wielding influence in the affairs of the west Mediterranean. By the fifth century it had fallen under Carthaginian domination, whence it later passed to Roman rule.

The largest ethnic group in the peninsula, the Iberians, were strongly tribal and warlike, qualities characteristic of the population of ancient Hispania as a whole. The most advanced of the Iberians and the people to whom the name Iberian was originally given (the word was extended in Greek usage to refer to the peninsula) lived in communities on the eastern coast. The eastern Iberians were considerably influenced by Greek and Phoenician merchants and immigrant colonies, who contributed much to their culture and political organization. Their communities never formed a major state, as did Tartessos, but were organized in a variety of small city-states not dissimilar to the Greek. In the east as in the south, forms of monarchy prevailed. The Iberian alphabet in the east was one of two alphabets found in pre-Roman Hispania; the other was the Tartessian alphabet in the south. Rather similar in structure, they were both alphabetic and syllabic in form.

Ancient Hispanic societies were increasingly primitive and less politically and technologically advanced the farther they were from the south and east and the nearer to the north and west. The tribes of the southern part of the central plateau revealed a transitional pattern; they were partly urbanized and semiliterate but proportionately more rural and pastoral than their counterparts to the south and east. The central tribes were also more representative in political and social structure. Their larger towns were governed by a form of republican assembly dominated by a semiaristocratic oligarchy.

The northern and western groups were almost completely rural and illiterate and never formed organized states. The most distinctive ethnic community among them was that of the Basques of the west-

ern Pyrenees and adjacent foothills. The origin of the Basques is
shrouded in mystery. Whether or not they were indeed the original,
pre-Iberian inhabitants of the peninsula, as is sometimes conjectured,
their language—which has persisted in rural regions to this day—is
unique and non-Indo-European. Their society was familial and tribal,
and their economy, like that of most of the peninsular tribes, was
essentially pastoral. They remained comparatively secluded in their
hills until late Roman times.

Celtic immigration spread through much of the northern part of the
peninsula during the eighth and ninth centuries B.C. In the northern
sector of the central plateau and in the Duero valley in the interior of
the northwestern area the Celts fused with the earlier population to
form so-called Celtiberian communities. Some of these practiced
extensive agriculture along with raising flocks and herds, and in the
Duero valley tribal collectivist social patterns prevailed. In the northern hills of Asturias and the central Cantabrian range tribal life was
more primitive. There the original population were mostly immigrants
from southern France and northern Italy and were apparently taller
and more muscular than the average Iberian. Partly because of the
poorer soil, the economy of the northwest was largely pastoral, and
social patterns tended toward matriarchy, possibly from Celtic influence.

The west, called Lusitania by the Romans, is set apart from the
northern and central areas by watersheds. The Lusitanians had a
better-developed agrarian culture than was to be found elsewhere
save in the sophisticated south and east. More prosperous than the
groups of the center and north, their society was also more sharply
divided by class. During antiquity, this western area was largely
ignored by the outer world and by the advanced eastern and southern
cultures. It had few metals, the principal commercial attraction of the
peninsula.

The complete lack of political or cultural unity among the disparate
societies of the peninsula impeded rather than facilitated their conquest by Rome. The incorporation of Hispania into the empire was a
long, slow process, lasting from 218 B.C. to 19 B.C. (though the major
part was completed by 133 B.C.). This was a much longer time than
was required to subjugate other major portions of the Mediterranean
littoral. The fact also that it was highlighted by celebrated examples
of diehard resistance—the most famous of which was the struggle to
the death of the town of Numantia in 133 B.C.—has led some Spanish
historians to view the ancient Hispanic tribes as already "Spanish" in
their cultural characteristics, particularly in their xenophobia and
obstinate resistance to foreign domination. In fact, the relative difficulties encountered in subduing Hispania stemmed in part from the

very absence of any such coherent entity as "Spain" or an "Hispanic culture." Many of the tribes had to be conquered separately, one by one, whereas in more advanced or unified regions defeat of the central government was enough to bring the whole area under Roman sway. The cultural particularism of the Hispanic tribes, together with the formidable geographic obstacles imposed by the peninsula, are as important as Hispanic xenophobia in explaining the long delay in consummating the Roman conquest.

Yet the discovery of enduring characteristics common to prehistoric Hispania and historic Spain may not be entirely the product of the cultural imagination. Then, as later, the peninsula was a marginal area culturally as well as geographically, and participated only with some lag in the major developments of antiquity. Most of the peninsula's societies were economically and technologically backward compared with the advanced areas of Mediterranean civilization—a gap that for the most part was never fully made good in Spanish history. The ancient population of the peninsula was less urbanized and not merely more agrarian but more pastoral than the more sophisticated regions of Mediterranean Europe. The social structure was obviously more archaic, and in much of the peninsula dominated by a kind of military aristocracy. The emphasis was on military much more than on productive values. In some respects, these qualities of ancient Hispania paralleled those of most of the rest of the ancient Mediterranean world, but in Hispania they were more pronounced and were less challenged by alternate developments. Historically, the tendency in the peninsula toward such ways of life has been more widespread and persistent than elsewhere in Mediterranean and western Europe.

Moreover, there is some support for the notion that the rather baroque quality of Spanish esthetics was also characteristic of ancient times. In the more developed areas there was considerable emphasis on the gaudy and sumptuous. Much of the gold in the ancient Mediterranean came from the peninsula, which seems to have been the "El Dorado" of ancient times, and Hispanic gold ornaments were known throughout the ancient world. It has even been conjectured that the valuing of gold as a precious metal originated in the peninsula. Certainly the opportunity to obtain gold and other metals whetted Roman interest.

The Romans brought political unity and juridical norms to the peninsula for the first time. Endemic warfare and raiding between the pastoral tribes and the more settled communities was brought to an end. The Roman road system was extended throughout, unifying Hispanic communications. During the golden age of Roman Hispania—from the first to the third centuries A.D.—the entire peninsula was incorporated militarily and most of the population was incorporated culturally into the Roman world. Linguistic unity was slowly achieved as Latin-derived dialects replaced the former native languages, even among most of the common people. This process encountered the least resistance and went forward most rapidly in the more cosmopolitan south and east, where the upper classes, who controlled most of the land, often made common cause with the Romans. In other regions, tribal chiefs were brought into the Roman property system as latifundists.

There was extensive Roman immigration to the more developed eastern and southern areas of the peninsula. In other regions Roman culture was spread by administrators, educators, soldiers, merchants, and technicians. Sons of the Hispanic upper classes were sometimes sent to Rome for education. During the early part of the second century A.D. Rome was ruled by emperors of Hispano-Roman origin, and there were three more emperors from Hispania in the late fourth and early fifth centuries. Several important philosophers and writers of the empire, including Seneca and Lucan, came from the peninsula. Yet it should be noted that nearly all these major figures were the offspring of Roman officials and colonists living there, not of Romanized native Hispani.

Large numbers of Hispanic troops served in the Roman forces; the closing phases of the conquest of the peninsula itself had been carried out to a considerable degree by Hispanic auxiliaries from the conquered regions. Indeed, the majority of the "Roman" troops that besieged Numantia had been Hispanic auxiliaries. (But conversely, the loss of life in the Hispanic wars had been a major factor in decimating the old Roman citizen army and converting it into a professional mercenary force.) Hispanic warriors had served abroad as mercenaries under Carthage, and later fought under diverse foreign banners after the fall of Rome. Altogether, the peninsula was the major source of mercenaries in the Mediterranean for nearly two thousand years.

The vital centers of Roman Hispania were its flourishing cities, and the key unit of local administration, the *civitas,* combined both town and countryside in a single district organized around the city. The boundaries of the civitas were often based upon ancient Iberian or Celtiberian tribal districts but under the Roman system were geared to the social and economic needs of the urban centers. In 73 A.D. the right of Roman law and citizenship was apparently extended to nearly all Hispanic towns. During the first and second centuries there was a great expansion of urban wealth and a fairly strong Hispanic urban middle class was formed. During the troubled final centuries of the empire the Hispanic cities seem to have been somewhat more orderly than those of the eastern part of the Roman world, and economic decline from the third century on apparently affected Hispania proportionately rather less than certain other regions of the empire, including the most advanced and prosperous sectors. Roman capital dominated commerce, in which Hispania played an essentially colonial role. Hispanic metals, especially gold, and Hispanic wool were imported by Rome in great volume. The peninsula also shipped large quantities of the three Mediterranean food staples, grain, olive oil, and wine, to Rome. By the fourth century, Hispania had begun to rival Egypt as the empire's most important granary and continued to sustain a considerable volume of Mediterranean commerce as late as the fifth century.

Under Roman rule much of the countryside was transformed. Extensive irrigation projects were completed and the area under cultivation greatly expanded. Yet despite extension of the latifundia system, a sizable proportion of the cultivated area was evidently exploited as small, individual properties during the first part of the Roman period, partly as a result of the Roman breakup of collective and communal patterns in the north-center and west. Moreover, Roman reorganization and expansion of agriculture relocated and stabilized part of the tribal population in the north and west, bringing the people down from the hills and settling them on small farming plots. In general, the concentration of land in large latifundia was not as extensive as in Italy or Gaul until the second or third centuries.

At its height Roman Hispania may have had a population of five million or more. This was concentrated particularly in the more urban south and east but was also fairly dense in the south-central region, in Lusitania, and in parts of the northwest. Yet the Romanization of the peninsula was far from complete. Much of the north and northwest was influenced little by Roman life. Resistance was always strongest among the more primitive, warlike tribes of the Cantabrian mountain range in the far north. A somewhat tenuous military dominion was maintained, but even at the height of the empire there were only a few Roman towns in the far north. The Basques offered less direct military resistance but remained even more impervious to cultural assimilation.

Christianity spread through Roman Hispania during the second and third centuries. There, as elsewhere, it was a predominantly urban religion. Large portions of the countryside remained for a long time almost untouched, as did most of Cantabria and almost all the Basque region. By the beginning of the fourth century, however, Hispania apparently had a Christian minority at least as large proportionately as that of the empire as a whole—upwards of 10 percent. After the official recognition of the church early in the fourth century, its following greatly increased, until almost the entire peninsula had become Christian. The pattern of Hispanic church organization was similar to that of most other parts of the empire: bishoprics became coterminous with the urban-centered civitas units and archepiscopal sees were established in provincial capitals. By the fifth century there had developed a distinctively Hispanic church, whose individual religious culture was most evident in the use of the special Hispanic rite (later inaccurately called the Mozarabic rite) in its services until the eleventh century. Theologically the Hispanic church was orthodox Catholic, though the Priscillian heresy of the late fourth century originated in Galicia (the northwestern corner of the peninsula) and Donatism was temporarily widespread in the fifth century. Yet the orthodox Hispano-Catholic church became increasingly strong and well organized, and provided spiritual and cultural leadership and identity which a faltering imperial government could no longer offer.

Hispania could not escape the general effects of the Roman social and economic decline from the third century on. If at first the economic decline seemed less severe than in parts of Gaul and northern Italy, this was because Hispanic agriculture had never developed to as high a level and because, aside from the barbarian devastation of 264-276, it did not at first suffer as much from the Germanic incursions.

The social changes that took place in the Hispanic countryside paralleled those of the rest of the empire. Latifundia increased in size and the pressure against small farmers and shepherds mounted. Inflation, taxes, warfare, and the drop in commerce produced great unrest, climaxed by sporadic peasant revolts in parts of Gaul and Hispania during the fourth and fifth centuries. Several efforts at land reform were made by the imperial administration in Hispania to protect and encourage small farmers, mainly in the central plateau, but institutional weakness and uncertain economic conditions frustrated these attempts. By the fourth century a significant minority of the peninsula's population lived as enserfed coloni on great estates, seeking shelter from the want and violence which the decline of imperial order and prosperity had left behind. Moreover, free peasants tended increasingly to place their land and labor at the service and the protection of large landlords by clientage relations known as *commendatio* and *patrocinium*.

The dissolution of Roman authority and its replacement by that of a Visigothic monarchy was a long, slow process. There was no sudden Visigothic invasion or conquest. The small host of the Visigothic ruler Ataulf that crossed the Pyrenees into Hispania in 415 acted as a federated army of the feeble Roman state, charged with expelling Vandal invaders from southern Hispania and subduing the Germanic

Suevi who had dominated the northwestern quarter of the peninsula for several years. From their principal base in southwestern France, Visigothic bands slowly began to extend their control over the more lightly inhabited central plateau of the peninsula, sometimes acting in the name of the emperor, sometimes merely advancing their own interests. The imperial government had broken down and the Hispanic population lacked the civil or military means to defend itself. The main body of Visigoths did not enter the peninsula until the reign of Alaric II (484-507), and then largely as a result of military pressure from the Franks to the north. They may have numbered no more than 300,000 in a peninsula with 4,000,000 inhabitants. The Visigoths were superior to the Hispani only in the application of armed force; economically, socially, and culturally the Hispanic population was in most regions far more advanced.

Though before their entry into the peninsula the Visigoths were culturally more Romanized than any other Germanic group, they were an essentially pastoral people, unlike the Ostrogoths and Suevi, whose societies were agrarian. The Visigoths settled in greatest numbers in the more sparsely populated, largely pastoral north-central area of the peninsula, and were thereby isolated from the main social and economic centers of the Hispanic population.

The Visigothic monarchy as an independent state was first proclaimed by Euric in southwestern France in 476, after the deposition of the last emperor in Rome by the Ostrogoths. The political center of the monarchy was not moved to the peninsula, however, until the reign of Athanagild (551-567), when a new capital was established at the town of Toledo in the central plateau, moving the axis of Hispanic life from the coastal regions for the first time. Visigothic authority was slowly expanded throughout the entire peninsula with the conquest of the Suevi during the reign of Leovigild (568-586) and the expulsion of Byzantine forces from their last remaining toehold in the southeast by Swinthila (621-631).

Like other post-Roman rulers in different parts of the former empire, the Visigothic kings of Hispania considered themselves the heirs of Rome and adopted Roman insignia and symbols of authority. They viewed themselves as successors, rather than destroyers or even replacers, of the empire. The Visigothic monarchy accepted the Roman theory of the state as a public power resting upon essentially absolute authority, though the official conversion to Catholicism that occurred during the reign of Leovigild accepted a modification of royal sovereignty by the religious and ethical tutelage of the church.

At the top of Hispano-Visigothic society there emerged an elite of some two hundred leading aristocratic families associated with the court and a broader aristocratic class of perhaps ten thousand people who held possession of most of the best land. Under the Visigoths, the aristocracy did not form a closed caste but were steadily recruited from below on the strength of personal achievement or royal favor. Over a period of a century or more there occurred a partial fusion of the original Visigothic warrior aristocracy and the socioeconomic elite of Hispanic society.

The Visigothic monarchy remained an elective institution, each new king nominally chosen or ratified by the aristocracy. The crown was assisted in decisions and administration by an *aula regia* or royal council, but until the next to the last generation of Visigothic rule broad assemblies of notables were called to ratify important decisions, a last residue of the earlier tribal assemblies of the Germanic peoples. Administratively, the Visigothic monarchy relied on much of Roman usage and employed Hispanic personnel in local administration. By the sixth century, however, the Roman administrative system had fallen into such decay that it could not be revived, and in place of the old provincial system there evolved a new pattern of regional and local overlordship based upon regional dukes (*duces*) and heads of smaller districts or *territoria* called counts (*comes*). The new ducal administrative regions tended to coincide with the old Roman provinces, and the territoria of the counts with the old civitas units. The old municipal system also fell into desuetude and was slowly replaced by a pattern of royal administration and local overlords nominally ratified by the crown. Most of the Hispanic population remained juridically free, but the process of commendatio continued, as peasants pledged parts of their land or services to local overlords for security, and the class of enserfed coloni grew larger. Yet there were still a number of relatively autonomous local rural communities that preserved their legal identity.

The cultural and economic life of Visigothic Hispania was carried on almost exclusively by the native Hispani, to whom was due the relative prosperity of part of the sixth and seventh centuries. Roman law had to be relied upon in administering the affairs of the social and economic infrastructure, and over a period of two centuries there evolved a slow fusion of Visigothic custom and Roman common law. The general trend was away from the Roman system of explicit private property toward more communal, reciprocal, usufructural relations in the ownership and use of property. The Hispano-Visigothic modus vivendi found codified expression in the promulgation of the *Liber Iudiciorum* (later commonly known in Castilian as the *Fuero Juzgo*) in 654. This fusion of aspects of Visigothic personal codes with Latin civil and property law superseded several less complete codifications and provided an organized code on which to base property rights and civil administration for the Visigothic aristocracy and, to some extent, the Hispanic common people.

It has sometimes been maintained that under the Visigothic monarchy a mode of theocracy developed that thereafter characterized Hispanic religion and government. Such a notion is considerably exaggerated. Even during the Arian period of the Visigothic monarchy, when a great theological gulf existed between the rulers and organized Christianity, the Hispanic bishops proved themselves to be obedient to legally established authority. They rarely hesitated to uphold the power of the state in the secular realm, even to the extent of supporting one Arian king against his rebellious (but orthodox Catholic) son. When finally the monarchy accepted Catholicism in 589, it was made clear that this conversion was not forced upon the state by the church but was freely decided upon by the monarchy to promote its own interests. The church lost a significant measure of independence by recognizing the right of the crown to appoint the members of the ecclesiastical hierarchy. The king became the nominal head of church councils and took a formal responsibility to see that church affairs were properly run. The subsequent Councils of Toledo were organized along more or less Byzantine lines as mixed assemblies of high ecclesiastical and state officials, with the clerics responsible for church affairs and the secular officials bearing primary responsibility for state legislation.

Thus rather than theocracy there developed a church-state symbiosis in which the power of the crown was uppermost but in which the church played a major role in trying to stabilize public institutions and authority. After the Fourth Council of Toledo in 633, approval by the councils was required to legalize succession to the nonhereditary Visigothic throne, anathematize usurpers, and ratify amnesties. Church leaders were increasingly employed by the crown in administration because they were the primary source of educated, technically competent, and trustworthy personnel. Yet the crown did not intervene in the theological affairs of the church; religious councils were presided over by an archbishop, not the king. The Christian church became the only cohesive institution in Visigothic Hispania.

The early Hispanic church reached its cultural height during the era of Isidore of Seville (first third of the seventh century), shining briefly as the brightest center of learning in western Europe. For the common people it provided the only identity and hope which they knew during this period. Hispanic monasteries played a special role, becoming quite numerous, and the most active force in raising spiritual standards, expanding the influence of the church, and providing a spiritual leadership for the church.

Toward the end of the Visigothic period the church had become a major property holder, with almost every parish and monastery of note possessing lands or rights that provided it with income. The church had achieved a special legal status, developing a code of canon law and special tribunals for the clergy and their affairs. The Hispanic church thus came to constitute a fairly well ordered state of its own within the poorly structured Visigothic political framework.

Yet despite its outwardly imposing strength, the Hispanic church failed to incorporate all the population of the peninsula within its following even as late as the seventh century. The peoples of the northern hills remained vague in their religious identification, while the Basques were almost untouched by Christianity. Even among the more densely inhabited southern and eastern districts, conversion of much of the rural population remained nominal at best. Hispanic Christianity was still to a considerable degree an urban religion, and tended to become weaker the farther one moved from the principal centers of population.

This was the more significant because it may be roughly generalized that throughout the Visigothic era the urban economy and society of southern and eastern Hispania continued to decline. The failure of administration, which the Visigothic crown was unable to restore, the absence of monetary order, progressive disruption of trade routes, and the decline of economic opportunities all continued even after the disorders of the fifth and sixth centuries had ended. The rise of Muslim power in the east Mediterranean during the seventh century presaged new commercial and military challenges. By that time Hispanic urban society had lost most of the vigor and prosperity that it had known during the high Roman period.

Even at its height, Roman rule had been unable to eliminate the strong regional and ethnic differences that divided the peninsula, and these became more pronounced again under the Visigoths. Fusion between the Visigothic elite and the Hispani population was never complete. The northwestern corner of the peninsula, ruled for two hundred years by the Suevi monarchy, remained a distinctive, not thoroughly assimilated region. The southwestern tip of France, known as Septimania, remained under Visigothic rule and tended to link northeastern Hispania with France. The sophisticated eastern coastal region had long been interconnected with the commerce and culture of the Italian peninsula, while the equally sophisticated towns of the south were closely associated with northwest Africa and with Byzantine commerce. In the far north, Asturians and Cantabrians were at best only partly assimilated, and the Basques remained almost entirely apart. Finally, there was a significant Jewish minority in the southern and eastern towns that played a major role in manufacturing and commerce. Subjected to attempted conversion and sporadic persecution by the Visigothic crown in the seventh century, Hispanic Jews were a politically disaffected and potentially rebellious element in the major towns.

The Visigothic monarchy never developed a cohesive polity. Visigothic aristocrats and military leaders deemed themselves part of a personal power association with the crown and resisted extension of juridical control. Royal succession remained elective, and the entire history of the monarchy was one of revolt, assassination, and internecine feuding. This insecurity placed a premium on military power, but the monarchy could not marshal resources to restore the independent standing army of Rome. Instead, a process of protofeudalization developed early and was expanded more rapidly in Visigothic Hispania than in Merovingian France. Decentralization was unavoidable, and power became a matter of personal relationship and example. The chief lieutenants of the crown were rewarded for their services by salaries or *stipendia* in the form of overlordship of land or temporary assignment of income from land held *in precarium,* that is, on a nominally revocable basis. This system was actually first used by the church to support local establishments, and by the seventh century was widely employed by the crown and also by the *magnates* (the high aristocracy) to pay their chief supporters and military retainers. The process of protofeudalization inevitably carried with it a splintering of juridical and economic sovereignty that further weakened political unity.

If the Visigothic aristocracy was unable to develop a unified, viable political system, it was nevertheless itself the beginning of the historic Hispanic master class. In this Visigothic caste the military aristocracy of the peninsula had its roots, creating a style and a psychology of the warrior nobleman that provided the dominant leadership for Hispanic society for more than a thousand years; this psychology ultimately managed to superimpose its values and attitudes on much of the society as a whole. Yet the success of the aristocratic ethos was a consequence of the experience of medieval Hispania, not of the rule of the Visigothic oligarchy, which largely proved an historic failure.

In the seventh century the caste relationship between the ruling group and much of the peasantry was little better than that of master to serf. A large proportion of the peasantry had been reduced to a kind of serfdom, and as the economy declined, economic exactions very likely increased. Evidence indicates that many Hispanic serfs and even many free peasants did not consider the protection and leadership they received worth the service demanded of them. During the last Visigothic century there were a number of peasant revolts and urban riots in protest against economic conditions.

In sum, the political and social structure of Visigothic Hispania was brittle and incohesive. It survived only until the first major challenge from without, then collapsed much more rapidly than it had been built.

2

Al-Andalus

It is difficult to determine in detail exactly what happened in Hispania during the crucial years after 700, for little direct source material has survived. Though the Visigothic aristocracy had achieved a degree of fusion with Hispanic society and had secured its dominance as a warrior caste, much of it was corrupted by wealth and power and it had at best a very feeble sense of political legitimacy. The Visigothic monarchy had failed to build stable institutions, successful means for transmitting power, or a stable and loyal elite behind the throne. Strife between rival pretenders and their supporters persisted throughout the history of Visigothic Hispania. Leovigild, the strongest of its rulers, had himself to face a five-year revolt by his son. Ratification of the elective, as opposed to the hereditary, right by the councils of Toledo in the seventh century sustained Visigothic law but guaranteed endemic civil war. It was not uncommon for factions to accept and encourage foreign intervention on their behalf. In part because of this, Byzantium had been able to control much of southern Hispania for approximately seventy years, from the mid-sixth century down to the third decade of the seventh century, and the Frankish monarchy intervened actively on several occasions in the seventh century. The quick and easy Muslim takeover is understandable only in terms of this persistent failure of political institutions, the accepted custom of foreign intervention, and the apathy or submissiveness of most of the

Hispanic lower classes, accustomed to nearly a millennium of rule by outsiders, first by the Romans, then by the Visigoths.

During the latter part of the seventh century the main antagonism was between the descendents of Chindaswinth (642-653) and those of a subsequent ruler, Witiza (702-710). Supporters of Witiza's clan refused to accept the election of a rival candidate, Roderic, in 710, and sought assistance from the newly established Muslim overlords of North Africa. The Visigothic dissidents obviously failed to appreciate the dynamism and integrative potential of the Islamic culture that had swept out of Arabia only a few generations earlier. Their miscalculation was probably due in part to the considerable difficulty encountered by the Muslims in subduing the Berber Kabyles of the Maghreb during the preceding half-century. The latter, like the Hispanic tribes confronting the Romans, had put up a more determined resistance than had most of the more civilized regions farther east. The conquest of the Maghreb had taken nearly forty years, and was nominally completed only in 705-710.

After a small exploratory raid, the Muslim commander of Tangier, Tariq, led a force of perhaps no more than 12,000 men, mostly Berbers from northern Morocco, across the straits in 711. Their goals were apparently ambiguous at first. The intervention was organized at the behest of the Witizan clan; the invaders probably hoped at the least to win booty and to exert some degree of Muslim influence in Hispania, possibly to make it a client state of the Arab caliphate. However, discovery of the hollowness of Visigothic power, both crown and oligarchy, coupled with a swift and decisive victory, expanded Muslim ambition. At that moment Roderic was engaged in trying to subdue Basque and Visigothic rebels in the northeast. He hurriedly marched south, where the invaders awaited him in July 711 at the Guadalete, a small stream in the extreme southern tip of Spain. There the Witizans arranged the withdrawal of the bulk of Roderic's forces; the outnumbered remainder resisted stubbornly but were destroyed. Roderic was killed, and the remnants of his army were shattered near Ecija, where they made a desperate attempt to bar the road to the north. Córdoba, demoralized and almost undefended, was quickly taken. Roderic's supporters in the Visigothic capital, Toledo, were then overthrown by the Witizans, who opened the gates to Tariq.

Civil war was at first even more debilitating to the Visigothic kingdom than the foreign invasion. By 712 the kingdom lay divided and virtually leaderless, its central military elite destroyed. Consequently the Arab governor of northwest Africa, Musa ibn Nusair, personally led a force larger than the first, some 18,000—a high proportion of them the best Arab warriors—in the second wave of invasion. Muslim armies had perfected a swift, flexible, hard-hitting style of battle that proved extremely difficult for Visigothic levies to cope with. Seville, the largest city in the peninsula and center of Hispano-Roman culture, fell easily after a short siege. The remaining elements of the Roderician faction withdrew to Mérida, which withstood a long siege but finally fell on June 30, 713. Much of the Visigothic aristocracy resisted little or not at all. Theodemir, duke of the Cartagena district in the southeast, made a treaty allowing him to retain control of his territory so long as the inhabitants paid regular taxes to the Muslim command. The spring and summer of 714 were then devoted to subduing the heavily populated northeast. Zaragoza was conquered and many of its aristocrats put to the sword. Nearly all the territory northeast of Zaragoza was rendered tributary, after which the main Muslim column apparently marched westward across north-central Hispania before returning southward.

The Muslim "conquest" took only three years, but the Muslims in fact made no effort to conquer and occupy the entire peninsula. That would have been impossible for an army of no more than 30,000 to 40,000 men. They occupied directly only the main strongholds of south-central and northeastern Hispania, the old centers of Roman civilization. The old Suevic district in Portucale to the west and Galicia to the northwest were rendered tributary but not occupied. The Witizan clan served as clients of the Muslims, who could in a sense present themselves as the protagonists of a legitimist cause. During the first generation of occupation, three thousand estates from the royal domain were bestowed on the Witizans.

The Muslims were concerned first with booty and secondly with the prosecution of the jihad—the holy war to extend Islamic dominion ever farther afield. By 720 an expedition had crossed the Pyrenees and seized Narbonne, and this was followed for the next twenty years by intermittent onslaughts into France. Conquest beyond the Pyrenees was the major new concern of the overlords of "Al-Andalus" (literally "land of the Vandals"), as the Muslims called their new peninsular domain. Between 721 and 732 three governors of Al-Andalus were killed leading expeditions into France, the last expedition culminating in a major defeat by the Frankish army at Poitiers in 732. This did not put an end to the Muslim offensives, however, for the Muslims were further encouraged by internal strife in southern France. The Gallo-Roman inhabitants of Provence stubbornly resisted domination by the Frankish monarchy to the north and summoned Muslim forces to their aid in 735. Two expeditions were dispatched into Provence during the next three years, but the expansion of Frankish military power threw the Muslims on the defensive, and they were barely able to retain a foothold in Septimania immediately northeast of the Pyrenees.

The relative ease with which Muslim domination was established over most of the peninsula can be explained by the fact that only some of the Visigoths resisted, and almost none of the rest of the population. Religious antagonism caused surprisingly little difficulty. Early Islam, despite its emphasis on the jihad, was comparatively tolerant of Christians and Jews as "peoples of the book." Moreover, there was little sense of racial antipathy; the majority of the first wave of invaders were not even Arabs, but Berbers who differed little in appearance from the Hispanic people. Some of these Berbers were themselves not yet fully assimilated into Islam. (For that matter, the Berbers of northwest Africa were not effectively converted until after the adoption of the local Kharijite doctrines in the eighth century.)

The Muslim invaders were greedy for land and booty, but the main targets of their rapaciousness were the Visigothic aristocrats who resisted them. To most of the population the conquest was represented as a liberation. Christians were promised free practice of their religion and in some cases greater social and economic justice as well. The rights of the minority of Hispanic smallholders were apparently respected. Though Christians were required to pay a special tribute, it was at first modest. In all, exactions were perhaps no greater than under the Visigoths. For more than a century, the Christians in the towns were permitted to live a semi-autonomous local existence, and in some cases shared their churches with Islamic worshippers.

People began to accept conversion to Islam almost immediately, in large numbers. The process went forward most rapidly in the population centers of the south and east, and in the meantime practically all the collaborationists among the Visigothic aristocracy embraced the Muslim religion. It is sometimes alleged that the rapid and comparatively facile Islamization of most of the peninsula was the result of the corruption and inattentiveness of the Hispanic church and the lack of piety and orthodoxy among the Visigothic aristocracy. In fact, it is difficult to demonstrate that the Hispanic church was significantly weaker than others of Latin Christendom or that the Visigothic nobles were appreciably less religious than their Frankish counterparts. Rather, Islamization probably stemmed primarily from the complete military and political defeat of the Catholic Visigothic state and from the prestige of the dynamic Muslim empire and its all-conquering armies. At first Islamic overlords did not encourage mass conversion, because it reduced the number of non-Muslims who paid heavier taxes, but once the Muslim authorities were firmly established in power many Christians converted simply to be on the dominant side, escape special taxes, and gain greater economic opportunity. It has also been suggested that a portion of the enserfed sector of the peasantry accepted Islam to be freed of their servitude. Moreover, it is doubtful that many ordinary people perceived the great religious gulf between Christianity and Islam that has subsequently been taken for granted. Rather than as the antithesis to Christianity, many probably saw it as a mere variant of simplification. Finally, according to a later claim of Muslim chroniclers, some Visigothic aristocrats were attracted by the opportunity under Islamic law for polygamy and legal concubinage.

The third religious group in the peninsula, the Jews, who may have numbered 2 or 3 percent of the population, eagerly collaborated with the Muslims. Hispanic Jews had achieved considerable wealth under the Visigoths but were subjected to intermittent persecution. Muslim rule promised greater freedom and security. Jews sometimes assisted the Muslims, and a detachment of Jewish soldiers (perhaps related to Hispano-Jews exiled to the Maghreb) accompanied the invaders. Several important cities were given to Jewish leaders to govern temporarily after the Muslims took over. During the next three centuries Jewish financial and cultural influence expanded in southern and south-central Hispania. Because of their unique position, and also because of their linguistic skills, Jews served for generations as mediators between sectors of the Muslim and Christian populations.

The Arabs, who formed a minority among the mostly Berber invaders, assumed the place of privilege from the beginning and began to set themselves up as a landed Muslim neo-aristocracy. Urban life in the peninsula, too, attracted many. Entering at a higher cultural level than had the Visigoths three centuries earlier, they formed an urban elite, and though at first only a small minority in the Hispano-Christian cities, sank deeper cultural and economic roots and helped expand the influence of Islam in the cities rapidly. The Berber warriors, the rank and file of the invaders, tended to be shunted toward the less productive highlands. Many were settled on territory seized from or abandoned by the Visigoths in the northwest-central region.

The destruction of the Visigothic system of state and society was one thing, and the building of a Muslim Hispania something else that was much more difficult and took more time—indeed, nearly two centuries. After the Visigothic collapse there was a tendency for the inhabitants of various parts of the peninsula to revert to the regionalism and localism characteristic of an earlier era. Muslim power advanced too far too fast to combine all these territories into a well-ordered system. The Arab clan leaders who formed the core of the new oligarchy quickly fell out with each other, and the heads of the caliphate in faraway Damascus revealed concern about maintaining control of their most distant dominion. The first official governor of Muslim Hispania, Abdul Aziz (who incidentally married Roderic's widow), was murdered by rivals in 716. During the four decades 715–755 there were approximately twenty different governors, many of them assassinated and only three retaining office as long as five years.

In addition to feuds between Arab clans and factions, a broad ethnic split emerged between the Arab aristocrats and the Berber population. By 740 a major rebellion was underway across the straits in the Maghreb, where the Berbers were adopting Kharijism, a new, heretical form of Islam that accompanied protest against Arab domination of the Muslim empire. The revolt spread to the Berbers settled in the northwest-central part of the peninsula. They marched against the urban-associated Arab aristocracy in south-central and southern Hispania, outnumbering them, for the Arabs could not depend upon their new Christian subjects to fight for them. It may be that only the arrival of some 7,000 Syrian cavalry saved the aristocracy. During the 740s, the new polity in the peninsula virtually dissolved. The spectacle of general Muslim civil war did not encourage Hispanic loyalty, and small elements of the Christian population took advantage of this opportunity to migrate to the unoccupied northern mountains, whence border warfare had been waged since 718. After 750, crop failures and raiding brought widespread famine to the Berber-inhabited Duero valley of the northwest, forcing the remainder of the invaders to withdraw farther south. When political order was finally

Rulers of Al-Andalus	
Abd-al-Rahman I	756– 788
Hisham I	788– 796
al-Hakam I	796– 822
Abd-al-Rahman II	822– 852
Muhammad I	852– 886
al-Mundhir	886– 888
Abdallah	888– 912
Abd-al-Rahman III	912– 961
al-Hakam II	961– 976
Hisham II	976–1009
Amirid dictators:	
al-Mansur	c.976–1002
Abdul-Malik	1002–1008
Taifa kings	1009–1090
Almoravid empire	1090–1147
Almohad empire	1147–1212

restored and the Berbers brought under control, the Duero valley south of the Asturian and Cantabrian hills had been evacuated, leaving a no-man's-land fought over by northern Christians and Muslims for the next two centuries.

Unified government in Muslim Hispania was finally achieved after 755 by its first independent ruler, Abd-al-Rahman I (756-788), last surviving heir of the traditional Muslim Umayyad dynasty in Damascus after it had been deposed by the rival Abbasid dynasty. In flight from the Near East, Abd-al-Rahman, whose mother was a Berber, sought to regain an independent kingdom at the far western end of the Muslim world. Arriving in the peninsula in 755, he won the support not only of the Berbers but also of the strongest Arab faction, enabling him to overthrow the forces of the erstwhile governor outside Córdoba, the Hispano-Muslim capital since 719. There Abd-al-Rahman announced the establishment of an independent Umayyad emirate based on "true justice" and toleration for all religions and ethnic groups. This stand greatly strengthened his position among the heterogeneous population of the peninsula. He was eventually recognized as heir of the legitimate dynasty by nearly all regions save the independent Christian hill country of the far north, but years of intermittent campaigning were required to subdue dissident Muslim regional overlords.

Little effort was made to conquer and occupy the northern mountain areas, because of difficult geographic obstacles, the poverty of those regions, and the resistance of their inhabitants. Instead, three frontier districts or marches were established to hold the border, and the emirate adopted or accepted a variant of west European feudalism in dealing with the frontier areas. The key spots were mountains, castles, or fortified towns difficult to incorporate into a central system. Loose personal relations akin to vassalage were worked out with Muslim and at times with Christian overlords in the frontier area. This meant an uneven border and an incomplete political system on the Christian fringe, but the offensive military strength and the economic resources of the northern Christian hill people did not seem great enough to warrant the expenditure of means that would have been required to subdue those harsh, backward regions.

It is impossible to calculate the number of immigrants who entered the peninsula during the three centuries of the emirate. All told they may have accounted for the ancestry of 20 percent of the peninsula's population by the end of the tenth century, yet the influx in most years was quite small. Moreover, the bulk of the immigrants were not oriental Arabs but Maghrebian Berbers. The prosperous, increasingly cultured Al-Andalus must have looked very attractive to the rude tribesmen across the straits. But the more cultured Arabs tended to monopolize the most important lands, posts, and perquisites, and relations with the Berbers and other elements were never very good. Muslim Hispania never achieved a fully homogeneous society. Descendents of Arabs jealously preserved their family and tribal identities, together with a distinct sense of superiority to the rest of the Muslim population. Many of the Berber immigrants did not at first speak Arabic and for some time retained their separate community identity. The majority of the Muslims were of course descendants of Hispanic converts and never managed to absorb fully the aristocratic Arab elements; rather, upper-class Hispano-Muslim *muwalladun* (or *muladíes*, as converts to Islam were later known in Castilian) later came to affect Arab ancestry or names for themselves. Interethnic tensions persisted throughout the history of Al-Andalus. They probably lay at the root of continuing internal political conflicts that were only temporarily assuaged, never eliminated.

The emirate was nevertheless free of such strong anti-Arab outbursts as occurred among the native Muslim populace of Iraq and Iran during those centuries. Abd-al-Rahman I encouraged the settling of Arab aristocrats directly on the land, overseeing the cultivation of estates, and by the tenth century the gap between the Muslim aristocrats and the *muladí* peasants was apparently not as great as that which had existed in much of the former Hispano-Visigothic society.

An Islamic culture in the peninsula developed with surprising rapidity. Though the first generation of Muslims had been relatively uncultured and had a rather weak grasp of Islamic theology, religious teachers arrived from the Near East soon after the conquest, and their numbers increased during the course of the eighth century. The roots of a genuine Muslim orthodoxy were established, in response to the problem of cultural heterogeneity and the challenge to the identity of the convert. Within three or four generations, Hispanic Islam was strongly identified with the Malikite rite. The religious teacher Malik (who died in Medina ca. 795) had propounded a rather simple and traditionalistic understanding of Islam, based on the formula of "the Koran, the words of the Prophet, and admitting that otherwise I do not know." The antirationalist conservatism of the Malikite rite was adopted as the semi-official observance of Muslims in the emirate during the reign of al-Hakam I (796-822). Malikite traditionalism, as propounded by local *faqihs* (jurists) throughout Al-Andalus, provided a degree of cultural unity for most of the Muslim population. Ultra-orthodoxy was characteristic of Islam in the peninsula throughout almost the entire Muslim period, and contrasted notably with the greater tendency toward heterodoxy in other parts of the Muslim world. This may perhaps be explained by the peripheral location of Al-Andalus at the outer limit of Islamic lands, adjacent to Latin Christendom, containing a Christian minority (at first a Christian majority), and usually in a state of tension with its religious and cultural rival. It is interesting, too, that during the Middle Ages western Christianity also emphasized pragmatic legalism, ethics, and orthodoxy in contrast with the more speculative metaphysics of the Christian east.

A wave of major "orientalization" began during the reign of Abd-al-Rahman II (822-852), who imported numerous oriental Muslim artists and educators. The high culture of the Middle East elicited a strongly eastward-looking orientation; though a few individual Hispano-Muslim art forms were developed by the tenth century (the *muwashaha* and *zéjel* songs and poems), the art and literature of Al-Andalus was established almost completely on oriental Arabic forms.

Christian society in the south and east was completely unable to hold its own. The independent Christians of the north came to call their counterparts in the south *Mozarabs,* derived from the Arabic *musta'rib,* meaning Arabized or Arabic-speaking. Mozarab culture became fossilized, its postconquest literature for example rhetorical and usually mediocre, deficient in dialectic and analysis. Of course it must be recognized that Mozarab culture was placed under increasing pressure and not able to develop in full freedom. Limited tolerance never meant equality, and Christians were never permitted to dispute publicly the teachings of Islam. Religious practice and cultural opportunity were increasingly circumscribed. It is true that some towns had Christian majorities for a century or more, that most Mozarab dioceses were able to continue an uninterrupted line of episcopal succession for nearly three hundred years, that all-Mozarab church councils were occasionally called, and that some religious and cultural contacts were maintained with other parts of western Christendom. Nonetheless, the strength and influence of Islam was increasingly felt. From about the beginning of the ninth century pressure mounted; taxes were raised and new restrictions were introduced, while the Muslim proportion of society steadily increased. One response to latent and then mounting persecution was the Christian "martyrs of Córdoba" movement of 850-859 in the course of which several score Christian spokesmen, confronting Islam directly, were put to death. A more common response was Mozarab emigration to the Christian principalities in the northern mountains. The Muslim state did not embark on a policy of extreme persecution until late in the tenth century, however, and the Mozarab minority persisted, in ever-dwindling numbers, until almost the end of Al-Andalus.

The growing strength and sophistication of Hispano-Muslim society was not reflected by political unity, for the ninth century was a time of political troubles for the emirate. Resentment among both Christians and Hispano-Muslims increased: against the overlordship of Córdoba by Muslims in other regions, against exclusivist Arab clans on the part of non-Arab Muslims, and against supposedly heterodox emirs by fanatical Malikite faqihs. A major revolt occurred among the lower classes of Córdoba in 814, when popular discontent took the form of an uprising against the emir himself. This reflected the uncertainty about political legitimacy that had existed in Muslim Hispania since the emirate broke away from the central caliphate in the Near East. After the revolt was quelled, one-fourth of the population of the Andalusi capital was expelled.

Muslim revolts grew serious during the second half of the ninth century. At times the emir controlled only the greater Córdoba region. Major rebellions occurred in the districts of Toledo in the center, Seville and Bobastro in the south, Mérida in the southwest, and Zaragoza and Lérida in the northeast. The partly Christian city of Toledo was more or less autonomous from 873 to 930, required only to pay a nominal tribute to the emirate. A more fully autonomous principality was carved out in the upper Ebro valley of the northeast by the Banu Qasi dynasty, descendants of the Visigothic overlord Casio (Cassius) of Tudela, who had accepted Islam in 714 at the start of the conquest. The Banu Qasi ruled the upper Ebro region for two hundred years, waxing at times rich and powerful. At their height in the late ninth century they were sometimes called "third kings of Hispania" (following the emirs of Al-Andalus and the kings of Christian Asturias-León). The most serious of the new revolts, however, was that begun by Omar ibn Hafsun at Bobastro in the hills above Málaga in 883. The descendant of muladíes, ben-Hafsun rallied Muslims and Christians alike and soon made most of the eastern Andalusian hill country independent of the emirate. In 894 he returned to Christianity, the religion of his ancestors. That cost the support of most of his Muslim following, but even so he held out in the Bobastro district until his death in 917. This domain was defended by his sons for another twelve years until it was finally reincorporated by the emirate in 929.

An effectively unified state was finally achieved during the long reign of Abd-al-Rahman III (912-961). The son of a Navarrese princess, this greatest of Cordoban rulers was a short, blue-eyed Muslim who dyed his red hair black to match that of most of his subjects. In 929 he took the step of raising his dominion from an emirate, or kingdom, to a caliphate, or empire. Originally the Islamic world had been unified under a single caliphate as the political successor to the prophet's authority. The Umayyad emirate of Al-Andalus had been nominally subordinate to the Abbasid caliphate in Baghdad, but establishment of a new caliphate under the aggressive Fatimids in

Egypt threatened military and political pressures through North Africa. Abd-al-Rahman III countered the claims and ambitions of the Fatimids by taking advantage of new Muslim theories to assert the imperial independence of Al-Andalus. This nominal authority also strengthened the claims of the Cordoban state over the local regions of the peninsula.

The caliph restored central control over all the Muslim population and carried on major border campaigns against the small Christian principalities of the north, receiving token submission from most of them. During the latter part of his reign he extended military dominion over part of the northwest Maghreb, briefly expanding Al-Andalus into an imperial domain.

The strength of the tenth-century caliphate was due as much to the efficiency of the state system as to the size and prosperity of its population, for the caliphate developed the best organized administration found anywhere in western Europe during that era. This had begun nearly a century earlier under Abd-al-Rahman II, who had commenced to refashion what had begun as a fairly simple despotism into a well-articulated structure patterned after the Abbasid caliphate in Damascus. Executive authority was nominally autocratic, administered by an *hajib* or chief minister through batteries of *visirs* or departmental ministers for varied aspects of administration, with complements of subsecretaries, scribes, and clerks. A fairly efficient treasury with some degree of central accounting was eventually developed. Theoretically, each district of the emirate was administered by a regional *wali,* or governor, responsible to the central government for the affairs of his province. The legal system was headed by a *cadi aljamaa* (chief justice), though his authority was restricted to the Córdoba district. The court structure was divided by region and municipality, with separate jurisdictions for different kinds of grievances according to civil need and Muslim custom.

Muslim military organization in the peninsula had long been rather rudimentary, resting upon the militia of the local Arab clans and other regional elites. Though originally made up mostly of infantry, Muslim armies came to rely especially on light cavalry, patterned in part on the Arabic model and armed with lances, darts, and small shields. Early in the emirate a permanent standing army had been begun with the formation of an elite corps of several thousand slaves from eastern Europe and Africa. Abd-al-Rahman III did not solve the problem of central military organization, but his forces were the most numerous yet employed by Muslim power in the peninsula and in their time were without peer in western Europe. The ports of the eastern, southern, and western coasts of the peninsula had long had large commercial fleets, but an armed navy of significance took form for the first time under Abd-al-Rahman II. For a brief time it was perhaps comparable to that of the Byzantines.

The political strength and military glory of this reign coincided with the first full flowering of the high culture of Hispano-Muslim society as well as its broad economic expansion. During the tenth century the state, society, and culture of Al-Andalus were more advanced than anything to be found in Christian western Europe. The studies in philosophy, astronomy, mathematics, botany, and medicine carried on by the intellectual elite of Muslim Hispania between the mid-tenth and twelfth centuries have earned standard references in medieval history textbooks. Economic achievements were equally impressive. During the ninth and tenth centuries new Persian and Nabatean agricultural techniques were introduced, old irrigation systems restored, and new ones developed. East Mediterranean fruits, as well as grain, olives, and rice, were important crops. Conditions of land tenure varied greatly. Most farms were family farms, many of them rented or worked on shares from aristocratic overlords but a not insignificant number held independently by Muslim smallholders. Exact measurement is impossible, but productivity, at least in the irrigated valleys and huertas of parts of the south and east, was apparently well above ordinary west European standards of the time. Grain production in the dry areas was less successful; from the ninth century on grain had intermittently to be imported from northern Africa.

The real strength of Al-Andalus lay in its cities, with their productive economies, skilled labor, technological development, and learning. Nearly all had been effectively Muslimized and culturally Arabicized by the tenth century. They excelled in the production of silk and other textiles, ceramics, leather work, armaments, and some types of fine steelworking. Al-Andalus had proportionately more artisans in its cities than had any other part of western Europe at that time. Commerce flourished well beyond the range of the peninsula.

Above all other cities, the capital, Córdoba, was the urban showplace of the caliphate. Textbook estimates of a population of one million people may be dismissed, but there were apparently well over one hundred thousand. In size, services, culture, and economy, the city was without a peer in western Europe and rivaled in the east only by Constantinople. Some of the enduring works of Hispano-Muslim architecture in Córdoba and other cities were at least begun in the tenth century. The architecture of Al-Andalus is often referred to as Moorish, yet its surviving specimens considerably surpass what was built in Morocco during that (or most subsequent) periods.*

* Although aside from the great mosque at Córdoba, the outstanding examples of Hispano-Muslim architecture are of a later time (for example, the Giralda of Seville, twelfth century, and the Alhambra of Granada, fifteenth century).

The population and cultural centers of Al-Andalus were for the most part the same towns and regions that had flourished under the Romans (and to a lesser degree under the Visigoths). Some of the people and atmosphere of the cultural vanguard of Romano-Christian Hispania were absorbed into Hispano-Muslim society, and it was not merely an accident that the high culture of Al-Andalus was superior to that of the Maghreb during the same period. It started from a higher base.

That Hispano-Christian culture affected Hispano-Muslim society cannot be doubted, yet its effect was negligible compared to the great impact of orientalization brought by the establishment of Islam in the peninsula. There are many regional variations in Islam, but the Hispanic peninsula was the only major part of western Europe that was for some time torn out of the matrix of western Christendom. All the culture as well as the religion of Al-Andalus was patterned on oriental norms and precedents. Non-Islamic Hispanic precursors for these ideas and trends are simply not to be found. The high culture of Al-Andalus was derivative, and oriental in inspiration. The only major exceptions lay in some of the arts: architecture, metalworking, and popular literature, where a synthesis of sorts was worked out between autochthonous Hispanic skills and motifs and oriental forms.

The sweeping effect of orientalization may be seen not merely in the high culture but in the common social patterns. Family standards and practices were patterned on those of the upper-class Muslim immigrants from the Middle East, and social customs were profoundly orientalized. A major example was the seclusion and restriction of women, something for which there was no parallel or precedent in Hispano-Christian society. The medieval Hispano-Christian family was distinctly more individualistic and egalitarian. Even the minor aberrations of Hispano-Muslim society were probably not as unusual as they have sometimes been made out. Fondness for wine has been presented as a triumph of the Hispanic over the Islamic, but there was also drinking in the Middle East. Sexual mores were typically Muslim as well, particularly in the apparently high incidence of homosexuality.

The Amirid Dictatorship 976/981-1008

The Cordoban state reached the height of its power in the middle of the tenth century under Abd-al-Rahman III, yet survived for only seventy-five years more. No state in Europe or the Mediterranean basin during the Middle Ages possessed the instruments to guarantee central government unless strong leadership and a continuous principle of legitimacy were preserved; by the eleventh century these were lacking in Al-Andalus. Abd-al-Rahman III's successor, al-Hakam II, ruled for fifteen years, but when he died in 976 he left as heir a twelve-year-old son who was recognized as Hisham II. The government was soon dominated by its vigorous and efficient hajib, an Hispano-Arab known to history as al-Mansur ("The Victorious"). In 981 young Hisham was forced to officially ratify the complete authority of the hajib over all aspects of government.

Al-Mansur relied on two factors to cement his dictatorship: religion and a strong centralized army. He allied himself with the influential Malikite faqihs in suppressing the few scattered expressions of Islamic heterodoxy that had appeared at Córdoba and won a reputation among the superstitious lower classes as a defender of the faith. He also expanded the standing army. Large numbers of Berber mercenaries were brought in from the Maghreb, and Christian mercenaries were accepted as well. The ordinary militia levies of Al-Andalus were reorganized by special regiment rather than by local district in an effort to counteract the centrifugal effect of regional loyalties. Al-Mansur built the most powerful military machine yet seen in the peninsula, but it broke the traditional service patterns of Al-Andalus and severed bonds between local leaders and the Cordoban government. It became to some extent an instrument of control over the rest of Al-Andalus and a resented agent of centralization.

The historic title al-Mansur was won in a long series of summer campaigns against the Christian principalities of the north. The motives were more political and economic than religious, but al-Mansur found it useful to strengthen his position by preaching the jihad against the northern Christians, little troubled by the fact that Christian mercenaries sometimes served in his forces. At one time or another he ravaged every major part of Christian territory save Navarre, with whose ruling dynasty he was allied by marriage. No ruler since the original conquest had inflicted such heavy damage on Christian Hispania. Moreover, at the very end of the century his son, Abdul-Malik, restored Cordoban authority over the northwest corner of the Maghreb, of which the city of Fez was the center. Al-Mansur died in 1002 at the height of power, exhausted by his triumphant exertions. He was succeeded by Abdul-Malik, who quickly obtained from the impotent Hisham the same plenary authority held by his invincible father. Abdul-Malik survived his father by only six years, however, dying in 1008, possibly assassinated.

The Amirid dictatorship* wielded by al-Mansur and Abdul-Malik from 976/981 to 1008 had raised the caliphate to the pinnacle of its military power, yet sowed within it the seeds of its political destruc-

---

* The title was derived from Al-Mansur's family name.

tion. For one thing, the dictatorship fatally weakened the principle of political legitimacy. Al-Andalus had always been difficult to rule, relying on both forceful leadership and administration and the legitimate authority of the Ummayad dynasty. In the long run, the dictatorship supplied force alone; it replaced the dynasty, yet could not develop a new principle of legitimate descent from Mohammed. By the tenth century Shiite doctrines in the Muslim orient had tried to establish a new principle of legitimacy on the basis of divinely appointed leaders, imams, who were nominal descendants of the Prophet and were held to enjoy divinely delegated charismatic authority. But the Amirids could claim no such descent from Mohammed. Appeals to the jihad proved insufficient to bolster what was eventually revealed as a purely opportunistic military regime. Traditional relations between the regions were disrupted, and replaced with purely military bonds.

Breakup of the Caliphate 1008-1031

Soon after the death of the second Amirid, the political unity and authority of the caliphate collapsed altogether. Once the legitimate succession had been interrupted it was never successfully restored. Many regions of Al-Andalus were resentful of their treatment under the dictatorship and refused to heed new leaders in Córdoba. The feckless Hisham was deposed in 1009, briefly restored the following year, then deposed again. Altogether, over a period of twenty-three years, six relatives of the Ummayads and three members of a rival, half-Berber family disrupted the throne. The slave pretorians functioned as a powerful independent faction and the bands of Berber mercenaries who had become more numerous during the preceding half-century usurped power in local districts. Regional Arab oligarchs and clans withdrew into local exclusivism, and the state system soon dissolved. Córdoba was wracked by demagogy, riots, and pillaging, while the educated and wealthy fled. In 1010 the city was sacked by a Catalan expedition brought in by Muslim dissidents at Toledo.

Had a leader as resolute and resourceful as Abd-al-Rahman III or al-Mansur emerged, he might have been able to restore caliphal authority. As it was, the caliphate had been unable to institutionalize political unity in the face of geographic obstacles, ethnic diversity, class divisions, and a persistent spirit of localism. The idea of Muslim unity had little currency, for Cordoban power in the tenth century had been based largely on political, not religious, standards and values. Nor did the small Christian states of the north seem very threatening in the early eleventh century; united defense of the faith was not an issue. Rather than undergo the Amirid experience again, the regions almost unanimously preferred to pull apart. The localism and factionalism that had proved an almost insuperable obstacle for the Visigothic monarchy also undermined the caliphate, and its official end was finally declared by a group of local leaders meeting in Córdoba in 1031. In the former capital it was replaced by a local government of notables ruling only the greater Córdoba district.

The Taifa Kingdoms

After the collapse of the caliphate, political power coalesced around local leaders, oligarchies, or ethnic groups and coalitions in the principal urban economic centers of Al-Andalus. Nearly all the first overlords were local commanders and notables who had achieved power through the political and military network created by al-Mansur. The result was a series of about thirty regional *taifa* (local faction) kingdoms that divided up approximately the southern 75 percent of the peninsula. Some of the taifas, chiefly Seville, Granada, Badajoz, Valencia, Toledo, and Zaragoza, quickly developed into fairly strong regional emirates or principalities, dominating large areas of the surrounding countryside and devouring their weaker neighbors. The taifas were typically governed by local dynasties of Arab aristocrats or local Berber military factions, but power was sometimes disputed by a variety of heterogeneous claimants: Arab oligarchs, Berber mercenaries or immigrants, the "Andalusian" or ordinary Hispano-Muslim majority, and other mercenaries or forces of slave pretorians. Political transition went most smoothly in border districts dominated by military leaders. In the Andalusian interior quarreling was more protracted.

The taifas managed to preserve most of the economic achievements of Al-Andalus and often to develop them further. Some of their capitals reached a greater level of prosperity and sophistication in the eleventh century than any towns under the caliphate save Córdoba. Hence the collapse of the Hispano-Muslim state did not bring the collapse of Hispano-Muslim culture.

Indeed, the famous "high culture" of Muslim Hispania, while building on the achievements of the tenth-century caliphate, was mainly a product of the new scholarship and writing of the eleventh and twelfth centuries. The same was true of the most enduring creations of Hispano-Muslim art and architecture. It was during the taifa and the subsequent Almoravid period that the popular Hispanic song

and verse forms—the muwashahas and zéjels—were formally incorporated into written literature and subsequently gained a vogue in
Islamic art.

A striking and dominant characteristic of Hispano-Muslim literature was its essential materialism and hedonism. Love lyrics and
erotic poetry in Al-Andalus often surpassed those of the middle East,
religious literature and mystical verse were rather poorly developed.
The society's religion remained hyperorthodox, but it did not lead to
a high religious culture in literature or theology. There were few new
religious ideas in Al-Andalus.

The taifa kingdoms and their successors were the late blooming of
Muslim Hispania's Indian Summer. Wracked by incessant factionalism, they divided and dissipated their civic and military energies.
When the military balance in the peninsula began to change in the
middle of the eleventh century, the taifas could not defend themselves
in regional isolation and were destroyed one by one. The dissolution
of the caliphate had been the political prelude to the political and
military decline of all of Al-Andalus.

Parallel between the Caliphate and the Later Spanish Empire

There are certain intriguing parallels between the circumstances and
historical patterns of tenth-century Al-Andalus and sixteenth-century
Spain. Both empires were launched, as is customarily the case with
expansionist systems, before their respective societies had reached
their fullest cultural development. Both emphasized imperial expansion and foreign issues to the detriment of internal problems. Neither
achieved a fully integrated civic entity: the Umayyad caliphate was
not effectively integrated, and the Habsburg monarchy was pluralistic, revealing centrifugal tendencies. Both strongly emphasized religious issues in mobilizing for expansion; religious orthodoxy was later
stressed by both in their periods of political decline. The renewed
assertion of reorganized military power marked the last generation of
strong government and the prelude to civic decline (compare al-
Mansur and Olivares). The full flowering of Andalusi culture came
after the collapse of the caliphate; that of Habsburg Spain, at least in
esthetics, after the apogee of politico-military power under Felipe II.
A major difference between the two was that the economic prosperity
of Al-Andalus survived the passing of the caliphate. Seventeenth-
century Spain exhausted its economy in war; the Muslim taifas never
organized the military strength that their economies could have supported.

3

The Early Christian Principalities and The Expansion of Asturias-Leon

The real dividing line between the Roman and medieval worlds came not with the Barbarian invasions of the fifth century but with the Muslim conquests of the seventh and eighth centuries. This interpretation, known to historians as the Pirenne Thesis, is more applicable to the history of the Hispanic peninsula than to that of any other part of western Europe. The historically enduring Hispanic kingdoms were those created in the aftermath of the Muslim conquest of most of the peninsula. The eight-century reconquest that followed was an historic enterprise without parallel in human history. Elsewhere invading forces and cultures have either been quickly repelled and eliminated or else as in Russia accepted as overlords by the native population. Exotic forces, once firmly implanted, have been absorbed by or have transformed the autochthonous culture. In Hispania, invading Muslim society could not be simply defeated and rejected, and much less could it be absorbed. Yet it was not completely accepted, either, and resistance by small independent groups of the indigenous population was maintained for centuries, becoming the major conditioning factor in the Hispanic cultures, until finally the Muslims had been completely defeated, subjugated, and ultimately expelled from the peninsula.

It should be remembered that the resistance of that minority of the population which remained Christian and independent was not in-

spired by any racial antagonism between Hispano-Christians and
Berber-Arab Muslims. For that matter, after a generation or so the
great majority of Muslims were Hispanic converts. Hence the antagonism was essentially cultural and religious.

Origins of the Kingdom of Asturias

The only parts of the peninsula relatively untouched by the Muslim
invasion were the mountainous regions of the far north in the Pyrenean and Cantabrian ranges. These areas had never been fully integrated into either of the preceding Hispanic political communities,
Roman or Visigothic. The native Cantabrian and Basque populations
stoutly resisted outside domination, though the Cantabrians had been
partially Romanized and had reached a modus vivendi with the
Visigoths. Small groups of native Cantabrians and Hispano-Visigoths
resisted Muslim dominion in the more inaccessible parts of Asturias
and the eastern Cantabrians (the latter, somewhat shakily organized
as the duchy of Cantabria under the Visigoths, roughly corresponded
to the modern province of Santander). About the year 718 they
recognized as leader a warrior named Pelayo, apparently a Visigothic
aristocrat. Pelayo's stronghold lay in the Picos de Europa district of
eastern Asturias, near the center of the greater Cantabrian range. In
722 his followers ambushed and destroyed a Muslim attack force
below the mountain of Covadonga, giving the Christians their first
clear-cut victory. After the death of Pelayo (737) and of his son Fáfila
(739), the military leaders of Asturias and Cantabria elected as successor Pelayo's son-in-law Alfonso, the son of the late Visigothic duke
of Cantabria. He subsequently became known to history as Alfonso I
(739-757), first regular ruler of the nascent kingdom of Asturias.

Rulers of Asturias-Léon

Pelayo	718-737	García	911-914
Fáfila	737-739	Ordoño II	914-924
Alfonso I	739-757	Fruela II	924-925
Fruela I	757-768	Sancho Ordóñez	925-929
Aurelio	768-774	Alfonso IV	929-931
Silo	774-783	Ramiro II	931-951
Mauregato	783-788	Ordoño III	951-956
Vermudo I the Deacon	788-791	Sancho I the Fat	956-966
Alfonso II the Chaste	791-842	Ramiro III	966-985
Ramiro I	842-850	Vermudo II	985-999
Ordoño I	850-866	Alfonso V	999-1028
Alfonso III *el Magno*	866-911	Vermudo III	1028-1037

The Muslim governors of the peninsula did not make an all-out effort to occupy the northern ranges. The number of Muslim fighting men was at first small, and operations against irregulars in mountainous terrain were extremely difficult, largely nullifying the Arabs' technological advantage in the open field. Furthermore, the few people living in the Pyrenean and Cantabrian ranges were economically and culturally backward. They had little to offer a conqueror and were scarcely worth the price, particularly when the most prosperous, cultured, and urbanized areas of the south and east had been occupied so easily. Moreover, after the first decade, the Muslim invaders were sorely distracted by their own internal quarrels, which gave the Christian resistance in the north further relief.

Under the leadership of Pelayo, the Asturians had been exclusively on the defensive. The first counteroffensive was begun by Alfonso I, taking advantage of the Muslim civil war between Arabs and Berbers that raged after 740, and of the great famine of 748-753, which temporarily weakened Muslim power and caused many of the Berber immigrants who had occupied parts of the northwest to leave. Alfonso's small forces, stiffened with modest cavalry detachments, descended from the mountains and raided parts of the Duero valley, killing or enslaving the small garrisons of Berber soldiers, liberating the Mozarabs, and in many cases moving them from the indefensible lowlands back into the hill country. With this and other immigration, the Asturo-Cantabrian hills acquired a slightly larger population. In the meantime, much of the Duero valley below Asturias, already hard hit by the famine of mid-century, was devastated and depopulated, turned into a thinly peopled no-man's-land between Christians and Muslims for the next century and more, forming something of a shield behind which the small kingdom of Asturias was able to forge its own institutions.

Apparently there was substantial immigration into Asturias and Galicia during the eighth and ninth centuries. This augmented the human and cultural resources of the small kingdom and enabled a distinctly institutionalized monarchy to form a nucleus of strength around its capital, first in the mountain village of Cangas de Onís, then in the town of Oviedo.

The new kingdom was ethnically heterogeneous. Its original inhabitants were a complex of Hispano-Visigoths (and Hispano-Suevi in Galicia), Hispano-Roman Galicians with strong Celtic residues, native Cantabrians and Basques, Mozarab immigrants from Al-Andalus, and a few small groups of Berber captives. Pre-Roman ethnic identities had still not been fully erased, and local or regional differences were strongly felt. In some cases they were reaffirmed or accentuated in the anti-Muslim resistance and the process of reconquest and resettlement that followed. The only unifying factors in the early years of the kingdom were the crown, the church, and above all the frontier, for it was common determination to resist Muslim domination that brought together the diverse population of Asturias.

Though the rudeness of life in the early centuries of Asturias-León may sometimes have been exaggerated, the society was simple and backward compared with areas of Al-Andalus, France, and Italy. Thrown back on the least-developed regions of the peninsula, medieval Hispano-Christian society began under the burden of a formidable lag in social and economic achievement. Rural communities were largely self-sufficient and lived mostly by herding sheep and cattle. The moist, hilly, nonfertile land did not encourage cultivation, and crops were limited. There were scarcely any skilled workers, and only simple clothing and rudimentary weapons and tools were produced. Society was completely rural; no city worthy of the name developed in greater Asturias for nearly two hundred years. During that period trade and commerce were extremely slight, and though some money was available, nearly all of it came from outside; no coins were minted by the kings of Asturias.

Formation of the Pyrenean Counties

Farther east, autonomous nuclei of Hispanic people survived in the interior valleys of the Pyrenees throughout the eighth century. Their numbers were slightly increased by Christian immigration from the south, and they were to some extent sheltered by the mountainous terrain. Yet their population was small, even compared with the kingdom of Asturias, and at first they were obliged to come to terms with Muslim authorities, accepting a kind of tributary status. The Pyrenees lay astride the route of Muslim expansion into western Europe, and because the northeastern part of the peninsula was more urbanized and productive than the northwest and also more Mediterranean and warm, it drew greater attention from the Muslims. All the main cities in the northeast—Zaragoza, Pamplona, Tarragona, Barcelona, Lérida, Gerona—were occupied directly, and the more southerly of them were soon in process of Islamization. Facing heavy military pressure and lacking any buffer zone, the small Hispanic population of the Pyrenees was at first completely hemmed into the mountain area.

As the Muslims had moved up into the peninsula, a number of Visigoths and lower-class Hispani had crossed the Pyrenees into Septimania. Though the Muslims established a tenuous subordination of Septimania in their destructive raids between 718 and 732, they were unable to extend their control permanently beyond the Pyrenees for reasons discussed in the foregoing chapter.

Frankish counterattacks from the north, followed by the outbreak of civil war among the Muslims, quickly altered the balance of power. After 742, part of Septimania renounced its tributary status, though the remaining Gothic overlords in Septimania sometimes preferred distant association with Córdoba to Frankish domination. In 756 Narbonne, the largest town in the region, acknowledged the sovereignty of the Frankish monarchy, which soon incorporated all the territory down to the Pyrenees. Charlemagne attempted to roll back the Muslim frontier by extending a Frankish protectorate over northeast Hispania at the behest of anti-Umayyad Muslim dissidents. In 778 a Frankish expedition against Zaragoza failed, but in 785 the Christian inhabitants of Gerona, in the northeastern corner of the peninsula, accepted Frankish suzerainty. In a series of limited campaigns fought between 785 and 811, Franks occupied and fortified the strongpoints of the southern Pyrenean foothills. The eastern and central Pyrenean regions were then organized on the Frankish principle into six counties—Urgel, Pallars, Barcelona (seized in 801), Ribagorza, Sobrarbe, and Aragón—under the Frankish monarchy.

The counties of the Pyrenees were more intimately associated with the culture and institutions of the rest of western Europe than was the semi-isolated kingdom of Asturias on the other side of the peninsula. Development of a semi-feudal political structure based on Frankish models, military reliance on Frankish assistance, the religious influence of Carolingian Catholicism, and cultural crosscurrents from France and Italy all drew the population of the Hispanic March into closer contact with the main forces shaping medieval western Europe.

The Basque Principality of Navarre

The Basque territory of the western Pyrenees had never been completely occupied and incorporated by an invading power. During the eighth century, its inhabitants maintained their customary hostility to outside domination and maneuvered between the Muslim emirate and Frankish expansion. Basques were probably responsible for ambushing the rearguard of Charlemagne's expedition of 778 when it retreated toward the north. In the course of a major expedition to restore the emirate's power in the northeast three years later, Abd-al-Rahman I occupied Pamplona, the only true city in the Basque country, and established Muslim control over lower Navarre (roughly in the area just south of the southwestern foothills of the Pyrenees). The Basques had all the less difficulty in establishing peaceful relations with the Muslims because few Basques had been Christianized and religious antagonism was not acute. The nearest Muslim power was not the emirate of Córdoba, but the semi-autonomous principality of the Hispano-Muslim Banu Qasi dynasty along the upper Ebro, from whence had come help against the Franks. An independent Navarrese state first began to take form in the final years of the eighth century (ca. 796–798) under a strong leader, Iñigo Arista. The history of Navarre for the next hundred years and more was turbulent, with fluctuating borders and a number of invasions from Al-Andalus. Nonetheless, an organized Navarrese state was created, and a close alliance was maintained with the neighboring Banu Qasi through interdynastic marriage.

Expansion of Asturias-León

During the height of Muslim power in the ninth and tenth centuries, the Pyrenean counties remained comparatively static and self-contained. The only dynamic, expanding power was the mountain kingdom of Asturias. With Galicia and most of the Cantabrian range organized within their territory, the Asturian rulers had the dual advantage of possessing greater resources than any single Pyrenean county and of facing less determined resistance to their immediate south, for the sparsely inhabited buffer zone of the Duero valley contrasted sharply with the strong, prosperous Muslim urban centers of the northeast that hemmed in the Pyrenean counties.

The struggle for independence in the northwest had at first been a desperate fight for survival, but it soon generated a broader ideal and a more comprehensive objective, at least for the immediate circle of the Asturian monarchs. Rather than considering themselves overlords of a parochial principality, the Asturian rulers tried to legitimize broader ambitions and a claim to increased sovereignty by identifying their throne with the lost legacy of the Visigoths. As early as 760, after increased Visigothic emigration to Asturias and the first generation of successful counterattacks, the "Neo-Gothic" idea of restoring the independent Hispano-Christian monarchy of the Visigoths was foreshadowed. During the course of the next century, a political identity and goal were developed by the Asturian court. The discovery of an impressive tomb in central Galicia early in the ninth century provided the kingdom with a spiritual patron. The tomb was soon labeled as the sepulchre of "Santiago"—St. James, the brother of Christ—and the saint subsequently adopted as the patron saint of Asturias-León. Whereas the leaders of the Pyrenean counties thought of themselves as autonomous within a broader political framework, the rulers of

Asturias began to identify themselves as heirs of the Visigoths charged with an imperial mission of reconquest.

The Neo-Gothic idea was developed during the reign of Alfonso III "el Magno" (886-911), apparently the first Hispano-Christian king to claim the title of emperor. If the title was indeed used by Alfonso el Magno—and the sources are by no means unequivocal about such a claim—it referred only to the lands of the Hispanic peninsula, which were held to be the legitimate patrimony of the successors of the Visigothic monarchy. From the time of Alfonso el Magno there was a conscious revival of certain Visigothic court forms, such as the traditional rite of royal consecration, employed to symbolize the continuity and legitimacy of the kingdom. It might be noted that in the ninth and tenth centuries the notion of regaining domination over the peninsula did not imply the expulsion or extermination of Muslim rivals. What was involved was political sovereignty and religious authority, something not incompatible with the limited system of "discriminatory toleration" practiced in Al-Andalus vis-à-vis Christians and Jews, save that the roles of superior and subordinate would be reversed.

The Asturian church played a major role in the development and diffusion of the Neo-Gothic idea. Its hierarchy, after freeing itself from any dependence on the Mozarab church, was ambitious to assert the sovereignty of Asturian institutions and expand their influence. Learned clerics and monks formed the only intelligentsia of that time; they prepared the arguments and discovered the precedents for Neo-Gothic legitimist ambitions on the part of the crown and served as its chief propagandists.

The expansion of Asturias was a slow, halting process. Advances were made during the long, constructive reign of Alfonso II "the Chaste" (791-842), but it was not until the time of Ordoño I (850-866) that the line of Tuy-Astorga-León-Amaya was effectively occupied, and then to some extent repopulated and fortified. During the long reign of Alfonso el Magno, severe internal conflicts within the emirate led the Asturians to believe at one point that destruction of the Cordoban state was imminent, and in 881 a royal expedition struck deep into the heart of Al-Andalus. Before the death of Alfonso el Magno a line of occupation was reached that stretched through the Duero and Mondego valleys from Simancas to Zamora to Coimbra. The formidable strength of the unified caliphate made further advance in the tenth century difficult, but Ramiro II (931-951) inflicted a crushing defeat on Abd-al-Rahman III at Simancas in 939 and was able to occupy, in a tenuous fashion, the regions of Salamanca, Avila, and Sepúlveda. Altogether, the one hundred years from the start of the reign of Ordoño I (850) to the death of Ramiro II (951) more than doubled the kingdom. Alfonso el Magno moved the capital from the hilltown of Oviedo to the more attractive city of León to the south, and the kingdom was henceforth known by the geographically more descriptive title Asturias and León, or simply León. It had grown larger than all the Hispano-Christian principalities to the east put together.

Thus the people of the northwest became the creators and protagonists of what was to be the historic Spanish tradition. The mountainous regions of Asturias and Cantabria had been peripheral and among the least sophisticated of the peninsula, though the districts of Galicia and Braga to the southwest were more developed. In the eighth century, of course, the notion of Spanish as distinct from Muslim or Moorish scarcely existed for the independent northern mountaineers. The adjective *Hispanic* had been from the beginning of Roman times a merely geographic term. During the early Middle Ages *Hispania* or *España* referred to the territory of the peninsula, most of which was dominated by Muslims. Consequently adjectives derived therefrom might refer more frequently to Muslims than to Christians. As late as 996 the term *espanesco* meant "Moorish" rather than "Spanish" in the modern sense. The word *espanyol* (in Castilian, *español*) was apparently first coined by Provençal merchants in southwestern France to denote all the people who lived south of the Pyrenees, Christian or Muslim. Thus the independent identity of the people of the northwest was not originally conceived of as Spanish but was defined in two different ways. One was by region (Asturian, Galician, Leonese), and the other was as Christian (or at least non-Muslim). Therein lay a second paradox, in that the Asturians and Cantabrians who became the first champions of independent Hispanic Christendom against the Muslims had been the least Christianized of the Hispanic population (save for the Basques, who later tended to react in the same fashion). They came to stress Christianity in part to distinguish themselves from the religion of their antagonists.

The Emergence of Castile

Because of the depopulation and devastation that prevailed for a century in the Duero valley, one of the few ways in which Muslim armies could strike directly at the heartland of Asturias-León was by travelling up the Ebro valley along the old Roman road northwest from Zaragoza. To guard against invasion from this direction, the Asturian monarchy built a series of castles and fortified villages in the mountains above the upper Ebro, where the route could be sealed off.

This territory (in the modern provinces of Santander, Burgos, and Alava) was known in ancient times as Bardulia after the Celtiberian tribe that had inhabited the region. By the beginning of the ninth century it was beginning to be called in the local vernacular Castiella or Castilla—"the land of castles"—from the Latin *castella.*

The people of the eastern Cantabrian range had been even less Romanized than had the inhabitants of Asturias. The effective Romanization and Christianization of Cantabria was not really accomplished until after the influx of a certain number of Visigothic and other Hispano-Christian refugees in the eighth century. Apparently there was also an ancient linguistic boundary between Asturias and Cantabria-Bardulia which persisted into the Middle Ages. Thus the Asturian-Leonese romance dialect, like the Galician (and also the Catalan), retained the normal Latin *f,* whereas the Cantabrian romance dialect apparently excluded it and included an aspirate sound. If this interpretation is correct, the influence of the Cantabrian dialect can still be heard in two of the linguistic pecularities of the Castilian language. Of the three major romance languages that were formed in the peninsula, Castilian developed into the most original, probably because of its beginnings in one of the remote and least cosmopolitan regions, a region whose linguistic individuality was already marked.

Communication with Cantabria-Bardulia and administration of that region always presented a problem for the Asturian monarchy, because of distance and rough terrain. As early as 804 a separate bishopric, that of Valpuesta, was organized to administer religious affairs in Castile. In the mid-830s Alfonso II the Chaste appointed several regional judges to administer the local affairs of Cantabria-Bardulia. After another generation passed, they were replaced by several regional "counts" to administer local districts, the most important of which was called the county of Castile, a name later given to the entire area. By that time the Castilians had come to constitute a separate territorial and social group within greater Asturias-León, a frontier society that was ruder, more militant, more egalitarian, and more self-reliant than the settled and developed areas of Asturias and Galicia.

Crown and Aristocracy

The Asturian state developed early a strong concept of royal sovereignty. Specific challenges of life in the peninsula, coupled with Neo-Gothic theory, resulted in a vigorous monarchy that did not succumb to the decentralizing effect of internal power struggles of the sort that were weakening other west European monarchies. The Hispano-Visi-

gothic law, the *Fuero Juzgo,* emphasized the overriding legal authority of the *rex* as ruler of the *regnum* (kingdom or public power), so
that in theory the Leonese crown held public authority over all its
domains. The royal state was viewed as sovereign in itself and not
merely the patrimony of a dynasty regulated by local custom, as in
the more feudalized areas of western Europe. Practice, however, was
something else, and de facto resistance by local districts, dissident
aristocrats, or even serfs against higher authority was not uncommon.
At first, succession to the throne remained semi-elective, though
within the original dynasty, and the principle of strict hereditary
succession was not fully established for nearly three hundred years.
The eighth and ninth centuries were marked by intermittent revolt
and at least one successful deposition of a sovereign. This notwith-
standing, the Asturian-Leonese monarchy proved more stable than
had that of the Visigoths, at least until the middle of the tenth
century.

Supremacy of the crown was reinforced by the need of its subjects
to maintain military unity in the face of a much stronger Muslim state
to the south. The Asturian monarchy raised military forces directly
and was not dependent merely on feudal levies. Most of the able-
bodied men, at least in the frontier areas, were under some obligation
to bear arms. Warfare was not the prerogative of a single class, and
the crown was able to maintain considerable control over military
power because it upheld the Romano-Visigothic principle that newly
conquered land that was unoccupied belonged to the royal fisc and
thus added regularly to its income. Retention of a moneyed economy,
augmented by military raids and border expansion, enabled the
crown to pay for some services and thus be less dependent on personal relationships. Organized administrative and judicial affairs
rested on the authority of the crown, which normally appointed
officials to their posts rather than recognizing such posts as the
personal patrimony of local feudal overlords.

In most of western Europe, the power of the medieval aristocracy
lay in its feudal politico-juridical dominion over local territories and
in its reciprocal military obligations toward the crown and the local
region. Only in Catalonia did the Hispanic nobility form along this
west European pattern, but actual social circumstances in the Hispanic principalities did not always differ as greatly from the norms of
feudal western Europe as the differing legal systems might imply. The
Leonese monarchy, for example, lacked resources to administer local
affairs throughout the kingdom, and in many areas local overlords
appropriated nominal functions of the crown, even if on an ad hoc
basis.

At any rate, a distinct hereditary aristocracy existed from the time
of Alfonso I, made up of vigorous Hispano-Visigothic elements and

the warrior elite of the local population. Though some aristocrats possessed hereditary estates, the establishment of such endowments was gradual and did not become general for almost two centuries. The aristocracy was largely a military class whose members enjoyed special privileges, such as exemption from taxes and ordinary labor. Military leaders and local overlords or administrators of the crown were frequently given grants of land or the income from herds of cattle or cultivated strips to maintain themselves, and in certain cases received special titles, but for the first century or so such grants were only lifetime awards and were not hereditary. The only original hereditary right of the aristocrats was that of transmitting special opportunities and legal exemptions to their heirs. By the tenth century, if not before, there had developed a system of vassalage whereby local aristocratic military leaders swore special fealty and vassalage to the crown, which in turn recognized certain privileges of its vassals, but this was not at first accompanied in Asturias-León by the granting or recognition of special feudalities—inherited fiefs under the permanent dominion of a local vassal who was free to govern them as a private domain. Only gradually did local barons and other aristocrats manage to establish inherited landed dominions and property rights, either by establishing their authority over local peasants in a reciprocal military and economic relationship or by gaining hereditary, rather than temporary, possession of the lands and rights granted as a reward for military or administrative service. It was not until the tenth century—the first "decadence" of León—that new benefices and grants of special income and exemptions were granted to aristocrats without the requirement of service in return.

There were at least two distinct classes in the nobility from the very beginning: the ordinary warrior aristocrats, those with horses and other accoutrements, who enjoyed special exemptions but received only minor *soldadas* (fees), and the high aristocrats, called magnates or *ricoshombres,* who enjoyed greater salaries or the income from larger grants of land. The difference between the upper and lower classes of nobility lay not in their legal status and exemptions, which were roughly the same for both, but in their wealth and the importance of titles and honors which they held. The size of soldadas or landed benefices and the category of positions held in royal service, or all these combined, were what raised the *ricohombre* (literally "powerful man") over the rest of the warrior aristocracy.

The Peasantry

The condition of the peasantry, particularly in the kingdom of León but to a lesser extent elsewhere, was varied and extremely compli-

cated. Perhaps most of the population of the north were originally
free peasants, free in the sense that they were recognized individually
under the law and were not bound to the land or placed under special
obligations other than taxes and normal community responsibilities.
In Galicia, which was more settled and traditionalist, however, a large
proportion held the status of *colonos* or *homines,* juridically free and
not fully enserfed but still bound not to have the land which they
worked. Moreover, in Galicia there was also a class of outright serfs,
augmented in the eighth century by a few captive Muslims.

A distinct social difference crystallized almost immediately between the inner and outer zones of the kingdom. The military elite
endeavored almost from the beginning to preserve the traditional
social hierarchy and subjection in the most settled, best developed,
and most secure parts of the kingdom, primarily in Galicia and in
some parts of Asturias. In the wilder or more exposed regions, such as
Cantabria-Castile, the outer parts of Asturias, or the new frontier area
of León, a rough sense of social equality or at least of tight functional
unity prevailed. In these regions the right of peasant proprietors to
their own lands or flocks was usually recognized, and in turn nearly
everyone had a common interest in the defense of the land against the
Muslims. New opportunities were created by the rolling back of the
frontier. The more disgruntled or enterprising from the settled zones
could often move to the most exposed areas, where they might normally expect land or cattle, better grazing opportunities, and fewer
special exactions upon them.

The first major instance of social unrest was a serf revolt in Asturias between 768 and 774. It was put down with the aid of the crown,
but many serfs are said to have run off to frontier districts where they
were allowed to live as free peasants. This in turn created something
of a labor shortage in the interior of Galicia, so that some of those
remaining in serfdom had to be granted the more lenient adscripted
status of homines.

At the time of the emergence of a separate county of Castile in the
tenth century, most of the Castilian population were free peasants.
Even the intermediate grade of adscription to the land as homines or
colonos was almost nonexistent among them. Early Castile was a
semi-egalitarian warrior community, whose members to a large degree shared the same responsibilities and the same opportunities. An
aristocratic class developed, but at first it was mainly a group of
military leaders chosen for achievement, not birth.

The situation remained more complicated in Galicia, Asturias, and
the new territories of León. In the southern region of León—the
Duero valley—repopulated slowly after the mid-ninth century, most

peasant immigrants established themselves as independent proprietors in *presura* (occupation) freeholds. Free peasant landholders were much less numerous in Asturias and the more settled parts of León, and soon were only a small minority of the population of Galicia, but changes in status occurred constantly. The situation of the Galician colonos or homines improved at the time of the major repopulation of the Duero valley in the first half of the tenth century. Some moved to new freeholds farther south, and many of those remaining had to be granted better terms to keep them on the land. Save for the small class of serfs, legal adscription to the soil became less and less common. One class of colonos, called *iuniores,* were recognized as being only renters and free to move whenever they liked. Eventually a decree of Alfonso V of León in 1017 officially declared all colonos free of legal adscription to the soil, leaving only the few serfs, concentrated in Galicia, still bound to the land.

Though the number of peasants legally bound to the land declined, it became increasingly difficult for independent peasant proprietors to maintain their position. From the first generations of the kingdom of Asturias, they had been under pressure in Asturias and Galicia to seek protection from warrior aristocrats by placing their land under *incomuniatio* (in later Castilian, *encomendación*), granting the overlord full use of part of it and keeping only a portion for themselves. This process of encomendación was soon widespread in Galicia, and later extended to the frontier districts of Portugal as well as to Asturias and León. It became increasingly common, until individual freeholders had disappeared as a class in Galicia.

The process of encomendación took a milder form in the newer districts of León, and later in Castile. The system there was called *benefactoria* (in Castilian, *behetría*) and at first required merely that collective peasant groups pay a sort of rent on their lands and pastures to support the military aristocracy. Under the terms of benefactoria, peasants normally retained their full personal freedom and the use of all their lands. Moreover, they were at first normally free to break the relation or choose a new overlord-protector. There was a tendency to tighten up these terms in León however, as early as the tenth century, and they became increasingly rigorous in later generations. Furthermore, there was always the possibility that because of debt, crime, or misfortune a peasant might sink from encomendación or benefactoria into *homone* status. On the other hand, there were occasional examples of serfs or homines being freed of prior obligations and given land by their overlords to hold in encomendación.

Some peasants were involved in dual status relationships. For example, in portions of León where peasant proprietors retained their land, they also might undertake obligations to work as laborers or homines two or three days a week on seigneurial plots.

In some districts, peasants could place their land under the protection of the church through a process known as *oblación,* but this came to involve varying degrees of financial obligation. Homines on church lands were normally better treated than those on the lands of the aristocrats, and in troubled times peasants sometimes voluntarily accepted homine status under a local church or monastery. By the twelfth century, however, new land management techniques had made clerical administrators more demanding, and there were occasional revolts of homines on church land.

From the beginning there was also a small class of free landless peasants who worked exclusively as salaried laborers. And in Castile, Navarre, and Aragón there was a class of *yunqueros,* peasants who owned oxen or other cattle but little or no land of their own. These became more numerous in the twelfth century.

By the twelfth century serfdom—peasants held in semislave status, tied to the land, without juridical personality under the law—was disappearing. By that time practically the only fully enserfed were Muslim captives, some of whom worked on the land but who were more commonly in domestic service. During the thirteenth century nearly all remaining landed serfs (found mainly in Galicia) were raised to *colono* status, giving them individual recognition under the law and in most cases freedom of movement, though under heavy obligations for the use of land.

Though slaves were numerous in affluent Al-Andalus, there were comparatively few outright slaves in Asturias-León. Again, nearly all held in this condition were captive Muslims, and the actual difference between Muslim serfs and Muslim slaves in León was apparently often complicated and unclear. The slave class became somewhat more numerous in the twelfth and thirteenth centuries as the Christian principalities grew in wealth and power.

Social Associationism

Very characteristic of medieval Hispano-Christian society was the predominance of various forms of associationism or communalism. It is true that, as indicated earlier, the occupation of new land by reconquest permitted the establishment of numerous new allodial freeholds as private property, but in the majority of cases the old Roman principle of complete, unfettered private property no longer prevailed. The main source of wealth was land, but most land was not owned, pure and simple, by a single party. The need for cooperation and division of responsibility for defense and the civil order was generally accepted, and a sometimes bewildering variety of claims, rights, shares, or interests were established relating to the use or production of a piece of property. Most land was held in a kind of condominium, part of the usufruct going to the overlord—whether aristocrat, church, or crown—and part to those who worked on it or otherwise "owned" it. Numerous kinds of sharecropping arrangements were worked out on lands that formed part of seigneurial or church domain, or were held under encomendación or benefactoria. This was the more common because part of the northern section of the peninsula had never been fully incorporated into the Roman property system and pre-Roman forms of communalism had not died out by the time of the Muslim conquest.

Associative arrangements functioned not only between members of hierarchic relationships but on the cooperative level of peasant village communes and pastoral associations as well. Particularly in Castile, but also to some extent in the frontier regions of León, much of the land was held by peasant villages that administered and reapportioned use of land and herds in common. In turn, local regional associations of villages and later of towns were formed for the regulation of common problems.

The medieval Hispano-Christian family was also organized along communal and associative lines, based on the joint rights of the parents. In place of Roman marital rights investing all power in the husband, medieval Hispano-Christian law in all regions held that marriage constituted a society of equal rights, based on half-and-half sharing and equal division of property among families and heirs. The same rule was normally applied to all income from or additions to community property. This reflected the greater emphasis on women's role in the post-Celtic society of part of the northern hill country, as well as the influence of Christian principles. Its sharp contrast to the norms of the orthodox Muslim society of Al-Andalus is obvious.

Early Extension of Seigneurial Domain

Even though the explicit feudal principle was not recognized in the legal structure of Asturias, and the military aristocracy at first was held to be more distinctly a service aristocracy than in other parts of western Europe, separate domains were built up by members of the aristocracy and by the church, probably starting as early as the second half of the eighth century. The origin of the seigneurial domains lay more in practice than in theory. As explained earlier, dominion over land was considered legally to be a temporary award in return for service or the maintenance of military strength. Legal jurisdiction by aristocrats was originally meant to represent the jurisdiction of the public power, which could only be administered through intermediaries.

In practice, however, there was an early tendency in the more settled parts of Galicia and Asturias for dominions of aristocrats to become permanent and inheritable and for aristocrats to exercise economic and legal jurisdiction by mere right of dominion, not as temporary lieutenants of the crown. This did not nullify the tendency toward sharing and associationism, for seigneurial domain was frequently limited by tradition and the local custom of peasants' rights. By the tenth century, at any rate, de facto relationships in much of the northwest were passing into law; seigneurial and church domain were recognized over most of Galicia, and parts of Asturias and old León as well.

Castilian Frontier Society and Resettlement

Of all regions of the peninsula, the one with the greatest social mobility, autonomy, and communal associationism was Castile. The inhabitants of Cantabria-Bardulia had never been subjected to as developed a social hierarchy as had obtained in the centers of Roman and Visigothic Hispania. The conditions of Castilian frontier society in the eighth, ninth, and tenth centuries precluded the growth of the degree of social subjection and hierarchy that were already established in Galicia. Local Castilian peasant villages and communities enjoyed district autonomy, and frequently made decisions by means of open village meetings. There were numerous examples of peasants proven in battle who outfitted themselves with horses and became knights (in Castilian, *caballero,* "cavalryman"). It might also be noted that until the broad southward expansion of the eleventh century, cavalry were rather less important in Castilian hill warfare than in some other regions, and peasant infantry more important. Indeed, the booty obtained in semiconstant warfare offered new property to whoever was able to take it, reducing the degree of social stratification.

Border districts were always the most democratic, not merely in Castile but in León as well, for peasant groups had to be granted better terms, often including peasant community autonomy, to induce them to settle the hazardous frontier. Enterprising peasant groups might resettle a district entirely by themselves on grants of *presura*, or with specific *cartas de franquicias* (charters of rights or immunities) from the crown, sometimes obtained ex post facto. The expansion of Castile was frequently a matter of osmosis. Most important of all was the establishment of new peasant communities as *concejos*, self-governing corporate councils, with *cartas pueblas* (charters) recognizing local rights and autonomy. Such practices were at the root of the system of local and municipal *fueros* (rights) that formed the basis of much of the historic Castilian legal structure.

It would be inaccurate to try to establish an absolute social and legal dichotomy between Castile and León. In the frontier districts of León there were semi-autonomous concejos just as in Castile. Not all local districts or peasant communities in Castile were autonomous, and by the eleventh century a trend had set in among elements of the new Castilian aristocracy to carve out their own seigneurial domains. Yet in general a difference in tendency and degree did exist, mainly because of the challenge and opportunity of Castile as a frontier region. It followed also that if Castilian society was freer, more autonomous, socially mobile, and egalitarian than that of greater León, it was ruder and more insular.

Immigration into the Hispanic Principalities

There were several currents of immigration into the northern principalities during the early Middle Ages, but the only one of significant proportions was the movement of Christian Mozarabs from Al-Andalus into the north, primarily into the major state, the kingdom of León. The flow of immigrants varied but continued fairly steadily for three centuries and more, the biggest influx probably occurring during the second half of the ninth century, when León was expanding and the pressure on Mozarabs in the south had begun to mount. It has been conjectured that Mozarab immigrants played a major role in diffusing sophisticated (sometimes Islamically-derived) cultural forms throughout the northwest, in the development of the Neo-Gothic and reconquest mystiques, and in the reestablishment or development of hierarchical institutions.

Up until the eleventh century, the Muslim population of the Christian states was small, consisting exclusively of prisoners carried back to the north. They were normally reduced to semislave status but were also more apt than not to be converted to Christianity. Conversion did not guarantee freedom, but it was the first step in the amelioration of their condition. In the more settled areas, particularly

Galicia, captured Muslims were frequently absorbed by the local society within a generation or two. No major centers of Muslim population were captured during the first three centuries of the reconquest; most Muslims in the path of the Christian advance withdrew, and only a comparative few were seized. Thus in the early Middle Ages they formed no ethno-religious bloc in the north.

The large Jewish society in the south played a significant role in the economic and cultural life of Al-Andalus, but few Jews lived in the Christian principalities before the eleventh century. The backward northern economy was unattractive, and the advantages of Muslim rule were appreciated, at least until the eleventh century, when conditions began to change. Even before then, however, very small groups of Jews were established in a few of the leading centers, engaged in commerce.

Aside from the Mozarabs, the most important group of immigrants in the tenth and eleventh centuries were the French, known as *francos* (Franks), who entered the peninsula in small but fairly continuous numbers from the ninth century on. The first notable Frankish immigration flowed into the Catalan counties in the ninth and tenth centuries, and during the eleventh expanded into the western principalities. The Franks were predominantly of three types—religious reformers and monks, who exercised a major influence on Spanish Catholicism (as well as government and economic development) and will be discussed in a subsequent chapter; military crusaders and adventurers, who sometimes lent decisive impetus to the reconquest, expecially in Aragón; and middle-class merchants and artisans, who played a major role in building up trade and urban economic life, to a greater extent during this period (the tenth and eleventh centuries) than did the Jews. Unlike the latter, middle-class French immigrants tended to merge with the general population after a generation or two.

Towns

Urban society only slowly began to develop in the north during the tenth and the first part of the eleventh centuries. During the period of caliphal splendor in Córdoba, León, the capital city of the northwest, had a population of scarcely 7,000. The only other towns of importance were Astorga, Oviedo, and the religious shrine of Santiago de Compostela. Farther east were Pamplona, Barcelona, and Gerona. Nearly all the towns that did exist had been laid out under Roman rule. What passed for towns in most localities were simply large churches or villages fortified for military defense. Significant change came only with the great expansion of the eleventh century and the economic stimulus of tribute payments and other newly incorporated sources of wealth.

León During the Tenth Century

For two centuries, a series of comparatively strong rulers, external pressures for unity, territory of manageable dimensions, simplicity of social forms, modest population, and strong natural frontiers combined to create relative unity and continuity behind the monarchy of Asturias-León. These conditions changed during the course of the tenth century. After the death of Ordoño II (924), domestic disputes multiplied. During the second half of the century the throne was occupied by a series of weak rulers whose ineptness encouraged particularism and dissension. At the same time, the kingdom faced the awesome challenge of the military might of the tenth-century caliphate, the sharpest threat from the Muslims since the original conquest.

Dynastic dissension in León was due in part to the active intervention of Navarrese diplomacy. Three successive Leonese kings were married to Navarrese princesses, all daughters of the redoubtable Queen Toda of Pamplona, who was the key to north Hispanic politics for twenty years and the principal organizer of the coalition of Christian princes that defeated Abd-al-Rahman III at Simancas in 939. Leonese dissension was compounded by the influence of aristocratic cliques and the failure of the crown to develop an administrative system beneficial to the domain as a whole.

Navarrese diplomacy encouraged the separation of Castile, and after the death of Ramiro II in 951, rival heirs from successive marriages of the late king plunged León into its first full-fledged civil war. Sancho I (known as Sancho the Fat or the Crass), the younger son of Ramiro's second (Navarrese) marriage, required help from Navarre and from the caliphate to retain his throne. He was forced to recognize the suzerainty of Abd-al-Rahman III and ruled feebly for ten years. Sancho was then succeeded by an underage son, Ramiro III (966-985), whose unhappy reign coincided with the rise of al-Mansur, a drastic contraction of Leonese frontiers, and years of devastation and misery. A Galician-Leonese reaction eventually established Vermudo II (985-999), a son of Ordoño III, on the throne, but the kingdom could not escape further suffering from the summer campaigns of al-Mansur. At times it seemed that all the achievements of two hundred years were being destroyed. Only toward the end of the reign of Alfonso V (999–1028) was domestic unity regained and the resettlement of border districts resumed. During the six harsh decades of 950–1010 León had lost its expansive momentum and had nearly broken apart.

The Autonomy of Castile

A major factor in the dissension of tenth-century León was the particularism of the region of Castile, where neither the regional counts nor the people felt close to the Leonese state system. Regulated by their own common law, largely free of social coercion, and often left to their own devices in the face of Muslim onslaught, the Castilians forged an identity of their own. Castile lay at the crossroads of diverse ethnic groups and principalities, but out of conflict and expansion had formed its own ethos and was developing its own language. The leader who first took effective advantage of this was a royally appointed count of Castile, Fernán González, in an attempt to assert Castilian autonomy during the reign of Ramiro II. Though several times defeated, he rallied most of the Castilian population behind him, and during the convulsed generation that followed the death of Ramiro II, established the full autonomy of Castile on terms of virtual independence. For twenty years, from 950 to 970, he governed as count of Castile, in conflict at varying times with the Cordoban caliphate, the kingdom of Navarre, and León itself.

Castile's chief reason for being was military, and it did a better job of defending itself against Muslim onslaught than any other Christian principality. The most redoubtable quality of Fernán González was his fierce military leadership. The vernacular Castilian *romances* later remembered that

Decíanle por sus lides el buitre carnicero.
(They called him for his battles the butcher vulture.)

The elite cavalry of lesser nobles was increased to 600 by González, and though it may have bent, the military structure of Castile did not crack under the Muslim onslaught. Most of the wealth of the land was in livestock, which was herded out of the way or into the hills, limiting economic loss. By the beginning of the eleventh century, Castile had weathered the storm of the "iron century" in rather better condition than the more sophisticated but less vigorous and more politically and socially divided regions of Old León.

The Expansion of Navarre

The small Basque region of Navarre (or Pamplona, as it is often called, after its capital and only real city) was originally one of the smallest but also the most ethnically homogeneous of Hispanic principalities. Its population was at first largely non-Christian, and only in its capital city and among the ruling class was Romance dialect spoken; elsewhere people spoke the isolated, autochthonous Basque tongue almost exclusively. The early history of Navarre is shrouded in mystery, for almost no records have survived. Though the region was not fully Christianized until the twelfth century, it may be inferred that Christian proselytization was carried on fairly continuously, particularly from the north, where Navarre lay more open to French influence than any other Hispanic region save the Catalan counties of the eastern Pyrenees.

Navarrese history took a new direction in 905, when a new dynasty was established in Pamplona under Sancho Garcés I (905–925). The one-hundred-year-old alliance with the Hispano-Muslim Banu Qasi rulers of the neighboring upper Ebro region was broken, and the Navarrese crown adopted an Hispano-Christian policy of expansion and reconquest. With military assistance from León, the Nájera district (in modern Logroño province) to the southwest was conquered between 918 and 923, though beyond that point the small Navarrese forces were unable to make headway. Indeed, the resurgence of Muslim power under the tenth-century caliphate soon forced the Pamplona rulers to return to their more customary policy of compromise and the renewal of marriage alliances, wedding a Navarrese princess to the heir of al-Mansur.

Somewhat paradoxically, the backward, non-Romance-speaking, still partly unchristianized Navarre nevertheless became by the end of the tenth century extremely receptive to new influences, in part because of its position astride the western Pyrenees. Navarre and the Catalan counties were the first Hispanic regions to be influenced by the tenth- and eleventh-century Catholic reform movements from France, which were transmitted through them to Castile and León. The eastern principalities served as channels of European modernization in a variety of ways: new forms of administrative organization, mercantile practice, training and functioning of clerks and scribes, artisanship, and military technology (particularly in the development of stronger horses, weapons, and chain mail for the new style of heavy cavalry) began to filter through the Pyrenean states. Though the Catalan counties in some respects may have been farther advanced culturally and economically, Navarre by the early eleventh century had become the peninsula's best-organized state politically, thanks in large part to a series of vigorous and capable rulers. Navarre was the only non-Muslim region unravaged by al-Mansur, and it was clearly the most unified.

The "modernization" of Navarre occurred just as the Muslim caliphate was crippled by the death of Adbul Malik. This provided a major opportunity, and Sancho III "el Mayor" (1004-1035) seized it to make Navarre briefly the leading Hispano-Christian state for the first and only time in its history. Sancho was unequivocal about the royal nature of his sovereignty; he was strongly influenced by French monarchist theory and feudal norms, and followed the French practice of claiming to rule "by the grace of God," a formula subsequently adopted by other Hispanic kings. His ambitions were greatly assisted by the weakness and division of León, which had not yet recovered from the civil turmoil and devastation of the century before. Sancho first annexed the three small counties to the east (Aragón, Sobrarbe, Ribagorza) and then extended Navarrese control over much of the Basque territory on the northwest side of the Pyrenees. When his father-in-law, Sancho García, third count of Castile, died in 1017 leaving only a small son as heir, Sancho of Navarre established himself as protector of Castile. This enabled him to incorporate the Basque-speaking districts of northeastern Castile (roughly modern Alava and Vizcaya) into Navarre. After the nephew came of age, he was murdered in 1028 by dissident Castilian nobles (perhaps with Sancho's encouragement), and Sancho incorporated all of Castile into his realm. From that point he pressed against the borders of León, fomenting rebellion by aristocratic dissidents and defeating the Leonese monarchy in battle. At the beginning of 1034 Sancho entered the city of León in triumph. Basing his claim on vague dynastic relations, support of fractious nobles, and the right of conquest, he asserted control over the Leonese throne and declared himself emperor of all the Hispano-Christian principalities. He died one year later, at the height of his power.

The Navarrese "empire" was no more than a personal creation of Sancho el Mayor, depending in large part on the weakness and disunity of its neighbors. Navarre itself lacked the resources to dominate the rest of Christian Hispania, and the empire immediately dissolved after Sancho's death. The dissolution, in fact, was arranged by Sancho himself, who gave vogue to French feudal theory and practice in the Hispanic states, introducing the term *vassal* into Castilian usage. He divided his three principal domains among his sons, with the understanding that the two younger sons in their separate patrimonies of Castile and Aragón would recognize the suzerainty of the eldest, García of Navarre (1035-1054), who inherited the dynasty's home principality. In the long run, however, the neighboring territories of Castile and Aragón benefitted more than did Navarre from new changes and techniques that were introduced during the eleventh century. In the decades that followed, the other states grew stronger, while Navarre remained comparatively static and no longer enjoyed leadership as effective as that of Sancho. When García tried to encroach directly on Castile, he was defeated and killed in battle in 1054. The Navarrese monarchy not only lost hegemony but subsequently encountered difficulty in maintaining the integrity of its domains.

Underlying Unity of the Hispano-Christian Principalities

The small Hispanic states of the early Middle Ages were divided by formidable geographic barriers, by linguistic differences, and at times by violent political conflict, yet these disparities were mitigated by undercurrents of religious and cultural unity. The Hispano-Visigothic liturgy was used not only by Mozarabs in Al-Andalus but also by Christians throughout the peninsula, and even for a time across the Pyrenees in formerly Visigothic Septimania, under French rule since the eighth century. The Hispano-Visigothic legal code, the *Fuero Juzgo,* was widely employed by the first generations of the Catalan Pyrenean counties, as well as in Asturias-León. Common artistic and architectural forms were followed, based on Hispano-Visigothic culture and the use of the peculiar Visigothic Latin script. All of this helped to keep alive the sense of a common Christian Hispania during the difficult centuries of Muslim hegemony.

By the eleventh century, the Hispano-Christian princes had also developed similar ambitions: the reconquest of territory and expansion to the south. Though this sometimes led to conflict, cooperation was more common, based on a common sense of historic mission. Yet the separate territorial political entities formed during these first centuries had laid deep roots, and expanded their frontiers southward rather than coalescing. Thus despite an underlying Hispano-Christian peninsular identity, monarchico-territorial pluralism became accepted as a legal and natural fact in the state systems of greater Christian Hispania.

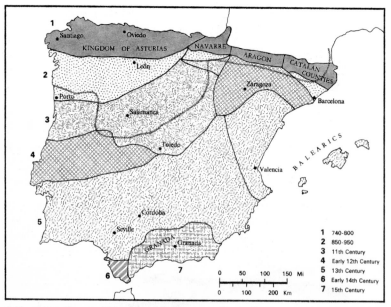

Approximate Stages of the Spanish Reconquest. Heavy line
indicates northern limit of major Muslim occupation

UWCL

4

Castile-León in the Era of the Great Reconquest

Stages of the Hispanic Reconquest

The Hispano-Christian reconquest and reoccupation was a continuing process of more than seven centuries, punctuated, however, by long pauses which Muslim strength, Christian exhaustion, or internal quarreling made inevitable. The reconquest may be divided into seven phases:

1. Ca. 740–790: conquest of the southern Cantabrian foothills and lower Galicia
2. Ca. 850–950: expansion into the Duero valley (in Catalonia, conquest of central Catalonia)
3. Eleventh century: conquest of the central plateau and central Portugal
4. Early twelfth century: conquest of lower Aragón and southwestern Catalonia and expansion of the southern and southwestern borders of Castile-León into Extremadura
5. Thirteenth century: climactic period of the reconquest, with the conquest of the Balearics, Valencia, all the south-central peninsula, and most of the south, save for the emirate of Granada and a few coastal points
6. Early fourteenth century: minor extension of Castilian territory along the southern coast

7. Fifteenth century: completion of the reconquest, ended by the occupation of Granada (1482-1492)

It should be kept in mind, of course, that there was often a lag of one hundred years or more between conquest and effective settlement or occupation.

The New Power Balance and Renewal of Leonese-Castilian Imperialism

The collapse of the Cordoban caliphate opened the way to a drastic change in the power balance of the peninsula. While Muslim leadership and strength splintered, the Christian principalities were expanding with a vigor only partially related to demographic changes, for the Christian states were still more lightly inhabited than the taifa lands. Key to the expansion were the recuperation of Leonese strength and unity and the reunification of Castile and León under the Castilian monarchy, accompanied by reinvigoration of the old Leonese program of imperial reconquest and Hispanic unity, first sketched out in the eighth century. A secondary factor of some importance was the development of mailed heavy cavalry, which had a distinct advantage over Muslim light cavalry and infantry, though it is not clear to how great an extent the Leonese-Castilian forces actually relied on heavy cavalry. Aragón and Catalonia also increased their military power, assisted by French adventurers and crusaders, but their forces remained much smaller than those of the large kingdom of León-Castile.

The reunification of León and Castile was accomplished by Fernando I (1037-1065), second son of Sancho el Mayor, who had inherited the county of Castile and raised it to the rank of kingdom after the Navarrese "anti-emperor"'s death in 1035. Meanwhile the young Leonese king, Vermudo III (1028-1037), had regained his capital after Sancho's death and begun to reassert the imperial sovereignty of the Leonese crown. In the process, he tried to reoccupy the territory in eastern León that had been seized earlier by Sancho for Castile, but was killed in battle by the Castilian forces of Fernando in 1037. Since Vermudo left no heir, he was succeeded by his rival, Fernando of Castile, who also happened to be Vermudo's brother-in-law, since Fernando was wed to a Leonese princess. Henceforth Fernando was ruler of "Castile-León," the younger and less-developed kingdom taking precedence in the royal title of the Sánchez dynasty because it was Fernando's inherited patrimony, whereas the larger and more important León was an acquired territory. In fact, the main role in the later reconquest by Fernando was played by the militant aristocrats and expansionist prelates of wealthier, more developed, and more imperial-minded León.

The united Castile-León of Fernando I fell heir to the historic Leonese imperial program, interrupted by a century of internal weakness and Muslim pressure. Nearly two decades were passed in recuperation, restoration of unity, and settlement of the border quarrel with Navarre, finally resolved in 1054 with the death of the Navarrese king, García. In the following year Fernando I launched the first of a series of assaults against the Muslim border taifas that filled the last decade of his reign. The major territorial conquests were made in the southwest, where Viseu was seized in 1057 and Guarda and Coimbra in 1064. More important geopolitically and economically was the reduction to tributary status of the three leading taifa emirates along the frontier—Badajoz, Toledo, and Zaragoza. Large annual *parias* (tribute payments) swelled the resources of the Castilian-Leonese crown and encouraged the military mercenary, overlord, ethos that was developing more markedly in Castilian-Leonese society than in the Pyrenean counties.

Though Fernando I had adopted the imperial reconquest program of the traditional Leonese monarchy, he proved unable to resist the feudalizing inheritance policy that had been introduced by his father. He divided his domains among his three sons and awarded territorial grants to his two daughters, giving them the title of queen. This created intense conflict and rivalry after Fernando's death. At the end of seven years of internecine strife, the second son reunited the dual kingdom as Alfonso VI of Castile-León (1065-1109) and, in Leonese terminology, "Emperor of Hispania."

Leonese imperial policy could now be resumed. Within another decade most of Al-Andalus had been subjected to tributary status under the Leonese crown, and in 1082 Alfonso VI led an expedition to the southern tip of the peninsula, where he rode his horse out into the water in a symbolic gesture to show that all of Hispania was under Leonese suzerainty. The city of Toledo was a major prize, and key to the peninsula's fairly populous and productive central plateau. That entire region had been seized directly by 1085, moving the boundaries of Castile-León far southward from the Duero to the Tajo river valley and establishing Leonese dominion in the very center of Hispania. Reoccupation of the Visigothic capital gave further impetus to the imperial pretensions of the Leonese crown.

Territorial expansion and the large income from parias also opened a new era in the economic affairs of León and Castile. Urban life developed, as new towns were founded and the few already established grew. Commerce increased and began to acquire a significance

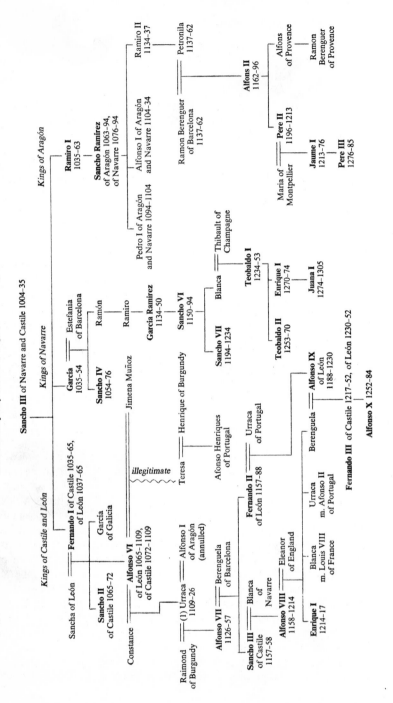

The Sánchez Dynasty of Castile, Aragón, and Navarre, 1000–1284

it had never known before. This was stimulated by Alfonso VI's encouragement of the immigration of monks, merchants, and artisans, who helped form the nucleus of a middle class in the towns of northern Castile and León. It was also assisted by the growth in traffic along the road to Santiago de Compostela, whose shrine had become the destination of thousands of west European pilgrims. The new prosperity stimulated building, the endowment of churches, the development of the arts, and the general growth of Leonese culture. Population expanded, and by 1100 the greater kingdom of Castile-León numbered approximately two and a half million inhabitants.

Resettlement of the Region Between the Duero and Tajo: The Concejos of Castile and León

Much of the newly acquired land between the Duero and Tajo was taken over by common soldiers and peasant immigrants, who formed communities that were given royal charters (fueros) as semi-autonomous concejos (council districts). The concejos covered most of the territory in the region. They were not so much municipal governments as governing councils of rural districts with a fortified village or small town in the center of each to serve as cattle market and military rallying point. The larger concejos thus included sizable tracts of land surrounding the main town around which they were organized. Concejos were organized on a semi-egalitarian basis; in some districts all the local *vecinos,* or permanent residents, had a voice in choosing the local council, though in others the most vigorous or wealthy soon formed a local oligarchy. Most of the land within the concejos was held under varying terms of condominium or communal ownership, though agricultural as distinct from pastoral land was sometimes set aside as strictly personal property. A considerable share of each district was held as *tierra concejil*—"council land" of the community. Other portions were classified as *bienes de propios,* semiprivate lands still subject to community regulation. Since animal-grazing was the basis of the economy, the principle of absolute private property was less useful. Under the terms of their fueros, most concejos were free to administer their local affairs and dispense justice, and were nominally responsible to the crown only for payment of taxes and military levies. The most important of the concejos were Salamanca, Avila, and Segovia. Though concejo settlement had begun by the mid-eleventh century, it was not complete for more than one hundred years, until after the frontier had moved south of the Tajo.

The founding of the eleventh-century concejos was accompanied by the establishment of an intermediate military elite in New Castile and lower León—the *caballeros villanos* or commoner-knights. This had already begun in Castile during the tenth century and had been hastened by two developments. First, there was the tendency, already marked by the tenth century, for the aristocracy in León and to a lessser degree in Old Castile to settle into an hereditary caste. What had earlier been a military and administrative service aristocracy had established itself as a privileged group, exempt from taxation and in some cases even military service, but enjoying hereditary dominion over lands and other perquisites, and among the high aristocracy over family titles as well. All this elevated its members into a feudal caste of regional socio-economic domination in Galicia, Old León, and Old Castile and deprived the crown of many of the services for which aristocratic status had originally been the reward. Second, the heightened warfare of the tenth century, followed by the renewed expansion of the eleventh, called for more mobile and offensive forces than had been needed for scattered raiding and defensive warfare in the northern hills. The Christian principalities had to expand heavy cavalry to secure military domination, but it was an expensive process.

The cheapest, most direct way was through broad expansion of the class of caballeros villanos, ordinary peasants who proved themselves in battle and were granted sufficient land or condominium shares in the concejos to maintain their expensive military equipment and retinue. Such expansion was made possible by the fact that horses were more available to commoners on the Hispanic frontier than anywhere else in western Europe. Formation of this nonaristocratic military elite strengthened royal power, discouraged aristocratic factionalism, and built military strength in the frontier areas where it was needed most. It recognized and reaffirmed the open society of frontier Castile-León, where common shepherds and peasants could rise to elite status.

Prominence of the Medieval Hispanic Venturero

During the eleventh century there emerged the Hispanic *venturero* (adventurer, professional soldier or mercenary), who for five hundred years was to be a common figure throughout western Europe and the Mediterranean and even parts of central Europe and northwest Africa. Ventureros came from all the Hispanic principalities, but the exorbitantly military style of Castile, coupled with its poverty, made professional warriors more often than not Castilian in origin, though probably the most famous of all were the special companies of Catalonia. Whether *campeadores* on land or *mareantes* on the sea, they were found in almost every theater of operations; Hispano-Christian mercenaries were the last elite corps defending the fanatically Muslim Almoravid empire. Generations of this kind of experience found their fruition in the epic *conquistadores* of the sixteenth century.

The Reconquest Checked: Rise of the Almoravid Empire

By the time of the incorporation of Toledo, Alfonso VI was collecting tribute not merely from Muslim frontier districts but from the taifas of Seville, Granada, and other important southern regions. He demanded that a lieutenant from among his officials be allowed to supervise the government of the emirate of Seville. Other military lieutenants occupied strategic fortresses in the south central, southern, and southeastern parts of the peninsula to ensure Castilian military dominance and continued tribute payments.

In 1085, there seemed nothing to hinder Castilian conquest of all the taifas of southern Hispania, though the economy and culture of the south continued to flourish. Silks, leather goods, cotton textiles, pottery, and farm products made the taifas the economic wonder of the peninsula, and their commerce remained extensive, but tribute payments were raised higher and higher, threatening to bleed away this prosperity. The only hope of respite from Castilian pressure was Muslim assistance from outside the peninsula.

Relief was available from the forces of a dynamic new Muslim power that had swept across Morocco from the western Sahara during the past generation. In 1039, a Maghrebi jurist and evangelist had been invited into the western Sahara to inculcate formal Islamic practice among the wild Touareg tribes of that region. This faqih, Ibn Yasin, preached a simple, ascetic, as well as militant interpretation of Islam and quickly collected a following calling themselves *al-murabitun* ("united for holy war"), westernized as *Almoravids.* In their fanatical fervor, the Almoravids preached the jihad and spread across the western Sahara like the early followers of Mohammed in the Arabian Hedjaz. The Almoravids' militant, puritanical doctrine—advocating strict, literal obedience to the Koran, daily ablutions, the shunning of money-making, the giving of alms and rejection of vice, and the fear of hell counterbalanced by hope of salvation through militant implementation of the will of Allah—caught fire among the fierce, half-pagan tribesmen. Within twenty years the Almoravids carved out a loose, theocratic state that covered much of the western Sahara. Though in theory submissive to the sovereignty of the Fatimid caliphate at Cairo, the Almoravid state actually constituted an independent empire. It conquered the tribes of the upper Senegal, spilled over into western Algeria, and invaded sedentary and more cultured Morocco. The Almoravids brought a promise of lowered taxes and relief for the poor, and by 1080 nearly all Morocco had been conquered.

As early as 1077, the Almoravids had been approached for military assistance by taifa representatives. The conquest of northern Morocco was completed in 1084, one year before Toledo was incorporated into Castile. The need of the taifas was desperate, and in 1086 an explicit invitation to cross the straits was tendered by al-Mutamid of Seville, who at the same time sought to make sure that the taifas would not fall under Almoravid domination. The invitation to do battle in support of the emir of Seville against Castile was accepted by the Almoravid leaders as a logical extension of their jihad.

As usual, Alfonso VI seized the initiative, meeting the Almoravids on Muslim territory at Sagrajas (near Badajoz). The Almoravid forces relied chiefly upon compactly organized, trained infantry, armed with lances and javelins and protected by hippopotamus-hide shields. In addition, they included an elite corps of black African guards, light cavalry interspersed with small camel corps to frighten the enemy's horses, and units of archers and crossbowmen. At Sagrajas the forces from Seville bore the brunt of the formidable Castilian charge while a mobile portion of the Almoravids flanked the Castilian host and struck their camp from the rear. Defeated, the Castilians retreated in fairly good order, and the Almoravids retired to Africa without exploiting their victory.

The only real prospect for independence of what remained of Al-Andalus—still nearly two-thirds of the peninsula—seemed to lie in a permanent Almoravid military presence. This left the taifa rulers in a dilemma, for they were no more eager to be taken over by the fanatical, somewhat primitive Almoravids than by the equally rigorous Castilians. By 1090, however, an Almoravid party had formed among the people of some of the larger taifa cities. It was led by fanatical faqihs and supported by Muslim traditionalists increasingly conscious of their Muslim identity and fearful of Christian domination; also by the poor, hoping for relief. The Almoravid leader, Yusuf ibn Tashfin, had gauged the feebleness of the taifa emirs, weak in religiosity, many of them steeped in self-indulgence. He returned to the peninsula in 1090 and within two years had seized the main taifa capitals in the south. Soon nearly the entire southern half of the peninsula had been incorporated in the Almoravid empire. The frontier then for several decades was stabilized south of the Tajo, since the Almoravids were not strong enough to assault the new line of Castilian settlements in the very center of the peninsula.

There seems little doubt that Almoravid rule was at first fairly popular among Hispano-Muslims. Yet the Almoravid military elite was culturally inferior to its appanage, and the Almoravid period is sometimes painted as one of intolerant suppression of the "high culture" of the taifas by the puritanical and fanatic Africans. It is true that secular poetry and the use of musical instruments were discouraged, but the decorative arts, song, and popular poetry continued to flourish. The achievements of Hispano-Muslim culture in the second half of the twelfth century attest its survival under the Almoravids.

With the eleventh-century shift in power and the subsequent establishment of the Almoravid empire in southern Hispania, the sense of ethno-religious identity among Hispanic Muslims and of intense hostility toward Christians was sharpened. The traditionalist Malikite rite, which had become less universal, was rigorously reimposed, and the *ulemas* (religious teachers) were employed as an instrument of policy. What remained of the traditional Hispano-Muslim "discriminatory toleration" ended with the Almoravids, who inaugurated a policy of direct persecution of the few remaining Christians in the south. Jews also suffered and for the first time were beginning to look to the Christian princes as saviors from Muslim persecution. This was a consequence of the Almoravid interpretation of the jihad, and something of the same degree of militance and intolerance was beginning to be shared by Hispanic Muslims as well. By the twelfth century the gap between Christian and Muslim Hispania was greater than ever before.

The Epic of the Cid

As Almoravid power grew, it veered away from the strongly-held Castilian center of the peninsula toward the prosperous urban centers and irrigated fields of the east coast. There at Valencia the greatest military figure of medieval Hispania, the legendary national hero Rodrigo Díaz de Vivar, known from the terminology of his Muslim subjects as the Cid, had carved out an independent protectorate.

As far as is known, the Cid was a renowned Castilian knight, vassal of Alfonso VI, banished from his native kingdom because of a misunderstanding. He entered the military service of the emir of Zaragoza and gained more laurels in the eastern part of the peninsula. As the Almoravid danger grew, he was accepted again into the service of the Leonese crown, and though Alfonso VI remained jealous and suspicious, he was granted hereditary autonomous dominion, under the crown of León, of all Muslim land that he could conquer in the peninsula's east. Between 1088 and 1092 the Cid carved out a domain reaching from the region of Lérida and Tortosa down to Valencia, and proved a shrewd ruler as well as a clever and ruthless warrior.

Large tribute payments were exacted from the Muslims, in keeping with the Hispano-Christian practice. In 1092 the pro-Almoravid party in wealthy, populous Valencia rebelled against their emir, who was a vassal of the king of León. Mobilizing his maximum force, the Cid took advantage of civil strife in Valencia to add that city to his domain after a long siege that decimated the Muslim population. Major Almoravid counteroffensives to regain Valencia were twice defeated, and even the Muslims admitted the extraordinary astuteness and military prowess of the new Valencian overlord. The Cid combined some of the prime characteristics of the new Hispanic society of his time. He represented the growing initiative of Castile, personified the ideal of the warrior overlord, and prosecuted the reconquest while demonstrating an understanding of Muslim psychology and ability to treat with and govern Islamic people. During the last decade of his career he cooperated with Leonese, Aragonese, and Catalans in the crucial struggle against the Almoravids. After he died in 1099, however, the Levantine regions could not be defended. Alfonso VI drove off a Muslim force that besieged the Cid's widow in 1102, but lacked the strength to do other than evacuate and burn Valencia. The surrounding district was immediately seized by the Almoravids.

The Succession Crisis and the Social Revolt of 1109-1117

The second half of Alfonso VI's long reign (1065-1109) was a painful anticlimax. At one point this Leonese-Castilian king who called himself emperor had seemed to be wresting nearly the entire peninsula from the Muslims, only to lose most of the remaining Muslim territory back to the Almoravids after his harsh tributary policies encouraged African intervention. He had been the most European of Leonese kings; he had tried to bring Castile-León fully into the orbit of European diplomacy for the first time and had encouraged the official Romanization of Castilian Catholicism (see chapter 7). During his long reign he had displaced both his brothers and outlived four wives, but after 1086/1089 his armies remained largely on the defensive. New Castile was devastated by Almoravid raids in 1097-1099 and 1108, suffering lesser incursions in between.

Despite his four marriages, Alfonso VI left only two daughters upon his death in 1109, one, Urraca, legitimate, and the other, Teresa, a bastard. Alfonso, who had established strong political and religious ties with Burgundy and had married three French princesses, had wed both his daughters to prominent Burgundian nobles seeking their fortunes battling the infidels in Hispania. Teresa and her husband,

Count Henrique, had been awarded the county of Portugal (roughly the northern third of modern Portugal), which formed the southwestern corner of the kingdom of León. Intent upon expanding their patrimony, they began to intrigue against the crown while governing their own territory independently. The resulting emergence of the independent kingdom of Portugal is the topic of chapter 6.

Alfonso's heiress, Urraca, was already widowed at her father's death. According to Leonese custom, the crown could not be inherited by a woman alone, so immediately after the death of Alfonso VI she was wed to the only reigning king in Hispania, Alfonso I "the Battler," sovereign of Aragón and Navarre (which was for several generations under the Aragonese dynasty). The marriage reunited the eastern and western branches of the Sánchez dynasty that had split in 1035, but it was a political and a conjugal failure from the beginning. Dona Urraca was stubborn, independent, and given to frequent changes of mind; the Battler was a pious crusader, apparently with a streak of misogyny in his nature, who devoted himself to a rarely interrupted series of campaigns against the Muslims. The powerful Leonese magnates resented a strong new king and were rebellious and eager to increase their own power. Conflict between king and queen and the machinations of grasping nobles had by 1110 led to civil war in León.

The struggle was deepened and complicated by the first major social revolt in Leonese history, led by the middle classes in some of the newly expanded towns of northern León and Castile and to some extent spearheaded by French immigrants. Their uprising against the exactions of regional overlords was much like the revolt of communes in France during the twelfth and thirteenth centuries. In a few regions there were also rebellions by peasants bound in servitude, supported by poor village priests who sympathized with their lowly parishioners against the wealthy prelates and big monasteries. Some of the townspeople looked to Alfonso the Battler as their champion, for he had been generous toward the towns and the small commercial class in his own kingdom, where there was not yet a large, powerful aristocracy or strong establishment of monasteries to dominate society.

Most of the Leonese aristocracy and church hierarchy struggled to isolate Alfonso from his new kingdom. The marriage between distant cousins was annulled by the papacy as incestuous, and after several years of political frustration and civil war Alfonso the Battler withdrew completely and returned to his raids against the Muslims, leaving Urraca's very young son by her first marriage to eventually succeed him as Alfonso VII of Castile-León.

The social revolt was not put down finally until 1117, but it ended with complete victory for the upper classes, and some of the townspeople active in the rebellion were forced to leave the kingdom. The outcome was frustrating to social and economic change. Towns in Castile-León remained comparatively few, small, and poor; internal affairs of the kingdom were dominated by the aristocracy to an extent greater than in the more rapidly developing areas of western Europe. The status of the concejos in the southern half of León-Castile was hardly affected, but the rural, agrarian character of the Leonese-Castilian economy was accentuated. The later twelfth century, marked by internal disorder and wars, was a time of relative economic decline. The society was still composed almost exclusively of aristocrats and peasants, warriors, priests, and shepherds, and was not developing the urban middle class and economy that were changing France, the Low Countries, west Germany, and northern Italy. The kingdom's primary export was wool to the textile towns of France, England, and the Low Countries, supplemented by other products of the countryside such as wax, hides, and honey. The extension of this rurally produced, partly aristocrat-dominated export trade in the second half of the eleventh century did, however, encourage commercial and maritime development along Castile's Cantabrian coast, where by 1200 a series of small but fairly active ports had been established.

The Crusade and the Crusading Orders

The first three and one-half centuries of warfare between Christians and Muslims in the peninsula were essentially a political power struggle having little or no ideological meaning and consisting of cattle raids or other depredations for booty by both sides. The Muslims normally did not practice the jihad and the main ideological justification for aggressive warfare by the Christian states, particularly by León, was the essentially political one of recovering the lost sovereignty of the Gothic monarchy. This was a major basis for the imperial claims of the Castilian-Leonese crown.

Among the Muslims, circumstances changed during the hegemony of al-Mansur, and the jihad was preached with great intensity during the Almoravid invasion. As for the Christians, the explicit ideal of the crusade as a holy war against Muslim usurpers was introduced from France and Italy during the Catholic religious renewal of the eleventh century. It was a consequence of the expanding population, military strength, and assertive spirit of western Europe, and of the increased power of the Hispanic kingdoms. The primary target of the western crusades was the Holy Land, but the struggle against the Muslims in the peninsula also received attention. As early as 1064, nearly three decades before the First Crusade to Palestine, the papacy promised indulgences to French knights who volunteered to assist an Aragonese campaign against the Muslims. From the twelfth century on, crusading expeditions against Hispano-Muslim states were common in the military life of the Hispano-Christian kingdoms, including the new state of Portugal. The advantages of papal authorization for an official crusade were threefold: it boosted morale, encouraged Hispano-Christian political unity, and provided financial and military support through special subsidies and indulgences. The institutionalization of the crusade and its accompanying religio-military psychology, which subsequently became an important motivating factor in Castilian and Portuguese expansion, can be seen as the consequence of two factors: extra-Hispanic religious influences, and the radicalization of the long Christian-Muslim struggle in the peninsula.

Branches of the two major military crusading orders, the Knights Templars and Hospitalers, were soon established in the peninsula. This was followed by organization of a number of strictly Hispanic crusading orders, of which the three most important were the Knights of Calatrava, organized on the southern extremity of New Castile in 1157, the Order of Alcántara, founded in Extremadura about 1165, and the Order of Santiago, formed near Cáceres in 1170. The military usefulness of the crusading orders was clear from the outset, for they played a major role in defending and expanding the frontier. Within a century of their foundation, the three largest orders had become wealthy institutions with large domains, and important economically and politically in the affairs of Castile and León and to a lesser degree in Portugal and Aragón.

Yet the institutionalization of the crusade still did not create an absolute and unbridgeable gulf between Christian and Muslim. Crusading was used for purposes that were in large measure political, and political circumstances were still sufficient to overrule crusading. At the end of the twelfth century, following the temporary division of Castile and León and a major defeat of Castilians by the Muslim Almohad state, the crown of León still found it expedient to form a temporary alliance with the Almohads against its own Christian rival, Castile.

Antipathy to Islam was never so strong as to preclude admiration for and adoption of certain practices of Hispano-Muslim society. Muslim baths were retained in some of the cities seized by the reconquest, the practice of veiling women was adopted and maintained by Christian society in some of the southern regions for several centuries, and hundreds of Arabic words were incorporated into the Hispanic languages. Polite ceremonious speech and even ways of referring to God were affected. To what extent certain facets of Hispano-Muslim psychology were also reflected in that of Hispano-Christians has been a matter of extensive debate.

Institutional and Social Change in Twelfth-Century Castile and León

Alfonso VII, the son of Queen Urraca's first marriage, came of age in 1126 and restored unified rule during a long reign that lasted thirty-one years, until his death in 1157. When the Almoravid empire broke up during the 1140s he extended the reconquest deep into the south, though he was unable to hold most of his gains. Like his grandfather, Alfonso VII claimed the title of emperor and with it the right to divide up his lands among his heirs; the experience of the past century had no effect upon the short-sighted practice of Castilian-Leonese sovereigns of this period. All of Castile proper was willed to his elder son, who in 1157 became Sancho III of Castile, while the lands of León were granted to a younger son, crowned Fernando II of León. Castile and León remained separate for nearly three-quarters of a century, until reunited by San Fernando III in 1230.

This division of the kingdoms marked the effective end of the Leonese claim to empire over Christian Hispania. León had long been the largest, most important, and most ambitious of Hispano-Christian states, but the eleventh-century reconquest had greatly expanded Castile, to almost equal it in size. Moreover, the southern territories of New Castile included the former ruling city of Toledo, encouraging Castilian claims to leadership in Hispanic affairs. After 1157 there existed a large and independent Castile, separate kingdoms of Navarre and Portugal, and a united crown of Catalonia-Aragón. León could no longer pretend to hegemony; when Castile and León were later reunited, Castile took precedence not merely in name but in political and military reality as well, until eventually the lands of Castile-León were called simply the kingdom of Castile.

Sancho III of Castile survived his father by a single year, leaving as heir a three-year-old son, Alfonso VIII (1158-1214). Throughout the Middle Ages effective monarchy depended on a strong king; with a three-year-old as ruler, power was violently disputed by factions of the Castilian nobility, who tended to coalesce around the two feuding houses of the Castros and Laras. The people of Castile suffered considerably during the next ten years, as authority was usurped by a lawless aristocracy. Seigneurial domain was extended, and the already powerful nobility of León grew more powerful. It had become increasingly common for the crown to make explicit grants of *seño-ríos* and *abadengos* (seigneuries and church domains) carrying with them social and economic jurisdiction over the land. Thus by the twelfth century much of León and some of Castile had become feudal in fact. The vogue of French ideas and French feudal terminology in Castile and León during the eleventh and twelfth centuries encouraged the trend.

It should be understood, however, that this de facto feudalization was not the same as the de jure feudalization of France and some other areas of western Europe. Seigneurial jurisdiction in León and Castile was with some exceptions limited to economic control, and governmental and juridical power over the seigneuries, at least in theory, still remained in the hands of crown. The authority of a strong monarchy was still predominant, and the process of economic feudalization worked from the top downward, through dispensations of the crown, as much as from the bottom upward, through the initiative or usurpation of local aristocrats. Moreover, in León, aristocratic holdings did not form the large compact semi-unified domains that they did in parts of France, but were usually made up of a patchwork of small territories, sometimes widely dispersed, over which economic seigneury had been recognized. Their crazy-quilt nature reduced the political or military power that could be exercised by aristocratic houses.

The system of benefactoria, by which local peasant groups recognized the overlordship of noble families and paid them shares of produce or rent, was extended considerably during the twelfth century. Both its name and nature were changing in the process. In Castile and eastern León the system, which had become known as behetría, was growing more restrictive. Under many original behetría arrangements the recognition of lordship might extend *de mar a mar* (from sea to sea), meaning that peasant villages dissatisfied with the protection and services of their overlord might switch their alliegance to another defender. By the twelfth century, the practice had become limited to one of *de linaje de linaje* (from lineage to lineage), meaning that any change of allegiance must be to a member of the same aristocratic family. Though behetría peasants were not homines or colonos, in many cases their freedom of movement was being limited to movement within their districts or to other domains held by their ruling families. Whereas the benefactoria system had originally been an arrangement for mutual defense, by the twelfth century it had become largely a means of institutionalizing aristocratic domination of the land. Exactions increased, as various forms of sub- and super-infeudation were practiced at different levels of the aristocracy, the more powerful overlords obtaining special *diviseros* or extra payments, from peasants who were already paying shares to their imme-

diate overlords. This extension of aristocratic control was a consequence of the insecurity and disorder of the twelfth century, and
particularly of the turbulent decade of the Castros and Laras. By that
time, autonomous local communities had disappeared in the greater
part of the kingdom of León. The greatest concentration of new
seigneuries and behetría arrangements occurred in the Duero plain of
Castile and León, the region which had been resettled between 850
and 1050. Behetrías also became much more common in Old Castile,
though their terms tended to be more liberal. Until the beginning of
the twelfth century, most of the peasants of Castile had escaped living
under direct seigneurial or behetría exactions, but by the end of that
century many were subject to them.

The region that preserved local liberties most fully was the new
concejo territory along the Tajo. The communities there, led by their
local elite of caballeros villanos, held the Castilian and Leonese
frontier firm against the onslaughts of the new Muslim invaders from
Morocco. Whereas, during the eleventh and twelfth centuries, the
peasant population of the Duero region had been depleted by emigration to the frontier and had fallen under seigneurial control, concejo
districts were being organized and populated on the southern frontier.
The concejos of the greater Tajo region and beyond became a major
stabilizing force in the kingdom.

Rise of the Muslim Almohad Empire

The strength of Almoravids lay in their military skill and religious
zeal. Their civil organization and culture were never sufficiently advanced to weld a unified empire. Their domains were heterogeneous
in the extreme, and in their most culturally sophisticated territory, Al-
Andalus, they never sank deep roots. To most Hispano-Muslims, the
Almoravids were foreigners who ruled by military power alone. The
social reforms promised rarely materialized, and after several decades
Almoravid rule came more and more to seem a mere military occupation. Furthermore it was opposed by local variants of Hispano-Muslim religious heterodoxy which had begun to show strength in the
eleventh century, religious trends that tended toward the mystical,
with populist and meliorist overtones. Reflecting the feelings of most
of the Hispano-Muslim population, they were also anti-Arabicist, but
one major result of this religious upsurge was to encourage opposition
to Almoravid political and religious orthodoxy. Revolts began in the
1120s in Hispania and later became widespread in Morocco, where
the last defenders of the Almoravid emperors were an elite guard of

Christian mercenaries. By 1147, the empire had been completely torn apart.

During the next twenty-five years, power in the south and east once more fell into the hands of local taifa rulers, much as during the preceding century. Their dominion lasted only one generation, for another militant Muslim empire was rising in Morocco. Known in the European languages as the Almohads, this new power was based on a Muslim reform movement that had begun, not among Saharan nomads, but among the agrarian Berbers of the Atlas Mountains. The Almohads (*al-muwahhidun,* "asserters of religious unity") preached a more sophisticated and mystical version of Islam in place of the simple, anthropomorphic religion of the Almoravids. By 1147, they had replaced the Almoravids as masters of Morocco and had begun to intervene militarily in the peninsula. Alfonso VII of Castile had made great gains in the wake of the Almoravid collapse, occupying Córdoba for three years (1146-1149) and holding the major port of Almeria for a decade (1147-1157), but nearly all his advances were wiped out by the Almohad counterattack. During the years that followed, the Almohads added most of Algeria and Tunisia to their realm, and by 1172 firmly established their control over all the neo-taifa territories in the peninsula. Their position in Hispania at first was stronger than the Almoravids' had been in 1100, and their territories in North Africa even more extensive, but they never rewon Christian territory save that of Alfonso VII's most recent conquests.

The Apex of Hispano-Muslim Culture

The Almohads came from a more advanced, more urban society and were considerably more sophisticated than their predecessors. Almohad emperors were quickly acclimatized to Al-Andalus and before the end of the twelfth century had established their capital in Seville. They were much more interested in the arts than were the Almoravids, and the last and in some ways the fullest blossoming of Hispano-Muslim culture came in the late twelfth century under their rule. This was the era of the great Muslim Aristotelian Averroes (Ibn Rushd), perhaps the greatest philosopher in the history of Islam. During this period secular and religious literature flourished, as did new rationalist and mystic religious expression. Art and architecture were vigorously pursued, and Hispano-Muslim architecture was introduced and copied with considerable success in the larger towns of Morocco. During the twelfth century the popular verse forms of muwashaha and zéjel, deriving partly from Hispano-Romance culture, were perfected and widely practiced. It was tragic and ironic that this most culturally syncretistic form of Hispanic literary culture flourished at the very time that the traditional political hostility between Muslim and Christian society was replaced by increasingly implacable religious and ideological antipathy.

Most of the Hispano-Muslim population under the Almohads remained traditionalist and orthodox Malikite in religious observance. In 1195, the cultured Almohad emperor, Abu-Yaqub Yusuf, had to order the burning of the heterodox writings of Averroes in order to assure the support of the populace in the struggle with Castile, and the learned philosopher fled to a more tolerant haven in the Maghreb at Marrakesh.

As with the taifas, the failure of the Almohad empire in the peninsula was not economic and cultural but military. Even though the Almohad rulers maintained political unity and won several important military victories over the Castilians, their wealth and following, though considerable, did not generate sufficient military power to face the large warrior kingdom to the north, which in the decisive struggle would draw assistance from other Hispanic kingdoms and other parts of western Europe.

The Reign of Alfonso VIII (1158-1214)

After Alfonso VIII came of age, he reasserted the authority of the crown in Castile, restored a degree of domestic order, and resumed the military contest with the Almohads. The treaty of Cazorla which he signed with the Aragonese crown in 1179 settled a long-standing border dispute between these neighboring Christian kingdoms and set a line dividing all remaining Muslim territory in the peninsula between Aragonese and Castilian spheres of conquest.

Developments in Hispanic military technology of the late twelfth and early thirteenth century brought a shift away from reliance on the massed charge of heavy cavalry and toward greater tactical dexterity, with the use of light cavalry for mobility and flanking maneuvers. From the thirteenth century on, light cavalry was in general use among Christians as well as Muslims.

Alfonso VIII suffered a major defeat at Alarcos in New Castile (1195), but gained complete revenge just before the end of his reign by virtually shattering Almohad military power at the great Christian victory of the Navas de Tolosa (1212). For more than half a century Castile and its Christian neighbors had been shedding each other's blood in border warfare, but in the crucial battle with the Almohads, large armies from each of the other four Hispano-Christian kingdoms supported the Castilians. In terms of numbers of men engaged—possibly 50,000 on each side—the Navas de Tolosa was the biggest battle yet to have been fought in Hispanic history. Loss of life was usually not great in medieval battles, but the decisive victory of 1212 was apparently accompanied by a slaughter of the defeated Muslims as they fled in disarray. The booty was enormous, replenishing the treasuries of the Hispanic crowns; for a short time Sancho the Strong of Navarre was the leading moneylender of western Europe from the investment of his share. However, the disease that followed the battle, engendered perhaps by the mass of rotting corpses, and the scarcity and famine of the succeeding year, discouraged the Christian forces from following up their triumphs and partitioning Almohad territory.

The Great Reconquest of San Fernando III (1217/1230-1252)

The crowns of Castile and León were finally reunited in 1230 under Fernando III, son of Alfonso IX of León and of the daughter of Alfonso VIII of Castile. When his uncle Enrique I of Castile died in 1217 without heirs, Fernando inherited the Castilian throne, then reunited it with León thirteen years later upon the death of his father. Meanwhile after about 1224 the Almohad empire, at a hopeless military disadvantage, began to break up, as had the Almoravid empire before it. After two decades of diplomatic maneuver and occupation of border zones, Fernando resumed major campaigns of conquest with the occupation of Córdoba and the surrounding countryside. Murcia in the southeast was taken in 1243, Jaén, the gateway to Granada, in 1246, and the imposing city of Seville in 1248. By that time the Catalan-Aragonese reconquest in the east had been completed, while the entire Cáceres-Badajoz region in the southwest had been occupied by Alfonso IX of León during the last years of his reign (1227-1230). By mid-century the only Muslim territory of any size that remained was the emirate of Granada in the far southeast. It was reduced to vassalage upon agreeing to pay a large annual tribute in precious metals. The pious, crusading Fernando III ("el Santo") was making plans to leapfrog Granada and launch a grand Hispanic crusade across the straits to overpower Morocco, when he died at Seville in 1252.

The Mudéjares of Castile

Large numbers of Muslims were first incorporated into the territories of the Castilian crown during the occupation of the Tajo valley and adjoining regions under Alfonso VI in the eleventh century. Muslims who lived under Christian rule were known as *mudéjares*. Most urban Muslims were deported to make room for Christian immigrants in the key economic and military centers; they were normally treated leniently and allowed to take all movable possessions with them. Only a minority remained behind, so that the great Muslim cities of the peninsula were converted one by one from mostly Muslim to mostly Christian communities, though the Jewish minorities usually remained fixed. This uprooting of most of the urban Muslim population and their culture guaranteed the Christianization of reconquered territories in the south.

The mudéjar peasantry were treated quite differently, for they were normally allowed to till the soil or practice crafts as before, subject only to a special crown tax and the payment of rent or shares to the new overlord. In most cases they received formal *garantías* from the crown, specifying such terms and freedom to practice their own religion, together with the option to emigrate if they preferred.

During the first two decades of Castilian rule in western Andalusia, the Christians remained a small minority concentrated in occupied towns which they lacked the numbers to fill completely. Encouraged by the invasion of the southern tip of the peninsula by the Merinid empire of Morocco, a great mudéjar rebellion broke out in the countryside during 1263 and at first threatened to overturn Castilian rule. After this major revolt was throttled, royal policy changed, and the majority of the Muslim peasantry, particularly in western Andalusia where they were most heavily concentrated, were driven out of the kingdom, some to Granada, others toward Africa. Portions of the mudéjar peasantry remained in some areas, but in general the medieval Hispanic advance did not absorb the Muslims or even incorporate them as a minority; it drove them before it. The reconquest was not merely a matter of military occupation, but of expanding the Hispano-Christian population and institutions southward.

Castilian Repopulation and Resettlement in the Thirteenth Century

The thirteenth-century reconquest greatly increased the size of Castile. In 1212, Castile and León together covered approximately 235,000 square kilometers, but by 1265 they had grown to approximately 355,000 square kilometers. The thirteenth-century reconquest was one of the most decisive developments in Castilian history not merely because of its military and territorial significance, however, but equally because of its social and economic consequences, for the resettlement policy of the thirteenth century differed considerably from that of the eleventh and twelfth centuries.

Most of the lands south of the Tajo-central plateau area were divided among the nobility, the crusading orders, and the church. Some of the Christian peasants who moved into the south during the late-thirteenth and fourteenth centuries worked as *braceros* or *jornaleros* (day laborers) on large estates or cattle lands, but the majority rented small plots from overlords or church institutions, or worked land as sharecroppers on tributary financial terms rather than on a traditional or associative basis, as in the north. In most of the north, "useful dominion," the right to work the land, was recognized as pertaining to peasants even on seigneurial domain; in much of the south, "useful dominion" was held by the overlords, and peasants worked plots on whatever terms they could get. Juridically, there was no question of homone or benefactoria status in the south; social and economic status there was more individualistic, and that was an incentive for immigration during the first few generations. Compared with the more densely populated north, terms of cultivation were often fairly favorable during the first century or so of resettlement but became more onerous as population increased.

There was, however, considerable variation between regions. A small minority of peasant immigrants managed to establish alodial property rights in a few areas, but more important were the formation of concejo districts in parts of the south-central region and the granting of autonomous fueros to a number of the repopulated Andalusian towns. The new concejos and some of the smaller towns were inhabited in part by stockmen who grazed livestock on a small scale on concejo land under royal, not seigneurial, domain. Such elements were only a minority in the south, but they were free of seigneurial domination, and their direct loyalty to the crown had a stabilizing effect on the southern regions of Castile and León.

The Triumph of Seigneurial Domain

Division of most of the reconquered south under separate jurisdiction of aristocracy, church, and crusading orders marked the triumph of seigneurial domain over the greater share of the peasantry and landed economy of Castile, accentuating the weight of the aristocracy and the church as institutions. The first codification of the rights of the aristrocracy appeared early in the thirteenth century (under Alfonso VIII) as the *Fuero Viejo de Castilla* (or *Fuero de los Fijosdalgo de Castilla*). This may have been the fruit of opposition to Alfonso VIII's effort to limit the granting of señorios and the terms of their jurisdictions during his reign.

There was never a truly concerted effort on the part of the Castilian crown to reduce the privileges of señorios, even during the reign of

Alfonso VIII, and amid the renewed internal difficulties that beset
Castile during the late thirteenth century, seigneurial domain was
extended. Most seigneuries during the thirteenth century, however,
still rested primarily on economic rights—to profit from the land and
its uses—and in the great majority of cases did not explicitly include
the juridical and fiscal (or tax-collecting) control of the overlord over
his peasants.

An indication of the wealth and influence of the aristocracy is
given in the tendency developing toward the end of the thirteenth
century for the nobility to limit entry and turn itself into a fixed caste.
Heretofore, the military aristocracy in Castile had been fairly open to
recruits, but from the late thirteenth century an increasing number of
suits were brought by nobles in opposition to those who claimed
aristocratic status.

The Economy of Thirteenth-Century Castile

Castile's twelfth-century economic stagnation was overcome in large
measure by the stimulus of the great thirteenth-century reconquest
and the subsequent expansion of the wool export trade. The invasion
of the Merinid dynasty in Morocco between 1263 and 1268 occasioned considerable economic loss in the south, checking commercial
expansion, but a period of growth commenced about 1280 and lasted
for approximately half a century, until the ravages of the Black
Death.

The Christian overlords of the conquered territory of Al-Andalus
did not attempt to maintain its traditional rural economy. Peasant
immigrants from the dry-farming regions of the north often lacked
the skills to maintain irrigation and other complex farming systems,
and the irrigated *alfoz* around Córdoba, for example, fell into considerable decay. Medieval Castile had always been the most pastoral
society in western Europe, and its expansion merely accentuated the
emphasis on cattle and sheep. Grazing and shepherding required less
manpower than agriculture, and this fact encouraged abandonment
of cultivation in some regions.

Extension of the wool trade made it the major single source of
wealth for the kingdom, and for the crown it had the advantage of
being easily taxed because of its increasing organization and concentration. One of the most important economic institutions in Castilian
history was created in 1273, when Alfonso X established the Honorable Council of the Mesta, a broadly based syndicate of sheep owners
that subsequently gained extraordinary influence.

During this period Castile failed to develop anything approaching the urbanization or town manufacture found in the Low Countries or north Italy—or even Catalonia. Its agriculture, largely because of soil and climate, was backward even by thirteenth-century standards. Its only invention was the precursor of the modern cattle ranch, developed in the south-central region between the eleventh and the thirteenth centuries.

The Castilian Sense of Wealth

By the thirteenth century much of Castilian society had formed a distinctive set of values regarding wealth and economic activity. The land of Old Castile was poor and unproductive. Insecurity and intermittent warfare had discouraged attention to long-term economic projects—agriculture, crafts, commerce—and cattle and sheep were its main wealth, mobile and self-generative. Income was the reward not so much of work as of conquest. Precious metals and manufactures flowed in considerable measure from alien territory in the south whose treasures might be appropriated by armed force. Thus in Castilian society riches were commonly considered not as something that one created or built, that is, worked for, but as something one conquered or enjoyed because of one's status as a warrior conqueror, a nobleman. The function of land was not as property with which to create wealth, but rather as dominion from which wealth might be extracted by superior right. Hence the notion of wealth and land as a result of military action and domination, rather than power and domination as a result of having land and developing its wealth. Hence also the particular importance of the aristocratic class as the military elite that enjoyed the full status and fruits of domination, and the identification of much of lower-class aspiration with the military style. The nobility was dominant in almost all of medieval Europe, but in most other regions there was a greater challenge to aristocratic values, at least among townspeople. Almost nowhere was there as wide an acceptance of the aristocracy and its particular sense of wealth, status, and dominance as in Castile.

The habit of living from imperial tribute began in the eleventh century with the influx of paria payments and continued in varying forms and degrees for almost eight hundred years. The first major inflation caused by a sudden influx of money and treasure came during the first generation after the major phase of the reconquest, during the reign of Alfonso X (1252-1284). The new income was concentrated in the military elite and groups of the aristocracy and resulted in an orgy of luxury goods buying and importing that unbalanced the late thirteenth-century Castilian trade equilibrium. To an extent, this foreshadowed the post-imperial inflation of Habsburg Spain in the sixteenth century.

The Incorporation of Hispanic Jewry

A major socio-cultural result of the thirteenth-century reconquest was the incorporation of the main body of peninsular Jewry into the Christian kingdoms. The Jewish population was concentrated in the towns of the south and east and prospered greatly during the early centuries of Cordoban toleration. From early times, however, there were also small communities enjoying toleration and legal protection in the leading northern Christian towns. Growth of Muslim intolerance, combined with the expansion of the Christian principalities, encouraged Jewish migration northward from the eleventh century on. Castilian Jews served in the forces of Alfonso VI at several of his major battles.

The thirteenth and fourteenth centuries were the heyday of Hispanic Jewry, and in some districts they achieved the rights of aristocratic fuero. The upper stratum of Jewish society grew wealthy, while Jewish intellectuals were the most vital and productive of the peninsula. The base of Hispanic Jewry, however, was composed of the artisans and craftsmen in the medium and large-sized towns, where they constituted a major source of skilled labor. In a few districts small groups of Jewish peasants tilled the soil or cared for vineyards.

Cultural Achievements of the Twelfth and Thirteenth Centuries

The most important cultural achievement of medieval Hispania was the transmission of classical knowledge and Muslim learning to the world of Latin Christendom. Much of ancient Greco-Roman knowledge had been lost to the western world during the Middle Ages, and for several centuries the scientific work done in Islamic countries considerably surpassed that of western Europe. The Hispano-Christian states, as the bridge between Christendom and the Muslim world, were able to translate and transmit a great deal of this from the Arabic. The work had begun in a few Catalan monasteries during the tenth century. It reached its peak during the twelfth century, when a number of monastic centers and clerical schools, led by that of Toledo, collected and translated large numbers of ancient Jewish and Muslim works of philosophy, philology, mathematics, medicine, law, botany, astronomy, and geography. Visiting scholars from other parts of western Europe, carrying these materials back with them, helped to change the course of medieval European culture and shape the form and content of its emerging philosophy and science.

Though the work in the main was done in the twelfth century, its most famous center was the royal school of translators that flourished in the thirteenth century in Toledo during the reign of Alfonso X, a sovereign known to history as Alfonso el Sabio, "the Wise," for he was the only philosopher-king to grace the throne of Castile. With the expanded income that Castile enjoyed after the great reconquest, he encouraged manifold undertakings in scholarship and the arts. Serious historical study, for example, was encouraged in the Castile of Alfonso el Sabio for perhaps the first time in medieval western Europe.

Castilian literature in the vernacular also emerged in the twelfth and thirteenth centuries. Castile had been one of the first regions in western Europe to use the vernacular in official documents, dating from the eleventh century. This was perhaps due to its simpler society or even to the linguistic complexity of an area in which Romance vernacular, Arabic, and Hebrew all came into play, encouraging the avoidance of Latin in public materials and manuscripts. By the thirteenth century the three main linguistic domains of the peninsula had been carved out: Castilian as the most broadly spoken language in the center (flanked by a parallel Leonese dialect in the west and Aragonese in the east), Galician-Portuguese in the far west, and Catalan in the northeast. The other two principal languages were also developing a vernacular literature, and in refined poetics Galician was more advanced than Castilian. With a long cultural tradition of the most fully settled society in the kingdom, Galician served as the court literary language of Castile itself in the thirteenth century.

The peninsula did not lag far behind the most advanced parts of western Europe in the creation of institutions of higher learning. The first peninsular university was founded in Palencia in 1212 and later moved to Valladolid. It was followed by the University of Salamanca, which subsequently became the outstanding school in the peninsula, in 1220, the Studium Generale of Lisbon in 1290 (which later became the University of Coimbra), two Catalan universities (Lérida, 1300; Perpinyá, 1350), and an Aragonese university at Huesca in 1354. There was no university in Navarre, but Navarrese students were not uncommon at the University of Paris.

Codification of Fueros and Expansion of Royal Law

The expansion of learning and revival of Roman law brought considerably greater attention to matters of law, administration, and legal jurisdiction. One consequence was a general movement toward the systematization and written codification of laws and rights, beginning with the *Fuero General de Navarra*, early in the century, followed by the *Furs de Valencia* (1240), the *Fueros de Aragón* (1247), the *Libro de Los Fueros de Castilla* (1248), the revised *Costumes de Catalunya*, and the *Costums de La Mar* for Catalan shipping.

Because of sustained efforts by the territorial aristocracy to encroach on the rights of town and peasant communities, there was a general trend toward the explicit regranting of fueros and local charters in all the peninsular principalities during the thirteenth century, to protect the local communities. Another equally important aim was the clarification and extension of the crown's authority. Thus some towns found that they were escaping aristocratic domination only to come under closer royal control.

Of all the intellectual undertakings of Alfonso X's reign, the project of greatest immediate importance was his effort to develop a unified system of royal law. In 1255, only three years after he came to the throne, Alfonso's jurists brought out a written *Fuero Real,* an only partly harmonized compilation of Castilian common law and new royal statutes not based on any clear precedent in the traditional *Fuero Juzgo.* Though the application of the *Fuero Real* was carefully limited, Alfonso's goal was a perfectly harmonized system of universal law, both theoretical and practical, that would satisfy social demands and enhance the authority of the crown, while resolving the limitations, insufficiencies, and contradictions of medieval legal practice.

The result of ten years of work by royal jurists was the famous *Siete Partidas (Seven Divisions of Law)* of 1265, a rationalized system of universal justice under central monarchy and the first great didactic literary classic in the Castilian vernacular. It was also revolutionary in that it would have done away with much of the common law and foral (local statute) practices. Thus it aroused such vociferous protests from aristocrats and towns that it was not promulgated until almost one hundred years later, and was never put into effective use.

The Political Failure of Alfonso el Sabio

The fate of the *Siete Partidas* was symbolic of Alfonso's reign. His primary achievements were cultural; in practical affairs his reign ended in disaster. He had pretensions to being the first extra-Hispanic Castilian imperator, for his mother was Beatrice of Swabia and he was encouraged by minor dissidents in central Europe to seek the crown of the Holy Roman Empire. A good deal of money was wasted on bribery in this venture which ended in complete failure. A few years earlier he had given away in a daughter's marriage dowry the claim to Gascony, inherited by the Castilian crown through his great-grandfather's marriage. In 1257 his forces played a major role in helping the Portuguese complete the reconquest of the southwest corner of the peninsula by occupying the Algarve, but Alfonso made no effort to claim part of that territory for Castile's crown or its aggressive aristocracy, some of whom rose in rebellion at what they considered Alfonso's sacrifice of their opportunity for aggrandizement. In 1263 came the beginning of the Merinid invasions and the great mudéjar revolt, followed by five years of border war, and then by another Merinid invasion in 1275.

During his last years Alfonso continued his effort to impose central Roman law, and he claimed the imperial right to divide his kingdom between his son and grandson. In 1282 the aristocracy and towns rose in revolt and deposed him in favor of his direct heir, Sancho, who was more respectful of foral right and seigneurial privilege. Two years later, the embittered philosopher king died in impotence and failure.

Origins of the Castilian Cortes

Spanish historians have derived considerable satisfaction from the fact that the first medieval parliament representing the three principal estates of society met in León in 1188, antedating the first parliamentary assemblies in all other European kingdoms. Medieval parliaments evolved in much the same manner in most parts of western and central Europe. The Leonese monarchy, like its Visigothic predecessor, was accustomed to convene periodic meetings of a royal council (*curia regia*) to advise on major policy matters and establish a sort of consensus. The curia regia was composed of leading aristocrats, royal administrators, and church hierarchs. By the eleventh and twelfth centuries it was occasionally supplemented by meetings of a *curia plena,* a broader royal assembly of lesser officials, nobles, and churchmen. As medieval society grew increasingly complex, the legitimization of changes in royal succession and in taxation and coinage became more difficult. By the twelfth century, the urban population in León and Castile had achieved some modest significance, as witnessed by the revolt of Urraca's reign and by the initiative of towns and concejos in some regions in forming juntas or *hermandades* to keep the peace and protect local economic interests. Since the aristocracy and church were exempt from ordinary taxation, the increasing costs of royal government could only be met by new levies raised from the towns and peasants, and such funds could be collected efficiently only if agreed to by taxpayers or their representatives.

Moreover, church leaders urged that town leaders be summoned to agree on means of limiting disorder on the roads and in the countryside.

In 1188 Alfonso IX of León faced major problems in consolidating his rule over an internally divided and disorderly kingdom, and he also faced mounting financial demands. To deal with these issues he summoned representatives of leading towns to meet with aristocrats and church officials at a royal assembly. He proclaimed a brief royal charter promising justice and recognizing local laws as well as the need to establish greater order. At a subsequent meeting he gained approval of a debasement of coinage to increase royal purchasing power. This *Cortes* (literally, "courts") was the first assembly representative of all three estates to meet in any European kingdom. Since the problems that induced Alfonso IX to summon this meeting were not unique to León, the introduction of a three-estate Cortes probably occurred there first because of the tradition of foral autonomies and rights for local groups in the Leonese (and Castilian) politicojuridical system. León accorded greater legal recognition to the interests of its various regions, towns, and classes than was to be found in the local-liberty systems of most of medieval Europe.

The meeting of the first three-estate Cortes in Castile cannot be dated as precisely as in the case of León. Such an assembly met in Castile in 1212, but there may have been an even earlier one. The respective dates for other peninsular kingdoms are: Catalonia, 1214 or 1218; Aragón, 1247; Portugal, 1254; Valencia, 1283; and Navarre, 1300. By comparison, the first regional parliament in Germany was summoned in 1232, the first English parliament in 1265, and the first estates-general in France in 1302. After 1250, Cortes meetings for León and Castile were usually joint meetings, but until the latter part of the fourteenth century there were also occasional separate meetings and several limited convocations of representatives from specific regions of Castile. After that only unified meetings of representatives of the three estates of León and Castile were held.

The original medieval Cortes had no institutional charters or rights and privileges as autonomous assemblies. They had no inherent legislative function, but were summoned solely at the convenience of the crown. Though in some periods frequent, meetings were often extremely irregular, and there was no legal specification as to which towns were to be represented. The composition of Cortes, particularly in Castile, often varied considerably from meeting to meeting.

Nevertheless, by the last years of the thirteenth century a philosophy of popular sovereignty was developing among some of the town representatives. There was at least one attempt, though unsuccessful, to codify the rights of representatives of the third estate, and some of the latter soon went beyond a mere response to royal requests and asserted their right to ratify new laws. The Cortes assembly of 1282 was used to legitimize the deposition of Alfonso X and the accession of his son Sancho. By the end of the century, the Cortes of Castile had established the unwritten right to vote on all new taxes, present grievances to the crown, and ratify succession to the throne. During the next century, the Cortes was important in regulating succession crises and royal regencies during the minorities of sovereigns. But unlike the parliaments of Aragón and Catalonia, the Castilian Cortes never institutionalized by charter its specific legal prerogatives and never developed juridico-administrative machinery to guarantee its precise jurisdiction over certain kinds of decisions.

Constitutional Status of the Basque Region

The Basque-speaking territories southwest of the Pyrenees remained culturally and politically apart from neighboring states. Navarre, which in its Hispanic domain comprised roughly the eastern half of the Basque region, preserved its independence of the other Hispanic principalities, but from the thirteenth century on was drawn more and more into the French orbit through dynastic marriage. Its institutions were similar to those of neighboring Aragón (see the following chapter), but it became a cultural backwater and by the close of the thirteenth century was one of the least developed areas of the peninsula.

The western half of the Basque country was made up of three distinct districts: Guipuzcoa to the northeast, Vizcaya to the northwest, and Alava to the south. These three provinces were never united, but for several centuries belonged alternately to the crowns of Castile and Navarre. By the twelfth century, the whole population had been officially Christianized. Its social structure was somewhat anomalous; the peasantry lived for the most part on family farms, though with strong extended-family or clan bonds. Local districts, villages, and peasant groups were quite jealous of their autonomy, but had not been able to escape a process of seigneurial subordination rather like that which had taken place in northern Castile. There had never been much (if any) outright serfdom in the western Basque provinces, but behetría relationships predominated.

Association with Castile became more attractive than subjection to the sovereignty of Navarre in part because of the greater degree of feudal subjection in Navarre. The Basque aristocracy was numerous and turbulent, but its powers were restricted by local custom. The most egalitarian region was Guipuzcoa, in which by the close of the

Middle Ages virtually the entire population had claimed aristocratic status, meaning equality before the law and exemption from many kinds of taxation. Guipuzcoans also claimed the right to choose their own overlord. In 1200 they renounced the sovereignty of the Navarrese crown under pressure and recognized Alfonso VIII of Castile as their king. The southern Basque "county" of Alava was conquered at the same time, but its provincial autonomy was fully recognized in 1332. Vizcaya, the northwestern district, was constituted as a señorío of the local aristocratic family of Lopez de Haro in the eleventh century under the suzerainty of Castile, and finally became a direct seigneury of the crown in 1379. The fueros of all three districts were officially recognized and guaranteed by the crown, which was represented in each by an *adelantado,* or royal governor, as in all other major regions of Castile. Local affairs were resolved mostly by regional or local assemblies of notables. There was no attempt to impose a Castilian royal law upon local customs, and save for a few limited taxes, the local assemblies of notables and town representatives (a sort of district Cortes without a sovereign) negotiated taxes with the crown.

From the beginning of Castilian history, Basque immigration from the north had been significant in the development of Castilian society. Though most of the population continued to speak their native Basque, a form of romance dialect akin to Castilian had been the official, legal, and cultural speech of the leaders and towns of the region from the tenth or eleventh century on. The Basques thus increasingly became a part of the Castilian world, and their emigrants played a major role in the expansion of Castilian society.

5

The Rise of Aragón-Catalonia

Evolution of the Catalan Counties

The crystallization of a common identity among the people of the border counties of the southeastern Pyrenean region was a comparatively slow process that took at least three centuries. The broadly regional term *Catalan* does not appear to have been used until the eleventh century. Geography and Muslim military pressure, as well as aspects of their cultural heritage, made the population of the nascent Catalonia a part of Christian Hispania. Other influences, however, reached across the Pyrenees to associate them with southwestern French society in particular and the Carolingian empire in general. It was the expansion of Carolingian France that had freed most of the Pyrenean region from Muslim domination and created the Catalan counties in the first place. The Catalan language that began to take shape faced no linguistic barrier at the Pyrenees, closely related as it was to the Romance vernacular of southwestern France. By the early ninth century the Carolingian script and Franco-Roman religious rite had replaced the Visigothic script and Hispano-Visigothic rite in the Catalan region.

During the course of the ninth century Carolingian political power contracted, and local overlords increasingly exercised de facto autonomy. In the Catalan region and southwestern France the old Roman system of direct ownership of land had been in large measure retained, so that in many cases local aristocrats and church establishments acquired full juridical title to their properties. A superstructure of personal political relationships in the feudal style of northern France was introduced during the ninth century, but such feudalism was slow to achieve full development in the south. Thus by the late ninth century this region had lapsed into extreme particularism under local counts and overlords and lacked any sort of general political system. Here for nearly two centuries there was neither the nominally strong monarchy found in León nor the overarching structure of rule by personal allegiance that characterized the classic feudalism of northern France.

During the first few generations after the Muslim conquest there had been a current of Visigothic and other Hispanic immigration into the eastern Pyrenees and beyond, reinforced by some slight Frankish emigration to the southwest. By the ninth century the eastern Pyrenean region held a fairly dense population, at least for its slight economic resources. The traditional property system and landlord domination remained comparatively unchanged; if the older form of serfdom tended to die out, stringent economic obligations of most peasants to their overlords remained. With the advance of the Catalan reconquest there was opportunity for peasants emigrating southward to till their own lands. Even newly occupied land, however, sometimes involved recognition of seigneurial obligations or payments, and when the expansion was resumed on a broader scale, some form of dominion by aristocrats or church institutions was established over most newly acquired land.

Formation of a single independent Catalan political entity was a slow and often confused process. The position of count in each of the original Catalan frontier districts was merely an administrative one, to which appointments were made by the Carolingian crown. Nevertheless, noble families were able to establish strong local positions, and they sometimes held offices for several generations. As the tendency toward local sovereignty spread during the latter part of the ninth century, their influence grew. By far the most powerful local dynasty was the house of Barcelona, descendents of Sant Guillem, count of Toulouse, one of Charlemagne's lieutenants. During the early and middle decades of the ninth century, members of this family at one time or another were counts of most of the small Catalan counties.

The roots of de facto Catalan independence have been traced to the time of Guifred el Pilós (Wilfred the Hairy), count of Barcelona from 878 to 897. After the overthrow of the main line of the Carolingian dynasty in 888, royal power was greatly weakened, and the

Catalan counties were farther from central control than any other part of the kingdom. Their relative stability in the tenth century encouraged the trend toward independence from the unstable French crown, as did the direct relations developed with the papacy by the counts of Barcelona. Yet the prestige of the crown was so great that there was no pretense of de jure independence by any of the Catalan counts until the end of the tenth century. Even as the county over-lordships settled into semi-independent hereditary dynasties, limitations of sovereignty prevented any of the counts from claiming the title of king, though it became common for the count of Barcelona to refer to himself as count "by the grace of God," in the formula of the French monarchy.

There were entire decades of peace along the Muslim frontier, but such periods of calm were interludes in a long and extremely costly struggle. During the reigns of Abd-al-Rahmann III and al-Hakam II, the count of Barcelona became a client of the caliphate, but this did not prevent a devasting attack by al-Mansur that resulted in the sack of Barcelona in 985. The first major counterattack of the eleventh century was the great Catalan expedition of 1010, which, with the assistance of the Toledo Muslims, briefly occupied Córdoba. After the collapse of the caliphate, the Catalan counties were able to assume the offensive, their impetus strengthened by the population density that had been built up in "Old Catalonia" by the eleventh century.

The hegemony of the county of Barcelona was strengthened during the reign of Ramón Berenguer I "the Old" (1035-1076). Sometimes in conjuction with the count of Urgell and the king of Aragon, he mounted a series of successful expeditions to the west and southwest, expanding and repopulating the borders of the Catalan principalities. Parias from the prosperous Muslim cities to the southwest—Zaragoza, Lérida, Tortosa—filled his coffers and helped to create what may have been the first wave of prosperity in Catalan history. At about the same time, Catalan maritime power began to be felt in the west Mediterranean. Ramón Berenguer I established Barcelona's dominion over most of the area southeast of the Pyrenees and began the trans-Pyrenean expansion of the house of Barcelona by acquiring the counties of Carcassonne and Rasés as well, coordinating most of the Catalan territory through the exercise of greater personal sovereignty and through politico-juridical agreements with local overlords, won by negotiation, bribery, or force. This period saw a major achievement in the beginning of the collection and codification of Catalan law and practice in the written *Usatges* (*Usages*), the first full compilation of feudal law in any west European state. The church also

contributed to keeping order in Catalonia by developing the institution of the "peace of God," which established a general truce among
warring feudal factions over a specific region for a specific time. This
was introduced at an earlier date in Catalonia (1027) than anywhere
else in western Europe.

Subsequent efforts by Count Ramón Berenguer II to expand westward toward Lérida and Zaragoza, made between 1082 and 1090,
were blocked. At the end of the eleventh century the Catalan frontier
was temporarily pushed back by the Almoravids, but the advance
recommenced under Count Ramón Berenguer III, who took Tarragona on the coast in 1118. This city, once great under the Romans
but ruined by the time of its reconquest, was rebuilt and soon made
the metropolitan seat of the church in Catalonia, relieving Catalans of
ecclesiastical dependency on the archbishopric of Narbonne beyond
the Pyrenees. Ramón Berenguer III, with the aid of a Pisan fleet, also
reduced most of the Balearic Islands to tributaries, though they were
subsequently lost again to Muslim domination for a century more.
The marriage of Ramón Berenguer III to the heiress of Provence
added significant trans-Pyrenean holdings to the house of Barcelona,
which during the next cuntury served as a barrier to the southward
expansion of the county of Toulouse, and more fatefully, the crown of
France.

Origins of the Kingdom of Aragón

At the time of the Muslim conquest, the central Pyrenean region that
later formed the nucleus of upper Aragón made nominal submission
to the invaders. Because of its remoteness and general poverty and
because of the small numbers of Muslim troops, it was left autonomous and was never occupied by a Muslim garrison. The two Pyrenean districts immediately to the east were called Sobrarbe and
Ribagorza. Lower Sorbrarbe was nominally occupied directly by the
Muslims, but Ribagorza was more remote and merely paid tribute.
Even in the Ebro valley to the south, Arab and Berber immigration
was lighter than in the main regions of Al-Andalus, and the subsequent Muslim population of the Ebro valley were mostly Hispanic
converts.

During the Frankish advance at the close of the eighth century, the
south-central districts of the Pyrenees were organized as the counties
of Aragón, Sobrarbe, and Ribagorza. The county of Aragón was
unique in that it soon became independent; it was only briefly an
appanage of the French crown. Moreover, unlike some of the Catalan
counties, Aragón was not by- or trans-Pyrenean; it was cut off by a

higher range from the French side of the Pyrenees than the others, more or less isolated from French influence, and consequently directed southward toward the more sophisticated and flourishing regions of Huesca and Zaragoza with their Hispano-Muslim populations. This reinforced a sense of Hispanic identity while reducing Mediterranean and French contacts.

The early society of Aragón was somewhat looser, simpler, and freer than that of the Catalan counties. The region was small, rugged, poor, and sparsely settled, inhabited mainly by shepherds and peasant farmers. By the middle of the ninth century a series of fortified villages had been erected as main points of defense, and many of the peasants took the protection of a *señor*—that is, a military leader—to defend themselves, but elaborate hierarchic forms and a rigid aristocratic caste were slow to take shape.

As the smallest, poorest, and weakest of Hispanic principalities, the little hill-county of Aragón at first had no hope of expanding southward against the prosperous Muslim cities of the Ebro valley, and for two centuries scarcely tried. The goal of reconquest or expansion was apparently first communicated to the Aragonese from the neighboring state of Navarre to the west, and the county momentarily lost its independence when it was incorporated into the "empire" of the Navarrese Sancho el Mayor early in the eleventh century. Yet Aragón emerged as the first of the Pyrenean counties to establish itself formally as a kingdom, when it was inherited by a bastard of Sancho named Ramiro, who invoked the authority of his late father the "emperor" to claim for himself the title of King Ramiro I (1035-1063). The real substance to back this claim was probably the increased income provided by tribute payments which Ramiro was able to exact from the wealthy taifa of Zaragoza. The Aragonese were rude and poor, but they developed the warlike qualities of their Castilian cousins to the west and by the mid-eleventh century had generated a military force disproportionate to their size or wealth.

The second king, Sancho Ramírez (1063-1094), strengthened his position, as had the counts of Barcelona in the preceding century, by aligning himself with the papacy. Support from Rome fortified Aragonese independence in the face of the imperial claims of the Leonese crown, and in 1063 introduced the first step in the development of the crusade, bringing military assistance from France that enabled the Aragonese crown to seize the key Muslim town of Barbastro in 1064. Sancho Ramírez formally recognized papal suzerainty over the kingdom of Aragón, and subsequently received papal ratification of the Aragonese dynasty's claim to an independent royal title. Sancho also established political and marital alliances with several important families of the feudal aristocracy of southwest France, reinforcing

Aragón's diplomatic position. Meanwhile, Muslim tribute helped build the Pyrenean village of Jaca, Aragón's original capital, into the first true city of the kingdom.

In the latter part of the eleventh century, the Aragonese crown and military leaders became more thoroughly imbued with the crusading ethos than their counterparts in any other Hispanic principality. They won a series of key points in the foothill country during the 1080s, but found it very difficult to break past the barrier of well-fortified cities into the Ebro plain below them. And whenever they seemed about to make a real breakthrough in the direction of wealthy Zaragoza, their more powerful rival, the Castilian crown, helped to prop up the emir of Zaragoza as a political client and tributary of its own. Consequently the ambition of the Aragonese crown shifted briefly to the southeast, in expeditions toward the Mediterranean coast. Conquest was easier there; in conjunction with forces of the count of Barcelona, the district around Tarragona was seized in 1095, then lost again. More important and lasting victories were finally gained, however, with the definitive seizure of the foothill towns of Huesca (1096), and for the second and final time, Barbastro (1101).

The great Aragonese reconquest occurred in the first part of the twelfth century during the reign of Alfonso the Battler (1104-1134), a pious crusader who devoted himself primarily to war against the Muslims. With decisive reinforcement from French crusading knights, Alfonso was able to occupy the key Ebro city of Zaragoza and practically all the surrounding Ebro plain. He nearly doubled the size of the kingdom, increasing its natural resources and economic potential several times over.

Before the twelfth century, most of the Aragonese aristocracy were relatively poor and lesser nobles (*hidalgos*), who sometimes had to work their own land and caused little trouble for the crown. As in León and Castile, but not Catalonia, military and administrative officials in Aragón had at first constituted a service aristocracy. There were few hereditary fiefs, though as early as the tenth century *tenencias* over land, with the right of jurisdiction as lieutenant of the crown, were held by some nobles in the *tierra vieja*, the hill country of old Aragón. Originally these were not hereditary, but merely rewards for military service. Already by the eleventh century, however, most nobles were claiming hereditary status for their honors and tenencias. During the expansion of the eleventh and early twelfth centuries, the crown had to recruit more heavy cavalry for lowland fighting, as the reconquest descended from the hills. The situation was broadly similar to that of Castile, and a similar solution was adopted. The class of caballeros villanos was expanded by the royal practice of granting *honores* of income from land as remuneration for military service. Alfonso the Battler relied primarily on a *caballería de honor* of petty hidalgos and military commoners, each of whom was normally assigned a certain amount of rent or income for each mounted warrior that he brought to the royal service.

The first kings of Aragón, and particularly Alfonso, were energetic in limiting the privileges of the hereditary aristocracy, while granting liberal terms of resettlement in the new lands and encouraging founding of new towns. Semi-autonomous concejos were established in parts of new Aragón just as in southern Castile and León during the same period. Moreover, better terms had to be granted to peasants in tierra vieja to keep them on the land. In general, there was a somewhat more equitable social balance in much of Aragón than in Catalonia during the twelfth century, though this changed. As early as 1164, representatives of Aragonese towns were invited to a Curia regia (the first clear instance of this in any peninsular kingdom), forming the precursor of the Aragonese Cortes that developed half a century later.

But Aragón was a small kingdom with scanty population, and even after the occupation of the *tierra nueva* its resources were not great. Most of its "towns" were simply rural village communities akin to those of Castile. The only true cities were the new capital, Zaragoza, Jaca, and Huesca. There were not enough people from the north to inhabit the new territory, and so many more newly conquered Muslims were allowed to remain in the Aragonese tierra nueva than in other reconquered territory of the twelfth century. The most productive rural districts of southern Aragón were inhabited and worked almost exclusively by Muslim peasants.

Thus the most notable development in twelfth-century Aragonese society was not productive new development for most of the population but rather a continued increase in the power of the aristocracy. This foreshadowed a similar pattern that would emerge in Castile at the completion of the major part of Castilian reconquest. Following the death of Alfonso the Battler in 1134, his hard-pressed successor was forced to recognize the right of hereditary seigneurial domain for the landed aristocracy in both the north and south. In old Aragón this amounted to full legal title and sovereignty for the nobility. In new Aragón the granting of large seigneuries worked by Muslim peasants only increased the power of new landlords who did not have to worry about the rights of Christian underlings. The aristocratic fiefs in the south were established on the principle of personal feudal loyalty to the crown, reflecting the growing French influence in the peninsula at that time. Whether or not they held direct title in the north or did feudal homage in the south, the Aragonese aristocracy was more powerful by the beginning of the thirteenth century than that of any other Hispanic kingdom.

The Aragonese Succession Crisis and the Union of Aragón and Catalonia

The first Aragonese succession crisis occurred after the death of the celibate Alfonso the Battler, who willed his crown and patrimony to the monastic orders of the Temple, the Hospital, and the Holy Sepulchre. This was blocked by the Aragonese elite. They elected as successor Alfonso's brother, Ramiro the Monk, who had to renounce holy orders and marry in an effort to provide an heir to the throne. The Aragonese succession immediately fell afoul of the strong expansionist ambitions of Alfonso VII "the Emperor" of Castile-León, who aspired to incorporate the entire Ebro district down to Valencia and the Mediterranean. Since Zaragoza had been tributary to Castile, he claimed sovereignty over many of the latest conquests of the Aragonese crown, seizing Zaragoza at the end of 1134 and forcing Ramiro to seek refuge in the Pyrenees. An international conclave of jurists, clerics, and neighboring princes forced Alfonso VII to retire, but not before Ramiro had been required to recognize the suzerainty of the Leonese-Castilian crown as well as Castilian occupation of the key fortresses of southwestern Aragón.

It was to save Aragón from domination by the powerful Leonese-Castilian monarchy that Ramiro turned to the highly capable young count of Barcelona, Ramón Berenguer IV (1131–1162), a strong military leader and the best Hispanic politician of his generation. Ramiro's infant daughter, Petronila, who was to have been betrothed to Alfonso VII, was instead pledged in 1137 to Ramón Berenguer, with the provision that their offspring would reign jointly over the two states of Aragón and Catalonia. In the meantime, the Catalan count was to exercise the powers of the Aragonese crown, and even in the event that the tiny Petronila died before the marriage could be consummated, the house of Barcelona was still to inherit the Aragonese crown.

This arrangement was the political masterstroke of the Hispanic Middle Ages. It guaranteed the independent succession to the crown of Aragón and strengthened the military and diplomatic position of both states, while providing that each would preserve its own laws, institutions, and autonomy undiminished. The two realms remained legally distinct, but federated under the rule of a common dynasty.

Rulers of the Crown of Aragón, 1137-1410

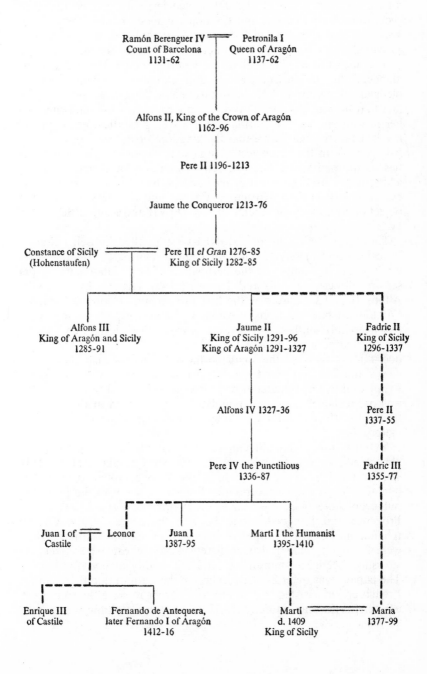

Ramón Berenguer IV
Count of Barcelona
1131-62
═══ Petronila I
Queen of Aragón
1137-62

Alfons II, King of the Crown of Aragón
1162-96

Pere II 1196-1213

Jaume the Conqueror 1213-76

Constance of Sicily
(Hohenstaufen)
═══ Pere III *el Gran* 1276-85
King of Sicily 1282-85

Alfons III
King of Aragón and Sicily
1285-91

Jaume II
King of Sicily 1291-96
King of Aragón 1291-1327

Fadric II
King of Sicily
1296-1337

Alfons IV 1327-36

Pere II
1337-55

Pere IV the Punctilious
1336-87

Fadric III
1355-77

Juan I of
Castile
═══ Leonor

Juan I
1387-95

Martí I the Humanist
1395-1410

Enrique III
of Castile

Fernando de Antequera,
later Fernando I of Aragón
1412-16

Martí
d. 1409
King of Sicily
═══ Maria
1377-99

Such an arrangement would have been impossible with Castile, whose strong monarchy and centripetal tendencies were inimical to equal federation. Both Aragón and Catalonia gained greater strength and security than either would have enjoyed alone, and Aragón was provided with a badly needed outlet to the Mediterranean. The measure of the skill of Ramón Berenguer IV was that he managed the union successfully and extracted Aragón from its pledged submission to Castile. In this he may have been aided by the fact that he was brother to Alfonso's queen, a princess renowned for her beauty and charm. Formation of a strong political entity in the northeast at the same time that the kingdom of Portugal broke away from Castile in the southwest gave greater balance to the principalities of the peninsula. The one left behind was of course Navarre, which found itself hemmed in territorially, had already lost its western and southwestern districts to Castile, and at one point was the object of a partitioning scheme of Alfonso VII and Ramon Berenguer IV.

The new ruler of the united dynasty still called himself count of Barcelona and merely "prince" of Aragón. During the middle years of his reign, he completed the occupation of new Catalonia with the seizure of Lérida (1148) and Tortosa (1149). His son by Petronila, Alfons II (1162-1196), was the first to call himself king of Aragón-Catalonia. Under the aegis of Alfons II, Catalan expansion across the Pyrenees into southwestern France reached its fullest extent, as the crown incorporated most of the territories of Provence and Languedoc, adding them to the small northeast Pyrenean districts of Cerdanya and Rosselló (Cerdagne and Rousillon). Emigration across the Pyrenees into Catalonia contined throughout the twelfth century, and was particularly useful in repopulating towns seized in the new districts of south and west Catalonia, and in expanding Catalan commerce.

Yet the trans-Pyrenean empire of Catalonia was brought to an abrupt end by the downfall of Pere II "the Catholic" (1196-1213). This resulted from the ambition of the French crown to overcome feudal division and reincorporate all territory down to the Pyrenees, but even more from the zeal for orthodoxy of Pope Innocent III. Provence and Languedoc had become the center of the Cathari religion in western Europe. Albigensianism, as the Cathari beliefs were frequently called, was an heretical Manichean type of religion stressing asceticism, moralizing, and the duality of body and spirit. The papacy was determined to extirpate the Cathari doctrine, and the French crown assisted this enterprise in order to seize the southwestern territories once more. Pere II of Aragón-Catalonia was a fully orthodox prince who pledged his kingdom a feudality of the Holy See (hence his nickname the Catholic) but could not allow French forces to conquer and expropriate the trans-Pyrenean domains. Whereas in 1212 this warrior king had played an heroic role at the great pan-Christian victory of the Navas de Tolosa, in 1213 he led his forces across the Pyrenees to eject the occupying forces summoned by the papacy from northern France. The odds at the battle of Muret were in Pere's favor, but his Languedocian vassals proved feeble allies, and fortune failed him. Pere was slain on the field, his forces fled, and ultimately all Provence and Languedoc were incorporated by the crown of France.

The fateful defeat at Muret had the positive effect of quickly terminating what might have been a long, difficult, and costly rivalry with the crown of France. It set a stable border between France and Aragón-Catalonia, and turned the Hispanic kingdom southward to complete the reconquest of the peninsula's east, and ultimately outward into the Mediterranean in the great Aragonese expansion of the late thirteenth and fourteenth centuries.

The Great Catalan Reconquest of Jaume the Conqueror

Pere the Catholic left a minor son as heir, Jaume I (1213-1276). During the minority of the new ruler, the power of the crown declined and the aristocracy usurped authority in both Catalonia and Aragón. But after he came of age, Jaume proved himself the first great ruler of the united dynasty. He seized the opportunity provided by the final decay of Muslim power to complete the conquest of all the territory assigned to the Aragonese sphere by the treaty of Cazorla with Castile in 1179. This coincided with Castile's reconquest of most of the south under Fernando III and won for the Aragonese ruler the historic sobriquet of Jaume the Conqueror.

Jaume's first step was to seize the Balearic Islands in a series of expeditions between 1229 and 1235. His second was to move into the entire central portion of the eastern coast, beginning with Morella and the Maestrazgo district in 1232, going on to Valencia in 1238, and by 1244 taking the coastal district south of Valencia as far as Játiva. The boundaries between Aragón and Castile were then reaffirmed in a treaty of 1244, and in 1265 Aragonese forces repressed a major Muslim revolt in the new Castilian region of Murcia in the southeast. Finally, the treaty of Corbeil in 1258 between the crown of France and that of Aragón-Catalonia wiped from the slate the old quarrels over the French regions of Provence and Languedoc.

Jaume's reign was important not merely because it expanded a dual kingdom of approximately 85,000 square kilometers to one of approximately 112,000, but also because of the growth of the Catalan economy during this period and the beginning of the formation of the classic political constitutions of the Aragonese realms. When the veteran Conqueror died at the age of seventy-eight in 1276, the political, economic, and territorial basis had been laid for the expansion of the Aragonese empire in the Mediterranean.

Constitution and Society of Aragón in the Thirteenth and Fourteenth Centuries

The thirteenth century was the age of consolidation of the political power of the Aragonese aristocracy. During the minority of Jaume I, the royal finances were exhausted (in part because of the extravagances of Pere the Catholic) and the resulting weakness of royal authority was used by some Aragonese nobles to divide among themselves the landed rents and other financial perquisites remaining to the crown. The expansionist policy of the Conqueror in his mature years was designed in part to remedy this weakness and restore a strong base for royal authority.

So long as the continental reconquest continued, ambitious and aggressive new aristocratic strata could be satisfied with new lands or rewards. After the reconquest ended, the nobility began to vie directly with the crown for control of the public power. The Aragonese nobility had already developed the myth of a pact which had supposedly originated the monarchy five centuries earlier through a compromise or contract between the chief noble, the king, and the leading ricoshombres (high aristocrats) to fight the Moors.

Much of the aggressiveness of the Aragonese nobility came from the fact that their position and power were in many cases of recent origin. Aragón had not been as thoroughly feudalized as Catalonia, where by definition most land was under the domain of the aristocracy or the church. Heading the nobility was a small group of ten or twelve families of ricoshombres, descended from or intermarried with royal bastards and the closest relatives of the crown. Most of their domains were of twelfth- and thirteenth-century creation and were the most productive areas in the Ebro and Jalón valleys and some of the most productive in the Valencia district. Below these few families was a fairly large group of middling-to-petty nobles, catagorized as *infanzones* and hidalgos. Though most of the landed aristocracy in Aragón exercised de facto civil and criminal jurisdiction over the people and territory of their domains, this jurisdiction was not fully recognized by law. Furthermore, the bulk of the Aragonese aristocracy remained poorer than that of Castile or even of Catalonia, where some of the petty nobility were involving themselves in commerce. It was clear toward the end of the thirteenth century that Catalonia was the more populous, wealthy, and important of the two principalities. Aragón, one-third of whose population were Muslim underlings (mostly semiserfs), was a social and economic backwater by comparison.

Most of the Aragonese aristocracy joined in a special "Union" of 1283 to press on Jaume's son and successor, Pere el Gran (1276-1285) their status grievances and protests against new taxation and the growing predominance of Catalan interests in royal policy. The opportunity was provided by a quarrel with the French throne over the inheritance of Sicily, leading to a French invasion of Catalonia. The crown's desperate need for help forced it to recognize part of the "General Privilege" demanded by the Union, promising not to arrest, execute, or confiscate the property of any noble without the approval of the Aragonese Cortes and to make no new laws without Cortes approval.

The subsequent Privileges of the Union, imposed on the crown in 1287, forced ratification of the prerogatives of the *Justicia* (chief judge) of Zaragoza, whom the crown had already recognized as supreme judge of the kingdom, primarily in protection of nobles' rights. The Privileges also established the principle of annual Cortes meetings and the power of the nobles to name several members to the royal council with a veto over royal policy. Though not all these concessions were fully implemented, they had the effect of converting the kingdom of Aragón into a virtual aristocratic republic for the next half century. In the process, the full fiscal, civil, and criminal jurisdiction of the landholding aristocrats over their domains and the peasants thereon was implicitly recognized.

One of the distinctive features of the power of the aristocracy was its place in the Aragonese Cortes, which contained two aristocratic *brazos* ("arms" or chambers): one for the ricoshombres and one for the infanzones or hidalgos. Decisions in the *brazo de ricoshombres* required a unanimous vote. The two aristocratic brazos and the *brazo popular* (which represented twenty-two towns and three rural confederations) were complemented in 1301 by a brazo for the church hierarchy, creating the classic four-chamber Aragonese Cortes.

So long as their domestic social and juridical privileges were respected, the Aragonese aristocracy normally did not contest the crown's policy of overseas expansion. During the fourteenth-century conquest of Sardinia, the contingent from lightly populated Aragón was as large as that from Catalonia and Mallorca combined.

The constitutional issue in Aragón was finally settled by the strongest king of the fourteenth century, Pere el Ceremoniós, who was determined to assert the authority of the crown in matters of general policy. He defeated forces of the aristocracy in a major battle in 1348 but reconfirmed many of the constitutional privileges granted by predecessors. Moreover, he ratified the authority of the Justicia, henceforth known as *Justicia Mayor*, to interpret the juridical rights of the aristocracy and safeguard the legitimate prerogatives of the Cortes. The Justicia Mayor was not, however, entirely above royal law; one who abused his authority was subsequently deposed, and another executed, by royal justice.

After 1348, the Aragonese nobility made little further effort to contest the sovereignty of the crown in the general affairs of the kingdom, in part because the crown accepted the social, juridical, and economic authority of the nobility on their local domains. The advance of Roman law gave them more exact legal tools to dominate the peasantry, particularly the lowest stratum of Muslim (and some Christian) peasants who lived in serfdom and were thenceforth treated under the judicial category of slave. New laws of the fourteenth century established the right of the señor to *maltratar* (punish) and even kill his serfs, if such authority was administered "justly." Thus by the fourteenth century the condition of most of the Aragonese peasantry, whether fully enserfed or simply *encomendado,* had declined from a hundred years earlier.

The towns and concejos of Aragón clung desperately to their charters under royal domain, to avoid falling under seigneurial control, and were frequently willing to pay large sums to the crown to have their status reconfirmed. Though the few Aragonese towns were small and poor, they were the only alternative under the crown to aristocratic authority. During the troubled twelfth century they had formed several regional juntas to help maintain law and order, but an effort was made from the thirteenth century on to incorporate jurisdiction over roads and royal domain in the royal administration, which appointed special judges and *paceros* (peacemakers) for policing.

The kingdom remained economically backward throughout the later Middle Ages. Some new irrigation was constructed in the river valleys, but the most productive farmland was for the most part the mudéjar (subject Muslim) regions of the tierra nueva. Sheep-grazing was almost as important as in Castile, and the Casa de Ganaderos of Zaragoza was the Aragonese equivalent of the Castilian Mesta. Compared with the extraordinary development of Catalan commerce, that of Aragón was insignificant. From about the eleventh century, the most important trade routes were those that led northward through Jaca and Huesca over the Pyrenees into France.

The Kingdom of Valencia

The most important of the new domains was the region of Valencia. The city itself had been one of the most populous and prosperous of the taifas, and the surrounding agricultural region, partly irrigated, was one of the most productive in the peninsula. The Muslim inhabitants of the city and of other towns in the district were expelled, but most of the Muslim peasants were allowed to remain, their lands divided to form new domains for Aragonese (and some Catalan) aristocrats. After a Muslim peasant revolt in 1263, however, some 100,000 Muslim peasants were expelled from the new kingdom as well.

Jaume the Conqueror had the creative foresight to establish the new region on an independent basis similar to that of Aragón and Catalonia, making constructive use of the federative and constitutional principles behind the Aragonese crown. The Aragonese aristocracy had provided most of the military strength for the conquest of the region, but the crown was eager to avoid adding the whole new territory to the possessions of that domineering caste and so kept it separate and encouraged Catalan immigration. Valencia and most of the other towns were repopulated almost exclusively by Catalan immigrants. The majority of peasant immigrants into some of the better irrigated districts that had been cleared of Muslims were also Catalans. They were mainly from the freer districts of New Catalonia and brought their own *furs*, or systems of local rights, with them, as well as the technical ability to keep a rather complicated agrarian system operating. The domains of Aragonese aristocrats were restricted to the north and northwest of the new kingdom, adjacent to Aragón itself, and the common language of most of the Valencian Christian population was Catalan, not the Aragonese dialect more akin to Castilian. A three-chamber parliament or Corts on the Catalan pattern was then created to represent the dominant elements in the new Christian population.

Immigration was slow, for the surplus population of Catalonia was not great, that of Aragón even less, and some immigrants were attracted to the Balearics. In 1270 the Christian population of the entire region, including the city of Valencia, was only 30,000, while there were four times as many subject Muslims in the countryside. By 1500, slow but steady immigration from the north and Muslim emigration to the south had increased the Christian proportion of an expanded population to nearly 50 percent: of a total of approximately 300,000 inhabitants, 140,000 were Christians, including nearly 70,000 in Valencia itself.

The rise of the city of Valencia as an important economic center dates from the height of the Aragonese Mediterranean empire in the fourteenth century. Its Catalan population brought with them the skills and values of Barcelona and other port towns, and ultimately, with the decline of Barcelona in the fifteenth century, Valencia became the leading commercial and financial city of eastern Spain. Its many skilled workers produced an important volume of manufactures, particularly in textiles. The principality's autonomy enabled the Valencians to maintain their own currency and protect it from the devaluations of the fifteenth century.

The two ruling classes in the principality were the urban oligarchy (*ciutadans honrats*) of the city and the landed aristocracy of the countryside. Early efforts to give artisans equal representation in the administration of Valencia were squelched, and strict sumptuary laws promulgated to keep them in their place; the dominance of the upper classes was maintained throughout. A degree of fusion between the urban oligarchs and the aristocracy occurred, particularly after an agreement of 1329 that allowed the lower aristocracy to hold office in the towns.

Valencia became in some ways the most cosmopolitan city in the peninsula and by the late fifteenth century was its primary center of sensual Renaissance esthetic and humanist culture, strongly influenced by Italian patterns. Yet Valencia remained a culturally bifurcate, religiously divided region, with half its population Muslim, for four hundred years, down to the final expulsion of the Muslims in 1613. Despite its prosperity and urban sophistication, it never developed a completely distinct, independent, and unified cultural personality.

The Balearic Islands

Occupation of the Balearic Islands was a major step in the expansion of Aragón-Catalonia in the Mediterranean. The largest of the islands, Mallorca, had supported a Muslim population of between 80,000 and 100,000, most of them peasant smallholders, but its Muslims were expelled en masse and the island redivided among the royal domain and members of the occupying force. Poor peasants from Catalonia were brought over in significant numbers to work the empty fields for the new overlords, at first on fairly favorable terms.

The key to Mallorca was its large and prosperous capital city of Palma. Endowed with a fine harbor and strategic position in the west Mediterranean, it became within two generations a new Barcelona and for the next century a rival of that capital. Through the first half of the fourteenth century the bourgeoisie of Palma built one of the strongest commercial and financial centers of the west Mediterranean, operating a large merchant fleet. After the middle of the fourteenth century, however, warfare, increased competition, the plague, and natural disaster combined to reduce sharply the commercial importance of Palma.

During the thirteenth and early fourteenth centuries, the society of Mallorca had been more or less open: the first positions after the conquest had been taken by petty *cavaller* and middle class conquerors and emigrants from Catalonia. The only feudal aristocrats were a very small group of nobles from Rosselló and Cerdanya. By the fourteenth century, Mallorca had developed an island parliament, the Consell General of three estates, with a special council for peasants and local councils for each district. Over half the land was originally under royal domain, and most of the original peasant immigrants enjoyed hereditary emphyteutic rights. By the fifteenth century, however, the urban oligarchy of Palma had come to dominate the entire island, buying up most of the land rights and establishing a kind of seigneurial domination over the peasantry, which was placed under growing exactions. Social tensions eventually erupted in several bloody civil wars between town and countryside.

The lesser islands were settled by Christian immigrants more slowly. Ibiza, the third largest, was occupied in 1235 and most of it divided among magnates (high aristocrats) from northeast Catalonia who led the expedition. The fairly dense Muslim population was reduced to serfdom, and in subsequent generations much of it was by degrees either expelled or sold into slavery. At the time of the original conquest the second largest island, Menorca, was merely reduced to vassalage. It was not occupied directly until 1287, after which most of the Muslim population of 40,000 were reduced to slavery and a large number sold throughout the west Mediterranean. Menorca may not have been fully repopulated with Catalan peasant immigrants for a century or more.

In his will, Jaume the Conqueror exercised the customary feudal right of division, and after his death in 1276, the Balearics were split off from the rest of the territories of the Aragonese crown to form a separate kingdom together with the north Pyrenean counties of Rosselló and Cerdanya. The logic behind this hybrid arrangement was that many of the original conquerors and emigrants to Mallorca had come from Rosselló. Though the separate kingdom of Mallorca, as it was called, was soon forced to recognize once more the suzerainty of Aragón, its territories were not fully reincorporated into the patrimony of the Aragonese crown until 1349.

The Economy of Medieval Catalonia

Aside from the commerce of Mallorca and the rise of Valencia in the late Middle Ages, the economic history of the Aragonese empire is mainly the economic history of Catalonia. Without the sea power of the Catalan ports, overseas expansion would have been impossible. Catalan maritime activity began to develop significantly in the eleventh century, and displayed major military importance in the successful expedition to Mallorca in 1229. During the thirteenth and fourteenth centuries, the shipyards of Barcelona vied with those of Venice and Genoa to build the finest vessels in western Europe.

The growth of the Catalan economy was probably stimulated by the flourishing urban economy of southwestern France in the twelfth century, then by the money, enterprise and technical ability of middle class Albigensian refugees who fled to Catalonia after 1213. Simultaneously, the ravages of the papal Albigensian crusade shattered the economic centers of Provence and Languedoc and eliminated much of their competition to the broadly expanding thirteenth-century Catalan economy.

The first great phase of commercial expansion came during the second half of the thirteenth century. It was built especially on the oriental spice trade through Sicily and the traffic in gold, wool, and slaves with northwest Africa. In the early Middle Ages, traffic in slaves—mostly white—may have been the core of Barcelona's commerce. After the middle of the fourteenth century, the slave trade became increasingly important in general Catalan commerce.

By the early fourteenth century, Catalan merchants had established themselves in all the major emporia of the Mediterranean. Barcelona's Consulate of the Sea regulated overseas commerce and supervised the trade of many lesser ports along the Catalan and Valencian littoral. Altogether, Barcelona merchants comprised one of the three largest groups of traders in the centers of Mediterranean and west European commerce. They were the principal European middlemen in the ports of northwest Africa, were second only to the Venetians at Alexandria and in the Flanders trade, and even ranged beyond Byzantium to the Black Sea ports. Traffic in the spices and drugs of

Alexandria was facilitated by a favorable gold balance in trade with northwest Africa and augmented by special tribute paid to the crown of Aragón by several states along the northwest African coast during the fourteenth century.

The Catalan towns became important manufacturing centers and were practically the only exporters of finished goods in any volume in the Hispanic peninsula. At the heart was the domestic textile industry, relying on woolens in Catalonia and silks in Valencia. It began a major phase of development at the start of the fourteenth century with the formation of several large concerns of textile producers, the first of which was established at Barcelona in 1304. Expansion was encouraged by the elimination of French competition during the war that raged intermittently from 1283 to 1313, and by the demands of a growing domestic population and export markets in Castile, the west Mediterranean islands, and northwest Africa. There was also a significant domestic metallurgical industry, whose main achievement, the "Catalan forge," was later copied for iron-working in other parts of western Europe. During the fourteenth century the Catalans held what amounted to control over the technique of extracting Mediterranean coral, and their production of leather goods was also important. At one point, early in the fourteenth century, Catalonia may have had the strongest local manufacturing complex of any one region in western Europe.

Equally significant, Catalonia led in the development of banking and finance. Unlike Castile, which for a long time kept some Muslim monetary standards, Catalonia functioned within the monetary system of the European west Mediterranean. Earlier than 1400, Barcelona's financiers and merchants had developed letters of exchange (the forerunners of checks), insurance, and other banking techniques that were major steps in the evolution of modern finance.

Science was used most impressively in the realms of astronomy, mathematics, and navigation, and it enabled Catalan mariners to make fundamental contributions to the fourteenth-century expansion of Europe into the Atlantic and around the northwest African coast. All told, thirteenth- and fourteenth-century Catalonia was probably the only society within the peninsula in all of Hispanic history to be ahead of most of its European contemporaries in technology and economy.

Society and Institutions of Medieval Catalonia

The economic and territorial expansion of thirteenth-century Catalonia was made possible by, and in turn encouraged, the heaviest concentration of people in the peninsula. Subsequent investigation has revealed, for example, that Catalan farming plots of the thirteenth century were only 20 to 50 percent as large as those of the sixteenth century because of the denser population in the earlier period. The population of the peninsula as a whole may have nearly doubled in the two centuries preceding the Black Death, between 1140 and 1340, as a result of improved agriculture and expanded commerce, but already by the mid-thirteenth century the population of Catalonia was nearly 500,000, or at least 10 percent of the peninsula's approximately 5,000,000. It is calculated that by the early fourteenth century Catalonia's population may have dropped to about 450,000, mainly because of heavy emigration. Altogether, two-thirds of the people of the home territories of the crown of Aragón were Catalan. The population of Valencia and Aragón combined, around 1300, scarcely exceeded 200,000, and that of the Balearics scarcely reached 50,000. Well over half the people of Valencia and Aragón were Muslims not integrated into the society. The Moorish population of the Valencia region amounted to 70–80 percent of the total of that area, that of Aragón to more than one-third, but it has been estimated at only 3 percent of all of Catalonia. The almost entirely rural population of bleak, landlocked Aragón was of secondary importance in producing food and raw materials (grain, wool, and hides).

Catalonia, however, suffered more heavily from the Black Death than did Aragón (or Castile), because it was more urbanized and the plague tended to follow the trade routes. The crest of the disease was followed by locusts, famine, and then its recrudescence, and according to some estimates nearly half of Catalonia died. By the latter part of the fourteenth century the population had declined to about 350,000.

There were two elements of the Catalan upper class: the feudal military aristocracy, established on the land, and the moneyed bourgeois oligarchies. By the late fourteenth century these two were beginning to merge, as more aristocrats chose to live in the towns and more wealthy merchants and financiers bought country estates. The urban patriciate or upper class were for the most part rentiers and the urban equivalent of the feudal seigneurs. These ciutadans honrats (honored citizens) wielded a disproportionate influence in town government.

Below them were the active middle classes, the *ma mitjana*, composed of several strata of *mercaders* (merchants and financiers), ranging from the *mercaders honrats* (enfranchised merchants), who might rival the oligarchic ciutadans in wealth, down to the ordinary *marxants* (peddlers). In wealth such categories might overlap with the *artistas* (professional men and skilled workers), below whom were the ordinary *menestrals* (artisans). The distribution of public power is revealed by the social background of the 200 elective members of the ruling Barcelona Concell de Cent in 1257: 89 were ciutadans, 89 were mercaders, and 22 were menestrals.

Despite strong status differences, this was a fairly open society with great mobility and considerable opportunity. There were definite social tensions, as demonstrated in an uprising by the *poble menut* of Barcelona in 1285, led by one Berenguer Oller and supressed with 200 executions. But in general the urban society of expanding Catalonia, with all its complexity, revealed a degree of social cohesion rivaled by few other regions of western Europe in the thirteenth and fourteenth centuries. The extent of opportunity is demonstrated by fourteenth-century menestrals who ultimately made so much money that they were able to buy landed estates in the countryside. It was only in the fifteenth century, after opportunity and mobility had decreased, that rebellion by the lower and middle classes against the oligarchy became endemic.

The condition of the peasantry improved steadily during the Catalan expansion from the eleventh to the thirteenth centuries. Genuine serfdom did not exist, though much of the peasantry was still liable to various kinds of feudal dues and services. However, after the Black Death reduced their numbers and placed a premium on labor, the upper classes began to tighten exactions and increase requirements, leading eventually to the great Catalan peasant revolts of the late fifteenth century.

The major political distinction of medieval Catalonia was that it developed the most effective parliament of any realm in western Europe. The constitutional structures of Catalonia and Aragón became more fully defined than that of Castile in part because of their more exact feudal separation of jurisdiction and rights. As in other kingdoms, the Catalan Corts that evolved in the thirteenth and fourteenth centuries were composed of representatives of three distinct *braces*. The Catalan parliament, like that of Aragón, was able to take advantage of the heavy fiscal and military needs of the crown to establish basic rights. Lacking the large royal domains of its Castilian counterpart, the crown of Catalonia-Aragón was constantly in need of funds, primarily to support military undertakings. Much of what was held in royal domain was sold to meet these needs, yet they were never fully satisfied and the crown was perpetually dependent on further grants, particularly from Catalonia. By the early fourteenth century, the Corts had used this hold over the crown to establish the principle of regular meetings of the Corts and its power of the purse, and it was on the way to achieving an explicit position of judicial and legislative sovereignty as well.

The Catalan system, unlike that of Aragón, was more than an instrument of aristocratic domination, but developed a broad constitutional structure that represented and protected the middle class as well. The principal reason for this difference was the much greater strength of the Catalan towns and middle classes, requiring that the landed nobility, which was involved in commerce, ally itself with the urban elite rather than merely usurping priority. Thus in Catalonia, as later in England, there developed a functional combination of interests between the aristocracy and the upper level of commoners.

A unique feature of the Catalan system was the establishment of a special institution, the Diputació del General de Catalunya, a committee of representatives of the three estates of the Corts. Its function was to apportion and collect taxes, interpret the laws, and guarantee observance of due constitutional process. The Corts made a rule of never permitting the crown to know the sources of its grants, which were presented in a lump sum after being collected among the population on the basis of periodic censuses. A special Diputació was usually appointed to supervise collection of taxes, and in 1359 the Diputació was summoned to permanent session. In addition to supervising taxes, it began to serve as a superior court, and in 1421 was recognized by the crown as bearing authority to interpret the laws and guarantee their proper observance by other authorities. The Catalan Corts not only established legislative cosovereignty with the crown but institutionalized the means of safeguarding constitutional process, something completely wanting in the Castilian Cortes. The institution of a permanent executive agency—though mainly restricted to fiscal supervision—was afterward adopted by the parliaments of Aragón, Valencia, Navarre, Mallorca, and Aragonese Sicily.

Yet the Corts and its Diputació were used by the dominant elements in late medieval Catalan society primarily as a protective device against the crown. The notion of legislative initiative or a positive economic or fiscal program by the Corts was almost entirely absent. The only programs that ever appeared in the medieval Corts were the annual *greuges,* usually long lists of juridical and financial complaints against exactions and abuses, designed mainly to hold down the tax bill.

Medieval Catalan Culture

The culture of medieval Catalonia was the most thoroughly "European" to be found in the peninsula. Its first significant intellectual center was developed at the monastery of Ripoll in the eleventh century. There and at several other schools in the northeast, the first work was done in transmitting aspects of Muslim science and culture to western Europe, antedating the more extensive efforts in Castile. In both Castile and Catalonia the major role in this was played by Jewish intellectuals, living especially in Barcelona, Huesca in Aragón, and Tudela in Navarre. Foreign students at the principal Catalan schools as well as the religious centers at Pamplona and at Tarazona in Aragón helped transmit Muslim learning across the Pyrenees.

The first major foreign esthetic influences in Catalonia came from Provence and Lombardy, to be followed by the common Romanesque art of western Europe, stronger in Catalan art and architecture of the eleventh and twelfth centuries than anywhere else in the peninsula. Largely from Provençal influence, formal vernacular poetry developed earlier in Catalonia than in Castile, beginning with such poets as Moncada in the eleventh and Arnau de Vilanova in the twelfth century. By the early thirteenth century, the Provençal mode of courtly lyricism (and topical satire), as spread by the trovadors and jongleurs, was widely practiced, and the poetic contest became an institution.

Throughout the Middle Ages, Catalan remained the language of the Aragonese dynasty and court, which itself produced the first great Catalan narrative in the *Crònica* of Jaume I. At the end of the thirteenth century, the Catalan theologian and philosopher Ramón Llull was the first writer in western Europe to compose philosophical and scientific works in the vernacular. The height of the medieval Catalan prose narrative was reached during the fourteenth century in Ramón de Muntaner's chronicles of the Mediterranean expansion.

Philosophical and theological study in Catalonia was the most advanced in the peninsula, and during the fourteenth century there were several teachers of Scotism in the region. The only new Catholic philosophical variant to appear anywhere in the peninsula during the Middle Ages was that of Ramón Llull. Llull is best known for a grand project to convert the Muslims that eventually led him to a martyr's death. He also developed a body of theology that differed from Thomism in its insistence that there was no function for philosophy aside from theology and that all theological propositions could be understood by reason. Llull was besides a poet, a mystic, and a writer of didactic romance, and was probably the first thinker in western Europe to propound the idea of an international association of states (Christian and non-Christian) to keep the peace.

Though open heresy was extremely rare, Catalonia was more noticeably touched by heterodoxy than other Hispanic realms. The Albigensians who fled into the region in the thirteenth century left few direct traces, but the more open and individualistic structure of

CATALAN-ARAGONESE EXPANSION IN THE 13TH AND 14TH CENTURIES

Territories of the Crown of Aragón-Catalonia

Aragonese-Catalan expansion in S.W. France prior to 1213 (lost militarily in 1213 and formally renounced in 1258)

Catalan duchy of central Greece

0   100   200   Mi
0   100   200   300   Km

Zaragoza · ARAGÓN · CATALONIA · Toulouse · Marseilles · Genoa · Florence · Venice · Rome · Naples · Messina · Palermo · SICILY · Athens

Valencia · VALENCIA · Barcelona · IBIZA · FORMENTERA · MALLORCA · MENORCA · SARDINIA

Catalan culture and society created a somewhat more critical-minded and questioning religious ambience than in Castile or Portugal.

Expansion of the Aragonese Mediterranean Empire

During the late-thirteenth and fourteenth centuries, the Aragonese crown developed the most clearly defined, conscious, and carefully planned imperial strategy of any power in western Europe. It first began to take shape during the reign of the heir of Jaume I, Pere III el Gran (1276-1285), who proposed active expansion on all fronts, to include restricting aristocratic power at home (particularly in Aragón) and establishing the indivisibility of the royal inheritance. Pere's queen was the daughter of Manfred von Hobenstaufen and heiress to Sicily. He proposed to claim this inheritance even though the pope had given the island to a branch of the French Angevin dynasty. An opportunity was provided by the famous "Sicilian vespers" of 1282, in which many of the French supporters of the Angevin claimant were massacred and the rest driven from the island, opening the way to Aragonese occupation. The claim to Sicily brought the Aragonese crown into direct conflict with the two major powers of western Europe in that era: the papacy and the crown of France. It led immediately to a major French invasion of Catalonia, under duress of which the Aragonese and Catalan parliaments exacted fundamental concessions from the crown. The invasion was blessed by the pope as a crusade but it ended in complete defeat (1285), leaving rich spoils to be garnered by the victorious Catalans.

Pere el Gran's successor, the weak Alfons III (1285-1291), was handicapped by the resistance of the Aragonese aristocracy. Sicily was given to Pere's second son, Jaume, who was hard-pressed to beat off the assaults of the French and papal forces but was assisted by the excellent Catalan navy of Roger de Lluria that smashed several French fleets. In 1291, Alfons was reconciled with the papacy and agreed to cease aiding the Sicilian branch of his family, but died six months later without a direct heir. The Catalans then offered the throne to Jaume of Sicily, who became Jaume II of Aragón (1291-1327), ignored some of his late brother's concessions to the aristocracy, and continued the struggle with the papacy over Sicily. After five years, however, a compromise was arranged: the Aragonese crown renounced Sicily, was lifted from interdict by the papacy, and was given sovereignty over Sardinia and Corsica (though it would be up to the Aragonese to conquer those islands to make such sovereignty effective). The compromise was not, however, accepted by

Jaume's younger brother, Fadric, the governor of Sicily, who was elected king by a Sicilian parliament in 1296. A settlement was finally reached in 1302, when the French crown agreed to accept Fadric as independent ruler of Sicily after he married a Neapolitan Angevin princess.

Jaume II, like his father, pursued a policy of calculated expansion, both in the west Mediterranean and in the peninsula as well. Royal policy was strongly supported by the Catalans, for it proved a stimulus to manufactures and commerce and offered advantageous new positions. Unlike his grandfather Jaume I, Jaume II did not regard the existing frontiers between Castile and Aragón as final. He took advantage of a Castilian minority crisis in 1296 to occupy the entire Alicante-Murcia region south of Valencia. Though unable to keep Murcia, Jaume did obtain recognition of the Aragonese crown's possession of all the Alicante district, which then became part of the kingdom of Valencia.

The most extraordinary single achievement of the expansion, however, was accomplished in the east Mediterranean by Catalan forces entirely independent of the crown. After peace was restored to the Mediterranean for an entire generation following the compromise of 1302, most of the *almogàvers,* the mercenary light infantry from Catalonia who had done much of the recent fighting, were left without employment. The greater share—a "Grand Company" of possibly as many as 6,500 under Roger de Flor—were hired by Byzantium to protect the eastern empire. Though they quickly established an extraordinary record in wresting Asia Minor from the Turks, the Byzantine court found the almogàvers potentially dangerous defenders; within two years Roger de Flor and many of them were tricked and massacred near Constantinople. The survivors of the Grand Company seized the Gallipoli peninsula, where they attracted allies, including several thousand Turkish mercenaries, and laid waste all of Thrace. In 1309, they moved to Thessaly in the employ of the French Burgundian overlord of central Greece but were soon dismissed. They turned on the Burgundian-Athenian forces and cut the latter's cavalry to pieces in battle near Thebes, then took over completely the "Latin" duchy of Athens. This independent Catalan dominion over central Greece lasted for three generations, and by 1370, one-third of the population of Athens was said to be Catalan. Catalan rule was finally overthrown in 1388.

The military and commercial power of the lands of the Aragonese crown waxed so strong throughout the west Mediterranean during the reign of Jaume II that at one point, in 1309, the Aragonese ruler was even offered the overlordship of the Italian republic of Pisa by its leading citizens. Given the intense rivalries in Italy, this was impractical, but during the course of his reign Jaume II prepared the diplomatic and commercial outlines of further territorial expansion, finally launched with the beginning of the Aragonese conquest of Sardinia in 1323. This brought the Aragonese crown into direct conflict with the powerful republic of Genoa, and the subsequent reign of Alfons IV (1327-1336) was full of conflict.

The outstanding Aragonese ruler of the fourteenth century was Pere IV "el Ceremoniós" (the Punctilious), whose long reign extended for half a century, from 1336-1387. He was a conscientious and devoted ruler and an excellent politician. Moreover, like most of the Aragonese kings of this period, he was cultured and well-read. Pere IV was extremely popular in Barcelona and enjoyed general Catalan support throughout his reign. His main accomplishments were to consolidate the constitutional system of Aragón and Catalonia and secure the domination of the Aragonese crown in the west Mediterranean islands. A showdown with the Aragonese aristocracy occurred in 1347-1348 when the leaders of Aragón and Valencia refused to recognize Pere's only child at that time, his daughter, as heiress to the crown. Momentarily in a weak position, Pere was forced to restore the privileges of the Union to the Aragonese aristocracy and to ratify the institution of a justicia mayor for the Valencian Corts. But the balance soon changed. After another outbreak of plague, Pere collected a largely Catalan army and broke the forces of the Aragonese aristocracy in pitched battle, bringing death to the leaders of the opposition. The Union was abolished, but, as explained earlier, Pere kept a respect for the traditional laws and did not try to alter the original prerogatives of the Aragonese Cortes. Moreover, it was during his reign that the executive branch of Catalan parliamentarianism, the Diputació, was permanently established (1359).

After settling the Aragonese constitutional issue, Pere forceably reincorporated the "kingdom" of Mallorca and its appendage of Rosselló under the Aragonese crown. The struggle with Genoa over Sardinia was then pursued more vigorously, but effective control of Sardinia was not achieved until the very end of his reign. Even after that, serious revolts had to be faced. The Catalan position in Sicily had remained strong, with eighteen commercial consulates ringing the island in an economic web, and in the last years of his reign, Pere was successful in regaining control of Sicily for the Aragonese crown. The Aragonese pattern of establishing autonomous local parliaments was also repeated in Sardinia and Sicily.

During the 1350s and 60s, many of the resources of the Aragonese crown were tied down in a protracted struggle with Pedro the Cruel of Castile. Aragonese interests emerged unscathed from this long contest with a powerful rival, thanks in large part to the diplomatic skill of Pere IV in finding allies and playing off Castilian factions against each other.

During the long reign of Pere IV, the Aragonese-Catalan empire reached its zenith, but the symptoms of decline were already apparent by the time of the old king's death in 1387. Earlier, the expansion of the empire and war with France had stimulated commerce and provided new opportunities for Catalan manufactures. By the middle of Pere's reign the effects of the plague, of population decline, and of constant warfare were beginning to tell on Catalan resources. The Barcelona financial collapse of 1381 was a warning of worse to come.

The achievement was nevertheless extraordinary. In the Middle Ages, only in Venice was there another example of economic development and commercial-military hegemony resting on so slim an original base. Given the complexity and difficulty of the problems faced and the elaborate political and technological developments that were realized in the process, the rise and temporary splendor of medieval Aragón-Catalonia surpassed the territorial expansion of militant Castile in scope and intricacy of accomplishment.

6

The Emergence of Portugal

The question of the roots of Portuguese individuality and the formation of a separate monarchy in the southwest has provoked considerable discussion. The two great Portuguese historians of the nineteenth century, Alexandre Herculano and Oliveira Martins, considered Portuguese independence somewhat accidental, the consequence of fortuitous political developments in the twelfth century. Spanish historians have stated such views even more emphatically. On the other hand, some twentieth-century Portuguese historians have stressed the distinctiveness of their region and what they interpret to be an underlying cultural identity and continuity that reaches well back into the Middle Ages.

The Roman province of Lusitania was not coterminous with modern Portugal, for it did not include part of the north but did embrace a portion of what was later southwestern Spain. The peninsula's southwest developed an economy with a special geographic basis oriented toward the Atlantic coast, but drew comparatively little attention because of the lack of mineral or other natural wealth.

The first separate polity organized in the western part of the peninsula in historic times was the independent kingdom established by the Suevi, a small Germanic tribe that invaded the region in 411. The Suevi settled primarily in the northwest, in Galicia and to the south of it. Their economic orientation was more agricultural than that of the

Visigoths, and they have been given credit for introducing the central
European quadrangular plow into the peninsula. The moist northwest
had a more fundamentally agrarian economy than the predominantly
pastoral dry central region of the peninsula, and after the collapse of
Roman power, cultivation of the land returned to smaller family
units, replacing much of the latifundia system. In later centuries,
more agrarian terms would be found in Galician than in any other
Hispanic language. By the sixth century, the best-developed agriculture in the northwest seems not to have been in Galicia proper but in
the Minho district just to the south. The role of the Suevi, however,
probably lay more in adapting to these conditions than fostering
them. There is little evidence of direct Suevic cultural and social
influence on the population of the northwest, and Portuguese has
fewer German words in it than any other peninsular language.

During the sixth century, the northwestern kingdom of the Suevi
was incorporated by the Visigothic monarchy, with subsequent fusion
of Visigothic and northwestern aristocracies, and there is no clear
indication of any separate political or ethnic identification by the
eighth century. During the first generation of the Muslim occupation,
there was little effort to establish Muslim colonists in the northwest.
Above the Mondego valley no more than a few small garrisons were
to be found. Almost all of Galicia was rewon in the Asturian advance
of the 740s, and between 751 and 754 all the Minho district down to
the mouth of the lower Douro (in Castilian, Duero) was temporarily
occupied. The Christian society of Asturias-Galicia lacked the
strength and resources to repopulate the northern part of the Minho
district until well into the ninth century, while the lower stretches of
the Douro valley constituted part of the no-man's-land whose inhos-
pitable wastes sheltered the north from Muslim attack. Though raids
might carry as far south as the Muslim centers of Coimbra and
Lisbon, effective Christian occupation during the ninth century
scarcely extended beyond the Minho River, the southern limit of
Galicia proper.

There was a large Mozarab population in the Muslim towns of the
southwest, as in other parts of the peninsula, and a significant emigration from the Muslim districts toward the north occurred in the
second half of the ninth century. Apparently Mozarab emigrants
from the south were primarily responsible for settling the city of
Porto in 868.

The difficulty of peopling the Minho-Douro region with Galicians
from the north, and the influx of Mozarabs from the Coimbra-Mondego region to the south, were evidently two factors of some importance in creating a separate regional identity for the area below the
Minho. At least as early as 841, the region was referred to as the
Provincia Portucalense, taking its name from the port of Cale (site of

the subsequent city of Porto), the main transit point between the settled region of Galicia to the north and historic Lusitania to the south. Hence *Portugal* or *portucalense* originally referred merely to an intermediate geographic district, not to a distinct cultural, political, or social entity. Toward the end of the ninth century this frontier district below the Minho River was established as a separate administrative territory by the Asturian monarchy, with a governor (later called *dux*) appointed for life by the crown, in much the same way as with the county of Castile. *Territorium portugalense* (changing *c* to *g* in ordinary usage) was the term used to refer to the entire area from the Minho to the Douro, and the succinct word *Portugal* can first be traced from a document of 883.

During the tenth century, the post of dux of the Portugalense was held by a powerful local aristocratic family which governed on an hereditary basis for a hundred years. The Viking raids and Muslim assaults of the tenth and early eleventh centuries, together with the contemporary decline of the Leonese monarchy, encouraged local identity and self-reliance. The center of the Portugalense tended toward its southern region, in the Douro valley, for the northern district below the Minho had apparently not been fully resettled even by the end of the tenth century.

Particularism in the Portugalense was reinforced by the mountain barriers and watershed—the region of Tras-os-Montes—that separated it from León to the northeast. Save for the Douro, none of the rivers that flowed through the Portugalense originated east of the mountains. There was distinct geographic separation and orientation toward the southwest and the Atlantic. Greater geographic and cultural continuity existed toward the north, for it appears that in addition to the climatic and agrarian similarities, a separate western dialect of vernacular Latin had been spoken in that part of the peninsula since late Roman times. This formed the basis for the modern language of Galician-Portuguese. Differences between Galicia and the Portugalense were not the result of dialect or important geographic barriers, but stemmed from political division, the sparseness of population below the Minho, and the frontier quality of the Portugalense. Galicia was a settled and sheltered society, oriented toward greater León and western Europe. Its spiritual center, Santiago, drew pilgrims from all over the western part of the continent. The Portugalense developed as a more exposed and peripheral area. Though it did not suffer from tenth-century Muslim attacks as much as did León proper, it was placed under heavier pressure than Galicia.

The Navarrese-Castilian hegemony of the early eleventh century shifted the power base in the kingdom farther toward the east, resulting in discontent among the local aristocracy of both Galicia and the

Portugalense. The *ricos homens* of Galicia and old León lost influence at the new Castilo-Leonese court, and in Galicia and the Portugalense their roles were increasingly taken by lesser nobles or royal
appointees. By the middle of the eleventh century the office of dux of
Portugal was no longer being filled; the Castilian-Leonese crown
simply appointed local *meirinhos* (royal administrators) to supplant
the influence of the local aristocracy. The Coimbra-Mondego region
to the south was retaken in 1064 and established as a new territory of
Coimbra, administratively separate from the Portugalense. It was
inhabited by a large and relatively cultured and prosperous population of Mozarabs and mudéjares, whose incorporation added a sophisticated element to the population of the southwest.

After the death of Fernando I and his division of Castile-León, the
barons of the Portugalense rebelled against the domination of the
new "king of Galicia," Fernando's younger son García (1071). This
hostility was exacerbated by the powerful archdiocese of Santiago,
which opposed independent authority for Braga, ecclesiastical center
of the Portugalense, whose bishopric had been restored in 1070. The
ephemeral kingdom of Galicia came to an end in 1073 when it was
incorporated by Castile-León, and Galicia remained close to the
interests of the kingdom, to which it had geographic access through
Asturias. Coimbra and the Portugalense, however, continued to be
relatively isolated by the rugged barrier of the Tras-os-Montes district
and increasingly at odds with their cultural cousins to the north, who
were under antagonistic political and ecclesiastical leadership.

New leadership was given the southwest in 1096, when Alfonso VI
of Castile bestowed the hereditary government of Portugal and Coimbra on the Burgundian aristocrat and crusader Henri (Port. Henrique), husband of Alfonso's bastard daughter and personal favorite,
Teresa. Though the administrative appointment was not necessarily
hereditary, Henri and Teresa were given the hereditary seigneury of
all royal domain in the region. As leader of the entire Hispano-Christian southwest, Henri established a capital at the town of Guimarais
in northern Portugal. He and his wife participated actively in the
quarrels over division of Alfonso VI's patrimony that followed the old
king's death. When Henri died in 1112, Teresa was left as governess
of all Portuguese territory. Her rule and that of her lover, a Galician
noble named Fernando Peres, provoked resentment among the local
aristocracy and town leaders, and they turned for hope to Afonso
Henriques, the heir of Henri and Teresa, who had been about seven
years old at his father's death. Overthrowing her in 1128, Afonso
Henriques took authority as head of Portugal.

In young Afonso's view he had inherited full hereditary authority
over all Portugal and Coimbra, and the Portuguese barons encour-

aged him to resist further political domination from Castile, León, or Galicia. In 1135, he refused to join other north Spanish princes in homage to Alfonso VII of Castile-León. He moved his seat of government southward to Coimbra and for eleven years used the title Prince of Portugal. Afonso was an aggressive military leader and won a notable victory in 1139 that reduced the Muslims of the Santarém district to tributary status. He took the title of King of Portugal on the basis of his autonomous authority, his conquests, and his descent from the Hispanic "emperor" Alfonso VI. The independence of his

Rulers of Portugal

House of Burgundy

Afonso I	1128-1185	Cardinal Henrique	1578-1580
Sancho I	1185-1211	Felipe I	1580-1598
Afonso II	1211-1223	Felipe II	1598-1621
Sancho II	1223-1246	Felipe III	1621-1640
Afonso III	1246-1279	João IV	1640-1656
Dinís	1279-1325	Afonso VI	1656-1668
Afonso IV	1325-1357	Pedro II	1668/1683-1706
Pedro I	1357-1367	João V	1706-1750
Fernando	1367-1383	José I	1750-1777
House of Aviz		Maria I	1777-1799
		João VI	1799/1816-1826
João I	1384-1433	Pedro IV	1826-1834
Duarte	1433-1438	Miguel	1828-1834
Afonso V	1438-1481	Maria II	1834-1853
João II	1481-1495	Pedro V	1853-1861
Manuel I	1495-1521	Luis	1861-1889
João III	1521-1557	Carlos	1889-1908
Sebastião	1557-1578	Manuel II	1908-1910

territory was further enhanced by establishment of the ecclesiastical independence of the archdiocese of Braga, giving the kingdom its own church hierarchy. For protection, Afonso subsequently swore fealty to the papacy and paid tribute to it, but the papacy did not officially recognize King of Portugal as a title and institution until 1179.

The establishment of the independent kingdom of Portugal coincided with a period of severe internal stress for Castile-León, as well as of renewed military challenges to it from the Almoravids and Almohads. This combination of pressures left Castile-León with little strength or energy for the reincorporation of Portugal. Afonso I's long reign of fifty-seven years ended with his death in 1185. During

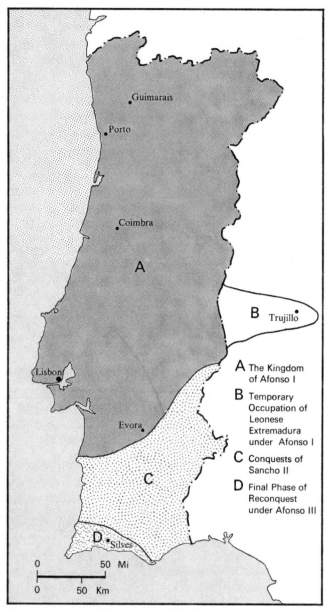

Guimarais

Porto

Coimbra

A

B Trujillo

Lisbon

A The Kingdom
of Afonso I

B Temporary
Occupation of
Leonese
Extremadura
under Afonso I

Evora

C Conquests of
Sancho II

C

D Final Phase of
Reconquest
under Afonso III

D Silves

0   50 Mi

0   50 Km

The Portuguese Reconquest   *UWCL* the middle years of his rule, the Portuguese border was extended well into the south. Though the strength of the kingdom, with its modest population of half a million, was comparatively slight, a passing force of English, French, and Flemish crusaders was enlisted to conquer the key Muslim city of Lisbon at the mouth of the Tejo (in Spanish, Tajo). Other foreign forces were recruited to aid in the occupation of much of the Alemtejo region to the southeast. The Knights Templars and four other orders of crusading knights, several of which were established expressly for the Portuguese reconquest, played a major role. Given their limited resources, Afonso I and his successors must be accounted among the most dynamic dynasts of their time.

The expansion of Portugal depended upon royal leadership, and the new state was fortunate in that all but one of its early rulers were adequate, and several were unusual. Basing the authority of the crown on strong royalist institutions patterned after those of León, and aided by the territorial compactness of its state, the Portuguese monarchy soon achieved greater internal political consistency than did most medieval kingdoms. Like León and Aragón, Portugal developed a largely seigneurial society, with most of its districts under the domain of church or aristocracy, but like León and Castile, its political organization was not strictly feudal. From the very beginning, the overriding sovereignty of the crown was clearly understood, and the monarchy also played a role in social and economic affairs, sometimes fostering the interests and representation of the third estate.

Afonso's son and heir, Sancho I (1185–1211), continued the military struggle, but devoted himself especially to institutional development, repopulation and the founding of towns, and the patronage of letters. The third king, Afonso II (1211–1223), was less concerned with military affairs. His principal achievement was the first systematic compilation of Portuguese law, clarifying property and personal rights and guaranteeing the overarching sovereignty of the crown. Afonso II's heir, Sancho II (1223–1246), was less successful. Dominated by a powerful aristocratic faction, his reign led to considerable internal conflict, and he was eventually deposed by his younger brother Afonso III (1246–1279), who was supported by the church, the crusading orders, the petty nobility, and the towns. Nevertheless, a major phase of Portuguese expansion was accomplished under Sancho II, and the reconquest was finally completed under Afonso III, who occupied the Algarve district along the southern coast, giving Portugal the approximate boundaries that it has had since. Altogether, between 1225 and 1250, the occupation of the Alemtejo and the Algarve increased the size of Portugal from 55,000 to 90,000 square kilometers. Afonso III was a notably successful administrator, promoting resettlement and summoning the first meeting of a three-estate Portuguese Cortes at Leiria in 1254.

The last ruler of the thirteenth century, Dinís o Lavrador, "the Farmer" (1279-1325), was in many ways the most impressive. He gained his nickname from efforts to promote agriculture, and it is especially because of his work that the period of the Burgundian dynasty in Portuguese history is often, and somewhat misleadingly, referred to as that of the "agrarian monarchy." Dinís devoted particular attention to the repopulation of the Alemtejo. He broke up a number of large domains in various regions to distribute among the peasants and discouraged the tendency of nobles to leave a part of their lands uncultivated. He reformed the terms of peasant land tenure in the north, stimulated food production and commerce, undertook the draining of swamps and the planting of the Leiria forest, and helped to develop fairs. His personal interest, however, lay in women and poetry. Dinís fostered Portuguese culture, and it was during his reign that the vernacular, rather than Latin, became the official language. His last years were troubled by a bloody civil revolt led by his legitimate heir and provoked by the honors Dinís had bestowed on the eldest of his nine bastards.

Medieval Portuguese Society

There was a notable increase in wealth during the main phase of the Portuguese reconquest, and for the next hundred years food production and commerce continued to expand, making it possible for the population of the kingdom to double between the twelfth and fourteenth centuries. Estimates of population in the Middle Ages are usually vague approximations, but it is generally believed that the number of Portuguese increased approximately as follows:

twelfth century	500,000-600,000
thirteenth century	800,000-900,000
fourteenth century	1,000,000-1,200,000

Unlike Castile, Aragón, and Valencia, Portugal contained no sizable Muslim minorities. Only in the Alemtejo and Algarve did small groups of Muslim peasants remain on the land after completion of the Portuguese reconquest.

Linguistically unified, the Portuguese people were socially and culturally more homogeneous than the population of Castile and Aragón. The small kingdom contained no ethnic subgroup of any importance save for a very slight Jewish population, and by the middle of the thirteenth century had become the first nation-state in Europe.

The structure of Portuguese society was originally quite similar to that of Galicia and León, though as it expanded southward it was more nearly like the frontier pattern of new León than the feudal pattern typical of Galicia. The dominant class in Portugal, as elsewhere, was the military aristocracy, rewarded by the crown with recognition of seigneurial domain and special grants of land or income as *honras*. Aristocratic seigneuries dominated the Minho and Douro regions of the northwest but were less common in central and southern Portugal. Moreover, Portuguese seigneuries were normally quite small in comparison with those of Castile. There were perhaps a half dozen truly powerful and influential aristocratic families, most of them related by blood to the ruling dynasty.

Most aristocrats did not have large incomes from their own domains, but depended for their wealth on subassignments of royal income known as *quantias*. The quantias assigned to nobles amounted, at certain times, to between 25 and 50 percent of the crown's revenue. One economic historian has calculated that the quantias were several times the total income from the nobility's seigneurial domain. The policy of assigning part of the royal income to the nobility was common in most late-medieval monarchies, and was a normal way of maintaining the social and economic preeminence of the aristocracy.

Below the nobility there existed, as in Castile, a class of *cavaleiros vilãos,* commoner knights, drawn from the middle or lower classes to supplement the military elite during the twelfth- and thirteenth-century reconquest. They held assignments of land or income sufficient to defray military expenses and occupied an intermediate social status, though their exemption from most taxes was a privilege that gave them near-aristocratic rank.

In the original *terra portucalense* north of the Douro, most of the peasantry, by the twelfth century, lived under terms of *cartas de incomuniaçao* or *pactos de benfeitoria* roughly similar to the *encomendación or benefactoria* of León. Though direct allodial possession was quite uncommon, so too was complete serfdom. Much of the peasantry was tied to the land under varying restrictions, but between the eleventh and thirteenth centuries such conditions of adscription largely died out.

The agrarian reforms of Diniś o Lavrador encouraged a tendency in the most heavily populated area of the kingdom, the Minho, toward family farms or *casais*. Diniś guaranteed the right of emphyteusis (hereditary transmission of cultivation rights) to peasant renters on most aristocratic and church domains in the northwest. The majority of Portuguese peasants operated petty farms either as hereditary emphyteutical renters or as sharecroppers, the terms exacted from the latter usually being considerably more rigorous than from the former. Below the sharecroppers or *parceiros* (roughly equivalent to the Castilian *aparceros*), there were the peasants who carried out various duties on aristocratic or ecclesiastical domains and sometimes had partial land-use rights of their own. In central and southern Portugal by the fourteenth century, with the growth in population and emigration from the north, there had also developed a class of completely landless rural laborers similar to the jornaleros of the southern districts of Castile.

In general, more of Portuguese society than of Castilian was devoted to agriculture. Grazing was not as important as in the neighboring kingdom, but sheep and cattle were of major significance in two of the newer, somewhat flatter regions of southcentral Portugal, Beira Baixa and the Alto Alemtejo. A greater communal access to land stimulated livestock production there.

The granting of special rights (*foros*) and charters (*cartas*) to small rural communities and municipalities soon became as widespread in Portugal as in Castile-León. In the mountainous northeast (Tras-os-Montes) that separated Portugal from León, the soil was poor and population sparse, encouraging communal social and economic organization. In that region, foros were sometimes granted by the crown to communal subgroups of no more than twenty households, recognizing local privileges, regularizing taxes and obligations, and specifying rights of self-government. The collectivist terms of much of the cultivation in the Tras-os-Montes region were ratified by the agrarian reforms of Dinís.

The most important semi-autonomous units were not small rural groups but the larger towns, like Porto and Coimbra, along the main rivers and coast, and the larger *concelhos* established mainly in the north-central region (Beira) and in west-central Estremadura (not to be confused with Leonese Extremadura). Concelho rights varied considerably in their terms, but the most common were similar to those of Leonese concejos such as Salamanca, though their privileges and organization were not as broad and strong as those of Castile. Towns formed by royal charter in the twelfth and thirteenth centuries received significant rights of autonomy, and some of the older towns broadened their prerogatives, as for example after a successful revolt for wider municipal rights at Coimbra in 1111.

In the broad plains of the southern Alemtejo, incorporated after 1238, much of the land was taken over by the church and the Portuguese crusading orders, just as in the southern districts of Castile after the great reconquest of San Fernando. There, as in southern Castile, autonomous communities were proportionately less common.

Portuguese Catholicism

Religion played a role in defining and sustaining Portuguese life rather similar to its role in Castile-León, though Portuguese religiosity did not become as intense as that of Castile. The crusade was officially introduced in 1100 with a papal bull calling all Hispanic monarchies to concerted action against the Muslims. Proclamation of the crusade was frequent in the Portuguese reconquest of the twelfth and early thirteenth centuries. The complex of holy war was encouraged by the nominal vassalage of Portugal to the Holy See during much of that period, and the aura of holy war came to be bestowed on a variety of military enterprises, including the struggle against Castile during the late fourteenth century, when the Portuguese and Castilian crowns supported opposing sides in the Great Schism of the papacy. Thus the idea of crusade became as firmly entrenched in Portugal as in Castile, and was intrinsic in the motivations of the subsequent overseas expansion, contributing to the ultimate doom of the monarchy in Morocco in 1578.

The earliest inhabitants of Portuguese territory, whether Mozarabs under Muslim rule or Galician immigrants, practiced the ancient Hispanic or Mozarabic rite, but by the time Portugal emerged as an independent kingdom, the entire Hispanic church had become Romanized in liturgy and organization. The establishment of the Portuguese monarchy coincided with the rise of papal political influence in the peninsula, and there was never any doubt of Portuguese religious orthodoxy, just as there was never any doubt of Castilian. As much as the Castilians, the medieval Portuguese defined their identity facing southward, against Islam, and found it almost impossible to conceive of heresy.

On the other hand, Portugal was more remote than Castile from the centers of European culture. Though stimulated militarily by European crusaders, the kingdom was less affected by medieval religious and cultural movements than was Castile, and there was less interest in transmitting or absorbing the achievements of Muslim intellectual life than in Castile or Catalonia. Portugal remained something of a cultural and spiritual backwater throughout the Middle Ages. The first major center of poetry in galego-português was not in Portugal, but was the thirteenth-century Castilian court of San Fernando and Alfonso el Sabio. The Visigothic script persisted in Galicia and Portugal until the middle of the twelfth century, even longer than in Castile. A Portuguese vernacular prose literature emerged somewhat late, in the fourteenth century.

Even among the clergy, educational standards were low, and compared with other areas in the peninsula and beyond, remained low during the fifteenth and sixteenth centuries. The only Portuguese university was founded at Lisbon in 1290 and later moved to Coimbra. It never became a major center of learning, and during the Middle Ages never employed more than some twenty-five professors. The three principal Portuguese religious thinkers and philosophers— Santo António de Lisboa, Pope John XXI, and Pedro Julião—all developed their careers outside of Portugal. The only dissenting philosopher of any note, the rationalist and Averroist Tomaz Escoto of the early fourteenth century (apparently not of Portuguese parentage) was eventually put to death.

Despite the orthodoxy and lack of dissent in Portuguese religion, thirteenth-century Portugal was wracked by conflict between the church and crown (the latter usually supported by the municipalities and concelhos) over church properties and jurisdictions. The church had gained greater political influence in Portugal than in Castile, because of the ecclesiastical support needed to assure Portuguese independence and because of the crown's tributary vassalage to the papacy in the late twelfth and early thirteenth centuries. The crown was frequently unable to control the election of bishops. During the reconquest, the Portuguese church amassed a great deal of land, especially in the center and south, and it has been estimated that during the thirteenth century its income was greater than that of the crown. The monarchy, which encountered great difficulty in taxing church property, viewed the influence and wealth of the ecclesiastical hierarchy as a danger. Church wealth and domains were resented by the autonomous municipalities and the concelhos and were coveted by the nobility.

The first measures to restrict or reexamine church acquisitions were taken by Afonso II, who in 1218 began a series of *inquiriçoes* (inquiries) into the legal titles of church properties. Relations with the hierarchy and papacy remained highly strained throughout the reigns of Afonso II, Sancho II, and Afonso III. The latter revived inquiriçoes into economic and juridical abuses by both the church and aristocracy, restoring a certain amount of church land to the royal domain. Four generations of conflict were finally brought to a close by Dinís, who instituted new inquiriçoes, recovered more property, and finally settled the longstanding dispute with the papacy and church hierarchy through a compromise concordat that was signed in 1290.

These political and economic clashes never involved issues of religion or the spirit, and the place of religion in daily life was little affected by them. There was always, however, a certain amount of anticlericalism in Portuguese society, encouraged by wealth, corruption, and ignorance among the clergy. During the fourteenth century, the relaxation of morals in Portugal was as marked as in the rest of Europe. Concubinage among the clergy was common, paralleling the licentious behavior of the aristocracy.

Portuguese culture progressed during the fourteenth century, with the growth of vernacular literature and the foundation of new religious schools. Though Portuguese achievements in architecture remained modest compared with the main regions of western Europe or with Castile, a number of impressive castles and Gothic churches and monasteries were constructed. Influences from France and England were probably more important in these developments than were those from Castile.

Maritime and Commercial Affairs

There may have been more usable small harbors along the Portuguese coast in the Middle Ages than in the twentieth century, and Portuguese maritime activity antedated independence. Before 1100, Portuguese merchants were already established in small numbers in the main ports of France and Flanders. The coastal and river towns joined the concelhos of south-central Protugal in the movement toward greater representation for the third estate in the thirteenth century and in the protest against overweening church wealth.

Urban handicraft never passed very modest proportions, and aside from some linens in the fourteenth century, Portuguese exports consisted of foodstuffs and raw materials: wine, oil, dried fish, hides, salt from Setubal, cork, and figs, raisins, and almonds from the south.

Growth of the Portuguese navy, taking advantage of the kingdom's unique geographic position, was slow but fairly steady, and by the fourteenth century it had become a minor force that could not be ignored in the Atlantic. In 1336 a Portuguese fleet ventured out into the Atlantic as far as the Canary Islands, establishing a claim that remained in contention for more than one hundred and fifty years until finally relinquished in favor of Castile. Maritime affairs, nevertheless, involved a smaller proportion of the Portuguese population than of the principal coastal regions of western Europe, and Portuguese strength could not be compared with that of the five or six principal naval powers. What compensated to some extent for the small size of the Portuguese fleet and the weakness of the domestic economy was the kingdom's strategic position at the outlet from the west Mediterranean to the Atlantic, central axis of the sea lanes from Italy to Flanders. The second half of the fourteenth century was a time of modestly growing prosperity for Portugal, and larger shipping companies were formed to pool capital and share risks. The crown played a crucial role in this development by providing protection and incentives. A royal decree of 1377 established shipbuilding subsidies, and another in 1380 set up a kind of compulsory maritime insurance. Neither in Lisbon nor in any other Portuguese port were there merchants or shipowners with the great resources of those in Venice, Genoa, Barcelona, or Bruges, but a basis for future expansion was being established.

The Sesmarias

Medieval Portugal was poor, even for its day. No more than a third of its soil was suited for agriculture, either because it was hilly, rocky, or infertile, and the rainfall, although heavier than Castile's, was unreliable. Despite such handicaps, Portuguese agriculture made some progress between the twelfth and fourteenth centuries and in the process adopted slightly improved techniques and was largely able to meet the needs of an expanding population. There were recurrent problems in provisioning Lisbon, but these arose because of the size of the capital, the inevitably bad medieval transportation, and the unavoidable bad harvests. Portugal suffered less from the Black Death of the early fourteenth century than other regions of Europe, but it did suffer a temporary decline in population, accompanied by a shortage of laborers and a drop in cultivation in certain areas. In the southern half of the kingdom, there was a growing tendency to take land out of cultivation and put it into the raising of livestock, which required less labor and drew higher market prices. By the second half of the fourteenth century, many of the coastal towns were importing grain, and there were exaggerated complaints over the "decay" of Portuguese agriculture.

Government intervention to regulate the cost of agricultural labor and production was common in mid-fourteenth-century Europe. The main Portuguese variant of this trend was the "Sesmarias" decree by the crown in 1375, taken from the term used to denote the dividing up of strips of land in the earlier resettlement of Portugal. It followed the tradition of royal encouragement of peasant agriculture, providing that two judges be named for each local district of Portugal to make sure that all arable land was being put to use. Lands of nobles or church foundations that were not being cultivated were to be confiscated, and all landless or unemployed peasants were to receive land on reasonable terms. At the same time, all peasants already working the land were required to remain there. Livestock raising, theoretically, was to be restricted to large properties only. The Sesmarias were not fully enforced and were largely under the control of the *homens bons,* or local oligarchies, of the concelhos and municipalities. The decrees were aimed particularly at latifundium districts of central and south-central Portugal, and did result in a certain amount of redistribution of land for peasant agriculture. They had some effect in raising food production and building Portuguese economic strength for the period of expansion in the fifteenth century.

The Monarchy in the Fourteenth Century

The long reign of Afonso IV (1325-1357) involved disputes and war with Castile, but this did not prevent the appearance of a large Portuguese contingent beside the Castilians at the battle of Salado (1340), in which the last invasion from Morocco was decisively defeated. Afonso IV's most famous act was his execution of Inês de Castro, Castilian mistress of his heir Pedro, for involving the Portuguese throne in the internal conflicts of Castile. Her execution brought Pedro into rebellion against his father, but the brief struggle was resolved by devolving upon Pedro certain functions of government, including that of dispensing justice throughout the kingdom. During Pedro's ten years as ruler in his own right (1357-1367), as Pedro I, he earned the nickname *O Justiceiro* (the Justicer) for his rigorous if capricious punishment of wrongdoing among all classes. The Justicer was in fact a merry and sometimes irresponsible monarch who loved to dance and sing with his subjects and devoted much energy to the hunt. However, he kept Portugal out of war and became perhaps the most popular of all medieval Portuguese kings.

The last king of the Burgundian dynasty, D. Fernando (1367-1383), was the least successful and the most unpopular, a ruler whose personality, policies, and reign were all contradictory. He instituted a number of constructive measures: the Sesmarias decree of 1375, regulations promoting shipping and commerce, and efforts to limit artistocratic jurisdiction on seigneurial domain. On the other hand, his foreign policy was disastrous. His government became involved on the Anglo-Aragonese side against Castile in the contemporary phase of the Hundred Years' War, and his forces were three times defeated, forcing him to sign three successive unfavorable treaties of peace. A great deal of Portuguese shipping was lost and a heavy economic strain was placed on the kingdom, leaving much of the population in growing misery by the 1380s. His queen, Leonor Teles, who had been legally wed to a nobleman, was extremely unpopular, identifying the throne with aristocratic and foreign intrigues. Moreover, Fernando increased the granting of *honras* to favored nobles at a time when the kingdom could least afford it. When he died in 1383, the towns and some of the aristocracy were seething with discontent.

The Succession Crisis of 1383-1385

Fernando left no male heir, and his only daughter, Beatriz, was married to Juan I of Castile with the provision that their offspring would inherit the Portuguese crown, introducing the danger of Castilian domination. Until such issue, however, the Portuguese crown remained under the regency of Fernando's widow, the hated Leonor Teles. The government of the queen regent and her new Galician lover was particularly detested by the townspeople and some of the lesser nobility. The queen regent's main rival was a bastard of Pedro I, D. João, grand master of the Order of Aviz (the Portuguese section of the Knights of Calatrava). An Aviz revolt drove Teles from Lisbon, but was immediately faced with an invading force from Castile.

The result was both a civil war and an international war between the Portuguese rebels and the crown of Castile. In general, the south and west rallied behind the Aviz banner. The coastal and urban areas, particularly, opposed the Castilian king, for they feared the imposition of a Castilian-style government which would favor the countryside and the aristocracy. On the other hand, the more traditional and aristocratic north and east rallied to Juan I. During 1383-1384 the Aviz forces were on the defensive but managed to hold fast in the central area around Lisbon, and early in 1385 the Portuguese Cortes at Coimbra officially recognized D. João as king. The struggle reached its climax in the summer of 1385, after the Castilian forces had been weakened by long campaigning. The battle of Aljubarrota, north of Lisbon, resulted in decisive defeat for the Castilian crown when the cavalry of Juan I failed to break the outnumbered ranks of dismounted knights, crossbowmen, and English archers led by D. João's brilliant military chief, Nun'Alvares Pereira.

Portugal's first alliance with England had been signed by Fernando, and it was renewed in a formal agreement of 1386, bringing nearly 5,000 English troops into the country. John of Gaunt, uncle to the English Richard II, had married a daughter of the former Castilian king, Pedro the Cruel, and pressed his own claim to the Castilian throne in opposition to the new Trastámara dynasty. Anglo-Portuguese forces temporarily occupied much of Spanish Galicia before the

Castilian crown paid off the English to get them out of the peninsula. Desultory hostilities between Castile and Portugal continued for years, especially at sea, until a definitive peace was finally signed in 1411.

João I (1384-1433)

The first ruler of the new Aviz dynasty enjoyed a long reign of half a century, during which the basis was laid for the expansion of the fifteenth century. He introduced nothing radical, but consolidated the institutions of the kingdom and continued most of the positive policies of his predecessors. The advent of João I did not mark the triumph of the middle classes over the aristocracy, as is sometimes stated, but a reorganization of the nobility and an elevation of new elements from the petty aristocracy (*infanções*) and middle classes. Indeed, it was during his reign that the Portuguese aristocracy began to be officially ranked by the categories and titles typical of the French and English nobility. Like most ambitious rulers, however, João I distrusted the high aristocrats and favored the lesser nobility.

The new reign brought with it an increase in the power and authority of the crown. João I's officials, like those of his predecessors, actively expanded the royal authority over seigneurial privilege and local custom. A Royal Council, with specific membership and functions, was established. Following the progressive custom of the later Middle Ages, middle-class jurists rather than aristocratic lieutenants were employed in royal administration.

João I was fortunate in possessing the qualities of a successful prince and in having ministers and a family of the highest quality. He was himself a cultured and learned man, prudent almost to a fault, and astute in his political dealings. João das Regras, the jurist who served as chancellor for many years, was perhaps the most effective administrator to assist the medieval Portuguese throne. His military lieutenant, Nun'Alvares Pereira, was a great leader and a model of knightly virtue. João I's English queen, Philippa of Lancaster, daughter of John the Gaunt, was a most exemplary princess, both as a wife and a queen. Their five sons were the most talented and imaginative generation of heirs in Portuguese history.

Since the middle of the fourteenth century, the monarchy had intervened increasingly in the government of Portuguese towns through the appointment of royal administrators and inspectors (*corregedores, regedores,* and *vedores*) to oversee affairs. João I continued this trend but at the same time broadened certain aspects of autonomy and representation. He rewarded town leaders who had backed his cause by granting them broader local property jurisdiction. This increased the influence of the *homens bons,* the middle-class oligarchs, who for more than a century had been gaining control in the larger towns and concelhos at the expense of the lower classes. Artisans never had much influence in Portuguese municipal government, but João I did open the government of Lisbon to representatives of the guilds (*mesteres*) in 1384, and during the fifteenth century the practice was extended to most other large towns.

João I was quite respectful of the Portuguese Cortes and summoned it almost biennially. The need to marshal national resources for large enterprises and enlist the support of the towns made the fifteenth century the golden age of the traditional Portuguese Cortes. Yet João I strove to avoid becoming altogether dependent on the Cortes for financial assistance, and for a period of ten years (1418–1427) he did not convene the Cortes at all. His government sought to expand both the royal domain and the royal revenues, incorporating a few sources of ecclesiastical income and restricting several perquisites of the nobility. Taxation became less unequal after the Cortes in 1387 voted general excises to be paid on certain goods by all social classes. These excises provided a significant share of the royal revenue during João I's reign.

The new dynasty assisted peasant agriculture less than its predecessor. Though peasant renters in the north benefitted from the inflation and devaluation that marked João's reign, landless peasants in the south were hurt. Social tension increased in the Alemtejo, whence a flight from the land was already evident by the fifteenth century. Moreover, the new nobility created under João I was often rapacious, and the *homens bons* of the towns too sometimes seized concelho land from the peasants.

The Aviz policy of strong royal government merely reaffirmed the tradition of the Portuguese monarchy, which had been to a large extent responsible for creating a Portuguese nation. Royal patronage of commerce and incentives for maritime development had already become traditional long before João I. What was new in Portugal by the beginning of the fifteenth century was not these trends of royal policy, but that the small kingdom had, after three hundred years, finally come of age. Though its population was no more than one and a half million, it had achieved strongly institutionalized government, a sense of national unity, a basis for modest economic development, commercial and maritime forces eager for a more expansive role in the world, a reorganized military aristocracy seeking new fields of adventure, and firm, calculating leadership able to guide the energies of its followers into major enterprises abroad.

7

Medieval Hispanic Catholicism

Before the Muslim conquest, the centers of Hispanic Christendom lay in the towns of the south and east and so from the very beginning of the conquest fell under Muslim control. At first it was perhaps not difficult to adjust to Muslim political domination. The system of "discriminatory tolerance" practiced during the first two centuries and more of Muslim rule made it possible to maintain the diocesan structure of the Mozarab church. Indeed, the hierarchy gained a degree of freedom, for unlike the Visigothic kings, the emirs of Cordoba let the ecclesiastical hierarchy call their own councils (with one exception in 851) and elect their own bishops. Yet within little more than a century, the Mozarab church had become fossilized, largely cut off from the Christian community of western Europe, more and more heavily taxed, and subject to restrictions and the pressure of a dominant oriental culture. It sank into decadence and its following dwindled, as the most vital elements emigrated to the Christian principalities of the north.

The northern hill districts that escaped Muslim domination had been uncertain in their Christian identity before the eighth century, but during that century much of their uncertainty was lost, apparently in part as a reaction against the Muslim faith of their adversaries. The Asturian church was by no means entirely cut off from Mozarab Christianity. When the border was not disrupted by fight-

131

ing, there was often a good deal of travel back and forth across the frontier, and Mozarab religious probably played an important role in the further Christianization and acculturation of the northern population.

The Asturian church, however, did not recognize the ecclesiastical overlordship of the metropolitan of Toledo, living under Muslim rule, and outright antagonism between Asturian and Mozarab Catholicism emerged by the end of the eighth century in the Adoptionist controversy. The customary Hispano-Visigothic religious definition of the two natures of Christ spoke of his "natural filiation" to the divine and of his "adoptive filiation" to the human, differing from the unified trinitarian interpretation that had become orthodox in most of Latin Christendom. After continued official usage of these terms at the Mozarab church council of 784 in Seville, the Asturian clergy protested. The issue was ultimately carried to Rome, perhaps the first such invocation of papal authority by Hispanic Christians, and in 794 the metropolitan of Toledo was excommunicated. Under Alfonso II (791-842), the Asturian monarchy created a separate ecclesiastical system independent of Toledo, thereby affirming the special identity of Asturias and the legitimate authority of its institutions as heirs to the Visigothic legacy.

During the ninth and tenth centuries, the Asturo-Leonese church grew in authority and wealth. It remained almost completely subordinate to royal power, for the Asturian kings dominated the selection of bishops and actually expanded the prerogatives of Visigothic rulers. But the clergy improved their own education somewhat, expanded parish and administrative operations, and increased their cultural and spiritual influence.

An important aspect of the expansion of the Asturo-Leonese church was the cult of Santiago (St. James) at Compostela in Galicia. The shrine there provided the main religious nexus with the rest of western Europe. By the tenth century, the pilgrim's route to it had become one of the most traveled in the west, and the thousands of voyagers along it provided stimulus for the development of the small northern towns. By the eleventh century the road to Santiago through the Pyrenees and across the north of the peninsula was a major force for Europeanization and modernization. The prestige of Santiago throughout Christendom was an important source of pride and identification for a monarchy that ruled over a poor, uncultured people subsisting on a largely pastoral economy. In turn, the bishop of Santiago de Compostela tried to assert leadership over the church in the kingdom of León. The diocese came to consider itself the equal of Rome, for the Leonese church at that time, though fully orthodox in

Catholic theology, clearly did not deem itself institutionally or organizationally subservient to the papacy.

From the earliest phase of Asturian territorial expansion, the church grew in wealth. Grants of land were made by the crown and by local overlords as well, and church property became especially extensive in Galicia. Monastic institutions also played an important role in taking over and resettling new territories. A definite contrast existed, however, in the social and economic pattern of Castile, where church endowments were proportionately much smaller and ecclesiastical leaders had a less imposing place in public councils than in Galicia and León.

The rise of the Leonese church in the ninth and tenth centuries contrasted with the steady decline of the Mozarab, a decline which first reached crisis proportions in the Cordoban martyrdoms of the 850s, at the very time when the cult of Santiago was beginning to take firm hold in the north. Sizable Mozarab emigrations to the northwest in the second half of the ninth century apparently made significant contributions to Leonese culture, but it is not clear that the influx of southern Christians had any very original effects on the religious structure and ethos, for these were fairly well defined in León by that time. Moreover, though there were instances of other heresies besides Adoptionism among the Mozarabs between the ninth and eleventh centuries, Leonese Catholicism remained rigidly orthodox throughout, as a militant frontier religion holding to a firm, rather narrow identity in tense opposition to a powerful spiritual foe.

By contrast to the theologically orthodox but regionally autonomous and somewhat archaic church in León, the church in the Catalan counties, from the end of the eighth century, was organized under the administrative system of west European Roman Catholicism. The native Hispano-Visigothic liturgy and forms persisted for a long time in León, but in Catalonia, which did not obtain a cis-Pyrenean metropolitanate of its own until the eleventh century, they gave way almost immediately to the more typical Roman rite. The economic endowments and the political influence of the church in Catalonia were more typically feudal. The church there, too, soon amassed considerable wealth, and enjoyed a greater autonomy because of the decentralization of political authority. Propertied monasteries in Catalonia remained strong supporters of the Frankish crown even after its decline, in opposition to the local power of the counts and overlords. Church-state tensions were more extreme in Catalonia than in León. Perhaps the most atrocious example was the fate of Arnulf, archbishop of Narbonne, who in 912 excommunicated Count Sunyer II of Ampurias (a district in northeast Catalonia). The count's henchmen waylaid the hapless archbishop, blinded and mutilated him, and tore out his tongue before he died.

Between Catalonia and Castile-León, on the other hand, a partly pagan territory existed for some time, since the Christianization of the bulk of the Basque population did not get underway until the tenth century. By the end of that century, most of the Navarrese had been converted, but the inhabitants of Vizcaya and Guipuzcoa were not fully brought within the sphere of Christianity until after establishment of the bishopric of Alava in the eleventh century.

The full institutional authority of the Roman papacy was introduced into the peninsula by way of southern France and Catalonia. The papacy's increasing diplomatic influence proved useful at the time of the Cordoban offensives in the tenth century, and the counts of Barcelona entered into regular relations with the papacy from the third quarter of that century on. They were followed a generation later by Sancho the Great of Navarre, whose political hegemony in northern Spain was to some extent assisted by papal diplomacy.

The effect of papal diplomacy on the Hispanic kingdoms from the late tenth century on was both centripetal and centrifugal, with the latter predominating. The papacy did exert some influence toward Hispanic political unity by trying to discourage internecine warfare and encourage cooperation in the struggle against the Muslims, but it also encouraged the independent or separatist ambitions of the several kingdoms in order to increase its own influence in each and gain larger contributions. Pope Alexander II (1061–1073) used his diplomatic influence to ratify the independence of the "kingdom" of Aragón, whose rulers were willing to recognize papal suzerainty. In the twelfth century, as has been seen, a similar relationship developed with the crown of Portugal.

Having established leadership over Latin Christendom, the papacy insisted on uniform liturgical practices. Another major influence for standardization was acceptance of the Benedictine monastic rule, which tended to reform behavior, improve administration, and straighten out frequently confused jurisdictions between monastic and secular domain. The Roman rite, together with monastic and ecclesiastical reforms, had first been accepted in Catalonia and Navarre, and then in Aragón under Sancho Ramírez. They were officially adopted for Castile-León at a church council in 1080, marking the full incorporation of the Castilian-Leonese church into the network of medieval Roman Catholicism. The state, however, continued to control indirectly the elections of most bishops.

French Cluniac monks, who entered León in significant numbers during the second half of the eleventh century, were important agents of religious Europeanization. Encouraged by the crown, they quickened the cultural life of the church, improved its administrative standards, and were especially concerned to purify morals. By the close of the eleventh century, many of the bishoprics in León, Galicia, and Portugal were occupied by Cluniac monks. They had much less influence in Castile, where there was some tendency to identify them with Leonese centralism.

The monasteries had played a key role in the early history of León and Catalonia, and in some respects their influence increased after the eleventh century as their organization and administration advanced. The conduct and preparation of the clergy were also improved. Immorality, violence, and participation in all manner of secular conflicts had been fairly common among high as well as low clergy, and were never overcome at any point in the Middle Ages. By the twelfth and thirteenth centuries, however, the influence of papal, Cluniac, and local church reforming movements seems to have helped effect a distinct improvement in the education and behavior of the clergy.

The development of the thirteenth-century universities was also related to Europeanization, for the main cultural, intellectual, and spiritual impulses in Christian Hispania throughout the Middle Ages came from western Europe, in particular from France and Italy. The influences from the Muslim south were either aesthetic—in architecture, clothing, language—or technical—in building, irrigation, crafts, medicine, and science. The modes of learning and the content of education were thoroughly Latin Catholic. All the universities were in the north, away from centers of Muslim culture.

The institutionalization of the idea of the crusade was another result of the Romanization and Europeanization of Hispanic Catholicism. The nature of and difference between the goals of reconquest and crusade in Hispanic history have become topics of considerable controversy. Some commentators have called the Leonese-Castilian reconquest of the early Middle Ages the first major example of the crusading impulse in Europe. Others, such as Menéndez Pidal, have denied that there was originally any conscious crusading sense. They have held that in the first centuries the Leonese and Castilians fought for concrete objectives of land, cattle, and booty. Ortega y Gasset went farther and uttered the well-known dictum that "something which lasted for eight centuries can hardly be called a reconquest." Américo Castro has pointed to the relative tolerance frequently found in medieval Hispania and has defined historically Hispanic society and culture as a unique blend of Christian, Jewish, and Muslim influences into which the crusading spirit was first injected from the outer world of Latin Europe after the eleventh century. These questions constitute one of the main problems in Hispanic history. It has now been fairly well proven by Menéndez Pidal, Sánchez Albornoz, and others that the early Asturo-Leonese monarchy did define itself as the heir of the Visigothic state and embrace a goal of reconquest, but there is no indication that this included the subsequent Latin Christian ideal of religious crusade. The evidence seems generally to support the contention that the idea of the crusade was fully implanted only after the end of the eleventh century and was generated by broader European influences.

Almost from the beginning, Leonese-Castilian society was marked by a degree of religious identification unknown in France or Italy, but the impulse to reconquest by Christian society was not synonymous with a crusading desire either to convert or to exterminate the infidel. At first, the reconquest was largely a political and military enterprise to recover what had been Hispano-Christian territory. The fact of the Muslim and Jewish religions was accepted by the northerners, just as was the example of partial tolerance shown by Al-Andalus. The acceptance of a degree of toleration did not imply relativism or equality, for Leonese-Castilian Christians were firmly convinced of the inferiority of the Muslim and Jewish religions, as they were of the legal inferiority of Muslims and Jews. This sense of religious superiority was in no way diminished by having to recognize the higher cultural and technological achievements of the Muslim and Jewish society of the south.

Américo Castro contends that centuries of contact or confrontation with Muslims and Jews resulted in a semitization of Spanish culture and religion. This analysis is used in part to explain the thoroughness and intensity with which religion became identified with nearly all aspects of Spanish life, including the ultimate quasi-totality of the church-state bond and the final rejection of pluralism of any kind. While Castro is unable to verify this contention fully, it is evident that historical confrontation with large, sophisticated, and in some ways culturally superior non-western, non-Christian societies could not but leave some impress. It is one thing, however, to claim that Spanish or Castilian society developed a unique set of values in confrontation with Muslims and Jews, and something else to contend that it absorbed an exotic psychology directly. This it did not do; specifically Muslim and Jewish values were overtly and categorically rejected. The resulting tensions, however, interacted to produce a unique culture and psychology.

Between the eleventh and the fifteenth centuries there occurred fundamental changes in the attitudes towards Muslims and Jews. For Alfonso VI of Castile, dealing with the Muslims was mainly a political, not a religious, enterprise, and in the thirteenth century, the tomb of Fernando III was inscribed with the title "king of the three religions." In some of the campaigns of the twelfth and thirteenth centuries, French crusaders either quarreled with or deserted their Castilian and Aragonese allies because of the latter's refusal to slaughter conquered Muslims. Ramón Llull and the Dominicans of Valencia proposed to educate and convert, not expel or even subdue, Muslims of neighboring regions. While Jewish communities were totally expelled from every other part of western Europe, they continued to flourish and multiply in the Hispanic kingdoms.

Attitudes and policies began to change during the course of the fourteenth century. Tolerance was above all a matter of official policy; the common people, both Christian and Muslim, were usually intolerant. The official position of the church, as distinct from that of the crown, was to accept the guarantees of tolerance but at the same time to put pressure on the crown to keep the Jews in their place and prevent them from becoming too influential in Christian society. The spread of the crusading ideal, with its violence and intolerance, may not have changed civic attitudes in the peninsula at first, but it left its effect over the course of six or eight generations. The anti-Muslim feeling of the crusades was accompanied by a great deal of anti-Jewish sentiment as well. The impact of the fanaticism and intolerance of the Almoravids and Almohads has been noted in a previous chapter. And finally, the total military superiority achieved by Christian society by the middle of the fourteenth century obviously lessened the need of Hispano-Christians for systems of discriminatory toleration.

Following the close of the thirteenth-century reconquest, the church's wealth and power increased. It held domain over at least 15 percent of the land in the Hispanic kingdoms, and of that 15 percent the crusading orders alone held more than one third. Over half of Galicia was under Church dominion. The church also collected a special tax from the Muslims and Jews of the Christian kingdoms. As the largest holder of capital, the church had even begun to invest in the royal debt in Castile, and the Cortes of Castile repeatedly petitioned the crown to prohibit acquisition of territories under royal domain by the church. Evidence of the wealth and splendor of the church by the thirteenth century was the construction of the great Gothic cathedrals of Castile (León, Burgos, Toledo, Cuenca), which was begun at that time.

Yet the church did not follow up the reconquest by extending parish organization and church facilities equally through the southern part of the peninsula, where the establishment of new churches lagged. In the eleventh century, approximately twenty episcopal sees had existed north of the Duero. During the next hundred years or so, approximately twenty new sees were created in the central portions of the peninsula, and often were given responsibility for leadership and defense in newly settled areas. During and after the thirteenth-century reconquest, only seven new sees were established in the south, where the crusading orders often filled the place of episcopal organization. By that time, the monasteries had become very active in the wool export trade, and many small churches were established in the sheep-raising regions of the central Meseta; in some of its districts there was a church for every one hundred people by the late Middle Ages. Churches were proportionately fewer in the south, where at first there was only limited immigration and less need. Even after the Christian population increased, church organization was thinner in regions of Extramadura, Andalusia, and Murcia. The slack was partly taken up by the mendicant orders, before their decline in the seventeenth and eighteenth centuries. In modern times, certain areas of the south would stand out as the major "unchurched" districts of the peninsula.

In the Hispanic kingdoms, as elsewhere, the wealth and influence of the medieval church aroused varying degrees of opposition. This stemmed primarily from the crown, the towns, and a few antagonistic critics and thinkers. Conflict with the papacy was common on the part of the Portuguese and Aragonese monarchies during the thirteenth and fourteenth centuries, though infrequent in Castile. At first, Jaume the Conqueror refused to pay the customary Aragonese tax to the papacy, and in Portugal a certain amount of church land was taken back under royal domain. In Castile, as well, a series of measures against church economic power were taken during the early fourteenth century, though the partial vacuum created in some districts by the Black Death resulted in further extension of ecclesiastical properties. During the fourteenth and fifteenth centuries, the church's economic strength in the Aragonese territories apparently did decline somewhat.

The fourteenth-century spiritual decline of European Christendom was reflected in the peninsula, where it was perhaps worse in the lands of the crown of Aragón and in Portugal than in Castile. The problem of the morals and conduct of the clergy was never solved during the Middle Ages; in thirteenth-century Catalonia Jaume the Conqueror had the tongue of the Bishop of Gerona cut out for revealing secrets from the confessional. One of the most common objects of protest by church councils—*barraganía,* or concubinage, among the clergy—was not necessarily looked upon as immoral by the common people, who accepted the common-law marriages of village priests as comparatively natural relationships.

All told, there were three major medieval religious reform movements in the peninsula, and they reflected those in Latin Christendom as a whole. The first was the Cluniac and papal reform of the eleventh century that has been discussed earlier. The second was the monastic reform movement of the thirteenth century: the Cistercians, Dominicans, Franciscans, Carmelites, and Augustinians. Most of the new thirteenth-century orders were composed of mendicant friars who came into close contact with the people and emphasized preaching and social service. They also encouraged learning and played a major role in development of the universities. Yet even the mendicant orders amassed property, and some came to be classed with the privileged and unconcerned among the clergy.

The last movement of reform took place in the late Middle Ages and was diverse and disunified. It began sporadically in the late fourteenth century, gathering momentum only one hundred years later. One of its first manifestations was the attempt of leaders of the Castilian hierarchy in the 1370s and 80s to purify morals, expand education, and encourage royal power in the hope that it would use its authority over other sectors of the church. A monastic movement of spiritual and moral revival known as the *Observancia* stimulated new interest in evangelicalism among the mendicant orders. The rise of the Jeronymite order in the second half of the fourteenth century, encouraging a more contemplative, internalized religion, was another significant new expression of reform. Late medieval spiritual ferment, though certainly not involving most of the clergy and the faithful, was expressed in new ideals of interiorism and antisacramental mysticism and in a growing vein of apocalypticism. In addition to the Jeronymites, the Carmelites and reformist Franciscans were active in trying to encourage spiritual change and growth. These elements played a major role in the subsequent "Catholic reform" of late-fifteenth- and early-sixteenth-century Castile.

Recruitment by the church remained comparatively democratic throughout the Middle Ages. Even after the aristocracy had become quite stratified, the clergy were still drawn from nearly all social classes and were the only institutional group in direct contact with and attempting to minister to all the population.

The Catholicism of Castile and Portugal retained its simple, direct frontier ethos and somewhat archaic quality throughout the Middle Ages. Hispanic religion was popular and vital but not intellectually creative. Nearly all its high theological cultural and structural-functional ideas came from western Europe. The nearest thing to an Hispanic school of philosophy and theology was that of the Catalan Ramon Llull. The Hispanic kingdoms were perhaps the most theologically and religiously orthodox in Latin Christendom.

Variant tendencies were definitely more marked in the Aragonese lands. Though during the Middle Ages scholarly studies developed in a more secular framework in Castile also, classical secular themes drew most attention in the northeast, thanks to French and Italian influences. Only in Catalonia and Valencia did religious thought and seeking lapse into serious heresy. Both Albigensian and Waldensian heretics penetrated Catalonia, but few reached Castile. In Aragon the *humillados* of Durando de Huesca developed ideas of religious communalism and were apparently influenced by both of the former groups, yet stayed within the Catholic system and were recognized by Pope Innocent III. The more radical forms of Franciscanism appeared in Catalonia, northern Aragón, and Vizcaya at Durango. In later times, the Spanish Inquisition would find little that was suspicious enough to examine or proscribe in Castilian religious literature, but a fairly large number of heterodox writings to delete from the religious literature of the Catalan-speaking regions.

It is possible to discern during the Middle Ages the establishment of a certain anti-objectifying bent in the Castilian mind that to some extent discouraged analysis. Religion provided total caste identification in much of the peninsula, and ultimately a sense of prenational group identity, the only unity in a divided and uncertain world. Yet if Hispanic Catholicism was on the whole fixed, incurious, and anti-individualistic by the end of the Middle Ages, this was true to an only slightly lesser degree in most of western Christendom. During the fifteenth century there was considerable religious ferment and questioning among small groups, and an extensive spirit of anticlericalism (directed solely against individual elements of the clergy and not against the church or Catholic theology). The closed, fanatical, caste Catholicism later thought of as typical of Hispanic religiosity did not come to fruition until the second half of the sixteenth century, and was more than simply a product of the Middle Ages. New pressures for religious redefinition and individual understanding of spiritual realities were perhaps no weaker in the peninsula at the close of the Middle Ages than in most parts of western Europe, and nowhere was religious fervor stronger.

8

Castile and Aragón in the Late Middle Ages

Preeminence of the Aristocracy in Castile

During the late Middle Ages, the affairs of Castile were dominated largely by the aristocracy, and especially by its upper stratum who by the fifteenth century were being recognized as *grandes*. This fact, together with many references in Spanish historical writing to the "feudal power" of the Castilian aristocracy, may seem to contradict the observation that Castile lacked a genuinely feudal political structure. As has been explained, however, the preeminence of the Castilian aristocracy was the result of social and economic power more than of formal political or juridical status. During the twelfth and thirteenth centuries, this power had been enhanced by changes in Castilian-Leonese society. Many local rights, small-property guarantees, and opportunities for self-government of an earlier period were being lost.

The formal powers of the Castilian crown were greater than those of the medieval French monarchy, but Castile lacked a well-articulated constitution or a balanced third estate able to maintain significant enclaves of autonomy. Thus it was without the institutions which could reinforce legal authority during the reigns of ineffective kings, leaving the field free for the aristocracy, as during the last part of the troubled reign of Alfonso X. The philosopher king was succeeded by

The House of Castile, 1252–1504

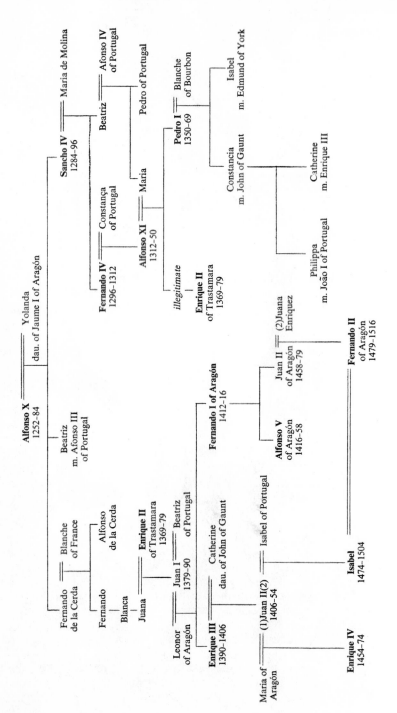

his son, Sancho IV (1282/1284-1295), nicknamed the Fierce because he was wont to fall into great rages. He renounced his father's efforts to reform Castilian government and extend royal law, becoming instead the champion of an aristocracy which desired to transform its seigneurial powers into political domination. If matters were confused during Sancho's weak reign, they became even more so during the reign of his son Fernando IV (1295-1312), who was only nine years old when he inherited the crown. Under a system of regency, the powerful regional aristocracy usurped political authority in many parts of the kingdom. When Fernando died young the situation deteriorated even further, since he left a son only two years old, Alfonso XI (1312-1350). The throne was disputed at one and the same time by an uncle, a grand-uncle, and a third cousin of the infant heir. The regency virtually broke down and for several years the kingdom was split asunder. At one point there were mutually hostile pretenders established in León, Toledo, and Seville.

Restoration of Royal Authority under Alfonso XI (1325-1350)

After Alfonso XI came of age (1325), royal power was swiftly reasserted, and in many ways the young ruler proved to be one of Castile's most capable kings. It was all the easier to restore royal authority because the Castilian aristocracy at no time developed a political program. They had no corporate goals other than to wield individual authority and gain personal wealth and prestige. During periods of royal weakness, the aristocracy never tried to supplant the crown but merely to usurp its regional authority. There was little effort to emulate the constitutional powers of the Aragonese aristocracy, who at times held their ruler legally checkmated. In Castile, neither the aristocracy nor any other class thought in terms of major political changes. The nobility was moved by a kind of normless self-assertion which did nothing to lessen the theoretically almost unbounded prerogatives of the crown. Thus when a strong ruler reappeared, all the legal structure remained with which to reimpose royal authority.

While moving against the anarchy of the nobility, Alfonso XI at the same time reduced the rights of the towns. Middle-class entrepreneurial elements were much weaker than in Catalonia, and as seigneurial jurisdiction increased after the twelfth century, powers of self-government had been progressively diminished in many municipal districts of northern and central Castile. By the fourteenth century, most towns were dominated by an urban aristocracy mainly of landowners and socially on a par with, sometimes actually drawn from, the lesser aristocracy. Fernando III had made efforts to counter the increasing influence of the aristocracy, and the crusading orders by establishing municipal councils in some of the territories of the thirteenth-century reconquest, but this probably affected no more than 10 percent of the reconquered land. Even so, the autonomy of the towns, though limited, had been the only force capable of checking to any degree the exactions of the aristocracy during the disastrous reigns of Sancho IV and Fernando IV; in another situation, the same modest influence could be used to limit the demands of the crown. Consequently Alfonso XI initiated a policy of royal intervention in municipal government, sometimes appointing royal officials to supervise affairs and help select Cortes representatives. This interventionist policy was eventually carried to a climax in the late-fifteenth and sixteenth centuries. Nevertheless, Alfonso XI generally enjoyed the support of the northern towns, the strongest, who realized that the ambitions of the aristocracy were more dangerous than royal authority.

Alfonso was not oblivious of economic problems; he reinforced wage and price legislation and tried to encourage easier cultivation terms for landless peasants. Castilian society as a whole suffered less from the Black Death than Catalan, since a greater proportion of its wealth was mobile and agrarian and less dependent on urban society. Nonetheless, shortages of farm labor developed in Castile as in other parts of western Europe, and in the later years of his reign Alfonso XI felt constrained to promulgate decrees controlling wages.

As a result of the inflation of the fourteenth century, the ambitions of royal administration, and continued military expenditures, the demands of the crown for funds increased steadily. Yet the economy of Castile remained unbalanced because of low agricultural production, limited manufacture, and the power and demands of the aristocracy. A fundamental change in Castilian fiscal policy occurred during the reign of Alfonso XI, when the crown began to find it easier and more profitable to raise money by its own taxes than to rely on periodic grants from the Cortes. An organized treasury, tentatively introduced in the thirteenth century, had its real beginning at this time. The *alcabala,* or sales tax, was established in its classic form; new levies on the wool trade were instituted in 1343, together with other new export taxes; new monopolies were set up; and the royal *quinta* (fifth) from the proceeds of Castilian piracy and *cabalgadas* (border raids) was regularized. Jews were widely employed in tax collecting and fiscal administration, inciting further hostility against them.

Alfonso XI's ultimate goal was to establish "pure" (and hence autocratic) royal sovereignty in Castile. He reduced some of the privileges of the *Fuero Viejo* of the Castilian aristocracy, and his jurists reorganized and codified Castilian law under four headings: 1) the new royal law that was to supersede much of previous practice in dealing with major questions; 2) the traditional *Fuero Juzgo* of the Leonese regions; 3) municipal statute law for the towns and much of commercial activity; and 4) the theoretical standards of the *Siete Partidas,* normally without practical effect.

The Southern Frontier

The territorial advance of Castile had been arrested after the reign of Fernando III. The rise of the Moroccan Merinid empire in the 1260s had given the Muslims a renewed foothold on the very southern tip of the peninsula around Gibraltar and reopened the possibility of invasion from Africa. Fighting and raiding raged intermittently in the far south for eighty years. During part of this period the emirate of Granada, which remained independent, continued to pay tribute to Castile, diminishing interest in the conquest of this last taifa. Inflation, economic depression, and commercial slumps weakened royal initiative in the late thirteenth century and again during the Black Death in the 1330s, while the internal division that preceded Alfonso XI sapped the strength of royal policy and diverted energy from external affairs. This dissension was a major factor in permitting the Aragonese to incorporate the Alicante district south of Valencia in 1304.

During the troubled regency of Fernando IV, the Merinids grew more belligerent. In a battle of 1319, they slew both regents of Castile and subsequently began to levy tribute on the southern frontier districts. In two major campaigns of 1340 and 1343, Alfonso XI succeeded in breaking Merinid power on the Spanish side of the straits and occupied nearly all the southern tip of the peninsula save Gibraltar itself. These victories ended the age of African invasions. Changes and strife within Morocco discouraged any later offensive actions across the straits; henceforth, it would be the Hispanic powers who carried their own raids into Africa.

Nasrid Granada

The last of the Hispano-Muslim taifas, the emirate of Granada, managed to preserve its independence for more than two centuries after the main phase of the great reconquest ended. It was a sizable state in the mid-thirteenth century, more than four hundred kilome-

ters long from east to west and extending well over one hundred
kilometers inland. During the reigns of Fernando III and Alfonso X,
the Nasrid emirs were faithful vassals of Castile; subsequently, their
closeness to Africa provided them with ready assistance from the
Merinids and from Berber mercenaries. Though the western tip of the
emirate was lost to Castile after the victories of Alfonso XI, the emir
Yusuf I (1333-1354) once more came to terms with Castile and
resumed tribute payments.

The most prosperous period of the emirate was the second half of
the fourteenth century, when it underwent a cultural and economic
renascence. Handicraft and agriculture flourished. There was active
commerce with North Africa and with the Genoese; Granada's chief
exports were silk, sugar, and fruit. Trade with the Sudan provided the
gold which was so useful in tribute to Castile. The Alhambra was
built and a major Muslim school of higher learning established.

As a remnant and a border culture, Granadan society was mili-
tantly Muslim. Much of the population were Muslim refugees from
other parts of the peninsula, though there was also a significant
Jewish community. The religious jurists exerted considerable influence and urged warfare against Castile. The Nasrid dynasty, however,
was inclined toward prudence, and war was unpopular among the
hardworking common people of Granada. The cultural vitality of the
society remained high, but the fifteenth century was a troubled time,
wracked with dynastic disputes and instability. There was intermittent border warfare with Castile, but during much of the fourteenth
and fifteenth centuries the Castilian crown's traditional goal of reconquest was replaced by a policy of tributary overlordship vis-à-vis
Granada. Crown and aristocracy in Castile tended to remain absorbed in internal affairs. The mountainous terrain of Granada,
shielded by fortified hill towns to the north and west, discouraged
reconquest until the Castilian crown finally reached its plenitude of
power after the union with Aragón.

Pedro the Cruel (1350-1369) and the Great Castilian Civil War

Alfonso XI died prematurely at the age of forty and was succeeded
by his sixteen-year-old son Pedro. The young ruler fell immediately
under the influence of a favorite companion, Juan Alfonso de Albuquerque, bastard of the king of Portugal and the first of a formidable
line of *validos* who in later reigns dominated Castilian kings. He
encouraged young Pedro to do away with the late Alfonso XI's
beloved mistress, Leonor de Guzmán, a possible source of rivalry.

The eldest son of Alfonso and Leonor, Enrique, was already a grown man and before his father's death had been made count of Trastá-mara (a district in Galicia). After his mother's murder, he came out in revolt against the crown, and later became the champion of a fractious aristocracy.

Pedro tried in large measure to follow the policies of his father, extending royal administration, restricting the privileges of secular señoríos and church abadengos, and employing middle-class jurists in place of aristocrats as administrators. He drew the hostility of most of the aristocracy, but the majority of the towns supported royal power as the alternative to aristocratic oppression. Pedro tended, however, to be somewhat unstable and vindictive, qualities that were exaggerated by the propaganda of his ultimately victorious enemies, who fixed upon him the nickname by which he is known to history—Pedro the Cruel.

The hostility of the aristocracy to Pedro turned the revolt of Enrique de Trastámara into large-scale civil war. Propaganda of the Trastámara faction presented Enrique as the "true heir" of the traditional monarchy, representing the real interests (the landholding aristocracy) of the realm. Trastámara propaganda strove to play on a narrow spirit of Castilian chauvinism, whipping up hatred of Jews and Muslims, whom it identified with the rule of Pedro. Jewish communities had been evicted from France and England nearly a hundred years earlier and were increasingly restricted in Catalonia from the mid-thirteenth century. Their elite status in Castile, where they were the major moneylenders to the crown and heavily involved in tax collection, made them an easy target for enmity. Enrique was also not above involving the French crown in the affairs of Castile, though French support of his struggle to overthrow the legitimate monarchy proved costly to the kingdom.

The great Castilian civil war swept across the peninsula, became involved in the Hundred Years' War between England and France, and prompted heavy foreign intervention. In the early years, Pedro had little difficulty driving the Trastámara forces from the kingdom. When both France and Aragón agreed to support Enrique's pretensions, Pedro carried the war into Aragón and briefly occupied Valencia. But royal financing for continuous campaigns was difficult, and the intervention of the French "free companies" under Bertrand du Guesclin tipped the balance in favor of the rebels. This was righted by English support for the Castilian crown: Edward, the Black Prince, with his English archers, severely defeated the Franco-Castilian rebel forces in 1367. Yet the English prince and Castilian king soon fell out over money matters, leading to an English withdrawal and a revival of Trastámara power. After the English ceased to support Pedro, the Trastámara forces moved in for the kill. Enrique showed great cruelty himself in his execution of royalist leaders in the northeastern towns during the decisive campaign of 1368. Pedro was captured and personally slain by his half-brother, who succeeded him to the throne as Enrique II (1369–1379).

Structure of the Trastámara Monarchy

The new Trastámara ruler was by no means a mere creature of the aristocracy. He was a politically intelligent sovereign who faced the task of constructing an effective monarchy on the basis of usurpation by a bastard branch of the royal family. His primary goals were to strengthen the power of the crown, to establish a loyal oligarchy of nobles as underpinning to the throne, and to strengthen the Franco-Castilian anti-English alliance that had won the war.

Enrique fully accepted the idea that a strong nobility was a necessary complement to a strong crown. Since much of the old Castilian aristocracy had been ruined by the civil war, he created a new one, chosen from his closest relatives, his military leaders, his chief supporters, and from backers of Pedro who had switched sides. This was the beginning of the classic Castilian high aristocracy of late medieval and early modern times, subsequently called grandes. Only six Castilian titles of later importance antedated the year 1369.

In addition to receiving major land grants and privileges, the new aristocracy paid increasing attention to establishing itself within the crown's state service. Contrary to the tendency of the preceding century to name middle-class appointees, the offices of the crown were filled with nobles. By the next reign, many of these offices were becoming hereditary, leading to further wealth and emoluments for the high aristocracy.

Yet Enrique II was not merely a "feudalizing" as contrasted with a "modernizing" monarch, for he claimed that he wanted to enforce the royalist laws of his father, Alfonso XI, and in some ways the crown did grow stronger. He organized a chancery for foreign affairs and set up a supreme royal *audiencia* of four jurists and three bishops to coordinate, apply, and interpret the legal norms codified by his father's jurists. He also made some effort to extend the royal administrative system, but was largely foiled by local aristocratic influence.

Enrique gained the support of nearly all the Castilian church hierarchy, standing as champion of law and order and reconfirming all privileges of the church. The monarchy was strengthened further by the decided support of the reform element temporarily dominant in the hierarchy, for church leaders tended to believe that stronger royal power was necessary to provide impetus and authority for effective reform within the church.

The towns of Castile were much less enthusiastic and more divided. In general, they suffered from the extension of aristocratic authority, although in some cases Enrique made minor concessions to the concejos. The most threatened element in the kingdom were the Jews. Pedro had leaned heavily on Jewish financiers, and Enrique came in on an anti-Jewish wave which he tried subsequently to check.

The second Trastámara king, Juan I (1379-1390), made some effort to limit the trend toward exalting the prerogatives of the high aristocracy. He continued his father's support of the church by agreeing, at the Cortes of Soria in 1380, to have most of the church land recently usurped by the aristocracy returned. He employed many petty nobles in royal administration and tried to avoid honors and appointments for the upper stratum. (The first years of the reign of his son Enrique III "the Ailing" [1390-1406] were to be marked by civil war between the upper and lower aristocracy, resulting in an almost complete, if temporary, victory for the latter.)

In his checkered reign, Juan I managed to give clearer form and function to the royal council, clarify and solidify the work of the several regional audiencias for royal law that had been established under Alfonso X, and establish central direction for a sort of rural constabulary, the Hermandad Nueva. For the first time in Castilian history, Cortes support was obtained for a royal standing army to be composed of 4,000 lances (backed by 3 to 5 men each) and 1,500 Andalusian light cavalry. No part of the royal forces or administration achieved the size, scope, or efficiency that was planned, but the structure, if not the practice, of royal government was advanced slightly under the Trastámaras in the late fourteenth century.

Apogee and Decline of the Castilian Cortes

The Castilian Cortes reached the height of its influence in the fourteenth century, culminating in the troubled years 1385-1390. During this time it strove to arrest the trends of unilateral royal authority and aristocratic domination, but ended during the fifteenth century largely succumbing to them. Originally, in the late thirteenth century all towns, concejos, or comunidades living under *realengo* (royal domain, as distinct from señorio or abadengo) had the nominal right to send representatives when Cortes were summoned. At the Cortes of Burgos in 1315, 101 Leonese and Castilian communities were represented. The Cortes' power of the purse was explicitly recognized by the Castilian crown for the first time in 1307, though it was honored somewhat unevenly in the course of the century. The other major function of the Cortes was to exert a degree of influence in ratifying the succession to the throne and the establishment of regencies during the minorities of young rulers.

The capacity of the Castilian third estate to organize was revealed in 1295 when sixty-six municipalities and concejos formed a *hermandad* (brotherhood) that organized district rural constabularies to maintain law and order and protect economic interests. This was the first important example of several *hermandades* formed by the Leonese-Castilian towns at various times in the late Middle Ages.

Representation of the third estate suffered from the administration of Alfonso XI, who intervened in the election of municipal council members and Cortes representatives. He employed bribery, sometimes appointed lifetime royal *regidores* (magistrates) to oversee town affairs in the event of difficulty or disorder, and named a series of royal *corregidores* to exercise authority, when necessary, over the town councils. Alfonso XI was a popular king and used his appeal to bolster arbitrary extension of authority. He succeeded in breaking up the Castilian hermandad, which he deemed too independent of royal sovereignty.

By the middle of the fourteenth century, the town meeting (*cabildo abierto*) was being used much less than in the past, and more and more the representatives to Cortes were chosen by municipal councils, often only from among council members. The inflation of the second half of the century made it increasingly expensive for small towns to send representatives to Cortes assemblies. The crown ceased to invite the less important towns, whose spokesmen often did not complain too much about their exclusion. This trend was reinforced by the rivalry of the larger towns, eager to exclude smaller communities.

The extension of señorio domain during the fourteenth century reduced the number of smaller autonomous towns and concejos, and the aristocracy exerted growing pressure on municipal government. There was a tendency for lesser aristocrats to take up residence in towns and seek to control municipal governments. Many towns fought back by refusing to let nobles hold office. These quarrels gave the monarchy an excuse to intervene in municipal government through appointment of corregidores.

Yet the autonomy that still existed in the northern half of the kingdom of Castile (exclusive of Galicia) was extensive. In addition to the self-government of most of the larger towns in royal domain, a census under Pedro the Cruel in 1359 indicated that approximately half the peasant villages in Old Castile still enjoyed partial autonomy under local terms of behetría.

Though the autonomous communities had been cool toward the Trastámara cause, the dynasty made no overt move to contest the somewhat cloudy prerogatives of the Cortes in which they were represented. The power of the Cortes rose dramatically during the last five years of the reign of Juan I. Disastrous campaigns in 1384–1385 to enforce his claim to the crown of Portugal, culminating in the historic Castilian defeat at Aljubarrota, left the king's treasury absolutely exhausted. A new Cortes assembly provided funds, but the crown was forced to acquiesce in a number of demands. Annual Cortes meetings were held between 1385 and 1390. During these years, Cortes representatives checked royal accounts and tax collections, tried to protect local rights, and made ultimately unsuccessful efforts to establish a delegation on the royal council.

Yet the meaning and consequence of these limited achievements were mixed, for they were gained by the active participation of the lower nobility. The goal of the latter was not to form a permanent political alliance with the upper stratum of the third estate but simply to check the power of the high aristocracy in favor of their own. During the reign of Enrique III, the petty nobility won a clear-cut victory over the high aristocracy, using the victory to advance its own power, especially in municipal government, and to create an artificial monopoly over part of the third estate's Cortes representation. It had little interest in developing the Cortes as an institution but instead exploited it for class interests.

Thus there did not develop in Castile the union of the lower nobility and upper middle class that later formed the backbone of the English parliament. By the beginning of the fifteenth century, all levels of the nobility and the church had effectively established their immunity to most taxation, and even the hidalgos lost interest in the function of the Cortes.

Since the Castilian Cortes relied almost exclusively on the towns, its possibilities were obviously limited at the outset by the small size and social and economic weakness of the urban population of Castile. Moreover, there was never a major effort to codify the rights of the Cortes as an institution. And finally, those of the third estate represented in the Cortes were almost completely unable to unite in their social, economic, and regional interests; towns, regions, and representatives of economic interests usually failed to develop broader goals. By the fourteenth century, artisans were almost completely excluded from municipal government. (Yet, unlike Catalan and Valencian towns, there were few class revolts in the towns of Castile after the early fourteenth century. Social struggle usually took the form of

Table 1. Periodicity of the Castilian Cortes, 1252-1520

Ruler	Years reigned	Cortes summoned
Alfonso X (1252-1284)	32	16
Sancho IV (1284-1295)	11	5
Fernando IV (1295-1312)	17	16
Alfonso XI (1312-1350)	38	19
Pedro I (1350-1369)	19	1
Enrique II (1369-1379)	10	8
Juan I (1379-1390)	11	10
Enrique III (1390-1406)	16	11
Juan II (1406-1454)	48	38
Enrique IV (1454-1474)	20	14
Isabel I (1474-1504)	30	10
Post-Isabeline, 1504-1520	16	10

Source: Piskorsky, Las Cortes de Castilla.

general revolts of local districts against their aristocratic or clerical overlords.)

Though Cortes assemblies were still called annually through the first half of the fifteenth century, their influence declined steadily. By the middle of the century, the crown had begun to indicate directly whom it wanted chosen as *procuradores* (representatives) in certain towns. From that time, only seventeen (later eighteen) towns were normally represented: Burgos, León, Seville, Toledo, Córdoba, Murcia, Jaén, Zamora, Toro, Salamanca, Segovia, Avila, Valladolid, Soria, Cuenca, Madrid, and Guadalajara. Large regions of the kingdom were entirely unrepresented, for the towns of Galicia (almost exclusively under señorio and abadengo), Asturias, Santander, Extremadura, La Mancha, and the Basque country were completely excluded.

Extension and Consolidation of Aristocratic Domain

The golden age of the Castilian high aristocracy may be dated from the start of the Trastámara dynasty, and the Catalan historian Vicens Vives has suggested six major factors for its rise to overweening wealth and power:

1. The *repartimiento,* or division, of vast territories in the thirteenth-century reconquest
2. The key importance of the wool trade in Castilian commerce, which offered great profit for grazing on aristocratic domain
3. The establishment of *mayorazgos* (entail), prohibited by Old Castilian law but legalized by Alfonso X

4. The tendency toward monopoly of royal and clerical offices by younger sons of grande families
5. Victory of the Trastámara aristocratic faction in the fourteenth-century Castilian civil war—the reverse of what happened in contemporary Aragón
6. Weakness of successive rulers of the Trastámara dynasty

Despite the concern of the first Trastámara kings to maintain the legal authority of the crown, their social and economic policy was regressive. Its feudal emphasis completed the reversal of the original trend of Leonese-Castilian history and exactly complemented that of Trastámara Castile's great ally, the feudal monarchy of France, in contrast to the trend in Catalonia and even Portugal. Though Trastámara policy did not devolve political jurisdiction, it increased the splintering of local social, economic, and even judicial power under an ever more powerful aristocratic caste.

The classic señorío jurisdiction of *mero y mixto imperio* carried with it general social and economic dominion, and usually meant juridical authority as well, and often the right of local religious patronage. New señorío grants of the fourteenth century frequently included special taxing privileges such as the right to collect local alcabalas, and in some cases, to keep all the proceeds. The ecclesiastical abadengo grants sometimes included similar rights. Rights to tax were especially common in the larger domains of the grandes, and at times they were usurped even when not specifically granted.

Seigneurial domain became more deeply rooted during the fourteenth century by the spread of mayorazgo—the entailing of family domains as inalienable inherited property. This principle of individual entail (*vinculaciones*), proclaimed under Alfonso X, was first invoked to an important extent under Sancho IV. Enrique II granted establishment of numerous large mayorazgos to his most favored nobles, and the principle of *vínculos cortos* for smaller domains was also established. Though the *mercedes enriqueñas* (grants of Enrique) were not as lavish as has sometimes been written, important concessions were made, and legal jurisdiction and entailment by nobles greatly increased. There was a parallel tendency to diminish the rights of communities and concejo land, awarding the administration and usufruct of portions thereof to aristocrats. In some cases, seigneurial domain was extended to hold peasants on the land in regions where population had been thinned by the plague.

Perhaps half the land in Castile was the domain of the aristocracy by the beginning of the fifteenth century, and a few grandes enjoyed incomes greater than that of the king of Aragón. During the course of that century the señoríos continued to grow, especially during the civil wars of the middle decades, and a shift of population occurred. The most powerful aristocrats could afford easier terms for peasant renters and sharecroppers than were customarily offered on royal lands, and there was a fairly steady transfer of population onto señorío land.

Save for the most powerful of the aristocracy, however, genuine fortunes were won not so much from the land and its rents as from honors and appointments in the royal administration. During the reign of the weak Enrique the Ailing, a new state oligarchy of petty nobles, entrenched in royal administration and enriching itself from the royal treasury, was consolidated. Grants of annuities from the crown had become common and were an important source of income for the aristocracy. Thus the rule of Enrique the Ailing became the golden age of a prosperous stratum of oligarchic-bureaucratic nobility.

During the minority of Enrique's son Juan II (1406-1454), Fernando de Antequera, younger brother of the late king, governed as regent and created a new cluster of titles and mayorazgos for his supporters. During his regency, the late medieval mystique of chivalry took hold in Castilian aristocratic society, influenced by French and Burgundian norms of pomp and ceremony. Here was the beginning of the vogue of *novelas de caballería* among the upper and middle classes, and a spur to further development of the crusading mentality, which had been largely in abeyance for the past seventy-five years. In this spirit, a border campaign captured the town of Antequera from Granada and earned Fernando his sobriquet.

After D. Fernando secured for himself the vacant throne of Aragón in 1412, the boy-king, Juan II, had to face a stormy reign. The Castilian monarchy began to founder, as the next two-thirds of a century were wracked by aristocratic civil wars. Juan II became the most literate and cultured ruler that Castile had had since Alfonso X, but political affairs were dominated by his *valido*, Alvaro de Luna, scion of one of the greatest Aragonese families, who was made constable of Castile (grandmarshal of the kingdom).*

For four decades aristocratic intrigues and revolts flared intermittently, and the Infantes of Aragón were the major source of factionalism. Younger sons of the new king, Fernando of Aragón, excluded from the Aragonese succession, they hoped to carve out dominions of their own in Castile, where their father retained much wealth and influence. Over the years, the domination of Luna at court roused the opposition of much of the native Castilian aristocracy, who several times forced his expulsion from the kingdom. Though the royal army defeated aristocratic rebels in a major battle in 1445, the anti-Luna forces and a new queen finally had their way. In 1453, Luna was

---

* Though the title *grande de España* was created in the early sixteenth century, the first elevation to grande of nobles who were not relatives of the royal family began around 1430, when signal honors were bestowed on the allies of Alvaro de Luna.

executed by royal order on a charge of having bewitched the king, who himself died—partly from remorse—within a year.

These internecine struggles were not actually civil wars between the aristocracy and the crown as much as conflicts between factions of the nobility for domination of the perquisites and power pertaining to the crown. The principles of royal sovereignty and a royal treasury were well established. The Castilian aristocracy accepted the fact that the path to influence and wealth lay not so much in combatting the sovereignty and income of the crown as in dominating the royal system.

The main thing needed to establish royal dominion was simply a capable ruler, and the first decade of the reign of the next king, Enrique IV (1454-1474), was moderately successful. Most of the aristocracy feared domination by fellow aristocrats more than rule by the crown, and even the Catalans looked to the Castilian crown for assistance and arbitration. Yet though Enrique IV was a humane and tolerant ruler, he tended to be weak, lazy, and indecisive. As the years passed, his shambling, uncouth appearance and exotic behavior increased his unpopularity with influential elements in the aristocracy, and by the middle of his reign the royal polity had broken down once more. In 1464 an uprising forced him to sign a pact that in effect guaranteed the dominance of the high nobility over the affairs of the crown. The next ten years were full of turmoil; portions of the aristocracy were in nearly continuous uproar; the towns had once more to form *hermandades* to protect themselves and keep the roads open; Castilian aristocrats intervened in Aragonese affairs and vice versa, and all the while smoldering border warfare with Granada continued.

The Castilian Economy of the Late Middle Ages

By the fourteenth century, Castile had become a major factor in west European commerce, but the economic structure that gave rise to this was quite different from that of the most prosperous parts of western Europe. Castile's economy remained a rural one stressing the export of raw materials: above all, wool, but also leather, wax, honey, wine, and olive oil. Transshipping of sugar and silk from Granada and northwest Africa was also of some significance after the Byzantine trade had been strangled.

It has been calculated that by the fifteenth century two-thirds of the productive land in Castile was devoted to grazing. Development of the curly-stapled merino sheep in the fourteenth century greatly increased high-quality wool production, and a huge trade was funneled by the Mesta through Burgos and on to the Cantabrian ports.

By 1477 the flocks of Castile numbered 2,700,000 head of sheep. Most stockmen in the Mesta could be defined as middle class or at least nonaristocratic, and the size of individual flocks was usually not great. Profits from the export economy by no means went entirely into middle class or protocapitalist hands, however. Grazing land and other perquisites were dominated to some degree by the aristocracy, which indirectly reaped a not insignificant share of the profits of Castilian commerce. In contrast to the increase in grazing, the proportionate value and productivity of Castilian agriculture may actually have declined in the later Middle Ages. The only significant irrigation to be found in Castile was in the Guadalquivir district around Seville and in La Rioja in the extreme northeast.

Castilian commerce was extensive enough to develop a significant urban mercantile class, though one living amost exclusively off the rural export trade. By the late fourteenth century, Castile's merchant marine was as large as that of any power in Europe, and was involved not merely in export cargos but in the carrying trade for other areas of western Europe and the western Mediterranean. The maritime foci were the Cantabrian and Vizcayan port towns, the Andalusian ports around Seville, and Cartagena to the southeast. Castile carried on something of a naval war with the Hansa ports from 1419 until 1443, when a treaty resulted in one-sided terms advantageous to Castilian commerce in the north. Throughout the fifteenth and early sixteenth centuries, Castilian merchants dominated trade along the French coast and were the leading element at Bruges. The development of new forms of credit and banking put Castilian merchants among the leaders in international commercial techniques, and Pirenne has shown their influence in the early sixteenth century in stimulating new kinds of production in Flanders. There new varieties of cloth were introduced, the breakdown in the guild system speeded, and production in larger, more efficient units encouraged. The crown assisted commerce with premercantilist navigation acts that helped weight Castilian trade toward raw material exports and cheap imports of manufactured goods and grains.

The economic base for the nascent Castilian bourgeoisie remained overwhelmingly the land. The only notable manufactures in most Castilian towns were textiles, and these were usually of low quality. The main exception, and the only significant finished producers, were Basque iron works in Vizcaya and Guipuzcoa, at the forefront of European metallurgy of their day.

The increasing influence of the local aristocracy in municipal government during the late Middle Ages reduced attention to economic problems and probably represented a significant hindrance to economic development. The Castilian bourgeoisie thus was able to amass wealth on the coast and in a few key trading centers, but had difficulty making headway in most parts of the kingdom. The development of commercial and financial resources opened the possibility for a new social and economic balance, but the Castilian bourgeois were even less interested than most in challenging the dominant aristocratic values. A major portion of whatever capital was accumulated went back into the land in the form of *censos consignativos*—pastoral and agrarian loans, much used, especially by the church. Wealthy merchants also began to establish their own petty mayorazgos with the spread of *vínculos cortos,* small entailments, during the fifteenth century.

The artisan classes of Castilian towns were always smaller and weaker than those of Catalonia and Valencia. The classic medieval guild system never developed fully in Castile, where it was restricted by royal law. The *cofradías* of artisans and laborers were essentially no more than charitable associations, though they functioned with relative efficiency. But if there were few guilds, there were also few restrictions in Castile. Because of the reconquest, land was more readily available than in some other realms, and the economic restrictions on town laborers and peasants were, with the exception of the region of Galicia, less severe and direct than in Aragón.

Though the income of the Castilian crown was much greater than that of the Aragonese, a large portion of it was drained away by inefficiency and the interposition of the aristocracy. In Castile, as elsewhere, the inflation of the late Middle Ages left the crown increasingly hard pressed to meet military and other expenses. One result was steady currency devaluation, beginning in the thirteenth century. Throughout the Middle Ages, Castile had retained the Muslim monetary system, using an orientally derived coinage and employing the Koranic gold-silver ratio of 10 to 1. During the thirteenth and fourteenth centuries, however, the actual gold value of the Castilian maravedí fell from a comparative ratio of 4.22 in 1252 to 2.87 in 1258 and to .47 by 1390.

The income of the royal domain was never sufficient in the late Middle Ages to permit the crown to "live of its own," and there was a persistent tendency to levy new taxes. The basic sales tax, the alcabala, was set at 5 percent in 1269 but had been raised to 10 percent by 1377. In addition, a *sisa* was levied, to be paid by the seller from the original sales price. It was set at 1 percent in the late thirteenth century but raised to 3 percent by about 1350. There were also a great variety of municipal, seigneurial, and transport taxes. From 1430 on, the emirate of Granada was obligated by treaty to pay annual tribute of 20,000 gold doblas (about 225 pounds of gold) a year.

The crown inevitably resorted to heavy borrowing, mainly from

Jewish financiers but also from the church. By the fourteenth century, Italian bankers, especially Genoese, had made their appearance at Seville and even some of the urban patriciate and merchants had begun, at least by the fifteenth century, to invest in the royal *juros* (bonds), which were reaching a significant volume. The tendency for capital-possessing elements to try to live off investment in the government rather than by economic development had already begun in Castile before the close of the Middle Ages.

Foreign Involvement: Castile in the Hundred Years' War; the Southern Frontier

During most of the Middle Ages, Castile had been turned away from involvement in the diplomatic and military affairs of western Europe, but completion of the major part of the reconquest broadened its horizon. Alfonso X's candidacy for the throne of the Holy Roman Empire was a remote and romantic ambition, however, entirely unrelated to Castile's primary interests. When order was restored to the internal affairs of Castile in the second quarter of the fourteenth century, Alfonso XI endeavored to pursue a logical policy of equilibrium between England and France while applying further pressure on the Muslims.

The return of internal disorder during the reign of Pedro I and the spread of the long Anglo-French conflict of the Hundred Years' War into the peninsula thrust Castile to the forefront of military-diplomatic affairs, and it remained deeply involved for the remainder of the century. For the two decades 1366–1386 the peninsula was actually the main theater of operations. During this period Castile was, for the first time, raised to the level of a major west European power. The alliance with France was solidified under the Trastámara dynasty, not merely because of similar political and social interests in France and Castile, but also because of the commercial rivalry between Castile and England in the Flanders wool market. The potential of Castile's Cantabrian ports had increased steadily through the thirteenth and fourteenth centuries, and by the beginning of the Trastámara period, Castile had emerged as a first-rank naval power. Castilian sea power started with the victory over the English at La Rochelle in 1372, followed by other victories off the English coast in 1377 and 1380. Castilian maritime strength thus assured development of the export trade through the fifteenth and sixteenth centuries, and it remained the major single force in the west Atlantic until defeated by Holland at the Battle of the Downs in 1609.

After the death of Enrique III in 1406, the Castilian crown withdrew almost entirely from the Anglo-French military rivalry, directing its energies toward expansion once more. For a short time in 1400, a Castilian force occupied Tetuán in northern Morocco. Three years later, the crown proclaimed its sovereignty over the Canary Islands; the Antequera district was seized from the Muslims in 1410, and two years later, a Castilian infante (D. Fernando) was placed on the throne of Aragón.

The Decline of Aragón-Catalonia

In contrast to Castile, the lands of the crown of Aragón, after their extraordinary history of imperial and commercial expansion during the thirteenth and fourteenth centuries, fell into decline. This was felt most directly in the great loss of population suffered by Catalonia after the 1330s, the result of war, emigration, natural disasters, including even a few earthquakes, but above all the plague, which recurred throughout the century. Though Catalonia was relatively free of the plague from 1400 to 1450, it returned in 1457 and periodically wracked the principality until the end of the century.

The epidemic deaths were important in breaking down the social cohesion that had been achieved in Catalonia during the thirteenth and early fourteenth centuries. Some land had to be left uncultivated, and not even all the land on the larger farms and those zones still under cultivation could be sown. Landlords were alarmed by the decline in the countryside, by the rise of rural wages and the improved terms that were being demanded and won by peasants, and they reacted with fairly systematic efforts to establish legal domination over much of the peasantry and tie them to the land. During the thirteenth century the remnants of serfdom had been disappearing, but by the late fourteenth century bondage to the land was increasing in some areas. Peasants increasingly resisted the tightening of feudal *malos usos* or special exactions. Many were eager for the opportunity to take over the strips of land left abandoned after the plague (*masos rònecs*) although in some cases they were denied the right to do so. Others occupied new land, increased their production, and sometimes were even able to hire poor Gascon laborers migrating from the other side of the Pyrenees. But still others remained in misery under the harsh neofeudal requirements. In 1370, the seigneurial right to *prendre e maltractar* that was being established in Aragón was also written into Catalan law. The church, which had been the most democratic of major institutions, adopted an equally exclusive polity; a Catalan church council of 1370 declared that children of serfs (*remences*) could not enter holy orders.

These pressures produced a wave of mysticism among portions of the peasantry. There was a burst of symbolic cross-building and the digging of public graves as the Catalan variant of the dance-of-death neurosis attending the social problems of the waning of the Middle Ages. The most popular sermon of Vicente Ferrer, the major Catalan-Valencian religious reformer of the early fifteenth century, was on the apocalypse. Interest in sorcery and magic increased during the reign of Joan I, in court circles as well as among others.

The depression in the countryside did not affect commerce for half a century or more; medieval Catalan commerce reached its apogee between 1350 and 1420. By 1350 Barcelona's financial institutions may actually have been more efficient than those of Venice or Genoa. Apparently capital was attracted to the most important commercial enterprises during the first decades after the Black Death, and Barcelona continued to improve its financial techniques, though by the early fifteenth century its earlier advantages were being lost to more rapidly developing rivals. All in all, the living standards of the urban workers in Catalonia and Valencia advanced during the later Middle Ages, for Hamilton's statistics show a net rise in real wages between 1350 and 1500.

The financial decline of Barcelona, however, began with the financial crash of 1381-1383, the result of exaggerated credits granted the royal treasury. This was part of an international economic slump that began about 1380 and was felt in Flanders, England, France, and Italy as well. The commercial crisis was overcome, but neither Barcelonan financiers nor those in Gerona and Perpinyá ever regained their former power. Social tensions were momentarily exacerbated, and among other channels found an outlet in the anti-Jewish riots of 1391. These began in Seville, spread through Andalusia and La Mancha, and then to the northeast. Jewish merchants and financiers were by no means as important in the Catalan-speaking towns as they had once been, for Catalan Jewry had declined from the height of its influence in the 1280s and the Jewish merchants and financiers were less numerous and wealthy than a century earlier. The riots in the Catalan towns were more than anti-Jewish; they were riots of the poor against the rich, bringing several attacks on wealthy quarters and the burning of some tax lists and debt records. Nevertheless they marked the beginning of the end for Catalan Jewry. The Jewish community of Barcelona was officially suppressed in 1401, and many Catalan Jews converted to Christianity.

During the second half of the fourteenth century, there was a growing tendency to invest in land and in state and municipal debts rather than in commerce and production. By the fifteenth century, the investment patterns of *censalistes* (mortgage- and bondholders) in a contracting Catalonia foreshadowed those of late-sixteenth- and seventeenth-century Castile. A second financial crash in Barcelona (1427) proved even more difficult to overcome than the first.

By the early fifteenth century, Genoese and Venetian fleets had begun to specialize in more rapid express traffic in spices and luxury goods for the central and west European market. Catalan commerce still relied on a great deal of slow, routine bulk traffic in cheaper commodities, and lacked the large commercial hinterland which central Europe afforded the Italians or the one provided Marseilles by the populous and productive kingdom of France after 1425.

Between 1427 and 1431, tax receipts on commerce in Barcelona dropped by half, and payments were 30 percent in arrears. A substantial recovery began in 1432 as a result of textile exports to southwestern France, expansion of the near eastern and Flemish trade, and renewal of the slave trade (which reached its height in Barcelona between 1440 and 1442). The final decline commenced about 1450. Average commerce for the years 1452-1456 was only 20 to 25 percent of that for 1432-1434. Barcelonan commerce lay prostrate for nearly four decades, until about 1490.

During those years, Valencia surpassed Barcelona as the peninsula's leading eastern financial and commercial center. Until about the middle of the century, Valencian commerce had dealt mainly in fruits, almonds, wine, raw materials, raw silk, and ceramics. As Catalan competition declined, the merchants and bankers of Valencia, living under an autonomous regime, were able to take advantage of the decline, concentrating their capital to expand production and the range of overseas commerce.

Catalonia's fifteenth-century economic decline can be traced to a number of factors:

1. Loss of financial control, accompanying the tendency to tie up capital in land and reject new enterprise and risks. Italian, especially Genoese, financiers played an increasing role in Catalan affairs
2. Counterproductive effects of the policy of maritime terrorism adopted by Catalan fleets after 1390
3. Loss of North African markets, in part as a consequence of the terrorism
4. Cost of the wars of the crown of Aragon, in both men and money, and the weight of taxation at home and abroad
5. Increased efficiency of foreign competition
6. Stagnation in Catalan society, which found itself overextended and tending to turn inward, much like Castilian society during the seventeenth century. Decline in population was accompanied by increased emphasis on status and rent
7. Economic debility of the principality of Aragon, which offered a minimal market for Catalan commerce
8. Growth of internal dissension eventually degenerating into civil war

The population of the city of Barcelona declined from a near 50,000 in the fourteenth century to only 20,000 by 1477. By contrast, the fifteenth century was a time when the population of most of the Hispanic peninsula and western Europe was growing. The principality of Aragón expanded from 200,000 to 250,000 people and the city of Valencia from about 40,000 to 60,000, surpassing Barcelona in both size and wealth as the leading city and commercial center of the eastern coast of the peninsula. In the thirteenth century, Catalonia had contained at least 10 percent of the population of the lands of Aragón and Castile. By 1500, that percentage was no more than 4; with its shrinkage came the decline of Catalan power and influence, bringing with it the decline of the crown of Aragón.

The last of the strong medieval Aragonese kings was Pere el Ceremoniós. His son, Joan I (1387-1395), was a learned and literary prince who introduced official jocs florals (poetry contests) in Barcelona but was less successful as a statesman. A major revolt in Sardinia in 1391 almost overthrew Aragonese rule, and a serious rebellion in Sicily was not suppressed for three years. When Joan was killed hunting in 1395, he left no direct heir and was succeeded by his uncle Martí (1395-1410), who had to face further trouble in the Mediterranean possessions and who also died without an heir in 1410.

The death of Martí precipitated the first severe succession crisis since the union of Aragón and Catalonia nearly three centuries earlier. The strongest claimant within the Aragonese empire was Jaume, count of Urgel, a close relative of the royal family, but opinion among the upper classes was strongly divided and the issue was further complicated by the intrusion of the religious politics of the papal schism. By far the strongest candidate outside the borders of the empire was the Infante D. Fernando, regent of Castile and a relative of the Aragonese royal family several generations removed. Internal dissension within Catalonia and Aragón, the strength of the Castilian regent, and the influence of large sums of Trastámara money finally told. At the Compromise of Caspe in 1412 a commission of nine jurists and theologians, representing the three Cortes of Aragón, Catalonia, and Valencia, selected D. Fernando by six votes to three as the new ruler of the Aragonese empire. The Compromise of Caspe was essentially a political decision to choose the only candidate who seemed strong enough to avoid civil war and hold the Aragonese polity together.

The reign of Fernando I,* the first ruler of the Trastámara dynasty

---

* In chapter 5, names of Aragonese rulers from the original dynasty of the Catalan House of Barcelona were given in Catalan. However, the names of the rulers of the new fifteenth-century Castilian-derived Trastámara dynasty are given in their Castilian form.

in Aragón, was limited to four years (1412-1416). The new king brought with him Castilian (and fifteenth-century) ideas of strong monarchy, yet his policy was comparatively diplomatic and conciliatory. The constitutions of the Aragonese principalities were respected, and though Fernando I brought with him many new Castilian appointees, the Aragonese aristocracy was able to regain a position of considerable political influence while the balance of power in Catalan affairs remained unaffected.

Fernando's son, Alfonso V "the Magnanimous" (1416-1458), enjoyed a long reign, the Indian summer of the medieval Aragonese empire in the Mediterranean. Taking advantage of the last generation of Catalan economic prosperity, Alfonso resumed expansion on a grand scale. Much of Corsica was reconquered in 1420 and held for fifteen years, and the Catalan fleet succeeded in smashing that of its nearest rival, Marseilles, in 1423. The great triumph of Alfonso's reign was the complete reconquest, by 1442, of Naples, which became the center and capital of the Aragonese empire until his death, for Alfonso never returned to the peninsula. He was one of the most cultured princes of the day, and his "magnanimity" supported a constellation of Renaissance litterateurs and artists in Naples. His forces were active in North Africa, and extended some assistance to Constantinople and to the Christian peoples of the Balkans in their resistance to Turkish expansion. Alfonso had finally succeeded in laying tight siege to his chief Mediterranean rival, Genoa, at the time of his death in 1458. The kingdom of Naples was then bestowed upon a bastard son, Ferrante, and not reunited with the Aragonese empire until half a century later.

Alfonso's Mediterranean policy relied, as usual, upon the people and resources of Catalonia. It endeavored to foster Catalan interests, and the principal appointments were given to Catalans. But by the 1440s, the Catalan economy was unable to stand the strain of sustained military and maritime expense. It was no longer stimulated, but increasingly overtaxed, by military expansion. Moreover, Alfonso's prolonged absence from the principality deprived it of leadership at a time when severe social and political splits were developing.

Juan II and the Catalan Revolt of 1462-1472

Lacking legitimate heirs, Alfonso was succeeded by his younger brother, Juan II (1458-1479), who had been born in 1398. The Infante D. Juan had had a stormy career as the principal of the "Infantes de Aragón" embroiled in Castilian politics during the turbulent reign of his cousin, Juan II of Castile. The Infante D. Juan had first been married to the heiress of Navarre, and after the death of the

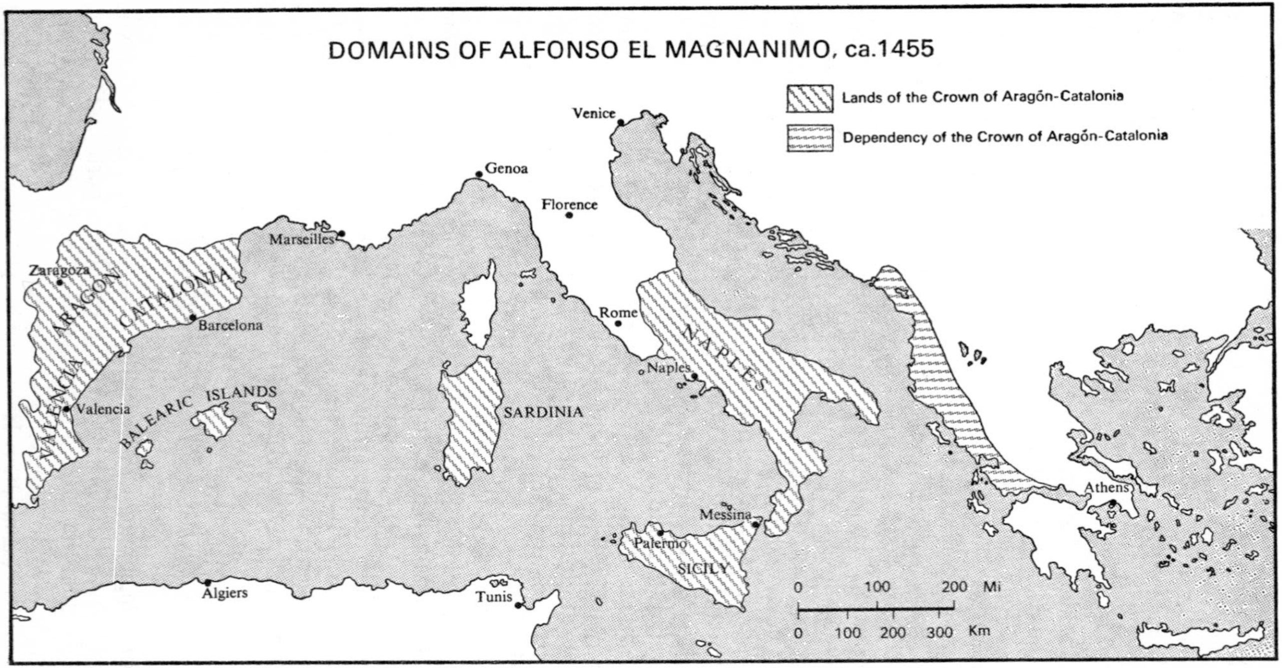

DOMAINS OF ALFONSO EL MAGNANIMO, ca.1455

Lands of the Crown of Aragón-Catalonia

Dependency of the Crown of Aragón-Catalonia

Venice

Genoa

Florence

Rome

NAPLES

Naples

Messina

Palermo

SICILY

Tunis

Athens

SARDINIA

Marseilles

ARAGON-CATALONIA

Barcelona

BALEARIC ISLANDS

VALENCIA

Valencia

Zaragoza

Algiers

0		100		200	Mi
0	100	200	300	Km	

Navarrese king in 1425 had held the title King of Navarre. After the death of his Navarrese princess he was married to Juana de Enríquez, daughter of the Admiral of Castile, one of the most powerful figures in Castilian affairs.

As king of Aragón, Juan II was immediately faced with the social and political turmoil that had been developing in Catalonia during the past generation. This had three main facets: the demands of the *remença* peasants; the revolt of the lower and middle classes in the Catalan towns, demanding reforms and an equal voice in municipal government; and the counterattack of the urban oligarchy and the rural nobility, who wanted to fortify their legal position against the crown above and the lower and middle classes below.

In the early fifteenth century nearly one-third of the Catalan peasantry were still tied to the land or at least held to continuing feudal exactions (malos usos); all peasants in such conditions were known collectively as *payeses de remença* (redemption peasants). Most remences were badly off, though some had sizable farms and were quite comfortable. All remences demanded an end to malos usos. Poor remences also wanted clear title to their land. Wealthier remences were less concerned about the tenure system per se but wanted opportunity to take over more wasteland. There had been noticeable unrest among the remences since about 1395, but the period 1420-1445 was one of moderate rural prosperity, stilling dissatisfaction and enabling some of the peasants to improve their status. After the return of bad harvests and hard times, grievances burst into the open. By 1448, the crown had granted remences the right to form local peasant syndicates to represent their claims and try to work out a settlement with landlords. Within one year, 25,000 peasant homes, representing most of the rural population of northern Catalonia, had paid the fees required to participate in the syndicates. The 1450s were years of increasing tension in the Catalan countryside.

At the same time, Barcelona and the other larger Catalan towns were the scene of intense socio-political conflict between the upper-class oligarchy on the one hand and the middle and lower classes on the other, represented in Barcelona by two political factions known as the Biga and the Busca. This conflict was the product of the Catalan economic depression of midcentury. The Busca represented especially the craft guilds, which had become fully developed and organized only in the late fourteenth and early fifteenth centuries. It demanded equal class representation in city government, money devaluation to reduce the tax load (since ciutadans honrats had invested heavily in municipal bonds in a deflated economy), and tariff protection for manufactured goods, in opposition to the import programs of upper-class wholesale merchants. The urban conflict had become severe by

1435, and finally, in 1455, the Infante D. Juan, as viceroy for his brother, came down on the side of the popular forces. The government structure of Barcelona was reformed to give equal representation to the four main social groups. Similar reforms had already taken place in a number of other cities. Furthermore, the obligations of redemption payments and malos usos in the countryside were suspended.

The urban oligarchy and the nobility then seized the initiative to effect a political counterattack. The nobles forced partial revocation of the suspension of remença obligations, so that the question of peasant obligations was still uncertain when the troubled reign of Juan II began. In meetings of the Catalan Corts between 1454 and 1458, representatives of the urban upper class and the nobility repeatedly pressed for constitutional reforms that would cement their control over the Catalan political and social system. Their goal was a strict system of constitutional laws establishing their prerogatives in relation to both the crown and the lower classes.

The Catalan upper classes were hostile to Juan II from the very beginning of his reign, viewing him as a champion of a strong crown as well as of the lower classes. On the other hand, the son of Juan II's first (Navarrese) marriage, Prince Carlos of Viana, acquired great popularity. Carlos of Viana had already been involved in a bitter civil war in Navarre against his father, but this made him appear as a champion of "rights" against the crown. When he was seized and imprisoned by his father in 1460, the Catalan Generalitat forced his release and recognition from Juan II of the overriding legal jurisdiction of the Catalan Corts. Carlos of Viana then died prematurely, but the Catalan upper classes remained in opposition to the crown and refused to accept Juan's second (Castilian) son, Fernando, as heir. Popular hysteria in that troubled age regarded Carlos of Viana as a saint; his bones were said to work miracles. In 1462, the Council of the Generalitat raised an army to put down rebellious remences, and purged their opponents in Barcelona. The struggle quickly expanded into civil war against the crown, lasting ten long and bloody years. The conflict ranged the urban oligarchy and most of the aristocracy and clergy on one side against the crown, most of the peasants, and part of the Catalan aristocracy on the other. The crown sought support from Louis XI of France, but this resulted in the French seizure of Rosselló. The crown's opponents turned for aid to Enrique IV of Castile, whom they proclaimed king of Aragón, but this gesture proved fruitless. The next candidate was Dom Pedro, Constable of Portugal and a descendent of the count of Urgel, but he was defeated in battle in 1465 and died soon after. The crown of the principality was next given to René of Provence, bringing French support for the revolt, but after his heir died in Catalonia, the principality was left without a ruler, and for the next two years Barcelona was the capital of a sort of constitutional republic on the Italian model. Meanwhile, the Burgundians had checked the power of the French crown and Juan II had neutralized Castile by marrying his son Fernando to Princess Isabel, half-sister of the Castilian king. Between 1466 and 1472, Juan II maneuvered an international anti-French coalition (England, Brittany, Burgundy, Naples, and even Castile) and finally captured Barcelona in 1472, but was unable to regain Rosselló from France. The peace settlement of 1472 was extremely generous, for it granted a return to the constitutional status quo of a decade earlier. Thus despite the great rebellion and civil war, the Catalan constitutional system was not altered in any fundamental way in the fifteenth century.

The struggle had become a virtual class war in the countryside, with many remences rising in revolt on the side of the crown. Both the royal forces and the rebel Generalitat made promises to the remences, and in general the poor remences of the hill country sided with the crown, while the more prosperous peasants of the coastal and plain areas supported the revolt. By the time peace was restored, landowners had largely ceased trying to collect regular remença (redemption) payments but still insisted on the old level of rents, dues, and shares for annual cultivation. The political and rural civil war left land arrangements in a state of great confusion. After 1472, many peasants were still armed and with military experience were more belligerent than before. Much of the countryside remained in a state of latent civil war.

The great Catalan revolt consummated the economic decline of the principality without solving any of the political and social problems that had led to it. Between 1450 and 1475, Catalan commerce declined another 20 percent and reached a secular low. The war had nearly exhausted capital resources and had killed thousands more of an already depleted population. By the 1470s the social and economic exhaustion of the principality was almost complete.

The only region of the Aragonese empire to suffer more severely than Catalonia during this period was the island of Mallorca, wracked by bloody, full-scale peasant revolts. During the course of the fourteenth and fifteenth centuries, the position of the Mallorcan peasantry had deteriorated as a result of bad harvests, price increases, growing taxation, and the increasingly harsh terms of the urban oligarchy of the port of Palma, who controlled most of the property and dominated the General Council of the island. Demands for more representative government increased. The great revolt of 1450 began with a tax strike by church leaders, then quickly spread to the peasantry, which had just suffered a bad harvest. In league with the lower classes from the smaller ports, the *foráneos,* or peasants, of Mallorca gained control of most of the island and three times laid seige to the capital. A similar movement developed on Menorca. Faced with social revolution, Alfonso V struck back with a decree of perpetual serfdom for all rebellious foráneos. The great revolt was finally put down in 1452-1453 by an expedition of Italian mercenaries, and heavy exactions were placed upon the peasantry in reprisal, further burdening rural society. Terms of genuine serfdom were not imposed, but many peasants emigrated anyway. A second foráneo revolt in 1462-1463 was suppressed with great bloodshed, as was a major rebellion on Menorca that flared between 1462 and 1466. Thus the great Balearic peasant revolts achieved no change, but ended in total failure and deep suffering for the peasantry.

Comparison between Castile and Catalonia in the Fifteenth Century

By the fifteenth century, Castilian society was proving more cohesive than that of Catalonia and less wracked by class struggle. It had suffered a proportionately smaller loss in population in the preceding century, and had enough land for most peasants to work on. The greater availability of the chief means of production, labor, enabled the Castilian upper class to take a more lenient attitude toward the peasantry and grant them comparatively easier terms. The Castilian high aristocracy was proportionately so much wealthier than the landed nobility of Catalonia that it felt less need to squeeze the peasant. The fact that so much of Castile's wealth was invested in livestock meant that its production, involving less labor, gave rise to less social tension. (The principal exception to this generalization is, of course, the situation in Galicia, where overpopulation, relative scarcity of land, and the demands of a more numerous and more powerfully entrenched seigneurial aristocracy produced vicious social struggle as intense as that of the Catalan countryside.)

Another important difference between the two societies lay in the greater unitarian tendency in Castile, in particular in the Castilian economy. Catalan economic enterprise tended to be individualistic, with a resultant rivalry and competition, sometimes of an extremely expensive and almost ruinous nature. In Castile, major corporations were formed for most of the significant areas of economic enterprise: the Mesta for wool production, the intercity Hermandad de las Marismas for north Castilian-west European commerce, municipal *consulados* for merchants and exporters, and even a widely organized teamsters freight corporation (the Real Cabaña de Carreteros), organized in 1497 on terms similar to those of the Mesta. Castilian commercial towns showed some tendency to cooperate, rather like the Hansa, whereas Catalan-speaking commercial towns competed against each other much like the Italians. Mallorca, which at the beginning of the fourteenth century found itself better situated and in some ways rather better organized for Mediterranean commerce than Barcelona, was nonetheless unable to meet head-on competition by its senior rival and eventually succumbed to it.

Another difference lay in the economic orientation of the oligarchies in Castilian and Catalan towns. By the fifteenth century, the Catalan urban upper classes were trying to live in large measure off the interest from shares of the municipal debt or from commercial operations that they could operate most profitably by underselling local production with cheap imports. The Castilians lived from land rent and the wool trade and thus did not find themselves in the same kind of social and economic conflict with the middle and lower classes.

By the latter part of the fifteenth century Castile was, more than ever before, the major Hispanic power. Castilian merchants in foreign ports were commonly accepting the term *Spain* to describe their own kingdom. At the same time, a greater degree of economic unity had been achieved in the peninsula than had been known since Roman times. Commercial ties were becoming stronger between Catalan and Andalusian ports, while Navarrese commerce had been made partly exempt from Castilian transit taxes and given an outlet through San Sebastián. The Castilian orbit extended even to Italy, for control of the Straits of Gibraltar after the mid-fifteenth century had developed close union of economic interests between Genoa and Andalusian ports, and relations with Genoa became a major factor in Castilian diplomatic and commercial policy.

9

The United Spanish Monarchy

The union of the crowns of Castile and Aragón was a consequence of the pressures of turbulent domestic politics in both kingdoms as much or more than it was part of a grand diplomatic design. Such a union had been attempted once before, after the death of Alfonso VI in 1109, and had failed completely. There were two main factors behind the marriage of Isabel of Castile and Fernando of Aragón in 1469: the desperate need of Juan II to garner Castilian assistance in the Catalan civil war, protecting against the danger of French intervention, and the need of the teenaged princess Isabel to have a royal mate on whom she could rely to strengthen her cause in Castile. Fernando was heir to an important Hispanic patrimony, but unlike Afonso V of Portugal, was not ruler of a firm, compact state that would have provided a base for intervention in Castilian affairs.

Isabel, born in 1451, was one year older than Fernando. Her life had been difficult and tempestuous, caught up in the political intrigues of the Castilian aristocracy and the succession to the throne. As the daughter of the second marriage of Juan II of Castile, she was originally far removed from the dynastic succession, ranking behind her half-brother Enrique IV, his daughter Juana, and her own elder brother the Infante Alfonso. Enrique IV was tolerant, easy-going, and peace-loving, and hence not the type of ruler who could most easily dominate the powerful, quarrelsome, and ambitious Castilian aristocracy. Despite lack of pronounced political ability, he strove to main-

170

tain order in the kingdom but after ten years became the victim, in 1464, of a strong aristocratic reaction which forced royal recognition of the predominance of the aristocratic faction and of his young half-brother, Alfonso, as heir to the throne. The propaganda that has blackened Enrique IV's historical reputation originated at this time, for he was labeled by dissident nobles impotent, sexually perverted, achristian, and promuslim. A campaign was waged to have his heiress, Juana, declared illegitimate because of Enrique's supposed impotence, and the unfortunate princess was given the nickname *la Beltraneja* after one Beltrán de la Cueva, a former court favorite who was without the slightest evidence tagged as her father.

Yet Castilian aristocratic conspiracies were notoriously fissiparous. Young Alfonso suddenly took ill and died, and the king regained the upper hand. Isabel then remained the sole candidate of the dissident aristocracy for the role of a more agreeable and manageable heiress than the legitimate daughter of the ruling king. Isabel's Portuguese mother had gone mad in her later years, and the constant intrigues and harassment by political factions to which Isabel's adolescent years were subject developed distinctly paranoiac tendencies in the princess. Isabel never doubted the justice of her cause and viewed herself the legitimate heiress of Castile, fully accepting all the propaganda about Enrique IV and his daughter Juana. A round-faced, plumpish, green-eyed girl with dark blonde hair in her youth, Isabel had been reared in the rural castles of Castile and did not receive a sophisticated education. She was vigorous and energetic, devoted to the hunt, and had a great sense of dedication to her responsibilities. She was also, as befit a fifteenth-century Castilian princess, extremely pious and committed to the cause of religion in her realm.

Fernando had been born in 1452 and literally grew up in the great Catalan civil war. Healthy and vigorous, he had a somewhat better education than Isabel and received much more practical experience at an early age, commanding military forces at thirteen. His political understanding was conditioned by the constitutional theories and practices of the Aragonese empire. Native instinct and long experience developed in Fernando one of the best European diplomats of his generation, yet despite the praise justly lavished upon him by Machiavelli, he was no unscrupulous Cesare Borgia. Unlike some of his contemporaries, his ideal was not absolute monarchy but political compromise and the constitutional monarchist state of Aragón. Though his religiosity was less obvious than that of Isabel, Fernando was also pious, and was influenced by the mystical strain of much of the religiosity of the fifteenth century, so that together with the prudent and calculating politician there existed a potential crusader.

The Castilian succession crisis began with the death of Enrique IV in 1474. Much of the aristocracy chose sides between Isabel on the one hand and (the supposedly illegitimate) Juana, backed by Afonso V of Portugal as her suitor, on the other. The succession struggle lasted five years, during which the cause of Doña Juana was supported by the entire southern half of the kingdom, as well as by some of the towns of Old Castile. Isabel herself saw the issue strictly in terms of black and white. The actual leader of the Isabeline party was D. Fernando, who brought in Aragonese military technicians to organize the somewhat backward Castilian levies that eventually brought victory to Isabel at Toro in 1476. Three years later, Juan II of Aragón died at the age of 81, and the Castilian consort ascended the Aragonese throne as Fernando II (1479-1516).

The union of the crowns established a dyarchy, but there was no attempt at constitutional fusion of Castile and the states of the Aragonese empire. Each principality remained autonomous and distinct with its separate administration, united only by the common diplomatic and military policies of the two rulers. There was never any question as to whether Isabel held authority in the constitutional systems of the Aragonese empire; the only point at issue was the influence of Fernando in Castile. It was ultimately decided that Fernando would enjoy kingly status and prerogatives even to the extent of exercising functions of government, but that only Isabel would receive homage as direct ruler and have power to disburse funds or make royal appointments.

The dynastic alliance worked with surprising harmony, and in Castilian affairs the two sovereigns frequently issued common decrees with a joint seal. The effectiveness of their royal administration permitted Castile to realize its size and strength for the first time since the great reconquest and to take the lead from Portugal in overseas expansion. In the Aragonese lands, Fernando's government finally checked the decline of Catalonia and encouraged a new era of modest prosperity.

The Ordering of Castile

Isabel could probably never have become queen of Castile (1474-1504) had it not been for the dissidence of the grandes and other aristocrats, yet she and Fernando planned to be anything but tools of aristocratic factionalism. Indeed, the Isabeline cause was able to take advantage of a certain current of democratic sentiment in Castile during the 1470s, for the petty nobility and townspeople wearied of the inordinate influence and ambition of the grandes and looked to a new ruler to provide order and justice.

Spanish historians often refer to the monarchy of Isabel and Fernando as the first modern state. This is an exaggeration. The distinctly new ideas of the royal couple were few, and the only radically different institution that they created was the Inquisition. Their political vision was to perfect existing monarchist institutions, but this in itself meant drastic change in the functioning of Spanish government. The establishment of genuine law and order, bringing internal peace and stability and the crushing of those divisive forces that had held Castile back for more than a century, marked a turning point from which the Spanish crown would move toward eventual European hegemony. If not the first modern state, the monarchy of Isabel and Fernando was the most effective reformed government in late-fifteenth-century Europe. Its reforms guaranteed the resources for final completion of the reconquest in 1492 and so won from the papacy the title by which the royal couple is known to history—the Catholic Kings.

Isabel and Fernando did not aim at the establishment of absolute monarchy in Castile and Aragón, for this concept was not introduced until the Bourbon dynasty of the eighteenth century. Their political ideal, according to the language of their documents, was the "preeminent monarchy," superior in authority to all other institutions, yet respectful of the laws of the kingdom and the rights of its subjects. The Castilian monarchy of Isabel built upon the traditional Castilian state—a strong royal executive with considerable scope for royal law, but functioning in harmony with a comparatively weak traditional Cortes that held a limited power of the purse and a nominal right to ratify the royal succession. These relations were the easier because most of the third estate looked to the crown to protect its subjects from the ravages of the aristocracy. The Castilian Cortes was summoned sixteen times during the reign of Isabel and Fernando—with one hiatus of fourteen years, between 1483 and 1497—and in almost every case proved quite docile. Unlike the Cortes of the Aragonese empire, those of Castile still made little effort to wring juridical or other concessions from their sovereigns.

The first objective of the new rulers was to assert royal sovereignty, put the aristocracy in its place, and restore public order. During the chaotic reigns of Juan II and Enrique IV, followed by the civil war of 1474-1479, murder and pillage had ravaged much of the kingdom. During the 1460s, a number of Castilian towns had revived the earlier tradition of forming a hermandad, a brotherhood for self-protection and the policing of roads. In 1476, this force was ratified by the crown, which authorized formation of a broad Santa Hermandad with crossbowmen and other armed policemen to serve as a rural constabulary. The Hermandad was deprived of any independent jurisdiction and kept subordinate to the crown, but it brought order to the central and northern parts of Castile. Before it was finally disbanded by the crown in 1498 it had done much to make Castile one of the most orderly kingdoms of western Europe.

The fractious elements of the aristocracy had to be dealt with by more powerful forces, and the royal military, with their new artillery, were used during the early years of the reign to put down disturbances. Subsequently, the building of new castles was prohibited. The monarchy of Isabel and Fernando was by no means an enemy of the aristocracy, but it brooked no challenge to royal authority. Large tracts of land recently alienated from the royal domain were reoccupied, but otherwise the crown ratified the economic jurisdiction of the señoríos and the latifundia that went with them. Grandes were encouraged to attend the royal couple and spend a great deal of time with the peripatetic court, in a policy that later became standard with royal states. Though the joint rulers were reluctant to appoint aristocrats to influential positions of government, there was ample opportunity to employ them more profitably in the foreign wars that filled the era. In 1512, a special Corps of Royal Guards, an early unit of what was becoming a Spanish army, was created exclusively as a place of special military honor in which young noblemen might serve the crown.

Some of the land alienated under Enrique IV was restored to the royal domain, and the territory of certain rebels was also confiscated. The royal patrimony in Castile was further enlarged by providing that D. Fernando would be elected master of each crusading order after the death of its incumbent leader. By 1494, the king had become master of the third and last order. Since the crown was in a position to accomplish those military tasks for which the orders had originally been established, most of their income and eventually their entire properties were incorporated into the royal domain.

In 1480, the Castilian royal council, which had existed since the reign of Fernando III and had held almost exclusive responsibility for affairs of state since 1385, was reorganized. Heretofore it had been a committee of aristocrats and church hierarchs, but under the Catholic Kings it was composed of eight or nine lawyers, only three nobles, and one cleric. The royal legal system was also revamped. There had been a royal audiencia (supreme court) since the reign of Alfonso X, but its jurisdiction was sometimes uncertain. In 1485, the royal audiencia was located permanently at Valladolid, and four regional audiencias were established as well. These measures, together with the reestablishment of order and security, were part of a general program of developing a rule of law in Castile. Compared with other states of that period, the system functioned well, for the extension of royal authority encouraged greater justice for the lower classes, and the right of appeal to the royal audiencia for certain kinds of cases was guaranteed.

The Catholic Kings followed the policy of intervention in municipal affairs that had become fairly common during the preceding two hundred years, sending out regular corregidores for one year's service in towns to report on local government and tax collection. Other royal agents, *pesquisidores* and veedores, were sent sometimes to check further on the corregidores. For general military and administrative jurisdiction, the system of frontier *adelantamientos* (forward border jurisdictions) was expanded into a series of nine to cover the entire kingdom, with one adelantado, or military governor, for each.

One of the great successes of the government of the Catholic Kings was their ability to select talent and employ it in the royal service. New leadership was provided for administrative, ecclesiastical, juridical, and military affairs. The reign saw no political or constitutional development in Castile, but accomplished great administrative improvement and brought into government new elite elements from the third estate. It was also a time of broad codification of laws in Castile, as in the Aragonese lands.

The only major social revolt in Castile during the fifteenth century was the rebellion of the peasant *irmandades* (brotherhoods) of Galicia, which are not to be confused with the constabulary of the Santa Hermandad of the main part of the kingdom. Formation of irmandades of Galician peasants and townspeople of the third estate had been authorized by Enrique IV in 1465 to check the overweening power of the Galician aristocracy. The irmandades were reasonably well organized by districts, and in some areas into groups of one hundred. They were sometimes led by elements of the petty nobility in opposition to the high aristocracy and church prelates. Their goal was basic social and economic reform, with better terms and an end to feudal residues for the peasants, and reduction of obligations for the towns on seigneurial and church domain. Rising in armed revolt, they took over large areas of Galicia and forced key prelates and aristocrats out of the region or into hiding. In general terms, the revolt of the irmandades, which may at one time have had fifty thousand not fully armed followers, was the Galician equivalent of the Catalan remença uprising and the foráneo revolts in the Balearics, generated by the pressures of feudal survivals in a late medieval period of social and economic change.

The irmandade revolt was put down, well before the general victory of Isabel in Castile, by a reaction of the regional aristocracy of Galicia, which finally concentrated its forces against the ill-armed peasants. In general, reprisals were not severe, and the Galician aristocracy split almost immediately into several feuding factions in a fight that degenerated into all-out civil war. In 1480-1481, the crown finally extended direct royal police authority into the region, broadening the scope of the Santa Hermandad to include all Galicia and sending a special royal commission to restore order and settle quarrels. A decree of 1480 explicitly canceled whatever residues of bondage to the soil existed in Galicia and a few other regions. Peasants in all parts of the kingdom were recognized as free subjects, and some minor reforms in Galicia ensued, but the social authority of the aristocracy and church remained greater there than in other parts of Castile. This reality, combined with population pressure and factors of climate and soil, left the peasantry of Galicia under greater stress than in most of the rest of the kingdom.

The one radical innovation in the state system of Fernando and Isabel, the establishment of the Castilian (or Spanish) Inquisition, was designed to maintain orthodoxy and unity among the Catholic subjects of the crown. Though the Inquisition was an instrument in state-building, it was formally a religious tool, and will be discussed in chapter 11. It became the ultimate guarantee of unity and orthodoxy in the realm.

The Ordering of Aragón and Catalonia

The rule of Fernando in Aragón was one of conservative reform that did not greatly alter the existing constitutional structure. The king spent little more than one year in ten in the lands of Aragón during his reign, for he fully appreciated the greater weight and importance of Castile in the affairs of the monarchy. From his youth he had been well versed in the constitutions of the Aragonese principalities, and accepted without hesitation the existing constitutional structure of Aragón and Valencia. He reorganized the Aragonese royal council and specifically ratified constitutional guarantees of safe-conduct and temporary sanctuary in that state. There was no attempt at new social regulation in Aragón that compared to what was worked out in Catalonia or Galicia, however. The Aragonese variant of the Hispanic social revolts of the period—several small peasant uprisings between 1507 and 1517—were simply suppressed. The dominance of the Aragonese aristocracy in its realm was even less questioned than that of the nobility in Castile, so long as no effort was made to contest specifically royal prerogatives.

The major problem was still Catalonia. During the last six years of the reign of Juan II, the crown had lacked the time or the energy and will to effect a complete settlement of the Catalan civil war. This complex problem was left to Fernando, and by the time he became king, nearly all factions were so exhausted that the entire principality looked to its able young sovereign for a lasting solution to the constitutional and social questions of the century. He did not disappoint these expectations.

Fernando explicitly reaffirmed Catalan constitutional rights and the limitations on royal power in his *Observança* of 1481. Many property disputes had been left unresolved at the end of the Catalan civil war, and Fernando finally settled them in 1481, largely on the basis of the status quo ante. Military jurisdiction over the principality was also ended. Fernando's original settlement, however, tended to confirm the rights of the landlords over those of the peasants, provoking a final remença uprising in 1484-1485. This was crushed, but its virulence convinced Fernando that fundamental reforms were needed in the Catalan countryside. His Sentence of Guadalupe in 1486 finally ended the remença controversy once and for all by establishing the juridical freedom of all peasants and abolishing all redemption payments and malos usos. The property rights of landlords were reaffirmed, but so were the usufructuary guarantees of the peasants. The result was a broad establishment of hereditary emphyteutical tenure for the majority of Catalan peasants and an acceptable social equilibrium in the Catalan countryside.

After many complaints about oligarchic domination of the Catalan Generalitat, Fernando decreed in 1488 the suspension of elections for Generalitat deputies and judges, henceforth to be named by royal order. Similarly, in 1490, he suspended further elections to the Barcelona city council and established the procedures of *insaculació:* the establishment of lists of qualified representatives for each sector of the population, from which councillors were to be selected by lot. Both these measures enjoyed general approval, because of the broadly felt need for royal intervention to break oligarchic and corrupt domination by sectors of the upper classes.

In the 1480s and 1490s, Catalonia began to find a new social stability that was to last for a century and a half. It was a stability based upon retrenchment and greater security, and upon a high degree of bureaucratization politically and economically. New arrangements had been worked out that satisfied most groups in the society, and almost every subject had a defined place. The result was a kind of neo-medieval corporatization, not a renewal of the risk-taking, expansive Catalan society of the thirteenth and early fourteenth centuries.

During the reign of Fernando the economic recovery of Catalonia began, supported by strong protective legislation that restricted foreign imports and guaranteed the market of the Mediterranean possessions of the crown for Catalonia and Valencia. However, Catalan merchants and financiers were unable to regain the vigor of one hundred and fifty years earlier. The modest prosperity of the sixteenth century did not provide them with the resources which they would have needed to participate in the major expansive ventures of the crown.

The Predominance of Castile in the United Monarchy

By the end of the fifteenth century, Castile had a population approximately seven times greater than that of all the Aragonese principalities combined. The predominance of Castile was apparent in the united crown from the very beginning, for Fernando was obliged by his marriage to spend most of his time there. The expanded commerce of late medieval Castile far surpassed even the potential of the smaller Aragonese principalities. Moreover, the greater authority of the crown in Castile, compared with its circumscribed position in the Aragonese lands, enabled it to marshal resources more effectively.

No single factor was more important in this than the increase of the royal income in Castile. New taxes were not levied, but the royal patrimony was extended and the tax collection system improved. Without seriously imposing on the domestic economy, the royal income—not allowing for a certain degree of inflation—increased some thirtyfold between 1474 and 1504. This made possible the conquest of Granada and a vigorously expansive policy overseas.

Castile thus became the base of Spanish monarchy, and its strength was gratefully acknowledged by Catalans, who now had less reason to fear French pressure. Catalans themselves sometimes addressed Fernando not as king of Aragón, or king of Aragón and Castile, but as *rei d'Espanya*—"king of Spain," meaning nearly all the peninsular principalities. At the same time, the institutional influence of Aragón and Catalonia did to some extent make itself felt in Castile. Certain aspects of the Catalan viceregal, consular, guild, and labor regulation systems were adopted by Castilian law in the late fifteenth and early sixteenth centuries.

The Sixteenth-Century Habsburg Monarchy

Of all the works of the Catholic Kings, none was more fateful for Spain than the dynastic marriage alliances arranged for the royal offspring. There was nothing unique in what Fernando and Isabel did, for such efforts were as old as international relations. But since no male heir survived to maturity, the succession passed through their

The Spanish Habsburg Dynasty, 1516-1700

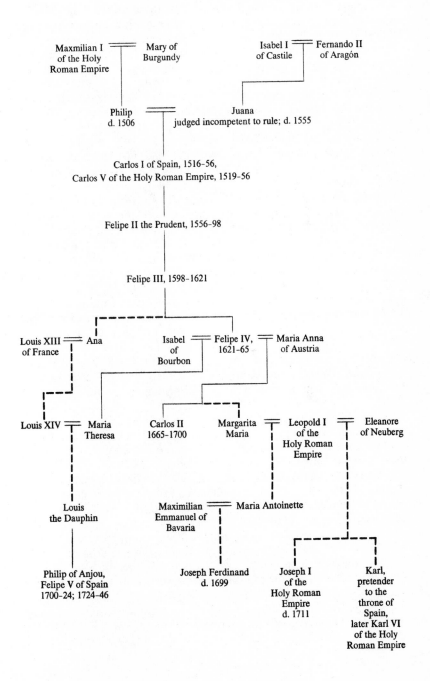

eldest daughter, the schizophrenic Juana (later called "the Mad"), who had been wed to the sole heir of the great Habsburg domains of central Europe. The resulting inheritance created an imperial complex of extraordinary dimensions, which raised the Spanish government to unimagined heights of power, complexity, and difficulty. In the short run, the succession in Castile once more fell into dispute after Isabel's death in 1504. The queen had been perhaps the most popular ruler in Castile's history, but little of this had rubbed off on Fernando, always distrusted as a foreigner and sometimes referred to as "the stingy Catalan." The aristocracy had been quelled but not eliminated as a power. Since Fernando had no personal right of succession, the nobles saw the opportunity for a political comeback during the reign of Isabel's successor, Juana, and her Habsburg husband, Philip the Handsome. The early death of Philip and the obvious incapacity of Juana, however, soon left the more responsible leaders of the Castilian upper classes no alternative but to accept the regency of Fernando once more until Juana's son Carlos came of age.

It is important to understand that by the time of Fernando's death in 1516 only the monarchy, and not the confederate kingdoms of Castile and Aragón (to whom southern cis-Pyrenean Navarre had been added by Fernando on an autonomous constitutional basis in 1512), had been unified. Though there was indeed a certain sense of association, and to some extent of Hispanic brotherhood, the various principalities of Spain remained intensely faithful to local identity and institutions. The appearance of the young king Carlos* in 1517 was greeted with distrust. Carlos was vaguely Germanic in appearance, Flemish in education, a rather callow, ungainly, and ungracious youth, ignorant of Castilian, and surrounded by a retinue of Flemish advisors who seemed eager to batten upon the Castilian treasury. The four parliaments of the united monarchy's realms rather unenthusiastically ratified the succession, and, in some cases subject to heavy bribes, voted new financial grants needed to support their ruler's candidacy for election as Holy Roman Emperor in Germany.

After Carlos left to assume that majestic office, resentment in Castile and in parts of the Aragonese territories boiled over into rebellion. None of the oligarchies in any part of the united kingdoms were anxious to be ruled by an essentially Germanic prince who had bought his way to the most prestigious title in Christendom. The most serious aspect of the rebellion was the *comunero* revolt of more than a score of towns and surrounding districts in the regions of Old and

---

* Carlos I of Castile, but known in Spanish history as Carlos V from the order of his imperial title as head of the Holy Roman Empire.

New Castile and eastern León. The *comunidades* of Castile had long since ceased to be the representative local communities of the early Middle Ages. Most of their wealth and government was dominated by an urban aristocracy, regulated to some degree by royal appointees. Yet the urban aristocracy, like the titled nobility, wanted to be left in control of its local perquisites and had no interest in seeing the urban economy taxed for the benefit of imperial designs. The rebellion of Castilian towns that began in May 1520 was poorly organized and had no central purpose. It was led in the beginning by the urban oligarchy, with at least some support from the aristocracy. Spokesmen in the various towns presented dissimilar goals, but common to almost every rebel element was the desire for regular Cortes assemblies called by law at the behest of the towns themselves, for the right of the towns and local districts to control their own affairs and choose their own Cortes representatives, and for their right to retain the power of the purse. In general, the *comuneros* had no specific national constitutional goals, but did want more explicit recognition and development of earlier rights that were no longer being observed. The neologisms *patria* and *nación* were employed by some of their spokesmen, who talked of a "republic" or "commonwealth" of Castile, not because they proposed to abolish the monarchy but because they were groping toward a vague concept of institutionalized representative government. The revolt was mainly an urban affair, though supported by part of the peasantry and by a certain number of hidalgos.

After several months, the revolt began to move toward the left, as the middle and lower classes became more prominent and started talk of economic and social reforms. The comuneros were vehemently opposed to the grandes, and apocalyptic and messianic views were voiced by some of the most radical. In areas where the revolt moved toward social revolution it was deserted by the urban upper classes and by rural hidalgos. After eleven months, influential aristocrats combined with the regents in charge of government during the king's absence to put together a military force that had little difficulty in decisively defeating the raw levies of the comuneros, in April 1521.

Meanwhile, an even more radical social revolt had broken out in Valencia, where the crown had authorized formation of a popular "Germania" (militia brotherhood) of lower-class volunteers to help protect the Valencian coast against Muslim pirates. At that time, Valencia was the city in the peninsula most influenced by the political and social ideas of the Italian Renaissance, and vague ideas of forming a representative republic on the Genoese model were in the air. The lower classes were as devout and superstitious as anywhere else in the peninsula, however, and a recent outbreak of the plague was interpreted as punishment for impiety and immorality. This led to a bloody riot against local homosexuals that spread into a general assault by the Germania against Muslim peasants in the countryside outside Valencia. Thousands were forced to be baptized, homes were ravaged, and some Muslims murdered. When officials tried to intercede, the Germania took over the whole city.

At first the Germania was supported by the Valencian middle classes, who interpreted it as a local reform movement to clean up the city and win greater independence from the rural aristocracy and the crown. The revolt turned into a social-revolutionary movement, however, as plans were made by radical leaders to redistribute property. Several small military forces led by aristocrats and officers of the crown were defeated, but after the local middle classes turned against Germania radicalism, a larger army was collected that suppressed the Germania with considerable bloodshed. The status quo ante was then restored. The rising of the Germania paralleled another revolt of the foráneos of Mallorca in 1520, which met the same dismal fate as its predecessors. All these Hispanic socio-political revolts of 1520-1521 were isolated local affairs, however, without any attempt at cooperation, thus making it easier for the crown and aristocracy to suppress them piecemeal.

In general, the revolts in Castile and Valencia should be understood as part of the general pattern of social, political, and economic unrest among the middle and lower classes that attended the transition from the last phase of the Middle Ages into the sixteenth century. They were one aspect of a broader process that included the irmandade rising in Galicia and the great Catalan and Mallorcan revolts of the second half of the fifteenth century, with European counterparts in the revolts of Bohemia, social risings in the Low Countries and France, upheavals in Switzerland, and the Peasants' War in southwest Germany. They were compounded of resentment against new exactions by the state and the aristocracy and rebellion against traditional inequities which the insurgents hoped to replace with freer opportunities and more moderate obligations. Most of the revolts failed, but some, like the Catalan rebellion, gained a mixed success.

In Castile, the crown was fairly lenient in punishing the comuneros, and only a few of the chief rebel leaders were executed. The eighteen towns previously represented in the Cortes were still seated, but royal intervention in local affairs gradually increased during the century as corregidores were appointed to more and more areas and were given greater authority. By the end of the sixteenth century, Castile was divided into eighty-six *corregimientos*, or local administrative districts, and autonomous handling of local affairs, save in a few special regions (especially the Basque country), had been greatly curtailed. Thus the comunero revolt turned out to be the last gasp of what remained of the medieval system of local autonomy and municipal representation. It had been encouraged by the relative prosperity of the Castilian economy during these years, though this prosperity was one measured by Castilian more than by Flemish or central European standards. Within another generation the Castilian economy showed symptoms of its great decline, and with that decline vanished any capacity of the Castilian urban population, never especially assertive, to show initiative. On subsequent occasions during the sixteenth century, the representatives of the third estate in Cortes did balk at raising new taxes, but that was the extent of their opposition to the crown, whose sovereignty and initiative remained absolutely uncontested.

The nexus of internal affairs between crown and subjects was public finance. A great deal of the royal funds were supplied by the church, primarily through the royal "thirds" of all tithes collected in Castile; the *subsidio*, a sort of income tax on the church in all Hispanic principalities; and the *cruzada*, a special contribution from laity and clergy in the form of an indulgence. These monies amounted to about one-fourth—sometimes more—of the royal receipts. Yet this did not constitute an Hispanic equivalent of the confiscation of much of church properties and wealth by sixteenth-century Protestant rulers to the north and east. Moreover, the territories of the crown of Aragón did not increase their regular grants to the crown in sums proportionate to the inflation and mounting royal obligations of the period. In the mid-sixteenth century, the eastern parliaments were voting no more than at the beginning of the century, which, in view of the price differential, meant that they were contributing a good deal less to the crown in terms of real value.

This meant that the crown had to rely all the more heavily on the central kingdom of Castile, where basic commercial taxes had escaped parliamentary control during the fifteenth century. The customs duties and the alcabala, the 10 percent sales tax, were collected throughout Castile and its overseas dominions directly by royal authority, and were probably the largest single source of revenue for the crown. After 1525, the Castilian Cortes gained the right to approve any further increases in the rate of customs and sales taxes, and the towns substituted payment of annual fixed sums from the Cortes for itemized individual duties, so that the proportionate value of the sales taxes began to fall behind as prices increased.

Even in its original form, the alcabala did not provide nearly enough money for the extraordinary military expenses of the crown. By the middle of his reign, Fernando had fallen back upon the already established device of requesting a servicio, a special appropriation, from the Castilian Cortes. These were transformed from extraordinary requests to regular demands made by the crown every three years. The royal attempt to exact extraordinary servicios as an ordinary request was one of the points contested by the comuneros. Their defeat meant that the crown would have its way, and by 1525 the principle of the crown's right to periodic extraordinary grants had been fully conceded. In return, the alcabala was consolidated and a permanent Diputación of the Castilian Cortes established on the Aragonese model, enabling the urban aristocracy of Castile to distribute the tax burden according to its own wishes. The defeat of the Cortes on the servicio issue was made possible by the increase of royal power in town politics, where the crown influenced selection of procuradores and their attitudes. It was made possible also by the delegation of authority in assessing the burden, whereby the urban aristocrats shifted the entire burden of servicios onto the middle and lower classes.

The tax shift was not desirable from the crown's point of view. Not merely did it weaken the kingdom's economy—something of which the crown was only vaguely aware—but it limited taxation to a restricted portion of the kingdom's wealth. For a century it had been customary for only the representatives of the towns to appear in Cortes, but in 1538 Carlos V explicitly summoned spokesmen for the aristocracy and the church hierarchy in order to attempt agreement on a more complete and equitable system of taxation. This was the last great opportunity after the comunero revolt for the representatives of all classes of Castilian society to establish a degree of political and legislative authority in return for financial cooperation with the monarchy, but the possibility never even entered the thinking of the upper classes. The idea of a binding representative constitution for all three estates was anathema to the aristocracy, interested only in the preservation of its privileges. A general excise on foodstuffs payable by all classes was blocked, after which the nobles and bishops were once more willing to be rid of Cortes, so long as commoners should continue to pay most of the taxes.

The Habsburg crown was successful in Spain during the reign of Carlos V because it accepted the institutional status quo of the Hispanic kingdoms, and because of the increasing Hispanization of the ruler himself, who eventually lost nearly all Flemish identification and came to associate himself more and more with the base of his empire, Castile. If rebel movements such as the comunero and Germania revolts were thoroughly suppressed, the Habsburg crown in return fully accepted the pluralistic "Aragonese" structure of the realms of the united monarchy, and even extended this system to the new domains conquered in Italy. There were no efforts whatever in the sixteenth century to unify the various Hispanic states; the existing constitutional integrity of the separate principalities was fully respected.

The second Habsburg king, Felipe II (1556-1598), was a Castilian prince born and bred. He represented the complete Hispanization of the new dynasty, as far as personal habits and values were concerned. He also accepted fully the constitutional pluralism of the empire, and projected no major innovations in public institutions. Like his father, Felipe II relied upon the broad royal authority in Castile and the lack of any strong constitutional spirit seriously interested in limiting the royal prerogatives. None of the great Castilian religious and legal theorists of the sixteenth century allowed for a genuine constitutional system of representation and legal limitations on the Catalan (or later, English) model. Francisco Suárez, greatest of the Castilian neo-scholastics, even held that the king could tax without consent, which was actually contrary to Castilian tradition. Thus when the Castilian Cortes persisted in complaining about royal fiscal excesses, Felipe II made no effort to restrict them, knowing full well that since the defeat of the comuneros there was little danger that this underlying resentment would find expression in organized resistance. He also permitted publication, in 1569, of the *Nueva recopilación* of the constitutional laws of Castile, including a codification of the Cortes's power of the purse. Cortes representatives had made it fully clear that there was no danger of their trying to use such nominal authority to restrict royal initiative, that they would do no more than haggle over the extent of further taxation.

Castilian society largely, though not completely, accepted the burden of imperial responsibility under both Carlos V and Felipe II, though the attitude of the crown's subjects in the Aragonese domains remained more resistant. Thus when in the 1570s two main factions developed in the royal council of state—one imperialist-expansionist, led by the Castilian duke of Alba; the other more cautious and less aggressive, led by the prince of Eboli—they came to be known as Castilian and Aragonese factions. This was an oversimplification, since there were aggressive imperialists in the Aragonese domains, and some voices in Castile advocated lower overseas expenditures, but they did represent genuinely contrasting attitudes toward the imperial affairs of the Spanish crown. During the 1570s the Eboli faction was dominant, until a scandal of 1578 that brought discredit to the "Aragonese" group and finally the arrest of the king's personal secretary, Antonio Pérez, on murky charges of plotting rebellion. During the remainder of his reign, Felipe II relied especially on non-Hispanic imperial advisers.

The crown's only conflict with Catalonia in the sixteenth century occurred in the late 1560s. Alarmed by the spread of Protestantism in the northern Habsburg territories and France and by the degree of French immigration in Catalonia, the crown tightened censorship in 1568 and prohibited French scholars from teaching in Catalan schools. When in the following year the Catalan Corts rejected a new religious tax which had recently been ratified by the Vatican, royal alarm resulted in swift action and the arrest of members of the Catalan Diputació, as well as of several leading Catalan aristocrats. Yet both sides soon had reason to draw back. Catalan society was fully orthodox religiously and had no desire to be confounded with heresy. Felipe II soon learned that his fears were exaggerated. Constitutional protocol was restored and remained unaltered during the rest of D. Felipe's reign.

Much more serious was the Aragonese crisis of 1590-1592. Up to that point the traditional feudal constitution of Aragón had remained virtually unaltered. During the sixteenth century, relations between the peasantry and aristocracy declined further, with new restrictions on peasants' rights to grievance and redress. The judicial sovereignty of the landed aristocracy over most of Aragón was uncontested, and the sphere of royal law still quite limited. During the 1580s, the crown attempted to bring the portions of northern Aragón that bordered on France under royal jurisdiction, partly for internal political reasons, partly for external security. This was resisted, but the Aragonese nobility was badly divided by feuds.

A crisis arose when the judicial authorities of Aragón gave sanctuary to an escaped prisoner from Castile, Escobedo, a sometime royal secretary accused of treachery. Uncertain royal efforts to get hold of him by means of the Inquisition sparked a small local rebellion. Neither the majority of the Aragonese nobles nor the majority of the towns in the kingdom supported the revolt of 1591, while the Aragonese peasantry seem to have favored the extension of royal authority as a shield against arbitrary usages of the nobility. The final settlement of 1592 reformed but by no means destroyed the structure of the Aragonese constitution. It was made clear that the crown might appoint a viceroy over Aragón, and the powers of the Diputación of the Aragonese Cortes over tax collection were reduced, but the Cortes retained the power of the purse as far as new taxes were concerned.

The *justicia mayor* or chief justice of Aragón was placed more directly under royal control, as was the supreme court of the kingdom, but most of the system of local law was left untouched. Representation in Cortes was slightly reduced by royal decree. Decisions in all four estates of the Aragonese Cortes were henceforth to be made on the basis of a mere majority (whereas earlier unanimity had been required among the upper aristocracy), save for financial matters.

The reform in Aragón was not dissimilar to the assertion of royal authority in Catalonia a century earlier, and established a workable compromise that made it possible to avoid major disputes during the final century of life of the separate Aragonese constitutional system. Thus throughout the sixteenth century the Spanish Habsburg monarchy remained faithful to the Catholic Kings' policy of pluralistic, preeminent monarchy, asserting the superior but by no means absolute authority of the crown, while basically respecting the multiple constitutional systems of the Hispanic principalities.

10

The Expansion

The expansion of Spain and Portugal overseas in the fifteenth and sixteenth centuries was one of the most important achievements in world history, an enterprise for which Hispanic people had been prepared by their past and by the changes and opportunities attending the close of the Middle Ages. The medieval heritage of a military society, frequently thinking in terms of divine warfare and crusading, used to living on the boundaries of Latin Christendom and ever pressing back these boundaries, provided cultural and psychological training that was no doubt indispensable for the role played by the Hispanic peoples in the expansion of Europe. Desire for glory and riches had been a major incentive in the reconquest since the eighth century, but fifteenth-century society had become more self-conscious about such goals and had better information about how to attain them. In Castile, especially, aspects of late medieval humanism developed a very conscious stress on individual fame and glory as inducements to great deeds. Direct striving for such goals was clearly in the minds of the sixteenth-century conquistadores.

For centuries the expansion of the faith was inextricably intertwined with military glory and economic profit. Because of this it is idle to ask, as is frequently done, whether the Portuguese pioneers and Castilian conquistadores were motivated more by greed or by religious zeal. In the Hispanic crusading-expansionist ideology, the two went together. In Castile, particularly, wealth was based on conquest and dominion, which in turn was the result of the expansion of Christendom against the Muslims. It was accepted by most as axiomatic that God made such wealth available because the expansionists were engaged in a righteous cause. Religious belief was whole and complete, and rarely admitted the possibility of any contradiction between worldly profit and religious aims in the expansion of Christian dominion, at least until the mid-sixteenth century. Crusading and profit were largely viewed as harmonious and complementary.

During the fourteenth and fifteenth centuries there had developed a new demand among the upper classes of Europe for luxury goods that could be supplied only from the Orient, goods such as cotton cloth (India), fine silks (China), exotic precious stones (India, Ceylon, Tibet), and pepper, cinnamon, ginger, nutmeg, and cloves to flavor foods, especially tainted meat. During the fourteenth century, Italian and Catalan merchants had enriched themselves as middlemen in the trade for such goods, channeled through the Near East. By the fifteenth century, achievements in maritime technology and navigation, coupled with demand from a broader market and the marshalling of economic and administrative resources for long-range enterprise, raised the possibility of direct communications overseas with the sources of exotic goods. In the process, new items of trade and wealth were acquired—west African pepper, Guinean gold, ivory, valuable new woods, and of fateful importance, African slaves.

The Catalans had been the first of the Hispanic peoples to expand overseas, in the creation of their Mediterranean thalassocracy during the thirteenth and fourteenth centuries. In the process, the Aragonese-Catalan empire developed key institutions—the viceroyalty and the organized consulate, or board of trade—that were imitated to some extent in both the Portuguese and Castilian empires. At the height of the Catalan expansion, some of their seamen and adventurers ranged far beyond the ordinary ambit of European commerce. Catalan explorers reached the Sudan and were among the first to get to the Canary Islands. In 1346, Jaume Ferrer rounded the northwest tip of Africa and sailed down as far as Rio de Oro (below southern Morocco). For several generations, Catalan commerce dominated the northwest African trade. Catalan shipping was basically Mediterranean in style and construction, consisting of galleys and sail-driven round boats, but at its height rivaled that of Genoa in skill and soundness of construction. Catalan technicians made significant contributions to the development of the rudder and to new navigational devices, especially in cartography. Italian and Catalan sailors were the first to use regular navigational charts, and the school of cartography at Palma de Mallorca, staffed mainly by Jewish experts, was the best in the world of the late fourteenth century, producing the outstanding Catalan Atlas of 1375. Yet by the fifteenth century, the economic decline of Catalonia made it impossible for seamen and merchants to exploit the broader commercial opportunities that the Catalans had done so much to open up, so that in general, Catalan activities did not transcend the traditional avenues of Mediterranean commerce.

The initiative of Portugal and Castile in transatlantic expansion was due first of all to the exceptionally favorable geographic position of the peninsula's western and southwestern coasts. By the end of the fourteenth century, the Castilian fleet had surpassed that of Catalonia in size and scope. It was most strongly developed in the Basque and Castilian ports of the Biscay coast of the north, whose shipping routed English naval forces several times, exploited the French and Flemish trade, and gave Castile its first age of maritime glory, helping to establish Castilian as a commercial lingua franca in some west European Atlantic ports. After the Christian population had become firmly established for several generations in the coastal regions of western Andalusia, a fleet developed there also, mainly in fishing and in coastal trade. By the early fifteenth century it had ventured farther, building an important commerce of the Canaries and later moving down the Guinean coast of Africa. Genoese merchants and entrepreneurs played a key role in the commerce of the southern coast, establishing themselves first when the Christians took Seville and then becoming more and more influential during the fourteenth and fifteenth centuries. Many Genoese commercial families were Castilianized or Lusitanized after several generations and became a major part of the new commercial elite.

It must be emphasized again that neither in Portugal nor much less in Castile did economic and mercantile affairs attain predominant importance. They were the concern of small commercial and maritime groups in the port towns. Society continued to be dominated by the aristocracy, and aristocratic ideals tended to dominate thinking and values. The maritime society of the southwestern coasts of the peninsula obviously could not compete with the genuinely important commercial centers of the period. The combined activity of these towns was very small beside that of the north Italian or Flemish towns, but they did develop nuclei of trained sailors and shipbuilders and just enough capital and commercial experience to provide a base for further activity. Though the coastal societies could hardly be called cultured or advanced in terms of the more developed regions of late medieval Europe, they developed significant technology, most notably in ship design and construction. By the fifteenth century the slender, graceful designs of the Basque pinnace and Portuguese caravel had produced boats much faster and more maneuverable than the slow, clumsy round boats traditionally used for Mediterranean commerce. These ships were planned for coastal navigation, but soon proved capable of a greatly extended radius of maritime activity.

C. R. Boxer has suggested that Portuguese expansion arose from four fundamental motives: 1) crusading zeal; 2) desire for precious metals (especially gold from Guinea in the fifteenth century); 3) the quest for Prester John (the mythic Christian prince of the East) and the establishment of a stronger geopolitical position in relation to the Muslim world; and 4) the search for commercial wealth, especially through the spice trade.

Under João I (1384-1433), Portugal achieved a unity and concentration of resources never before realized. It was still a small kingdom that counted for little in European affairs, but it was modestly prosperous and in a unique strategic position. Moreover, the crown's tradition of patronizing shipping and commerce was expanded under the new Aviz dynasty.

Direct and continous outward expansion was begun with the Portuguese conquest of the north Moroccan port city of Ceuta in 1415. This expedition had been encouraged by the Moroccan civil war of 1411-1412 that left Ceuta without support from the interior. Seizure of Ceuta offered an attractive prospect because it opened the door to a variety of new opportunities: a) its position opposite the straits of Gibraltar gave its possessor leverage in the Mediterranean trade and control of one of the main outlets of the trans-African Sudanese gold trade; b) it could serve as a base for naval activity and piracy in several directions; c) it offered a new outlet for the petty nobility to win wealth and glory, an important consideration in view of the limitations on domestic income for much of the Portuguese aristocracy in the fifteenth century; and d) it could enable Portugal to flank its most dangerous rival, Castile, whose further expansion to the south and west might choke off Portuguese opportunity. The chief promoter of the Ceuta expedition was João Afonso, royal overseer of finance and principal representative of the bourgeoisie in the government. The expedition required a major mobilization of Portuguese resources but won a quick, dramatic success and established the Portuguese in a lucrative and strategic trade mart.

Expansion into the Atlantic was actually begun a few years earlier by Castile, when soon after 1400 several small groups of adventurers of Norman and Castilian origin occupied and began to settle three of the outlying Canary islands. They did official homage to the Castilian crown, which had won a vague title to the archipelago two generations before. In the 1420s, the transoceanic Portuguese expansion began with the settlement of the Madeira Islands, which at first were prized for their wood (whence the name). In little more than thirty years the Madeiras were converted into a lucrative source of cane sugar, for which there was a great market in Europe. In the mid-1420s, the Portuguese crown sponsored efforts to occupy the largest island in the Canary archipelago, Gran Canaria, but these expeditions were beaten off by the warlike islanders. A half-century of competition with Castile ensued for control of the Canaries, until Portugal finally withdrew in 1479 according to the terms of the Treaty of Alcaçovas. Occupation of the larger islands was not completed by Castile until 1493. The land and native population of the Canaries was divided up among the Castilian conquerors by a semifeudal system of bequests (*encomiendas* and *repartimientos*), which foreshadowed the subsequent system of land grants and division of the native population in much of Spanish America. The Canaries played a growing role in Castilian commerce in the 1480s and 1490s.

During the greater part of the fifteenth century, the main target of Portuguese expansion was not transoceanic dominion but the coast of Morocco. Within Morocco itself there were a variety of useful goods: grain, cattle in the north, sugar, some textiles, as well as fish, hides, wax, and honey. These helped compensate for the grain deficit that had developed in Portugal and were added to the lure of the Sudanese gold trade.

Almost more important was the fact that under the Aviz dynasty there had arisen an aristocracy of modest origins with commercial connections and looking for honor and profit overseas. For much of the nobility, the income from new *senhorios* or from raiding and piracy would compensate for the relative decline in their modest seigneurial dues. It is scarcely an exaggeration to speak of an early-fifteenth-century Portuguese crisis of the nobility, whose small fixed-rent income from land was being reduced by inflation. Whereas the military aristocracy had opposed the Ceuta expedition of 1415, advocating instead a direct land expedition against Granada, within two decades its position had changed and it became a champion of raiding and expansion in northwest Africa. Along with this grew a new sense of chivalry and crusading spirit among the fifteenth-century aristocracy, the product of conscious cultivation of aristocractic norms by fifteenth-century culture. The ideal of the crusade against the infidel had been less prominent in Portugal than in Castile, but it received emphasis in late medieval chivalric culture.

Royal policy under King Duarte (1433-1438) was more strongly sympathetic to the military aristocracy than it had been under João I. A firm money policy—unlike that of João's reign—was adopted, accompanied by an attempt at revaluation which benefitted a nobility living from rents. Royal decrees established the inviolability of the entailment (*morgadio*) of aristocratic estates. Moreover, new establishments in the Madeiras were set up on the basis of seigneurial domain, contrary to the practice of João's reign. Until 1433, the crown had received one-fifth of the profits of all expeditions, but after that date the royal fifth was limited to the profits of commercial voyages and did not accrue from military raids, and nobles became more active in outfitting pirate expeditions. Younger sons began to concentrate on fighting in Morocco, for which they expected special *mercês* (endowments) from the crown even though they might not be able to establish seigneuries in Morocco.

Thus the territorial aristocracy played a major role in the second great Moroccan expedition—the disastrous campaign against Tangier in 1437, an ill-organized, poorly led campaign designed to provide booty and lay the foundation for direct territorial expansion. Since it was not supported by merchants and moneylenders, the crown had to raise taxes to finance it.

After Duarte's premature death in 1438, Portuguese affairs were plunged into crisis. His heir, Afonso V, was but six years of age. The middle classes and townspeople in general were eager to affirm the regency of Duarte's eldest brother, Pedro, who was well educated, clear minded, and prudent. Dom Pedro was opposed by the territorial aristocracy, led by João I's bastard Afonso, for whom the duchy of Bragança, the first dukedom in Portuguese aristocratic history, had been created by the crown. A revolt by the Lisbon population in 1439 was necessary to win the regency for Pedro. Under his leadership navigation and overseas expansion received decisive encouragement.

The key period of maritime innovation was the half-century between 1420 and 1470. During these years the rapid, long-ranging caravel was perfected, and lateen sail rigging, greatly increasing speed and flexibility, was developed. Navigational devices, chiefly the perfected astrolabe, were introduced which made possible the great voyages of the last years of the century. The greater share of this technical achievement was accomplished by the Portuguese, though with considerable assistance from Spaniards and Italians.

The most celebrated figure in Portuguese maritime development was the Infante D. Henrique, one of the younger sons of João I. Dom Henrique was not, as he has sometimes been painted, a monomaniac, nor is it clear that he himself knew much about the science of his day. He did possess geographical curiosity, and he was concerned about prosecuting the offensive against the Muslims and converting the heathen. He was also keenly interested in profit from gold, sugar, and slaves, and since he was not in line for succession to the throne, in building the honor and power of his own household. As govenor of the port of Lagos and grand master of the Order of Christ, wealthiest and most important of the Portuguese crusading orders, he led in the outfitting of expeditions into the Atlantic and down the west coast of Africa. Had it not been for special resources of the Order of Christ and sometimes of the crown, these exploratory voyages could not have been continued, for during the first decades they were operated at a considerable loss. Keen professional cost accountants like the merchants of Venice would probably never have developed the facilities for circumnavigating half the world, as did the fifteenth-century Portuguese, for it was not a profitable business. In this respect, the Hispanic crusading impulse was a factor of great significance, encouraging the expansion during its most difficult phase. Prince Henrique's influence was probably most important in the early 1430s during the effort to round Cape Bojador, successful in 1434. The difficult currents in that region made voyaging past the cape unattractive to commercial enterprise, and without special incentive and encouragement Portuguese mariners would surely not have ventured so far at that time. In 1436 Henrique turned his attention toward leading the expedition against Tangier the following year, however, and its crushing failure cast grave doubt on his capacity as a military leader.

More concerted encouragement to Atlantic exploration was given by the regency of Pedro, who had traveled widely, collected maps, and was a classical scholar. Dom Pedro opposed destructive raiding and fighting in Morocco, and championed commerce and exploration instead. Until 1441, there had been only three long Atlantic voyages down the African coast, but during the six most active years of Pedro's regency (1441-1447), there were twenty such major expeditions, and no new military ventures in Morocco.

Meanwhile efforts were going ahead to colonize more distant Atlantic islands. The Portuguese reached the Azores either in 1427 or 1431 and began to settle there in 1439. Settlement progressed more rapidly during the 1450s, and the Cape Verde Islands, farther down off the northwest coast of Africa, were colonized in the 1460s.

In 1443, D. Henrique was given sole authority to approve further African voyages, but expeditions were in fact inspired by a variety of initiatives, and the prince was personally responsible for only one-third of the maritime explorations organized during the seventeen years until his death. During eight years of D. Pedro's regency, 198 leagues of African coastline were discovered. Subsequently, during the last twelve years of D. Henrique's career (1448-1460), only 94 leagues of new coastline were explored. There were no major expeditions between 1448 and 1456, and when they were resumed, it was not primarily at the initiative of D. Henrique.

The regency of D. Pedro was ended in 1449 by a reaction of the military aristocracy, who encouraged the pro-aristocratic Afonso V

(1438/1449-1481) to seize the reins of government himself. Afonso was an attractive prince but given to rather irrational decisions in matters of major policy. He was urged to imprison or banish his uncle, and in a brief battle that followed between the royal forces and retainers of the ex-regent, the learned, prudent, and far-sighted Pedro was killed.

During the reign of Afonso V, the Portuguese nobility enjoyed great influence and prestige. They were recategorized according to the typical rankings of the French aristocracy, and for several decades the bastard ducal house of Bragança was the wealthiest and most influential force in the kingdom. There was further concentration of land in seigneurial estates, and more estates in the south were cultivated as latifundia with peasant (and later sometimes African slave) laborers.

During the mid-fifteenth century, the Portuguese nobility succeeded in fully imposing its consciously developed style and values on Portuguese society and culture. The ideals of chivalric honor and crusading developed by the early fifteenth century, together with a living standard of great luxury, became the norms of aspiration and achievement. It was within this psychological framework of elite society that the technical achievements of the expansion were carried out. Such a scale of values, still questioned during the reign of João I, carried the day in Portugal during the second half of the century. The wisdom and justice of an attack on Morocco had to be seriously analyzed in 1415, but during the reign of Afonso V and for the century following, such enterprises were accepted as self-justifying crusades for religion, chivalry, and honor. The justice of Negro slavery was debated in the first years when slaves were brought back from the Guinea coast, and children of the first African slaves in Portugal were set free, but by the end of the fifteenth century the ethics of perpetual slavery for Negroes were rarely questioned.

Afonso V reflected fully the zeal of the military aristocracy for carving out a land empire in Morocco. During his reign there was proportionately less interest in oceanic exploration and expansion, but so much energy was spent on raiding and territorial expansion in Morocco that the king became known as Afonso *o Africano* (the African). With their metal accoutrements and firearms, the Portuguese enjoyed a certain advantage in military technology over the Moroccans, but their attacks upset economic relations and limited the possibilities of commerce. As early as the 1440s, this had diverted the vital Sudanese gold trade from Morocco down to the Guinea coast. Nor did the Portuguese military aristocracy give up plans for a major campaign against the emirate of Granada; in 1465, the Granadan port of Málaga was briefly besieged.

Yet commerce and exploration continued to prosper even though

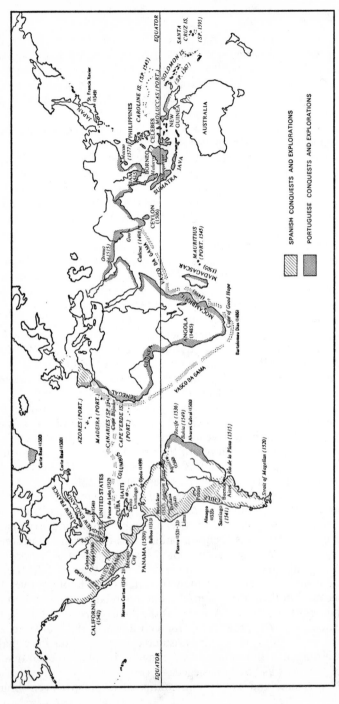

Hispano-Portuguese Expansion in the Fifteenth and Sixteenth Centuries

they received secondary emphasis from the crown. In 1455, the papal bull *Romanus pontifex* commended to the Portuguese a crusade to the East around the continent of Africa, and granted the Portuguese crown a monopoly of trade in eastern regions. New articles of commerce were becoming important: by 1450, African voyages were bringing back seven to eight hundred slaves a year, and after 1455, coarse malagueta pepper from Guinea was being sold on the European market.

Portuguese enterprise received great encouragement from the shrewd and far-sighted João II (1481-1495), one of the ablest European rulers of the century. D. João was first placed in charge of supervising Atlantic expeditions in 1474 as a nineteen-year-old prince. By this time a very profitable gold trade was beginning along the Guinea coast, where contact was made with caravans from the Sudan. In 1475, the crown established a royal monopoly over the Guinea trade, through the Casa da Guiné. Two years later, D. João was made de facto ruler of the kingdom by his elderly father, and the Treaty of Alcaçovas with Castile in 1479 brought Castilian recognition of the Portuguese monopoly of African coastal trade and exploration. In 1480, the crown officially adopted a policy of absolute secrecy concerning knowledge gained from Portuguese explorations and completely excluded subjects of other powers, on pain of death. To protect the increasingly profitable commerce in gold dust, slaves, pepper, and ivory, the major trading fortress of São Jorge da Mina was built on an island off the Guinea coast in 1482.

During the last quarter of the fifteenth century, the two main sources of overseas income were the lucrative sugar production of Madeira and the gold from Mina. It has been calculated that from 1481 to 1495 Portuguese production of sugar increased forty times over, so saturating the European market that prices fell 60 percent. Despite steady production by central European silver mines, enough gold was returned by Portugal to hold the ratio of gold to silver fairly steady in western Europe during the latter part of the century.

Columbus's first petition to the Portuguese crown (1484) to support a westward expedition to the Orient across the Atlantic was rejected because Portuguese experts were developing a fairly accurate estimate of the earth's circumference. It was realized that Columbus had probably considerably underestimated the length of a westward voyage to the Orient; moreover, Diogo Cão was nearly due to return from a long voyage (1482-1484) that they hoped would show the way around the southern end of Africa. The results of Cão's voyage were disappointing, but by 1485 the Portuguese had perfected calculation tables for charting positions of longitude and latitude. In 1487, three expeditions were dispatched: another major voyage eastward through the south Atlantic led by Bartolomeu Dias; a small land expedition across Africa and the near east by Pedro da Covilhão (1487-1493) to gather information about the Indian Ocean; and a private voyage northwestward from the Azores by the Flemish mariner Van Olmen. The latter apparently either never got started or ran into late winter weather in the North Atlantic and was never heard from again. The very useful reconnaissance mission of Covilhão did not get back for six years, but in December 1488, when Columbus was about to renew his plea, Bartolomeu Dias sailed back into Lisbon after an epoch-making voyage that rounded the southern tip of Africa and opened up the route to the East.

João II was succeeded by a twenty-six-year-old cousin and brother-in-law, Manuel I (1495-1521), called the Fortunate, who presided over the most glorious reign in Portuguese history. After nine years of hesitation, four vessels were outfitted for the voyage of Vasco da Gama to the Malabar coast of southwest India (1497-1499), vindicating the Portuguese claim to an eastern sea route to the east. The startling success of Columbus five years earlier was a major incentive for the Portuguese to press their efforts to a climax. Though one-third of the crew on da Gama's epoch-making voyage perished, the expedition's total profit was said to have surpassed 600 percent.

Yet the mere fact of getting ships across a ten-thousand-mile route to India hardly established a profitable commercial position for Portugal. The trinkets and cheap textiles that were used for trade with west Africans held no attraction for sophisticated Asians. The spice trade of south Asia was almost completely monopolized by Muslim middlemen who sold their goods through the Middle East to north Italian traders, and the Muslim monopolists were in no mood for competition from Christian interlopers. The very aspect of the Portuguese, mostly filthy and bedraggled after six months or more at sea on their small, ill-provisioned vessels, repelled the Asians.

In the Mediterranean and in south Asia, the expansion of Portugal and Castile was not carried out in the face of decadent, yielding nonwestern societies, but was met head-on by dynamic, conquering Muslim sultanates that were victorious throughout most of southern Asia, like the Turks in southeast Europe. As far as the conquest of territory inhabited by civilized people was concerned, the expansion of the Hispanic kingdoms appeared for a long time relatively insignificant beside the seemingly invincible expansion of the Ottoman Turkish empire after the seizure of Constantinople, the establishment of a Muslim empire in India, and the spread of Muslim sultanates through and across the Indonesian archipelago.

In view of the commercial weakness of the Portuguese economy and the militarily supported monopoly of the Muslim traders in the spice-producing areas, only force of arms seemed capable of breaking the Muslim hold and creating a profitable commercial position for the

Portuguese. The third voyage to India, again led by Vasco da Gama (1502-1504), was the first major Portuguese military expedition to the east, consisting of fourteen heavily armed vessels with as many soldiers as they could carry. In 1503, it fought and won the first pitched sea battle against the Arab naval forces and blasted its way into the spice trade.

The enormous distance from Portugal of these commercial-military operations meant that direct royal supervision was impossible, and within a few years the office of viceroy of India was created to administer trade and strongholds throughout the litoral of what was being called the Indian Ocean. The second viceroy, and the real founder of Portuguese power in the East, was Afonso d'Albuquerque (1509-1515), a Portuguese nobleman who must be considered the outstanding strategic planner of the sixteenth century. Albuquerque and other leaders realized that Portugal's position could not be secure until it had acquired permanent bases, not merely to guarantee acquisition of spices and other commercial articles, but also to safeguard its lifeline to Europe and to protect Portuguese operations from Muslim counterattack. The base for Portuguese power was laid with the capture of the island city of Goa off the southwest coast of India in 1510. From that time forward "Goa the Golden" served as capital of Portuguese activity in the East. To ward off Arab naval forces, Albuquerque had already partially occupied the key island of Ormuz (1509) at the mouth of the Persian Gulf, whence competing fleets could easily be harassed, and he completely conquered it in 1515. The year after Goa was taken, the viceroy massed most of his small resources for another strike far to the east, seizing the strategic base and spice center of Malacca on the Malay Peninsula (1511). From here the Portuguese could dominate the route to the Indonesian archipelago. Within two more years, Portuguese vessels reached Canton harbor on the Chinese coast, and subsequently obtained commercial rights on the nearby peninsula of Macao, where they remained.

Albuquerque not only staked out the key points of the Portuguese commercial empire in the East but tried also to provide the necessary logistical base for its prosperity. He planned permanent garrisons, reserves of naval manpower, stores, and even shipbuilding facilities, to make the Indian forces partially independent and able to survive long sieges and extended onslaughts by their numerous foes in the east. He did not live long enough to pursue his even more grandiose ambition to use Portuguese naval superiority in a crusade against the Muslim Middle East from the opposite side of the globe. Albuquerque had dreamed of landing an expedition on the eastern shore of the Red Sea to capture Mecca, or diverting the source of the Nile to ruin Muslim Egypt. He died prematurely in 1515, but what he accomplished during the climactic last four years of his life established him as one of the greatest, perhaps the most extraordinary of all, of the Hispanic conquerors.

The military success of small Portuguese forces on the other side of the world, virtually cut off from reinforcement, in a hostile environment populated by scores of millions of potential foes, was in some ways more remarkable than the sixteenth-century Spanish conquests in the Western Hemisphere. In India the Portuguese had to face not religious ascetics of Hindu culture but members of dominant military castes. The giant war junks of China and Java were frequently larger than Portuguese ships and sometimes as strongly constructed. Unlike Amerindians, Asians were well acquainted with guns and gunpowder and were capable of laying cannon which far surpassed those of the Portuguese in size. Nor can it be contended that Arab merchants, Hindu princes, Mogul emperors, and Malay sultans were awestruck or nonplussed by the sudden appearance of a handful of Europeans.

Nonetheless, the Portuguese did possess certain advantages of a military, political, and psychological nature. Portuguese ships, if not always larger, were faster, more maneuverable, and in most cases more stoutly constructed than those of the native peoples of the Indian Ocean. Secondly, the Portuguese were the only armed force in the East to mount long-range naval artillery. Installing light cannon on ships apparently originated with the Venetians, but at the beginning of the sixteenth century the Portuguese had developed this tactic further than any of their contemporaries. Such naval artillery was extremely weak by later standards and could not be used to blow most ships out of the water at long range, but it sufficed to kill enemy soldiers and sailors at a distance, cripple ships, and demoralize foes who were unable to reply in kind.

Psychologically, the morale, vigor, and self-confidence of the Portuguese, like that of their Castilian contemporaries, was incomparable. Products of a heritage of expansion and victory, they were ready to tackle the enemy at any odds in full expectation of triumph. In most of their major conquests, the first Portuguese assault failed but was renewed with greater spirit. Their ferocity and determination may not have been more than Asians had the potential to resist but in many cases was more than they were able to withstand psychologically.

Finally, the Portuguese benefitted from the political disunity of the south Asian states. Though several local alliances were formed at various times against the Portuguese, these rarely lasted. The major Portuguese bases held out and were as prosperous as ever at the end of a hundred years. It was eventually competition from European rivals rather than an upsurge of Asian opposition that broke the back of the Portuguese thalassocracy.

The rise of Portuguese naval power in the East paralleled the discovery and settlement of the West Indies by small detachments from Castile between 1492 and 1515. The momentous deeds of the Hispanic powers in those years—the conquest of Granada, the discovery of the Western Hemisphere, the carving out of major Portuguese and Castilian footholds on the Moroccan coast, the opening up of the East—stood out in western civilization during a period in which the primary dynamic expansion was found in the major powers of the Islamic world.

By comparison with the arduous preparation and cost of Portuguese enterprise, Columbus's epoch-making voyage of 1492 cost relatively little money and was undertaken when the Castilian crown was in an expansive mood, immediately following the conquest of Granada. It was financed not by Isabel's crown jewels but by private capital from Zaragoza, Valencia, and the Genoese of Seville. The first voyage to America was made by ordinary small Castilian coastal vessels sailing in extraordinarily propitious weather. In recent years there has been some tendency to downgrade Columbus by emphasizing his ignorance of some of the principal scientific findings of his time, particularly in the calculation of distance. Columbus was indeed not a professional mariner but an imaginative entrepreneur. His intellectual orientation was not thoroughly empirical, and he did not know everything that it might have been possible to learn about his expedition. He persistently misrepresented the reality of what he had discovered. Yet when all is said and done the importance of the voyage can scarcely be overestimated. It is true that if Columbus had not sailed westward successfully, someone else would probably have done so within the next few decades, but the point is that Columbus was the first to accomplish the feat in 1492.

His success precipitated a potential crisis in Portuguese-Castilian relations, for the Portuguese crown had for half a century been trying to maintain a monopoly of transoceanic routes to Africa and the Indies. The bull of 1455 had specifically granted them control of the eastward route around Africa, but after Columbus had shown that new land might be reached by sailing westward, the Portuguese crown insisted on a major share of that. The issue was resolved by the Treaty of Tordesillas (1494), which when amended drew a boundary between Spanish and Portuguese zones of dominion in the west Atlantic at a line 370 leagues west of the Cape Verde Islands.* It has been conjectured that the Portuguese already had information that the eastern tip of South America lay within the Portuguese zone. If that is so, they made no haste to take advantage of it. It was not until

---

* This agreement was not altered until the Castilian occupation of the Philippines in the 1580s, during the period of dynastic union between Spain and Portugal (1580-1640) when the rules of demarcation were no longer so clear.

1500 that Pero Alvares de Cabral, while making the second major voyage to India, swung far west with the prevailing winds and touched the eastern coast of South America, laying the first direct claim to the vast area subsequently known as Brazil.

One of the principal differences between the Portuguese and Castilian expansions was that the Portuguese were more thoroughly in control of their own activities. For example, Geonese bankers, merchants, and entrepeneurs played a major role in the affairs of Seville, the Andalusian ports, and Spanish America, but there was comparatively little foreign influence among the Portuguese. The latter financed most of their own expansion, despite slender resources, and built up their own state-regulated trading system. They learned comparatively little from the mariners of other countries, whereas Columbus and his lieutenants learned much from the Portuguese.

The arrangement made by the Spanish crown with Columbus was an essentially archaic one, based on medieval precedents. He was invested with the offices of viceroy and governor general of whatever new dominions he might discover, and with the hereditary office of grand admiral of those regions for his family. In his second voyage, the customary Castilian pattern of expansion and settlement was essayed. The discouraging result of that voyage caused a great decline in interest, and it was not until after the turn of the century that enthusiasm for the Indies was seen again in southwest Castile. In following years it mounted steadily. By 1515 most of the West Indian islands had been staked out, and the following thirty years were the great period of continental conquest.

The explorers and conquerors of Spanish America were drawn mostly from the people of the southwestern quarter of Castile, though there were some from almost every region of the peninsula. The soldiers of conquest were for the most part ex-peasants led by relatively undistinguished, frequently impoverished hidalgos. To that extent they were a representative cross-section of Castilian society. The grandes were not represented in the conquest, though during the second half of the century, younger sons from almost every great family of Castile, and from a few of Aragón, were to be found in Spanish America. Though everything done in America was done directly or indirectly under license from the crown, the initiative was relatively spontaneous and came in almost every case from below rather than from above. The conquest was not carried out by organized military units, for the regular Spanish army was not found in America until later in colonial history. Many of the conquerors had fought against the Muslims or Italians or in Castilian civil war. They were products of a process of competition and survival, and their toughness and endurance revealed it.

For the crown, the conquest of America was a mere sideline to its major preoccupations in Europe and North Africa, and it is surprising to note how few men and little material were involved. During the first half-century of Spanish activity, in which most of the two continents plus a series of major islands and archipelagos were staked out for occupation, fewer than fifty thousand Spaniards left the peninsula. The amount of capital involved was also small, for there was relatively little available, even in Seville. Other maritime and commercial centers, such as the Basque region and Catalonia-Valencia, were already well occupied in the Flanders and Mediterranean trades, respectively. Moreover, Catalans and Aragonese were soon prohibited by statute from participating in American ventures.

The resourcefulness and vigor of west European initiative was immediately made manifest, though the difficulties involved in dealing with the more scattered and backward aboriginal groups also became apparent. The military superiority of the conquerors was a matter of psychology and leadership more than of weapons alone. Firearms played a comparatively small role. Horses were more important, though most of the fighting was hand to hand, where the superiority of steel to stone might have been offset by the immensely greater numbers of the aborigines had it not been for the vast cultural differences between them and their conquerors.

Comparisons have occasionally been drawn between the Hispanic expansion and other voyages to or from Asia between the twelfth and early fifteenth centuries, raising the question of why the fifteenth-century European expansion achieved the consequences that it did. This question has been answered by referring to certain social and psychological characteristics of the people of Castile, Portugal, and other west European states. The overland travels to Asia of Marco Polo and others in an earlier period had no immediate results simply because the effort involved was absolutely prohibitive. The major Chinese expeditions westward across the Indian Ocean between 1405 and 1433 were something else, but the Chinese obviously lacked the naval technology to make long-range transoceanic activity possible. The hermetic, subjective exclusivism of their culture discouraged the sort of interest in the outside world generated in Christendom with its intellectual curiosity and evangelical zeal. Certainly, the qualities of spontaneity and individual initiative which played a significant role in the expansion could not have been found in the more authoritarian or traditional-communal societies of other parts of the world. But perhaps as important as anything was the closer proximity of the Western Hemisphere, with large, reasonably fertile, temperate territories inhabited by much less developed societies. The monopoly of the new world was thus a logical consequence of geography and culture.

For an entire century, the Portuguese and Castilian overseas empires stood alone. They had no direct competition until the beginning
of the Dutch and English colonies at the start of the seventeenth
century, and that of the French a bit later. What the Dutch did was to
replace the Far Eastern commercial thalassocracy of Portugal with
one of their own. The English ultimately achieved the same sort of
thing even more effectively, while emulating the Castilians in the
development of large scale continental colonization.

The superseding of the Portuguese in Asia by the Dutch and
English and the enormous political and technological superiority of
Anglo-North America over Hispanic America have raised some serious questions about the historical efficacy of Luso-Hispanic expansion. English colonization was a product of the seventeenth and
eighteenth centuries; that of Portugal and Castile was, it must be
emphasized, a product of the fifteenth and sixteenth centuries, that is,
of the late Middle Ages. Portugal and Castile never completed the
transition into modernity in the eighteenth century, but they were of
course even less developed, by any standard of modernity, in 1500.
Thus the Hispanic expansion was a projection of medieval Hispanic
society and culture, not a development of the new society conceived
of by so many English emigrants. The "new world" for Spanish
conquistadores and Brazilian settlers was to be an extension of the
old, a projection of societies which had failed to develop their earlier
representative political forms and were unable to sustain the rate of
social and economic progress that they achieved momentarily in the
latter part of the fifteenth century. Added to this was the overwhelming problem of a populous aboriginal society in much of Spanish
America, a vast mass which was difficult to move.

The unique achievement of colonial Hispanic society was the development of an original, hybrid society, but it was not a dynamic
society that was born with or quickly developed the finest tools of
modern government and technology. It was rather a kind of colonial
feudalism which recreated, often in more extreme forms, many of the
problems of peninsular society which had not been solved before the
expansion and grew only more severe afterwards. The ideals of glory
and conquest were effective in part because they raised their practitioners out of the civil community of the merely functional or legally
conformist. This brought a kind of aristocratic status, which was
considered desirable because among other things it lifted one above
the common law. Hence the worst aspects of aristocratic dominion in
the peninsula were reproduced socially and psychologically in His-
pano-America.

11

The Apogee of Hispanic Catholicism

The age of expansion has sometimes been called a period of Glory, Gold, and God, the precise order of priority varying from writer to writer. This assumption that religion was one of the main driving forces of Hispanic life during the imperial period is undeniably accurate. The expansion of Castile was accompanied by transformation of certain aspects of Castilian Catholicism, as the reforms carried out under the Catholic Kings brought to a climax some of the efforts for renewal that had been underway since the end of the fourteenth century.

Reform of the clergy was part of the general program of Fernando and Isabel to unify and reorganize the main institutions of the realm. The Catholic Kings objected strongly to large payments to Rome and to the appointment of foreign prelates, mainly Italian, to Hispanic posts. During their reign they won from the papacy the right of *patronato*, complete patronage, over the newly conquered territory of Granada (bull of 1486), a right subsequently extended to all of Spanish America. The more limited right of nomination to all dioceses within Spain was granted to the crown only in 1523, however.

The position of the Catholic Kings was not that which in the eighteenth century came to be called regalism. They recognized papal authority and did not insist on full royal domination, but they constantly petitioned and protested to the papacy concerning aspects of policy and administration affecting the church of Spain, and occasionally even used force to contravene specific papal acts. The question of royal authority and right of nomination was closely linked with spiritual reform, as well, for the religious zeal and rigor of the Catholic Kings was greater than that of most Renaissance popes. Fernando and Isabel were determined to bring in model prelates who would improve the quality of church life, and consequently royal authority was supported by the most zealous and reformist elements in the Spanish church. The greatest resistance to change came not so much from the hierarchy itself, but from routinists and bureaucrats in the middle administration of the clergy.

The first major reforms of clerical conduct and organization in Castile were carried out in the 1480s by the Franciscan provincial of the kingdom, Francisco Jiménez de Cisneros, who became the outstanding figure in the Hispanic church of the imperial age. Learned, intensely pious, severely ascetic, and full of endless zeal and energy, Cisneros was elevated to the archbishopric of Toledo (the primal position of the Castilian hierarchy) in 1495 when he was nearly sixty years of age. His leadership was crucial in six important activities during the next twenty-two years: a) Catholic reform; b) furthering religious unity when he became inquisitor-general; c) encouragement of learning; d) advancing the anti-Muslim crusade; e) maintaining political unity under the crown, especially in the last year of his life when he served as regent of Castile (1516-1517) following the death of Fernando; and f) helping to establish the beginning of a regular Spanish army during that same year. These great tasks were accomplished for the most part when he was between sixty and eighty years of age.

Permission was obtained from the pope to extend to others in the clergy the reforms first carried out within the Franciscan order. In this enterprise, Cisneros used a wide broom. Concubinage, often a form of common-law marriage, was so taken for granted that its abolition led to physical violence by the clergy in some towns; nearly four hundred friars in Andalusia emigrated to Morocco and converted to Islam rather than give up their women. The Cisnerian reforms had a strong effect, but it is misleading to represent them as having transformed the conduct of the Castilian clergy overnight. Nearly two decades later, at a church council in Seville, in 1512, the presiding archbishop Deza recommended that local clergy at least try to give an outward appearance of chastity and virtue, abstaining from attending the marriages of their grown children or officially deeding their personal property to concubines. In Portugal the situation may have been worse, and the record of sexual promiscuity and slave-

running by the Portuguese clergy in the tropics later became one of
the major scandals of the time. Indeed, nearly a century was required
before the reforms in conduct and education began to be generally
effective in Castile.

The Inquisition

The importance of Catholicism in Castile actually increased at the
close of the Middle Ages as a result of new social and cultural
problems. The new political principles of the fifteenth century were
unity and security, cornerstones of the "modernization" of that period. For the Catholic Kings and most of their subjects, it had become inconceivable that political unity should not be reflected in the
religious realm, for the two were inextricably intertwined and reinforced each other. Thus the united Spanish monarchy became the
first major state in Europe to impose the principle of both political
and religious unity that became the standard of governments
throughout the continent in the century that followed.

The Muslim question was temporarily settled by the conquest of
Granada, but the issue of Hispanic Jewry was qualitatively entirely
different. Jews played a more important role in Castilian affairs than
they had in any other kingdom of western Europe. They were the
major single group, though by no means the whole, of the Castilian
financial class. Jewish intellectuals, physicians, and specialists had
composed a large part of the Castilian intelligentsia of the late Middle
Ages. Jews also performed major functions in royal administration,
particularly in tax collecting, an activity much hated by the people.
The upper class of Castilian Jewry had become extraordinarily
wealthy by the late fourteenth century, while popular hatred of the
Jewish community grew. That Jews were protected by the crown in
the peninsula for a century and more after they had been expelled
from other kingdoms in western Europe is explained by the weakness
of Hispanic society (save for Catalonia) in conducting its own financial operations and the importance of Jews to royal administration.

Though there were a number of anti-Jewish riots during the course
of the fourteenth century, the first great outburst against Hispanic
Jewry was the great pogrom of 1391, precipitated by a combination of
financial pressure and religious revival in southern Castile that
preached puritanism, strict observance, ultra-orthodoxy, and segrega-
tion of Jews and Muslims (the last point having first been demanded
by the Castilian Cortes in 1387). The lead in suppressing Jewish
communities and placing heavy pressure on Jews to convert was
actually taken in Catalonia, where Jews were proportionately much
less numerous and important than in Castile. Practically the entire

Jewish community in Barcelona was converted or forced to leave, and by 1435 the same was true in Palma de Mallorca. Almost equally heavy pressures for conversion were felt in Castile in the 1390s, and a second wave of semivoluntary conversions followed between 1411 and 1415, prompted in part by the evangelism of the Dominican Vicente Ferrer and some anti-Jewish legislation by the crown. (It might be noted that Jews also held a dominant and usurious financial position in the emirate of Granada, where they suffered a number of pogroms in the fourteenth and fifteenth centuries.)

In the 1390s, the Jewish population of the peninsula was probably more than 200,000. During the next generation over half formally converted to Catholicism. The step was all the easier because of the position of so many Hispanic Jews among the elite, and the opportunity for further gain that conversion brought. Conversely, in the case of Aragonese Jews with more modest resources, conversion made it possible to escape heavy taxes. To this must be added the fact that linguistically, and in some aspects culturally, Hispanic Jews had become quite Hispanized.

The paradox of the history of Castilian Jewry was that mass conversion was not a step toward solving the religious problem but only made it more intense. The Conversos, as the converts were termed, usually advanced further in wealth and status in their new situation as Christians. Intermarriage of wealthy Conversos with the aristocracy became increasingly common, and the number of descendants of formerly Jewish families placed in influential positions in or out of government was impressive. Suspicion and hatred of Conversos grew more intense as their wealth and influence increased.

The first major riots against Conversos occurred at Toledo in 1449. During the next quarter-century feeling against them spread among the zealots in church leadership, among their rivals in the upper and middle classes, and among lower-class people inflamed against "false Christians" and genuine or supposed oppressors. The most common charge against Conversos was that of Judaizing, that is, of falsely pretending conversion and secretly practicing Jewish rites. Their enemies insisted that Conversos constituted an insidious force of subversion within Spanish Catholicism, corrupting the faith and conspiring with the enemies of a united Catholic state and society. By the 1460s this antipathy led to major riots and outbursts in many towns, where conditions verged on local civil war. The Jewish question had become the main source of internal discord in the kingdom.

Traditionally, Castilian Jews had relied upon the support of the crown, and most Conversos supported the cause of Enrique IV and later of Juana in the Castilian civil struggles of the 1460s and 1470s. Thus they found themselves on the losing side when the Catholic

Kings ascended the throne. Two centuries earlier, Fernando III el Santo had broadly termed himself "king of the three religions," but in the 1470s Isabel and Fernando could not conceive of unity and security in anything other than a staunchly, ultimately monolithic, Catholic society. The strong, expanding Castile of the late fifteenth century had destroyed the Muslim menace and no longer needed the Jews as it had a century or two earlier. The existence of a powerful financial caste closely associated with influential (and potentially antagonistic) groups in the aristocracy, all the while vaguely identified with an alien religion, stood as a theoretical menace to political and spiritual unity. Conversos were also a major part of the urban oligarchy—another special power group—and were on good terms with certain wealthy prelates. They constituted a sort of state within a state, but Isabel and Fernando would permit no more than one state and no more than one conceivable religious identification. After a ten-year campaign by the head of the Jeronymite order in Castile against Judaizing, and a new series of anti-Converso riots in Andalusian towns in 1473, the crown applied to Rome for approval of a special ecclesiastical inquisition under the patronage of the monarchy.

The Spanish Inquisition was conceived as part of the process of building a united state as well as a defense and purification of religion. Hence the insistence on royal patronage in naming the tribunal of a separate Castilian institution, rather than merely reviving a branch of the medieval papal inquisition in Castile. In the 1470s, most of the Castilian hierarchy were too corrupt and too political to be trusted with resolute action on their own. Moreover, a royal-ecclesiastical institution would identify royal initiative more closely with the common people, whose antipathy to the Jewish and Converso oligarchies was intense.

Pope Sixtus IV was extremely reluctant to approve an inquisition under state rather than ecclesiastical control, but at the opening of the modern age, heresy was the worst of all political and religious crimes. Since it was held to require organized detection and correction methods rather than mob rioting, a Castilian inquisition was authorized by papal bull in 1478 and went into operation two years later. It was extended into the kingdom of Aragón in 1484, and subsequently, against great opposition from protectors of local constitutional rights, into Catalonia in 1487, becoming the only politico-administrative institution common to all the principalities of the united crown. The work of the Inquisition got under way in Seville, a major center of Conversos, in 1480. Seven hundred Conversos were, after execution, burned there during the next eight years, and many more received lesser punishment. Though the Inquisition was nominally on the lookout for "Judaizers," all Conversos, whether remaining crypto-Jews or not, were immediately suspect. Altogether, under the direction of the first major inquisitor-general, Tomás de Torquemada (1483-1498), approximately 2,000 Conversos were burned and some 15,000 subjected to lesser punishment. Moreover it was soon being alleged that operations against Conversos could never be fully successful unless the remaining Jewish community was gotten rid of as well. The first orders for expulsion of Jews from selected areas came in the mid-1480s, but were not fully enforced.

The thesis has been advanced, most notably by Américo Castro, that the Inquisition itself was to a large degree created and prosecuted by lesser Conversos in the Spanish clergy, eager to prove their orthodoxy and zeal in an outburst of Jewish anti-Semitism which has found echoes in modern times. It is true that a number of Spanish clergy of Converso background were prominently associated with the Inquisition, a prime example being Torquemada himself. No doubt some Converso clergy were motivated especially to persecute Judaizers. Castro is also correct in pointing out the particularly Jewish identity of the *malsines,* or informers, of late medieval Spanish history. Yet the Inquisition was scarcely a Jewish institution, as this line of reasoning would have it. The institutionalized inquisition was a special feature almost unique to the Roman Catholic Church in the late Middle Ages. In constructing their own special tribunal, Spanish clerical and government leaders were merely reemphasizing their ultra-Catholic heritage. The reason why the Hispanic peninsula was the only part of western Christendom to develop a separate inquisition in the fifteenth century is clear: it was the only part of western Christendom that did not have a religiously and ethnically homogeneous society. So long as the peninsula was divided between four Christian states and fairly powerful Muslim domains, some degree of toleration was necessary both in the interest of Christians living under Muslim control and to prevent wealthy Jews from passing over the border into the domains of royal competitors. By the fifteenth century, Hispanic society was coming of age and having to identify itself as a unique and independent entity in the world, free of the restraints of the Middle Ages. The latent tendencies of five centuries then clearly won out, resulting in absolute insistence on religious conformity.

More recently it has been pointed out that the motivations for the Inquisition were as much social and economic as religious. It is difficult to weigh the exact force of various motivations in the elimination of the Hispanic religio-ethnic minorities, for this was a process that began in 1391 and was not completed for a quarter-millenium, until 1613. It has been seen that the religious and cultural ideals of

Castilian, and to some extent Portuguese, society had direct social and economic consequences, in that they tended to discourage financial and economic activity, encouraging a peasant-aristocratic continuum. Insofar as the Jews were a bourgeois elite and especially hated and envied for this, their elimination can be seen as a process of social and economic repression. There is evidence in the documents to indicate that desire to expropriate Jewish wealth was indeed a motive in the establishment of the Holy Office. But of course religion, culture, and social and economic ambition were not separate or exclusive ideals or spheres of activity. They were intimately associated and to a considerable degree responsible for each other.

The establishment of an inquisition to purge suspect Conversos was a prelude to the elimination of the regular Jewish communities in the Hispanic kingdoms. Because of their financial importance, this was delayed until the ten-year Granada campaign was finally concluded. The final decree for the expulsion from the kingdoms of the united monarchy of Jews who refused to convert was issued in 1492. It is not possible to know exactly how many people were affected. Both the Jewish and Converso populations increased even more rapidly than that of Castile as a whole in the fifteenth century. By 1492 there may have been nearly 150,000 Conversos and 150,000 unconverted Jews in the kingdom of Castile, which had a total population of nearly 7,000,000. This would mean that people of Jewish background made up about 4 percent of the whole. There were only about 30,000 Jews in the Aragonese principalities, but perhaps 40,000 Conversos there, since more poor Jews had converted in the eastern kingdoms. Under pressure of the 1492 decree, approximately 50,000 more chose conversion, but well over 100,000 made the best arrangements they could to leave the country. Subsequent expulsions and flights from persecution probably resulted in the departure of at least 150,000 Jews from the peninsula over a period of several decades.

Most of those expelled accepted their fate passively, though there were a few minor attempts at fomenting an aristocratic revolt against the crown. The expulsion and accompanying persecution struck a major blow against the financial elite of Castile, and though it can hardly be said to have had crippling effects, it did reduce the pool of resources and skills that could meet the economic challenges of the sixteenth century. In some regions Jews and Conversos had in the past two hundred years acquired dominion over land, and most of these territories were apparently gobbled up by the aristocracy, further increasing the socioeconomic imbalance of Castile.

The Spanish and Portuguese inquisitions had a variety of functions, for they were widely used for enforcing morality, particularly among the ranks of the clergy. They also combatted sorcery, witchcraft, and blasphemy, sins which elicited similar repression in many other parts of Europe during the sixteenth and seventeenth centuries. Their focus, however, was on the descendants of formerly Jewish families, for there never emerged an Hispanic Protestant minority of any size to be repressed.

The ability of the Converso community to endure was remarkable. Though perhaps only a minority remained crypto-Jews, a large proportion continued to marry only within their own circles and so preserved their identity for five or six generations or even longer. It has been argued that the great bulk of Conversos had originally been sincere in accepting Christianity, and that protracted persecution actually encouraged rather than discouraged Judaizing. In certain places, such as Palma de Mallorca, the entire ghetto area of converts was ostracized, and despite its militant formalistic Catholicism, the community was forced to continue its separate existence for centuries. Segments of the Converso community thus survived as identifiable units into the eighteenth century and beyond.

The Holy Office inspired fear and terror because of the secrecy of its operations. Those arrested were not allowed to communicate with the outside world and seemed temporarily swallowed up. The fact that the names of informers and accusers were not divulged made it all the harder to disprove charges. Servants and lower-class people, however, were less troubled by the Inquisition than were the wealthy and powerful, particularly in the sixteenth century. This was because of the Holy Office's concern for influence and example, and possibly also because of venal interest behind some of the prosecutions.

During the first century of the Inquisition's activity approximately 50,000 Conversos were condemned in one manner or other. Altogether, the Inquisition executed a grand total of some 3,000 (including a small number of Protestants) over a span of three hundred years, the last handful of executions taking place in the eighteenth century, ending with one final execution in 1826.

It is worth pointing out that the number of executions for heresy in Spain was less than the number of people destroyed in Germany by Protestants and Catholics alike during the witchcraft craze of the seventeenth century. Between 1562 and 1684, 3,200 were executed in southwest Germany alone.* On those occasions when witchcraft mania did break out in Spain—as in Navarre and Catalonia in 1527-1528 and in Navarre in 1610—the Inquisition acted to calm the hysteria and accurately diagnosed the tendency to mass psychosis.

* H. C. E. Midelfort, *Witch-Hunting in Southwestern Germany, 1562-1684* (Stanford, 1972).

The Inquisition clearly reinforced an increasingly narrow and rigid concept of Catholicism. Yet its own Index of Prohibited Books was operated with greater restraint than the Papal Index in Rome. The Spanish Index often did not suppress books in their entirety but published lists of excisions and corrections.

Ignorant twentieth-century commentators have likened the secret police terror of modern totalitarian regimes to the Spanish Inquisition. Such comparisons have at best very little foundation. Most of the lurid publicity about the Inquisition is greatly exaggerated. Most of those arrested were not tortured; the tortures that were employed were rather mild and sometimes were successfully resisted, and scarcely anyone was burned alive. The Holy Office did not operate as a modern totalitarian police system, but had to abide by a series of rules as a legal institution. Those accused were permitted to name advocates and sometimes managed to mount a successful defense. The worst excesses were the result of greed and corruption among the inquisitors themselves during the sixteenth century, for the Holy Office was entitled to a proportion of all goods confiscated from heretics. During the reign of Isabel, the Inquisition operated under fairly strict royal supervision, but became more independent and temporarily more corrupt during the early and middle decades of the sixteenth century.

The destructive effects of the Inquisition on Spanish society and culture are obvious. It reinforced narrow ethnocentric, caste-oriented, and anti-intellectual values. It also strengthened the united monarchy and the subsequent Habsburg state, and was probably the most popular single institution in Castile (if not in Aragón and Catalonia, where it was viewed with greater suspicion) during the sixteenth and seventeenth centuries.

The Moriscos

Jurisdiction of the Inquisition included only heretics; it did not cover those who were recognized followers of another, non-Christian religion. There were already a quarter-million Muslims in Valencia and Aragón; conquest of Granada added as many more to the population of southeast Castile. At the end of the fifteenth century, the Muslim and quasi-Jewish minorities numbered nearly 10 percent of the population of Castile and Aragón. The eastern principalities, with their mixed social and constitutional structures, were accustomed to a degree of diversity. For Castile this was a comparatively new experience. Though the terms of 1492 guaranteed the Muslims of Granada freedom of religion and some security of property in the traditional medieval pattern, this had become very difficult for the zealots in the Castilian church to accept. A campaign for the conversion of the Granada Muslims was launched, yet according to the agreement this could only be carried on by educational and evangelistic means. Some Castilian missionaries, led by the new archbishop of Granada, Fray Hernando de Talavera, made a sincere effort, but these modes of activity were only beginning to be developed by the Hispanic clergy. The obdurate resistance of Muslim society maddened the zealots, and Cardinal Archbishop Cisneros decided to speed up the conversion process. High-handed acts provoked military revolt in part of the Muslim region near Granada. This in turn raised the question of security, finally solved to the satisfaction of the zealots by a decree of 1502 which required the conversion to Christianity of all Muslims within the kingdom of Castile. Many thousands left, but the large Muslim minority remaining became Moriscos, or Christianized Moors, and as such, subject to the rigors of the Inquisition.

For more than half a century, the Morisco population was bothered comparatively little. The Moriscos were a compact and exclusive group, limited to a corner of the kingdom and not at all associated with Christian society to the extent of the Conversos. Whereas the latter had been a financial elite, with sometimes important social and political associations, the Moriscos were almost all peasants and artisans. They threatened Christian society only in the sense that they inhabited a certain territory, but they were in no position to subvert that society, as many feared the Conversos would do. The Moriscos were thrifty, productive, and hard-working. The Inquisition, on its part, was like other sixteenth-century Spanish institutions in that it was agreeable to at least a certain degree of corruption. Periodic payments to high officials and members of the crown's Council of the Inquisition preserved Morisco society from direct persecution for more than six decades.

The traditional system of tolerance in the eastern principalities was altered by the revolt of the Valencian Germania in 1520. The violence and enforced conversions carried out by the militia of the Germania reflected the intensity of feeling of Levantine Christians against Muslims. Of all the revolutionary changes attempted by the Germania, the only one that was subsequently adopted by the crown was the official Christianization of Muslims, as extended to all principalities of the crown of Aragón by a decree of 1526. Henceforth the peninsula's entire Muslim population were catagorized as Moriscos, or converts. The religious uniformity of the Spanish kingdoms had theoretically been made complete. It was not merely a negative process of eliminating diversity, but also a part of the broad expansion of Hispanic society and religion, an expansion carried out on the cultural and spiritual plane at home and on a continental territorial plane abroad. Yet, in fact, the decrees of nominal conversion changed very little; with very few exceptions, the Moriscos preserved their traditional religion and culture.

Expansion of Catholic Learning

The age of the elimination of religious diversity in the peninsula was also the age of the greatest expansion of Catholic education and learning in Hispanic history to that time, another expression of the vitality of Catholic culture in the early imperial period. The first printing presses in the peninsula appeared in the major eastern towns—Valencia, Zaragoza, Barcelona—that were closer to the mainstream of west European commerce and culture than most parts of Castile and Portugal. In most of the peninsula the towns were so small and weak that urban secular humanism on the Italian (or even Valencian) pattern failed to develop, and church leaders, with large incomes at their disposal, became the major patrons of learning. During the era of Cisneros, schools of higher education were begun at Valladolid, Avila, and most important at Cisneros's new University of Alcalá de Henares (1508), not far from Madrid. Cisneros was especially concerned with developing theological studies, but Alcalá also stressed the humanities, languages, and medicines. Cisneros also patronized translations into the vernacular of some of the most important new foreign works of Catholic devotion, in the vein of the *Imitatio Christi* literature. A main feature of the new spiritual learning in Spain was Bible study, the principle achievement of which was the massive Polyglot Bible, which published original and complete texts of both Old and New Testaments in all the classic languages in which they had been rendered, complete with a vocabulary and an analysis of grammar. The first volume of this work, the most complete comparative study of the scriptures ever made in Christendom, was published, paradoxically, in 1517, the same year that Luther nailed his ninety-five Bible-inferred theses on the church door in Wittenburg, starting the Protestant Reformation.

The expansion of religious learning within the Castilian church paralleled the expansion of Castilian vernacular literature in the early sixteenth century. During this era the Castilian language established itself as the dominant tongue for cultural expression throughout the principalities of the united monarchy. Castilian cultural hegemony marched pari passu with the political and military hegemony of the Castilian crown. Castilian thus came to be the main Spanish language, known among foreigners as Spanish, pure and simple. By the mid-sixteenth century it had become the dominant vernacular cultural tongue in western Europe, and retained that position for one hundred years and more until replaced by French in the latter part of the seventeenth century. Within the peninsula, it remained the dominant literary vehicle until the coming of nineteenth-century romanticism gave new impetus to Portuguese literature and revived the vernacular literatures of Catalonia, Valencia, and Galicia.

Spanish Erasmianism

During the 1520s, the Catholic humanism and moderate reformism of the Dutch scholar Erasmus enjoyed great vogue among Spanish intellectuals and religious thinkers, and inspired the major new current in the Spanish Catholic thought of the decade. The centers of Spanish Erasmianism were Barcelona, Zaragoza, and above all Valencia and the new University of Alcalá de Henares. The chief of Spanish humanists, Juan Luis Vives, son of a Valencian Converso family, proved to be one of the most profound disciples of Erasmus in Europe. At one point Cisneros had offered Erasmus a chair at Alcalá, and whereas the Sorbonne combatted Erasmian tenets, a Castilian theological conference at Valladolid upheld them. At that time Spain was probably the center of European Erasmianism, particularly between 1527 and 1532 when Erasmian humanists were the chief religious advisers of the crown and Carlos V hoped to encourage Catholic and papal reform in a moderate humanist direction. His failure to accomplish this, together with the radicalization and polarization of religious positions in Europe by 1532, led to a reaction in Castile and an erosion of the influence of such Erasmian counsellors as Juan and Alfonso de Valdés. In an intensification of this reaction, Erasmian doctrines were repressed under the weight of the Inquisition.

Counter-Reformation Religious Policy in Spain

The Catholic humanism of several thousand clerics and university sophisticates had scant effect upon a united kingdom of nearly ten million people, most of them illiterate peasants. Confrontation with Judaism and Islam had already led the great majority of Spanish people to take a stand for absolute Catholic orthodoxy and homogeneity. The split that developed in European Christendom after 1517 was absolutely inacceptable for Spaniards, whose institutions and culture were totally identified with Hispanic Catholicism. The fact that Protestantism was adopted by societies and states that were enemies of the Spanish crown and sometimes rivals of the Spanish themselves accentuated the rejection of religious alternatives. The only non-Catholics whom peninsular people had known were Muslims and Jews, perceived either as mortal enemies or exploiters. The same attitude was easily transferred to Protestants. Few of the religious, cultural, social, economic, or political features that encouraged Protestantism in northern Europe were present in Spain. Before 1558, the Inquisition could discover only 105 potential exemplars of Lutheranism in the united kingdom, and two-thirds of these were foreigners.

By the late 1550s, however, two small groups of Protestants were discovered, one in Valladolid in the north and the other in Seville. The news of this, along with many other rumors from home and abroad, was enough, after the experiences of the last three generations, to accelerate what was already emerging as a sort of collective paranoia. A royal decree of 1559 forebade Spaniards to study in foreign universities—even Catholic ones, for foreign Catholicism was considered flaccid and untrustworthy. The process of turning the Hispanic peninsula into the cultural Tibet of western Europe was by this time under way. During the next year or so, the Inquisition tried some 800 persons suspected of Protestantism, including many "Old Christians" of high social standing never suspected of Jewish background. The Holy Office reached so far as to purge one archbishop of Toledo, holding the primate of the Spanish church in jail for seven years before he was finally cleared and released.

From this time on, the cloak of orthodoxy became increasingly heavy. In the reign of Felipe II, which was just beginning, Spain would emerge as the champion of the Counter-Reformation and the sword arm of international Catholicism. Many historical commentators have interpreted Spanish policy in Europe during the sixteenth and seventeenth centuries as having been dictated mainly by religious motives, with the result that the practical interests of the Spanish crown were often sacrificed in the crusading fervor of the Counter-Reformation. This impression is strengthened by the central role of the Spanish delegates to the Council of Trent in maintaining the authority of the papacy.

Such an interpretation, frequent among Hispanic Catholic zealots and foreign anti-Catholic commentators, is quite wide of the mark in a number of respects. The coincidence of royal policy with Catholic objectives is in most cases at least as easily explicable by political motivations, because the religious split between portions of European society during the sixteenth century coincided with a political and military antagonism that found most of the enemies of the Spanish crown identified with Protestantism or the anti-Christian Turk. Carlos V did not move to crush Protestantism in Germany when it emerged, and took military action only after political and military tensions had built up over a quarter-century. Felipe II was rigorous against Dutch and Flemish Protestants, but would not have acted so severely had they not been political rebels against his crown. The Protestant Elizabeth was left unmolested for nearly three decades, and the great Armada was attempted only after severe military and political rivalry had developed. Both kings let operations against the Turk slip more often than not in order to prosecute their intra-Catholic imperial rivalry with the crown of France.

Relations between the papacy and the crown of Spain were bad throughout the century and sometimes violent. Rebel mercenaries of Carlos's forces sacked Rome in 1527. Several times popes joined or even led anti-Spanish coalitions. Paul IV (1555-1559) was the bitterest foe of the Spanish crown, whose subjects he called "those dregs of the earth, that breed of Moors and Jews." During his reign the crown found itself for a short time in the embarrassing position of operating a royal army in Italy against the forces of the papacy itself, though the piety of Felipe II was ultimately expressed in his orders to the Duke of Alba to kneel before the Spanish-hating pope to ask forgiveness.

Felipe II followed what might be termed not inaccurately a dynastic policy of orthodox Catholic nationalism. Locked in a struggle for the hegemony of western Europe, he saw religious orthodoxy as a mainstay of Spain and the empire, and the Spanish crown as the mainstay of orthodoxy within its realms. Foreign prelates, even the pope himself, were not to be trusted in political, administrative, and financial matters, where they might be representing other interests. Even more than the Catholic Kings, he tried to Hispanize the church in Spain. Foreign appointments became even rarer, and he asked that Aragonese Franciscans and Cistercians be freed from French control, because of the suspected heterodoxy and divided loyalties of the leaders of those orders. Later he endeavored to establish a completely separate Spanish section of the Jesuits. He delayed publishing the Trentine decisions in Spain for fear that they might endanger the royal control of church appointments. Ecclesiastical affairs were more fully dominated by the crown in Spain than in any other contemporary Catholic kingdom of Europe. In turn, the papacy sometimes looked upon the Spanish crown's frequent expressions of concern about church affairs and the repression of heresy as pretexts for the extension of Spanish royal power.

Though there was little reason to doubt the sincerity of the Spanish desire to avoid or eliminate heresy, the papacy was rarely able to identify its political interests with those of the Spanish crown. Spain was simply too powerful; having won hegemony in Italy, it was sometimes in a position to coerce the papacy politically, and the papacy was not always disappointed when Protestant or other Catholic interests managed to check the might of the Spanish crown. Clement VII, for example, might have been able to head off the English schism had he not been under the coercion of Hispanic dynastic interests. This purely political tension between the papacy and the Spanish crown lasted throughout the century, and resulted in another breakdown of relations in the early 1590s over the question of the French royal succession. Rome preferred an ex-Protestant Frenchman to a hyperorthodox member of the Spanish ruling family, for reasons of political balance in Europe.

Whatever the reasoning or motivation of the Spanish crown, the situation was much simpler from the viewpoint of its subjects. The Spanish popular mind of the sixteenth century did not distinguish sharply between religious and secular activities in the modern sense. Ordinary Spaniards continued to confound their cause with that of God; much of the time they did indeed believe that they were engaged in a crusade when making war against non-Catholic powers. Through the sixteenth century, the notion was sustained that the Hispanic cause enjoyed the special favor and protection of God. Hence the corresponding depression and disillusion that set in after 1588, when evidence started to accumulate that this was not exactly the case.

The most important institutional development of Spanish Catholicism during the Counter-Reformation was the creation and expansion of the Jesuit order. Its founder, the ex-soldier San Ignacio Loyola, was rooted not in Hispanic orthodoxy alone but also in the introspective trend of sixteenth-century Basque religiosity, which differed somewhat from that of most of Spain. He was also influenced by the methodic, systematized spirituality of the *Devotio moderna* as practiced in the peninsula especially by the monks of Montserrat in Catalonia. The Jesuit order became, as is well known, the sword arm of allegiance to the papacy, emphasizing religious teaching and proselytizing among non-Christians and in the second half of the century the Counter-Reformation's prosecution of heresy.

The imperial age was also a great era of Hispanic missionary activity. The best-known figure in this was the Basque Jesuit San Francisco Javier, but his nominal conversions of great masses of Asians in southern Asia and the Far East were perhaps less important than the work of many hundreds of obscure Spanish (and Portuguese) monks and priests who accompanied seamen and conquerors. The work of the Spanish clergy among American Indians, particularly in

parts of Mexico, was extensive and did more than anything to build
the uniquely symbiotic culture of Hispano-Indian America.

Sixteenth-Century Spanish Thought

During the sixteenth century, the peninsula became the center of
Catholic thought. The intellectual life of the Spanish universities and
cultural elite did not merely freeze into a negative, reactionary pattern before the new ideas of the sixteenth century, as has sometimes
been suggested. In the first half of the century, particularly, there was
a sense of newness and the development of culture, in which the
discovery and conquest of America played a major role. The word
progreso was first employed in Castilian in the 1520s and the term
moderno was first used at about the same time. The sense of cultural
unity with the ancients persisted, but with a feeling of continuity and
of surpassing their achievements both in the arts and in practical
affairs. Among writers and scientists there was a new emphasis on
observation, and the experience of America provided one of the first
examples in Europe of a sense of the comparative history of civiliza-
tions, as it developed among church writers and thinkers in sixteenth-
century Spain and Mexico. Among these same elements was first
expressed the early modern myth of the "noble savage," as applied to
some of the American Indians.

Spanish theologians and philosophers recognized the breakup of
the medieval cultural and philosophical unity, but they strove to
avoid the complete secularization of culture by stressing the primacy
of religious thought, not merely on the basis of authority, but as
accepted by individual minds and consciences. The imperfections of
Rome were recognized, while the religious values and authority of
Catholicism were affirmed. The idea of the overarching imperial unity
of the Middle Ages was abandoned for new norms of natural law
and, in the political sphere, of international law. The Spanish theorists and moralists of international relations, led by Francisco de
Vitoria, have thus been frequently given credit for initiating modern
concepts of international law.

The thrust of sixteenth-century Spanish theology lay in the elaboration of neoscholastic thought, culminating in the work of Francisco
Suárez, the outstanding European neoscholastic of the age. While
endeavoring to reconcile freedom and law, modernity and tradition,
Spanish neoscholasticism recognized that the modern principle lay in
a stress upon the role of conscience as well as authority. Emphases
varied: whereas the Dominican Domingo Báñez tended to be a full-

fledged predestinationist, Luis de Molina in his *Concordia* attempted to harmonize individual freedom and God's will.

Though there was nowhere any foreshadowing of modern representative political theory in the thought of sixteenth-century Spanish philosophers and theologians, a key work such as Suárez's *Defensa de la fe* (1613) was explicitly anti-absolutist, emphasizing the authority of the laws of the kingdom and the function of delegation of power by the crown. It was held in theory that power and legitimacy lay only in the community, though the ideal of direct community representation was not advanced. Suárez did not go beyond advocating greater participation in the royal government, under which the civil power could be altered and mediated by the administration of laws and juridical institutions.

In the doctrines of natural law that formed the basis of social theory, private property was not held to be an inherent part of natural law, but to be a logical consequence of it. The most radical of Spanish civil theorists, Juan de Mariana, who advocated tyrannicide in dealing with cases of severe oppression, suggested that property holdings should be redistributed if they became excessively or unjustly concentrated.

This period was also one in which clerical historians laid the foundations of modern Spanish historiography, particularly in the use of original documents, as in Jeronomo de Zurita's *Anales de Aragón,* and in the scope of their study, as in Mariana's *Historia general de España* (1601).

The Struggle for Social Justice in the Colonies

Church missionaries and theorists also led the struggle for social justice for the American Indians. Some Spanish jurists sustained a rather primitive theory of the "right of conquest" over the Indian population, but this was not accepted by the best minds in Spain. Francisco de Vitoria carried out an independent and penetrating analysis of the moral and legal problems of empire and of dominion over alien, non-Christian peoples. For Vitoria and his colleagues, Spanish dominion in the Indies could not be founded on mere conquest or assumption of superiority or divine right, but required a complex of historical, religious, and legal factors, and only as restricted and mediated by the tutelage of natural law under a moral restraint.

Missionaries of the regular clergy carried on intensive struggles to protect the Indians from exploitation by Spanish colonists. The most famous of them, Bartolomé de las Casas, the Apostle to the Indies, was so outspoken in his denunciation of Spanish treatment of the Indians that he has even been accused of having founded the "black legend." During the reign of Carlos V, the arguments of church moralists were written into imperial policy when the New Laws of 1542–1543 forbade further enslavement of Indians and made provision for eventual liberation of all those held in peonage. However, the New Laws could not be enforced, and it became ultimately impossible to control many of the ravages of the colonists. Church advocates of the Indians' rights had a significant mitigating effect on conditions in Spanish America, but they were unable to dominate the mores of colonial society.

Spanish Religiosity in the Later Sixteenth Century

Just as the church did not rule a theocracy, so the monarchy did not enjoy caesaropapist domination over the church. The crown controlled major appointments, but it could not fully dominate the ecclesiastical hierarchy or all important church institutions. The sixteenth-century Spanish church bore within it resources for many spontaneous initiatives. The church was not a monolithic institution but one divided by considerable internal strife. Rivalry between orders, struggles for preferment, appointment, and jurisdiction, the administration or use of church properties and income—all provoked considerable dispute. Wealthier orders like the Benedictines tended to identify with the aristocracy, whereas the Franciscans and Dominicans were closer to the common people. The foundation of the Jesuit order provoked a good deal of hostility. Animosity toward hierarchs was keenly felt, leading in one case to the fraudulent imprisonment of an archbishop by the Inquisition. Within the universities there were bitter contests for chairs, which involved extremes of slander and intellectual distortion.

It is undeniable that Felipe II's effort to seal off Spain from regions of heresy and heterodoxy had a somewhat traumatic effect on Spanish culture, closing up many of the avenues of thought pursued by the much more open pro-Erasmian culture of the early decades of the century. Yet the prohibition of foreign study for Spaniards never became fully effective, and ties always remained with Italy and Flanders. The flowering of Spanish culture in the latter part of the century actually led to a growing cultural influence of Spain on most of the rest of western Europe, at least in literature and the arts.

The repression of outside ideas that reigned in the 1560s and 1570s was eased after the more moderate Cardinal Quiroga became inquisitor general in 1577. During the last two decades of the century there was greater liberty for a more critical vein of scholarship, and many of the new foreign scientific concepts were accepted and taught in the Spanish schools. For example, Copernican doctrine was well established at Salamanca, the queen of Spanish universities, by the 1590s.

During the reign of Felipe II there developed a great intensification of religious feeling whose most direct literary expression was found in the writings of the Spanish mystics, led by Santa Teresa de Avila and San Juan de la Cruz. Though in 1559 a number of mystical works had been placed on the Index, this persecution later ceased.

There was also an increase in practical religious work and in charitable activity. The most important order established for such ends was the Hermanos de San Juan de Dios, but reforms of this sort were carried out in some of the older orders, and further efforts were made to improve the educational level of the clergy. Though the new Jesuit order was not favored by the crown, it increased its influence considerably in the 1580s and 1590s, particularly in education.

The end of the sixteenth century witnessed the neoscholastic movement at its height at Salamanca and other schools, a revival of a Spanish Christian humanism which emphasized reason and natural law. The influence of religiosity was keenly felt in the great Spanish literature of the late sixteenth and early seventeenth centuries, which was saturated with a sense of human sin, themes of moral psychology, and expressions of mysticism. Never in the history of the West has the culture and art of a people been so thoroughly identified with its religion.

12

Sixteenth-Century Portugal

The expansion first began to have noticeable domestic effects on Portuguese during the reign of João II, when the gold from the Guinea coasts and profits from other trade and enterprise produced a wave of prosperity among the minority involved in overseas activity. If the Portuguese expansion was less dependent on foreign assistance and investment than was that of Castile, it was also less "popular," in that Portuguese activity and commerce were stringently regulated by the crown, functioning under the monopolies of the Casa da Guiné and the subsequent Casa da India established for the eastern trade. Given the small amount of capital in Portugal, opportunities for participation were inevitably limited. Unlike their counterparts in Castile, many Portuguese aristocrats were not at all reluctant to involve themselves in commerce as well as piracy. Portuguese maritime expansion was to a large degree led by aristocrats. Those of the middle-class who achieved success were in turn co-opted into the nobility, and the whole process remained largely under the economic control of crown and aristocracy. Consequently the prosperity of Portuguese enterprise in the late-fifteenth and sixteenth centuries had comparatively little effect on the structure of Portuguese society. Monopoly military commerce overseas did not develop an independent bourgeoisie but enriched the elite of a still quasi-medieval society.

224

Restoration of Strong Central Authority
under João II (1477/1481-1495)

João II, "the perfect prince," raised the power of the Portuguese throne to a new height. He was the Portuguese equivalent of the late fifteenth-century "new monarchs," paralleled by such rulers as Henry Tudor, Louis XI of France, and Fernando II of Aragón. After the slack reign of his father, João II lost no time in reasserting the sovereignty of royal law and administration, which was ratified by the Cortes. The practice of appointing royal corregedores to supervise affairs in towns and larger districts was extended, and the broader administrative positions (*adiantados*) held by aristocrats in the south were taken over by royal *ouvidores* (judges). João II broke the power of the duke of Bragança, whose house held sovereignty over fifty towns and who controlled a strong private army. After numerous intrigues with the Castilians to compromise the Portuguese crown, Bragança was brought to trial and beheaded in Evora. A similar fate befell the duke of Viseu, first cousin to the king, who was dispatched by João himself. The growth of royal sovereignty and the cowing of the high aristocracy was greeted with general approval by urban leaders and the lower classes. João II made no effort to reduce the social and economic status of the aristocracy, however. His concern was simply to subordinate it politically and juridically to the crown.

João II carried on an active diplomacy with the west European powers, designed to keep Portugal out of European wars and assure its monopoly over west African trade and exploration. This policy was completely successful, and it was during his reign that the foundations of the sixteenth-century thalassocracy, as explained in chapter 10, began to be clearly laid.

Manuel I the Fortunate (1495-1521)

D. Manuel inherited the strong royal position built by his cousin and predecessor, João II, who had left no direct heirs. During his reign all the fruits of a century of trading, exploration, planning, and hardship were harvested, and before his death the boundaries of the thalassocracy had been extended beyond the east coast of Asia. Manuel I was less hard and cunning than João II, but he had many fewer obstacles to face. By 1470, the barren adventures and aristocratic favoritism of Afonso V had reduced the royal income to a level lower than at the beginning of the century, but the thrift and initiative of João II, combined with the Guinea trade, had increased the royal income greatly. Expanded gold trade with Guinea made Manuel, in the

tian baptism. The comparatively tolerant Manuel, however, had little interest in enforcing this edict. Only a minority of the 80,000 or more Jews in Portugal left the kingdom, a large group departing after a massacre of Jews in Lisbon in 1506. Most accepted a vague, nominal conversion, becoming *cristãos-novos* (new Christians), and all legal discrimination against them was abolished in 1507.

Some three decades passed before the crown developed the determination to press the issue of minority heterodoxy. The reasons for the founding of the Inquisition in Portugal are less clear and apparently even more complicated than in the case of Castile. At least four factors were involved. 1) There was a climate of religious compulsion, paranoia, and ethnocentrism brought on by the struggles of the Protestant Reformation and the example of Castile, as well as by the expanded warfare with renascent Muslim forces in Morocco and elsewhere. 2) The nominal cristão-novo minority was large, proportionately larger than in Castile. Many accepted Catholicism sincerely, but others remained Jews. 3) The cristãos-novos comprised the bulk of the Portuguese middle classes and remained the principal financiers, entrepreneurs, and craftsmen in the kingdom. They were virtually the only social and economic competition to the dominant elite, the military landed aristocracy, whose preeminence was otherwise uncontested. Hence it has been argued that the Portuguese Inquisition, more directly than that of Castile, was founded to eliminate the wealth and socioeconomic influence of the only nonaristocratic elite in the kingdom. 4) The Portuguese Inquisition was meant to give the crown greater control over the hierarchy and clergy of the church, establishing a degree of supervision over the church seigneuries and providing an instrument to attempt the reform of the clergy, some of whom in Portugal remained dissolute and corrupt.

The papacy issued the first bull for the establishment of a Portuguese inquisition in 1531, but wealthy cristãos-novos intervened to win temporary pardon from Rome for alleged crypto-Judaizers. A second bull was obtained by the crown in 1536, but its powers were temporarily revoked by the papacy in 1544 after evidence of gross abuse, and it was not fully reestablished until 1547. During the late-sixteenth and seventeenth centuries the Portuguese Inquisition showed itself to be more zealous than its Spanish counterpart. According to the best investigation of its records, 1,379 people were burned between 1543 and 1684. This was more than the Spanish total for the same period, which was considerably less than a thousand, and was much higher in proportion to the population. In Portugal, however, the Inquisition was even more exclusively directed against cristãos-novos than in Spain, for in Portugal there were no Protestants at all, not even the handful to be found in Castile and Catalonia. The animus against cristãos-novos was if anything more intense, perhaps because in Portugal they were proportionately more numerous as a result of the Spanish immigration.

In the process, the Catholic orthodoxy of Portugal was reinforced, the social and economic dominance of the aristocracy solidified, and the prospects for the development of a prosperous and independent middle class in Portugal greatly retarded. Persecution of the cristãos-novos reduced Portuguese economic resources at a time when the country was facing increased difficulty meeting the military and economic challenges of empire. The cristão-novo population of Portugal was by no means eradicated, however. Though a rash of *limpeza de sangue* ("purity of blood") regulations were passed in Portugal, as in Castile, to exclude descendents of Jews from all major positions, "new Christian" money was more than acceptable to a steadily impoverished aristocracy. Intermarriage proceeded at a rapid rate, and by the seventeenth century probably most families of social or economic prominence in Portugal counted some Jewish ancestry.

Despite the unquestioning religious orthodoxy of the Portuguese, political and financial relations between the Portuguese crown and the papacy were occasionally strained. Ever since the inquirições that had been conducted three hundred years earlier, the crown had endeavored, often without success, to gain greater control over appointments to the church hierarchy. From the mid-fourteenth century, the crown had held the *beneplácito regio,* the right to confirm and ratify official proclamations of the church leadership, but even in the sixteenth century it did not gain the full control of patronage achieved by the Spanish crown. Taxation of church rents remained a major bone of contention. In the sixteenth century, church income in Portugal was about 50 percent greater than the domestic income of the crown, but much of it was not regularly taxable. In addition, the crown was interested in gaining power to regulate the clergy. During the sixteenth century, more and more able-bodied men in Portugal without real religious vocation or training entered the clergy to achieve a bureaucratic niche and avoid military or naval service. D. Manuel's heir, João III, was eager also to take steps to reduce the immorality of the clergy.

During the subsequent reign of D. Sebastião (1557-1578), coinciding with the flowering of the Counter-Reformation, the most important new religious influence was the Jesuit order. Jesuits achieved a strong position, especially in education, and Portuguese Jesuits opened a second university at Evora in 1558 and remained the major single influence in Portuguese education for the next two centuries.

The Thalassocracy

The golden age of the spice trade from the Portuguese thalassocracy was the three decades 1510-1540. The royal mercantile consulate, the Casa da India, which was established about 1503 to regulate the eastern trade, maintained a royal monopoly on the trade in pepper, cloves, and cinnamon, and levied a nominal 30 percent tax on the profits of regulated trade in other articles. For about thirty years, from 1503 to 1535, the Portuguese breakthrough to the east substantially reduced the volume of Venice's Levantine trade, hitherto the main source of oriental spices for Europe. By 1510, the crown was gaining a million cruzados per year from the spice trade alone, and it was this profit which led François I of France to dub Manuel *le roi épicier*—"the grocer king." The second major source of overseas wealth, the gold trade with the Guinea coast, fell into decline after 1521, however, because of renewed competition in northwest Africa, especially from a resurgent Morocco. Furthermore, after a decade or so the volume of Portuguese spice exports was so great that it began to depress the spice market in western Europe, forcing prices downward. Finally, after about 1535, Venice began to rebuild its own trade as east Mediterranean middleman for oriental products, and competition became more severe.

Ultimately, Portugal lacked the resources to maintain and develop its military and commercial position. The costs of the thalassocracy were enormous, and rose yearly, as military pressure in the East became heavier. The Portuguese maritime expansion did not rest upon a broad, expansive domestic economy capable of accumulating and investing large amounts of capital. It was more in the nature of a series of royal military expeditions. The most lucrative commerce was monopolized by the crown and did not serve to foster the growth of a large and productive middle class. Profits were absorbed primarily by the court and aristocracy, which occupied the best positions in the thalassocracy, and hence income was drained off by consumption, leaving little to reinvest to meet the mounting costs of warfare, trade, and competition. By the 1530s it was becoming increasingly difficult to raise loans, even for the crown. Portuguese merchants lacked the resources to distribute their imports on a large scale, and much was sold wholesale at a reduced profit to Italian and German merchants. By the middle of the century the quantity of spices being sold through the traditional Middle Eastern channels to Italian merchants was almost as large as before the Portuguese breakthrough, and after that time Portuguese profits were considerably reduced.

The cost in material and manpower of the *carreira da India* (passage to India) was enormous. It is doubtful that Portuguese naval resources numbered more than 300 vessels at any one time, but it has been calculated that altogether, during the half-century 1500-1549, approximately 472 ships left for the east, carrying possibly as many as 180,000 men during that time span. By the time huge four-deck carracks were constructed, it was feasible to carry as many as 500 to 600 men on an outward-bound voyage though the voyage might last eight or nine months. Sanitary conditions on the long voyages were abominable, and it was no novelty to lose at least half the crew on a round trip.

The best estimates have been that an annual average of some 2,400 Portuguese left the home country for overseas during the course of the sixteenth century, making a total of nearly a quarter million. By contrast, the kingdom of Castile, with five times Portugal's population, sent only some 1,500 a year to its American colonies during that period. Few of the Portuguese who shipped out ever returned in good health; many did not even survive long enough to take up a career in Asia. Much of the Spanish American population was concentrated in temperate regions where the climate was reasonably salubrious, but the Portuguese were stationed in pestiferous tropical posts with inordinate mortality rates. Though the Portuguese emigration, almost exclusively of healthy young men, drained the vitality of the home population, it was scarcely sufficient to compensate for the extremely high death rate in the thalassocracy, whose strongholds were always thinly held.

A contemporary source in 1600 listed Portuguese in Asian ports as numbering 16,000, half of them soldiers and half *casados* (married men, meaning civilian traders and settlers). This figure may well have been too high; certainly the number of Portuguese in Asia during most of the sixteenth century was not so large. It is probable that there were rarely more than 10,000 Portuguese in the most important area, from Ormuz to Ceylon. By 1515, the fighting strength had increased to 4,000 men, but there was always a tendency for soldiers to drift away either as well-paid mercenaries in the employ of Asian princes, who prized them highly, or as semi-independent merchants or freebooters. In later years, there were rarely more than 5,000 soldiers in the East, though nearly all able-bodied civilians served in a militia in times of emergency. About 2,000 Portuguese lived in southeast Asia during the late sixteenth century (the East Indies, Malacca, and Macau), but nearly all of them were engaged in purely commercial activity.

Portuguese society in the East, as later in Brazil, was built largely on the basis of *mestiçagem* (miscegenation), together with the incorporation of a certain number of native Christian converts. It has been calculated that by the end of the sixteenth century the Portuguese could augment their forces in the East with militia units of 4,000 *lascarios* or *peões* (native mercenaries), 10,000 armed slaves, and 20,000 *cristãos da terra* (converts and half-castes).

Living conditions in the tropics brought an even higher death rate than the constant fighting in which the Portuguese were involved. Nevertheless, the Portuguese imagination was captivated by dreams of fame and wealth, especially wealth, and for several decades there were often more aspirants for extremely hazardous voyages to the Indies than could be accommodated. At first, crewmen had come especially from the Algarve, but after the beginning of the sixteenth century, when large numbers of men were needed, the main source of soldiers and sailors was the heavily populated Minho district.

During the second half of the century, those directing Portuguese activity in the East became even more obsessed with commercial profit, which brought sounder business activity but often led to profligate maritime practices. Huge carracks were constructed, ranging up to a thousand tons, becoming the largest merchant vessels in the world at that time. The degree of overloading on homeward-bound ships reached fantastic proportions. Deck space was crammed with boxes and crates, other goods were tied over the sides, and many ships were so heavily laden that they were almost under water before they left port.

Though the search for Christians as well as spices was given in the chronicles as the original motive for the Portuguese presence in India, for several decades little was done by the Portuguese to evangelize the East; they were too busy establishing their military and commercial position. The first major effort was made by the Jesuits, beginning in 1542, and from that time proselytizing monks became increasingly active and influential in the major Portuguese ports. During the second half of the century the most numerous were the Franciscans, and at times as many as five hundred members of this order, from Portugal and elsewhere, were laboring in the East. The only lasting conversions, however, were made in the enclaves of Portuguese civil and military domination, and the statistics for converts given by the Spanish Basque St. Francis Xavier and others cannot be taken at face value. In Brazil the main attempt was made by the Jesuits, who dispatched some twenty-eight missions to Portuguese America between 1549 and 1604.

The Portuguese cannot be said to have shown much respect, in the beginning, for native society and religion in the East. Hindu temples in the Goa district were closed in 1540 and the Portuguese Inquisition was introduced twenty years later. After the Synod of Damper in 1599, the native Nestorian variant of Christianity adhered to by small groups on the west coast of India was proscribed in the Portuguese enclaves and driven underground. In other areas, however, when the local balance of power dictated, the Portuguese followed a more prudent course.

The basis of Portuguese strength in the East was sea power and the disunity of the native states. During the course of the sixteenth century, the power balance in India shifted greatly in favor of the Muslim forces, always the strongest foes of the Portuguese. The rise of the great Moghul empire exerted heavy pressure after mid-century, but the Moghul rulers did not develop naval forces to match the Portuguese, and the long siege of Goa (1565-1571) was withstood successfully.

Despite the size of the Portuguese bureaucracy in the sixteenth century, administrative control over the thalassocracy was never well developed, and the office of viceroy of India never functioned as effectively for Portugal as similar posts in America did for Castile. The Castilian institution of the audiencia was unknown, and the degree of corruption was probably greater in the Portuguese empire than in that of Castile. Distances involved were longer, and there was less administrative experience and skill to draw upon in the Portuguese elite. The situation was compounded after mid-century by a general crisis of leadership in Portuguese society as a whole. Throughout this period, discipline among the Portuguese in the East was poor, and the thalassocracy never operated as a single coordinated organism. Portuguese adventurers and entrepreneurs became increasingly autonomous in their small enclaves, and had to rely on the local half-caste society they were engendering and on their armed slaves. During the second half of the century, local intra-Asian trade became more and more important for the Portuguese in the East. A variety of subsidiary channels were opened, especially for Indian textiles. Though the commerce with China and Japan flourished for only fifty years or so, Portuguese local trade in south Asia was solidly established by the close of the century and had indeed become the major source of income for Portuguese in this part of the world.

In contrast, though its volume continued to increase, the eastern trade became proportionately less significant for metropolitan Portugal during the second half of the century. It had never done much to stimulate Portuguese production and exports at home; outbound Portuguese vessels were often deadheaded, loaded mainly with ballast and men, since Portuguese goods had little value in the East. Spices and other imports were paid for by bullion at first derived partly from Portuguese Africa but later mainly from Spanish America, or the imports were exchanged for other Asian goods.

The thalassocracy became increasingly costly to Portuguese society as the century wore on. Not only was the loss of life on the naval routes and in the Moroccan conflicts very great, but it resulted in a process of inverse selection. The sturdiest, most daring men left in large numbers and comparatively few of them returned. Despite the importance of naval enterprise to Portugal, ordinary seamen were treated with contempt, and almost nothing was done to guarantee their training. The shortage of trained sailors in the second half of the century became severe and was reflected in growing shipping losses. The loss rate on the eastern voyages between 1500 and 1550 was close to 12 percent but rose to between 16 and 18 percent in the years from 1550 to 1650. Losses were due in part to competition from other European powers: French piracy had become a problem from the 1490s, and by the end of the sixteenth century conflict with Holland and England caused heavy losses. The situation was aggravated by the scarcity or high price of good materials in domestic ship construction, declining quality of workmanship, and poorer leadership.

Toward the end of the century, naval production in both Spain and Portugal was increasingly handicapped by lack of materials. Wood and other naval stores had more and more to be imported from northern Europe, giving Holland and England a natural advantage, for their vessels could sometimes be constructed for about one-third the cost to Hispanic naval yards. Ships were built in Portuguese India as early as 1510. Teak, a superior wood, was available there, and labor was plentiful and of a reasonably high quality, but other supplies were lacking and qualified engineers were in short supply, especially after the close of the century. Even so, a certain number of large ships of reasonably good quality continued to be built in Portuguese Asia until about the middle of the eighteenth century.

An equally grave handicap to Portugal was the failure of its social framework to adjust to the increasingly rigorous demands of maritime activity during the second half of the sixteenth century. The dominance of the aristocracy did not lessen but grew more complete. The political and social patterns of Portugal and Castile still required that leadership normally be given to noblemen rather than to better-qualified professionals. This situation was not limited to Castile and Portugal, but it was being overcome by the foremost maritime power of the late sixteenth century, Holland. Command and performance in Dutch naval enterprise were increasingly dominated by strictly technical considerations.

After the middle decades of the century, the Portuguese enclaves in Asia were left increasingly on their own, and the flow of manpower diminished. Later, in the seventeenth century, most of the men sent out would be jailbirds and rabble rather than the sturdy and ambitious adventurers of the first generations. As time passed, surprisingly little echo of the *carreira da india* would be found in Portuguese folk literature and culture. In one way, the impact of Portugal on Asia was greater than that of Asia on Portugal, for a sort of pidgin Portuguese became the commercial lingua franca of the south Asian seas for the next two centuries.

The Atlantic islands—Madeira, the Azores, and Cape Verdes—were more important to Portuguese life, for they became authentic extensions of metropolitan Portugal, incorporated politically and economically into the affairs of the mother country. Madeira proved to be one of the most profitable of all Portuguese possessions, though later surpassed in importance by the larger island chains. The introduction of American corn was eventually important in making possible the full settlement of the Cape Verdes, where cultivation was more difficult. The outstanding quality of Portuguese society in the Atlantic islands was that it became the most successfully interbred society of white and black people anywhere in the world. Negro slaves, at first imported from Angola, were freed over the course of three centuries, many of them intermarrying with peasant immigrants from Portugal. Only in the Cape Verde Islands was this carried to the point of almost complete mixing and equality, more so than in Madeira and the Azores. In general, however, the racial history of the Atlantic islands developed at variance with the pattern in all other parts of the Portuguese thalassocracy, where a strict policy of white racial supremacy was the rule.

In the late sixteenth century, it became increasingly clear that the real future of Portuguese commerce and colonialism lay not in the Indian Ocean and Asia but in the Atlantic Ocean and Brazil. The colonization of Brazil had begun slowly in 1531. The first economic attraction, Brazilian wood, gave way, as in Madeira, to sugar production, which began to achieve significant proportions after about 1570.

The rise of Brazil in turn led to intensified Portuguese activity on the Angolan coast of southwest Africa, where Portuguese penetration began in earnest in 1575. Though the Portuguese also sought silver deposits, their main interest was in slaves for Brazilian plantations, and later for Spanish America as well. The demand was great enough to encourage the shipping of some five thousand slaves a year to the western hemisphere by the 1570s, and the slave trade spread to the Moçambique coast of southeast Africa as well as expanding in Guinea. Most slaves were not captured by the Portuguese but simply bought from native slavers and enemy tribes. The death rate on the Portuguese African slave trade was high, not merely among slaves but also among crewmen on the unsanitary slave trips, but the profits to owners and slavemasters were great, making the slave trade one of the most lucrative of Portuguese oceanic commerce. Portuguese slavers had a head start in this deadly business, and traders from other western countries did not provide major competition until the seventeenth century.

Portugal under João III (1521-1557)

João III ascended the throne at the height of Portuguese power, but before the end of his reign this power had already noticeably begun to decline. Like his father Manuel, João III "the Pious" was a serious and diligent prince. He took personal responsibility for directing affairs of state and lent them much attention, but he lacked the imagination—and also the advisers—to institute the major policy changes that might have maintained Portugal's position. In domestic affairs he continued to expand the scope of royal administration. By this time the nobles posed no threat to royal sovereignty, but their social and economic position was if anything further enhanced during the reign. Much of the profit from overseas enterprise was spent in conspicuous consumption at court and in aristocratic luxuries rather than in the investments needed to meet the multiple responsibilities of empire. João III was a Maecenas, and Portuguese culture reached its height in the work of such humanists and writers as Gois, Gil Vicente, and Luis de Camoens.

The domestic economy, however, entered a phase of relative stagnation. Certain domestic export products, such as wine, olive oil, and fruit, maintained their volume, but cultivation of the key staple, wheat, declined as land was taken out of use. This was due to partial depopulation in some rural areas in central Portugal, as a combination of low wages, seigneurial oppression, and the lure of an easier life drew peasants to the larger cities or the empire. The food problem was made worse by intermittent bad harvests and several severe plagues during the reign, requiring food imports that weighed heavily on the exchange balance. The population of Portugal, which had expanded to possibly as many as 1,400,000 early in the century, ceased to increase and for the rest of the century was in danger of declining.

By contrast, Lisbon grew enormously. It became the mecca of Portuguese society for both the wealthy and the poor or ambitious who wanted to attach themselves to the center of wealth in the kingdom. The royal monopoly system concentrated trade disproportionately in Lisbon, leading to hypertrophy of the chief port and a decline of most of the small coastal cities. By 1550, Lisbon had reached a population of 100,000 (10,000 of them African slaves), making it the largest city in the peninsula. (Seville did not equal that figure until the 1580s.) By 1620, Lisbon had grown to approximately 165,000; it was the third largest city in western Europe, after Paris and Naples. Leisured wealth, a flowering of the arts, the presence of exotic articles from Africa and the East, and its African servant class made it perhaps the most colorful city in Europe. Lisbon more and more became a parasite on the Portuguese economy and empire, for rather than being a center for new enterprise, it was increasingly a center for consumption of profits.

At one of the increasingly rare meetings of the Portuguese Cortes, in 1525, there were strong protests about the waste incurred by court parasites, the increasing appointment of nobles to well-paying sinecures, and similar abuses. Corruption in administration was rampant, and the crown made only feeble efforts to restrain it. Measures of economic reform were halting and intermittent. There were some modest attempts to restrict the powers of aristocratic and church seigneuries and bring more land back under cultivation. On several occasions during times of famine in the countryside the excise taxes on food were suspended, and a series of sumptuary decrees tried to restrict conspicuous consumption and encourage productive labor, but had little effect.

As early as 1506 some 65 percent of the state income was derived from taxes on overseas activity. After 1540 the total income began to decline, though the proportion derived from overseas revenue dropped only slightly. The main problems did not come from the costs of maintaining the eastern trade but from exorbitant and futile expenses in Morocco combined with waste at home. The failure to develop a competent entrepreneurial bourgeoisie was accompanied by lack of productive investment and an inadequate commercial substructure, leaving Portugal unable to derive full profit from its overseas trade. During the reign of João III only about one-third of Portuguese commercial enterprise was actually financed by foreigners, but foreign merchants and financiers received a higher proportion of the profits and disposed of a much higher proportion of goods. In 1549 the Portuguese trade center in Antwerp had to be closed because of bankruptcy. By the 1550s the crown was desperate to cover its obligations and relied increasingly on foreign finance. By about 1560 the Casa da India, clearing house for the Asian trade, was no longer able to make payments, and by that time the Portuguese monarchy had become, in Garrett Mattingly's phrase, proprietor of "a bankrupt wholesale grocery business."

The Portuguese in Morocco

Throughout this period the major center of Portuguese activity was Morocco, where the main phase of Portuguese expansion had begun in 1471. After the conquest of Ceuta, the chief Portuguese target was the other important coastal city of northern Morocco, Tangier. The expedition of 1437 had ended in disaster, but Alcácer Ceguer, east of Tangier, was taken in 1458, and after Arzila to the southwest was seized in 1471, Tangier was abandoned to the Portuguese, leaving all the northwest coastal region of Morocco under Portuguese control. Subsequently three of the ports on the southern Moroccan coast, only loosely associated with the Moroccan sultanate, accepted Portuguese suzerainty.

During the exciting decade of 1505-1514, at the same time that the thalassocracy was being established in the Indian Ocean, seven new coastal fortresses were built or occupied, and the port of Safim as well, drawing almost the entire coastline of Morocco under Portuguese control. Safim also brought Portugal the commerce of the Suz district of southwest Morocco. Three Catholic bishoprics were established for the Portuguese ports, and a local Moroccan administration functioned under the Portuguese in the Doukkala coastal district west of Marrakesh. One cultural product of Portuguese military and commercial control was the use of *aljamia,* Portuguese written with Arabic characters. But Portuguese dominion in Morocco rested on slippery ground, for in most port and fortress districts it extended only a few miles inland, without any real foothold in Morocco itself. In general, the Portuguese coastal hegemony cost more than it produced, but was attractive as an outlet for the military aristocracy, imbued with the hybrid crusading ideology made popular by late medieval Hispanic chivalry. There was little manpower and money to divert to Morocco, and most Portuguese posts were poorly manned. They had increasingly to rely on Castilian mercenaries and native Moroccan auxiliaries.

Had the Portuguese dominion concentrated on commercial relations, it might have survived longer, but it remained oriented towards military raiding. The most proficient leader in this was Nuno de Ataide, military governor of the Safim district from 1510 to 1516, who ranged far and wide on raids inland, with the assistance of local Moroccan auxiliaries. The sultan in Marrakesh preferred peace, but Ataide was bent on conquest. This, plus the reaction to the slave trade and slave-raiding based at Agadir, eventually called forth a Muslim counter-crusade. There was strong resistance in the Chaouia district west of Fez, where in 1515 the Portuguese lost 4,000 men in trying to establish themselves at the coastal fortress of Mamora. After many exploits, Ataide himself was killed in 1516 while leading a raid far inland past Marrakesh.

A major Moroccan resurgence began in 1524 when the Sadid dynasty, sweeping in from the Sahara, established itself at Marrakesh. By the 1530s, Portuguese fortresses on the central and southern coast were under heavy pressure. In 1534, João III called a royal confer-ence to consider strategic withdrawals and a concentration of Portu-guese resources, but the Africanists had their way and the crown continued to try to defend all its far-flung coastal fortresses. After Agadir fell in 1542, however, Safim had to be abandoned the next year, and after five more years only the fortress of Mazagão was left to Portugal on the southern coast of Morocco. The new Moroccan dynasty incorporated the Fez district in 1549 and placed heavy pres-sure on the Portuguese possessions along the northern stretches of the Atlantic coast of Morocco, so that after 1550 only Ceuta, Tangier, and Mazagão remained.

D. Sebastião (1557-1578) and the Disaster of Alcázarquivir

At the time of João III's death in 1557, Portuguese resources were sorely taxed. The heir to the throne, D. Sebastião, was only three years old. For five years government was directed by the prince's grandmother, D. Catarina, widow of João III. In 1562, a regency council was established under his great-uncle, the Cardinal D. Henri-que, and it governed until Sebastião was declared of age at fifteen in 1568.

The boy king was poorly educated and of no more than mediocre intelligence, with two passions, war and religion. Though of uncertain health, Sebastião was given to violent sports, mainly riding and hunt-ing. He showed no interest in women, even when older, and spurned numerous offers of marriage alliance. Completely impulsive, he was bored by affairs of state and administration and refused to heed any sort of disagreeable counsel. He had no interest in the people and affairs of Portugal and no program for their government and well-being. The obsession of his life was the idea of a grand crusade against the infidels, perhaps to India or the Near East, or at the very least through Morocco. The fate of this incompetent, emotionally unbalanced prince has been seen by some historians as a not inappro-priate symbolic climax to the history of sixteenth-century Portugal: a nation whose elite had forged far beyond their resources to build a thalassocracy around half the world, lacking the means, policy, or interest to use their resources rationally, wastefully diverting much of their income to conspicuous consumption, yet presuming all the while to maintain society and empire unaltered, bolstered by the ideological assumption that their place in the world was the result of their devotion to "the crusade."

Efforts were made to strengthen the armament of Portuguese mer-chant vessels, especially after French pirates sacked and held Madeira for two months in 1566. Decrees were issued requiring the movement of Portuguese goods in Portuguese ships whenever possible, to stimulate shipping. In 1570, the system of royal monopolies in the African and Eastern trade was relaxed, though not the general system of regulation.

All the while, D. Sebastião was attempting to prepare an invasion of Morocco, but for ten years the steady decline of Portuguese resources made it impossible for him to mount an expedition. His opportunity increased after 1574 when the sultan of Morocco, Muley Muhammed, was deposed by his uncle Muley Abd al-Malik, with some slight help from Turkish forces. In 1577 the port of Arzila, near Tangier, surrendered to Portuguese protection, and Muley Muhammed sought Portuguese assistance to regain his throne. Dom Sebastião in turn tried to gain support from both the papacy and Castile against the "Turkish menace" in Morocco, while Muley Abd al-Malik endeavored to buy peace by offering to return the port of Larache to the Portuguese. D. Sebastião ignored this offer, in order not to complicate his own invasion plans.

In 1578, with financial assistance from the church, he managed to assemble an expedition of perhaps 14,000 men, including many aristocrats. Hiding his true aim, which was an all-out battle with the Moroccans, he led this force inland from Arzila and on August 4 was met near the town of Alcázarquivir by Muley Abd al-Malik's whole force, which may have numbered as many as 40,000. The Portuguese expedition and its foreign mercenary allies had little chance in a desperate fight. Most were slaughtered, but many of the important nobles of Portugal were taken prisoner. In this "battle of the three kings" all three sovereigns died: the young ruler of Portugal, the elderly sultan, and his deposed nephew.*

The Portuguese Succession Crisis and the Union of the Crowns

The death of the king and the slaughter or capture of the flower of the aristocracy threw Portugal into crisis, and there followed two years of confusion and growing economic distress. Collection of a huge ransom to gain the freedom of the captives in Morocco completed the exhaustion of financial resources; jewels, plate, and silverware had to

* It also marked the end of Portuguese expansion in Morocco. Of the four remaining Portuguese towns, Arzila was relinquished by Felipe II in 1589, Ceuta remained with the Spanish crown after the restoration of Portuguese independence in 1640 (and remains Spanish to this day), Tangier was included in the marriage dowry given England's Charles II in 1661, and the last, Mazagão, was evacuated under siege a century later in 1769.

be pawned on a large scale to raise the funds. Domestic leadership had failed, and a power vacuum existed within the kingdom. The late king's sixty-six-year-old great-uncle, Cardinal D. Henrique, was left regent but lived only a year and a half. The strongest claimant to the throne was Felipe II of Spain, for he was the uncle of Sebastião and his first wife had been a Portuguese princess. The lower classes were depressed and resentful, and many of the upper classes feared social revolt if strong government were not restored. Thus most of the aristocracy and church hierarchy quickly accepted the candidacy of Felipe II, whose agents distributed large bribes in 1580. He was recognized as king by a meeting of the Portuguese Cortes—the first in nearly three decades—in 1581. The introduction of Habsburg sovereignty was made easier because the Portuguese elite had not lost a sense of broader Hispanic identity. Manuel I had protested when Pope Alexander VI granted Fernando el Católico the title King of Spain on the grounds that Portugal was also part of Spain (the entire peninsula) and Fernando was ruler of only Castile and Aragón. Cultural Castilianization reached extremes in sixteenth-century Portugal, where every educated man was either bilingual or could at least read Castilian, and Camoens had affirmed that "we are all Spaniards."

The Spanish monarchy sought incorporation of the Portuguese crown not only to consummate the long-desired dynastic unification of the peninsula, but because by 1580 Spanish policy was turning strongly toward the Atlantic and western Europe. Despite the economic and military decline of Portugal, the kingdom still had an ocean-going fleet of some consequence. Lisbon was the peninsula's leading city, and Felipe II established his government there for two years, 1581 to 1583. During the preceding half-century, the Portuguese and Castilian economies had become increasingly interconnected and complementary. Silver from Spanish America was indispensable to the balance of Portugal's eastern trade. The Algarve had become so involved in the commerce and shipping of southern Castile that it functioned as a sort of economic colony or appendage of Andalusia.

There was never any question of the institutional incorporation of Portugal into the Castilian system of government. The union of crowns was carried out strictly on the basis of the system that prevailed in the Spanish Habsburg empire, the Aragonese federative system of separate principalities. Felipe II swore not to interfere in the laws, customs, or system of government of Portugal and not to appoint Spaniards to Portuguese offices. This pledge was largely respected during the reigns of Felipe II and Felipe III, and even afterward under Felipe IV, so that the kingdom and its overseas empire remained completely separate and essentially autonomous under the Hispanic crown.

For nearly half a century, this system was fully accepted by the Portuguese upper classes. The only native pretender who continued to seek the throne was a bastard of a younger son of Manuel I who had taken holy orders, Antonio, the prior of Crato. Dom Antonio had the sympathy of the lower classes, who preferred a Portuguese king, but he was easily routed by Spanish troops in 1580. He made two major attempts to gain a foothold in Portugal, once with French help in the Azores in 1582 and later with an English expedition near Lisbon in 1589, but was beaten off both times.

Sebastianism

Many in the Portuguese lower classes responded to the loss of independence, and their own economic decline, with the development of a messianic faith that their young king was not dead but would return to lead them. Alternately, in later generations, it was hoped that a new savior, the "desired" or "hidden" king, would restore his people to greatness and prosperity. These messianic hopes have been termed Sebastianism, and they lingered on in various forms into the early nineteenth century, with echoes in Portuguese literature almost to the present day. The first and strongest wave of Sebastianism, from 1580 to about 1600, was influenced by three factors: a) dismay among the lower classes over the loss of independence; b) the influence of the cristãos-novos among the lower middle classes and their great fear that Felipe II would intensify the already rigorous Inquisition in Portugal (though he never did). This led to a rebirth of Jewish-derived messianism centering on the Portuguese, anti-Castilian (and less inquisitorial) savior; and c) the depression of the peasants, squeezed by inflation and seigneurial pressure, with little hope for alleviation of their plight. Their situation was typical of most of the peninsula, and indeed of most of the Mediterranean basin and eastern Europe, by the end of the sixteenth century. In Portugal, the dominance of the seigneurial system was merely ratified by the Castilian hegemony.

Sebastianism may also have been a reflection of the level of popular culture. The Portuguese peasantry were among the most ignorant of the peninsula, and indeed of western Europe. Little benefited by the wealth of empire, which was drained off by the upper classes, they remained extremely superstitious well into the twentieth century. Mythic fixation on the symbol of an intemperate prince was an expression of the *saudade* (sadness, longing, nostalgia) of a depressed people who had once accomplished great deeds but whose culture, social structure, and natural resources frustrated their transition to a more modern way of life.

The Continuity of Portuguese History under the Habsburg Crown

Sixty years of nominal Habsburg rule provided an era of recuperation for Portugal. The spice trade had begun to decline in mid-century, and the revenue from the eastern empire dropped at least one-third in the years after 1587 but temporarily recovered at the beginning of the seventeenth century. Portugal's position in Brazil expanded steadily. The domestic economy began to grow once more. Exports of domestic wine, olive oil, fruit, and salt mounted, and the growth of the population, temporarily halted or at least slowed after mid-century, resumed. By the middle of the seventeenth century the Portuguese numbered nearly two million.

In the Habsburg period cultural Castilianization reached its height; Castilian was the language of the majority of literary works published in Portugal during these decades. The Habsburg crown actively fostered a new pro-Habsburg high nobility, expanding the number of titled houses in Portugal from about twenty-five in 1580 to sixty-nine by 1640.

None of this, however, had the effect of blurring Portuguese political identity or the sense of Portuguese interests. Autonomy for domestic government and for the Portuguese empire maintained steady continuity of basic Portuguese institutions, and the occasional Habsburg attempts at interference provoked sharp discontent. In the late sixteenth century association with the Habsburg crown seemed to benefit Portugal's primary interests. When that ceased to be the case a half century later, national spirit came to the fore and seized the first good opportunity to end the dynastic association.

13

The Spanish Empire

The crown of Castile had conceived of itself as imperial since the
eleventh century, and the crown of Aragón had created a Mediterranean empire on land and sea. During the later Middle Ages a whole
series of institutions had been built to cope with imperial expansion.
The Catalans had dealt with the problem of controlling far-flung
territories by creating the office of "vice-roy" (sub-king) for direct
representation of the crown. This office was used also in administering peninsular principalities of the Aragonese crown. Commerce was
regulated by the Consulat of Barcelona, which chartered and administered maritime activity. In Castile, border governors (adelantados)
had been appointed since the thirteenth century to govern and defend
the frontier territories. The outfitting of individual expeditions against
the infidels (or others) in imperial enterprise or reconquest had been
common since the early Middle Ages, though the most extraordinary
example until the sixteenth century had been the conquest of Athens
by the Catalan Grand Company of Almogàvars. Subjects of all the
major Hispanic states had participated in the repartimiento, or division, of conquered territories and the tutelage of alien ethnic groups.
The Castilian crown for four centuries had been accustomed to intermittently augmenting its income, somewhat artificially, by bullion
shipments in tribute from the remaining Muslim territory. In all three
major kingdoms the reconquest had encouraged a massive flow of

colonizing emigrants outward (southward). Local social and urban structures had been developed or redeveloped, with varying representation or self-government.

Even more important than any particular aspect of historical experience was the continuing psychic mold which patterned the thinking of the people of Castile in particular. The crusade psychology rose to its height in the late fifteenth century. The paradoxical consequences of this orientation have frequently been pointed out, for the *guerra divinal* for God and the crown had the added appeal of making some of its practitioners rich. It was the opportunity for renewed military aggrandizement that had enabled Hispanic society to remain socially mobile over a period of eight hundred years. Thus at the end of the fifteenth century no societies were better prepared for imperial expansion than those of the Hispanic kingdoms.

The completion of the reconquest, absorbing the entire emirate of Granada after the ten-year struggle of 1482-1492, was a galvanizing deed that gripped the imagination of nearly all Castile and much of Aragón as well. It extended royal power and satisfied popular aspirations at the same time. Once completed, however, the straits hardly served as a stopping point. The Maghreb and the Hispanic peninsula had formed a geographic unit in African expansion throughout the Middle Ages, and were perceived in the same terms when the tide began to flow in the opposite direction. The Spanish crown received the blessing of the papacy and special tax rights over church and laity for expansion into North Africa. Portugal had begun its offensive in Morocco in 1415, and the Castilian phase began with the capture of the northeast Moroccan port of Melilla in 1497. Several minor ports and fortresses were seized during the next few years. In her will of 1504, Isabel commended to her subjects the continuation of the offensive against the Muslim world as their main international objective, and a major expedition in 1509 seized the key Algerian port of Oran.

Yet the grand Hispanic counteroffensive into northwest Africa did not fully materialize, for almost from the beginning it was shoved into the background by other considerations. The united crown had inherited not one but two imperial traditions: the crusading drive of the Castilians against the Muslim world to Africa and beyond, and the Mediterranean thrust of the Catalan-Aragonese monarchy. Even during Isabel's lifetime foreign affairs were mostly the prerogative of the more experienced, sophisticated Fernando, who had every intention of restoring, and if possible extending, the Aragonese sphere of influence in the west Mediterranean, though that would bring the Spanish crown into conflict with other Christian states.

The rise of the united monarchy in Spain coincided with the last great burst of vigor of medieval Europe. The French monarchy, always potentially the most powerful force in western Europe, had greatly consolidated its position during the second half of the fifteenth century. This was done partly at the expense of its traditional enemy, Aragón, as the French crown incorporated Catalan border territory and pressed its imperial ambitions in Italy. By the treaty of Barcelona of 1493, Fernando skillfully avoided immediate conflict with the French in the Italian peninsula, winning in return, as a bloodless concession from Charles VIII of France (1483-1498), restoration of the former Catalan dominions of Cerdanya and Rosselló.

At no time during the Middle Ages or after could even a united Castile-Aragón equal the economic and organizational potential or manpower reserves of a unified kingdom of France. France was the most densely populated major power in Europe, and if not always ahead economically, was never too far behind, enjoying the medieval and early modern equivalent of the largest gross national product in Europe. France's population was at least 50 percent greater than that of Castile-Aragón; its domestic economic superiority was potentially even greater.

In contrast, medieval Aragón had built its position in the west Mediterranean by exceptional military, naval, and commercial skill, at times abetted by clever diplomacy and the intermittent breakdown of French political unity. Fernando made more effective use of diplomacy than perhaps any other king in Hispanic history. He was assisted by the first regular cadre of diplomats, agents, and spies used by an Hispanic government, and it may not be too much to say that he developed the first regular royal diplomatic service in late medieval Europe.

The union of Castile with the Aragonese Mediterranean empire meant that the Spanish monarchy almost inevitably inherited an anti-French orientation. After Charles VIII established French hegemony in the Italian peninsula in one swift campaign (1494), the balance of power was so greatly changed that the Spanish crown had no alternative to direct action unless it was ready to relinquish the entire sphere of traditional Aragonese activity. Fernando labored to restore the broad international anti-French alliance first fashioned by his father, Juan II of Aragón. There followed the campaigns of 1495-1497 and 1501-1504, in which the Spanish forces, aided by Italian allies, drove the French from the peninsula, regaining Sicily and Naples for the Spanish crown.

These contests were triumphs of skill and leadership over superior French manpower and were the training ground for what would become the royal Spanish army. Though the medieval Castilian forces had more often than not been paid soldiers, and the crown maintained a few small mercenary units, there was no more a standing royal army in Spain than elsewhere. The Spanish army did not develop fully until after the reign of Fernando, but prolonged confrontation with the leading military power in western Europe hastened its organization.

The early Italian campaigns made famous the name of Gonzalo Fernández de Córdova, the Andalusian grande called by Italians "the great captain." One of the most chivalrous spirits of his time, Fernández de Córdova led Spanish forces in Italy and began the tactical transformation that created the classic military operations of the imperial age. The Catalans had been used to employing professional infantrymen in their Mediterranean operations, and foot soldiers had been used to great advantage in the siege warfare of the Granada region. By the fifteenth century, the dominance of armored cavalry was nearly ended. The new military elite of Europe were sturdy infantry pikemen, usually Swiss or German mercenaries, who wielded compact rows of long, heavy lances. Such a well-disciplined foot formation had broken many a cavalry charge, though it was not itself very mobile. Fernández de Córdova's achievement was to build a diversified force, incorporating firearms, that could deal with both cavalry and infantry.

The standard Spanish unit developed in the Italian campaigns was at first made up of some 6,000 men. These large sections were later broken into *tercios* (thirds) or brigades of approximately 2,000. Until the 1530s, pikebearers, infantry armed with short swords, and arquebusiers firing a sort of matchlock were combined in proportions of 3-2-1. The pikemen guaranteed the defense, the swordsmen carried the offensive against the enemy infantry once the latter had been engaged, and the arquebusiers provided what was perhaps the first portable long-range missile force in modern history, able to strike at a distance before the enemy was ready to engage. Small light-cavalry companies also accompanied the tercios. The soldiers were almost entirely volunteers, but they normally served for long terms of ten years or more and were paid by the royal treasury. Discipline and organization became strict, for only careful coordination could ensure success in increasingly complex battles.

During the sixteenth century, the regular army became a popular institution, and even younger sons of the gentry sometimes served brief periods in the ranks. The officers were almost exclusively Spanish subjects, until the latter part of the century, and these professionals provided the best leadership to be found in their time. Spanish military superiority in the imperial age was not simply a matter of tactics, organization, and leadership, however; moral and psychological qualities were almost equally important. Spanish troops were among the most committed and self-sacrificing in Europe, for victory or a totally dedicated effort toward it were inseparable from that

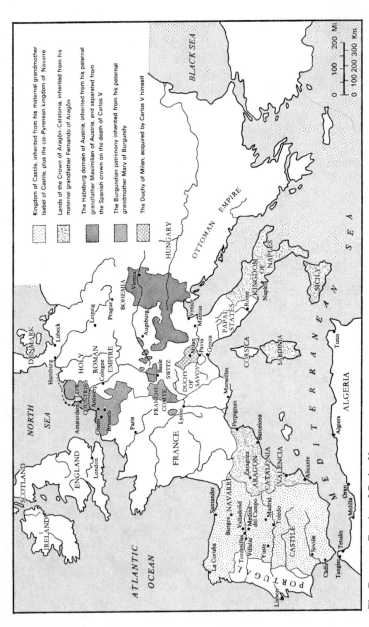

The European Empire of Carlos V

UWCL

Legend:
- Kingdom of Castile, inherited from his maternal grandmother Isabel of Castile, plus the cis-Pyrenean kingdom of Navarre
- Lands of the Crown of Aragón-Catalonia, inherited from his maternal grandfather Fernando de Aragón
- The Habsburg domain of Austria, inherited from his paternal grandfather Maximilian of Austria, and separated from the Spanish crown on the death of Carlos V
- The Burgundian patrimony inherited from his paternal grandmother Mary of Burgundy
- The Duchy of Milan, acquired by Carlos V himself

ethos of Hispanic honor in which they had been steeped almost from birth. Coming from a poorer, less indulgent society, they tended to be more spare and ascetic in many of their habits than other Europeans. It was observed early that Spanish troops could get by on less and could keep going longer in the face of greater miseries than soldiers of outwardly more imposing physical appearance from other lands. The short, sinewy Spanish regulars, together with mercenaries from other areas who were later used more and more to fill their ranks, were undefeated in major encounters from the first Italian campaign of 1495 until the disaster at Rocroi in northern France in 1643.

The military history of western Europe from the late fifteenth to the seventeenth century can be seen in retrospect as a prolonged duel between France and Spain, in which Spain was heavily distracted by other responsibilities in northwestern, central, and southern Europe. The eventual and definitive French victory, despite the superiority of individual Spanish units, is not difficult to explain in light of the increasing demographic and economic superiority of France, which was also ultimately able to concentrate on warfare near its own borders, while Spain exhausted its energy on widely separated fronts. Because of the extraordinary resilience of the French people and economy, none of the many Hispanic victories of the reign of Carlos V were effective for more than a few years.

The European empire of Habsburg Spain was composed of two main parts. The first was the dynastic patrimony of the Habsburg-Burgundian inheritance, comprising the Low Countries with several small adjacent territories and the large region of the Franche-Comté in eastern France, together with the original Habsburg crownland of Austria. The second was the Hispanic imperial conquests in Italy, primarily Sicily and Naples in the south and later the duchy of Milan in the north. To this was added the crown of the Holy Roman Empire, won by Carlos V in 1519, making the Spanish ruler nominal emperor of central Europe.

Consequently Carlos V faced imperial responsibilities on three fronts: against France in southwest Europe, against the Muslim world and the Turkish empire in the Mediterranean, and against rebel Protestant princes of Germany in the north. The expenses in manpower and money were so great that the resources of Spain and the Habsburg principalities of Europe would not have sufficed had it not been for the increased flow of precious metals from America by the middle of Carlos's reign. It has been argued that most of the responsibilities assumed in the titanic Hispano-Habsburg struggle of the sixteenth century were those of Habsburg dynasticism, and not properly Hispanic problems or responsibilities at all. There is considerable truth in this, for the complications in central Europe were brought on entirely by dynastic inheritance and ambition, as was the hideously expensive conflict in the Low Countries that later dragged the Spanish crown into direct confrontation with England. Though the military rivalry with France was traditional in Aragonese policy, it was made worse by the Habsburg inheritance of the Franche-Comté, which would remain a bone of contention for more than one hundred and fifty years. Yet once the dynastic union had been completed, it was no longer possible to define Hispanic as distinct from Habsburg interests, for the two became inextricably intertwined.

The wars and diplomacy of the reign of Carlos V may for the sake of convenience be divided into three general periods: 1) the struggle for Habsburg hegemony in southwest and west-central Europe on the basis of a reformed *Respublica cristiana,* from 1519 to 1530/1533; 2) the primarily Mediterranean phase of military conflict, from 1530/1533 to 1544; and 3) the major phase of Habsburg struggle for continental hegemony and Catholic unity in western Europe, from 1545 until Carlos V's retirement in 1556.

During the first decade of his reign, Carlos V's policy was dominated by the universalist ideal of the Holy Roman Empire, reinforced by the claims of the Flemish-Burgundian inheritance of his grandfather. The basis for this policy in terms of the religious conflict with Protestantism was a reformist Catholic humanism that would achieve the goal of a reformed Respublica cristiana under the civil leadership of the Habsburg dynasty and the religious leadership of a reformed papacy. This goal was influenced and encouraged by humanist ideas from the Low Countries, northern Italy, and the Spanish states, and the key diplomat charged with the administration of policy was Carlos's Piedmontese Italian chancellor, Mercurino Gattinara.

The important military contest during this first phase was with France over control of the Milanese region in northwest Italy, the territory binding the northern Germanic and southern Hispano-Italian Habsburg possessions. The two main rounds of fighting (1521-1525 and 1526-1529) resulted in victory for Carlos V, who gained the Milanese and assured Habsburg control of the Italian peninsula. The major ally in this conflict was Genoa, historic rival of Catalonia, which sided with the pluralistic Habsburg crown against the threat of French domination. Naval assistance from Andrea Doria and the Genoese fleet was important in defeating the French in the second round of fighting.

It should be remembered that the imperial orientation of royal policy in Europe was originally opposed by the third estate of Castile in the comunero rebellion of 1520-1521. Once this had been crushed, however, the great power of royal authority in Castile, along with the kingdom's military vigor, its considerable population, and wealthy, expanding American possessions, made it the base of Habsburg power in Europe.

The first main phase of Carlos V's struggle for reformist hegemony in Europe ended in frustration. French military power and ambition, though repeatedly defeated on the battlefield, could not be permanently contained. Despite Carlos V's second imperial coronation at Bologna in 1530 by the pope, the papacy was too strong and resistant to be dominated. It thwarted the emperor, evading major attempts at reform and the calling of a new church council. This, in turn, made it more difficult for the emperor to deal with the Protestant princes of Germany, who united their forces in the Schmalkaldic League of 1532. By this time religious positions were becoming radicalized and lines of contention firmly drawn. Meanwhile Carlos V's personal secretary, Francisco de los Cobos, who was more or less in charge of the administration of the kingdom of Castile, pressed for greater attention to direct Castilian interests instead of pan-Habsburg imperial ambitions.

Thus the second major phase of the reign of Carlos V began in the early 1530s when imperial military policy turned to face the threat of Muslim expansion in the Mediterranean. The Turkish advance northwestward through the Balkans and westward across the Mediterranean, reviving and reinforcing the hostility of the sultanates and pirate fleets of North Africa, could no longer be ignored. The eastern coast of the Hispanic peninsula suffered more than any other part of western Europe from Muslim attacks, and it was inevitable that the Spanish crown, as the leading Christian power in the Mediterranean, would bear the brunt of resistance. This aroused the expected enthusiasm in Castile, whose Cortes representatives repeatedly urged Carlos V to "make peace with Christian kings" in order to prosecute the war against the Muslims. The need was all the more pressing when the empire's greatest European rival, the crown of France, completely unmoved by crusading ideals, concluded a military alliance with the Ottoman sultan in 1534.

During the respite in the recurrent campaigns against France, the Spanish forces, assisted by the Genoese fleet, took the offensive and scored a spectacular series of triumphs between 1530 and 1535, climaxed by the capture of Tunis, the most important African port west of Alexandria. Yet renewal of the European struggle with France again drew attention and resources away from the Mediterranean contest with the Muslims. In the third round of French wars (1536-1538), France managed to seize and retain Savoy, marking a slight decline of Habsburg continental power. During the fourth round, Carlos V had to face the French and Turks at the same time, and suffered defeats at Algiers (1541) and on the French border. Peace was temporarily restored to Europe in 1544 on the basis of the status quo ante.

During the last decade of the reign of Carlos V, from 1545 to 1556, imperial resources were heavily engaged on the borders of France and in the effort to impose imperial and Catholic authority over the Protestant rebels of Germany. Coordination of such dispersed energies proved increasingly difficult. The final campaigns of 1554-1556 ended in virtual defeat. The emperor was forced to accept the compromise Peace of Augsburg (1555) in the Germanies and failed in his final effort to promote Catholic reform. The years 1554-1556 were probably the time of the highest shipping and economic losses to Muslim attacks in the Mediterranean. Setbacks between 1541 and 1556 offset all the earlier victories of Carlos V's forces in that area, so that his reign resulted in a slight net loss for Spanish power in northwest Africa. Thus it is understandable that the emperor, worn by gout and worry, resigned his responsibilities two years before his death to retire to the monastery of Yuste in Extremadura and meditate on the vanity of worldly striving.

The reign of Carlos V in Europe was a mixed success at best. The emperor can perhaps be remembered for his physical courage, his sense of chivalry, his feelings of imperial and religious responsibility, and his personal commitment to duty. Aside from being a glutton he was a sober prince, persevering in his labor but weighed down and partly overcome by the military and political responsibilities devolved on him from the empire.

Administration of the Spanish Habsburg Empire

Beside these titanic struggles on the European continent and in the Mediterranean, the great transatlantic empire developed as a marginal activity. It has sometimes been observed that the Spanish conquest and partial colonization of so much of America—and of a large swathe of the western Pacific as well—was a matter of private initiative. There is considerable truth to this, yet it must be remembered that all the principal expeditions of exploration and conquest were conducted under royal license, though not usually at royal initiative or expense, and that the crown was always careful to reserve for itself all political sovereignty in new areas brought under Spanish domination. Properties and a few positions were granted on an hereditary basis, and toward the end of the sixteenth century it became increasingly possible to purchase local administrative offices in Spanish America, whether or not on an hereditary basis, but all this merely followed Castilian precedent. Every town established in the overseas empire had to be chartered by the crown, and the entire administrative structure was organized from Castile. Thus the overseas empire was not at first a fully Spanish empire but an empire of the Spanish crown and more precisely of the crown of Castile. For several generations, subjects of the Aragonese principalities were nominally prohibited from participating, though in one guise or another a small number had been involved from the very beginning.

The government of the Spanish crown was organized on the basis of a series of separate councils for various regions and branches of governmental activity, expanded over a period of one hundred years. In 1494, a general royal Council of Aragón to deal with the affairs of all the Aragonese principalities was established parallel to but separate from the royal Council of Castile, which dealt with the internal affairs of Castile. This, in turn, required formation of a new Council of State, to help formulate the foreign policy of the royal government as a whole. The conquest of Mexico made it necessary to set up a new organ, the Council of the Indies, to supervise the American possessions. This body was officially constituted in 1524 and retained its authority until most of Spanish America had gained its independence. The council was not officially dissolved until 1834.

Since the Spanish Habsburg empire in Europe was governed on the Aragonese pluralistic principle, further councils were added to supervise its affairs. A Council of Italy was organized between 1555 and 1558, a Council of Portugal in 1580, a Council of Flanders in 1588, and finally, a separate Council of Finance in 1593, to try to bring order to the crown's highly complex and overburdened financial system. Smaller royal councils administered royal justice in Castile and the affairs of the Inquisition. The pluralistic conciliar system guaranteed considerable autonomy in the affairs of various regions of the empire and certain branches of government, but it also discouraged cooperation and coordination in the whole. It resulted in the duplication and overlapping of functions and the entrenchment of vested interests that became increasingly pernicious during the seventeenth century.

There was a basic difference between the structure of the Council of the Indies and those which governed the crown's European principalities. The latter were composed for the most part of influential inhabitants of the regions with which they dealt and were guided and limited by the local constitutions or laws and usages of the area. The Council of the Indies was staffed exclusively by peninsular Spaniards, mostly Castilian, and was not bound by any colonial charter, tradition, or constitution. For three hundred years its power was nearly absolute. It must be said, however, that the council's members were more often than not able and hardworking, and even during the seventeenth century tended to escape the pervasive corruption that was by that time weighing down most branches of Spanish government. Their legislative and judicial activity was prodigious, for they constantly felt called upon to regulate life in the most minute detail. By 1635, over 400,000 edicts were nominally in force; an abridgment of 1681 reduced this number to a more digestible 6,400.

Under the Spanish Habsburg empire, the executive powers of the crown were vested in regional viceroys, more or less on the Aragonese pattern. Viceroys represented the crown in Zaragoza, Barcelona, Valencia, Palermo, and Naples, and after the incorporation of Hispanic Navarre (1512), in Pamplona as well. Overseas, powers of viceroy were delegated to Columbus in the first charter of 1492 and subsequently divided between two viceroys in Mexico and Peru. All commerce and navigation with Spanish America was controlled and administered by the Casa de Contratación (House of Trade), an agency of the Council of the Indies established in Seville and modeled, to some extent at least, on the medieval Catalan consulate, though its powers were more extensive and arbitrary. The colonial judicial system, by comparison, was a direct extension of the Castilian. Regional audiencias were formed in America from 1511 onward, expanding the audiencia system slowly elaborated in Castile since the thirteenth century and reformed by the Catholic Kings.

The empire was administered by the largest bureaucratic apparatus in the western world. This vast mechanism, which sometimes worked with surprising effectiveness, was eventually overwhelmed by its own size, by distance, and by the volume of its work. By the end of the sixteenth century it was becoming ossified, but even during the seventeenth-century decline it continued to serve its main purpose of holding the empire together administratively.

The overseas empire, of distinctly secondary importance during the first third of the sixteenth century, became more significant after the increase in shipments of precious metals in the 1530s. By the reign of Felipe II, American resources were a vital mainstay of the crown, even though the overseas territories still received much less attention than did the European principalities.

The Reign of Felipe II

Felipe II (1556-1598) has been the most controversial ruler in Spanish history. Foreign and Protestant writers gave him a long and enduring reputation as the arch-fiend of Counter-Reformation iniquity, blackening his fame outside of Spain for three centuries. To Spaniards, he has been the great ruler who guided the empire at the height of its power, the sword arm of Catholicism, defender of the faith and unity of Europe. He has also been called *el prudente*—"the wise" or "prudent."

Felipe II was a Spanish king in a way that Carlos V could never become. Born and bred in Castile, he was thoroughly imbued with Castilian values and knew no other language well. After the retirement of Carlos, the central European Habsburg ("Austrian") domains were split off from the Spanish crown. They remained the patrimony of Ferdinand, younger brother of Carlos V, who decades earlier, as the Castilian-bred Infante D. Fernando, had been much the more Spanish of the two sons of Juana and Philip the Fair. Ferdinand also succeeded his brother as Holy Roman Emperor. This title henceforth would remain exclusively among the Austrian Habsburgs.

Freed of the central European imperial title and obligations, the empire of Felipe II was much more a Spanish empire than that of his father had been. Its base was the kingdom of Castile, whence came the bulk of its manpower, the largest share of its income, the tenor of its religious policy, and even to some extent the spirit of its politics. Felipe II was most similar to his father in his sense of duty. Yet whereas Carlos V had been a military and cavalier king, devoted to battle, the hunt, and the pleasures of the table, Felipe was a bureaucratic ruler. He did not personally lead his armies and was averse to hunting, but he himself attended to the vast paperwork and correspondence that held together the huge diplomatic and administrative network of the empire. He served as the first clerk of the imperial bureaucracy. The amount of detail to which Felipe applied himself was truly prodigious, but even his tireless application was inadequate to the task. Refusing to delegate central authority, he fell farther behind each year, and the backlog of imperial paper work became even greater.

The imperial affairs of the reign of Felipe II fall into five general periods: 1) the peaceful Spanish hegemony of 1559-1565, inaugurated by the treaty of Cateau-Cambrésis in 1559; 2) the imperial crisis of 1566-1570; 3) the Spanish response of 1571-1572; 4) the relatively static period of 1573-1580; and 5) the concluding era of the crown's great struggle for the unity and hegemony of western Europe, 1581-1598.

The last round of the Franco-Spanish wars of Carlos V had begun in 1552, and was climaxed by the major Spanish victory at St. Quentin in northeastern France in 1557. The peace of Cateau-Cambrésis (1559) putting an end to these Hispano-French wars, proved the longest peace agreement of the century between the two crowns, lasting for thirty-seven years until 1596. Felipe II was eager to have the costly struggle over, while the French crown found its kingdom weakened by internal division. Cateau-Cambrésis was a "Catholic" peace, designed to promote harmony between the two major Catholic powers and enable them to concentrate their energies on internal and religious unity. It coincided with the first measures of Felipe II to seal off Spain from foreign books, and with major persecution of Castilian crypto-Protestants by the Inquisition. It also recognized, in effect, the hegemony of the Spanish crown, for France renounced its ambitions in Italy and evacuated the duchy of Savoy, which it had occupied for more than two decades. Felipe II thus began his reign in a stronger position in western Europe than his father had ever enjoyed.

Four years later the Council of Trent completed its work, providing reformed Catholicism with a strong doctrinal base from which to launch a counteroffensive on wavering borderlands. The political difficulties of Felipe II with the papacy have been discussed in chapter 11. In his own dominions, the Spanish king took an even more ruthless and uncompromising stand against heresy than some church theologians felt was necessary. Toward other powers, however, he followed a more prudent line, ignoring all pressures from the papacy to pursue a hostile policy toward Elizabeth of England so long as Elizabeth avoided an outright declaration of Protestantism.

For nearly fifteen years the center of attention for Felipe was not western Europe but the Turkish menace in the Mediterranean, which had been a major factor in his desire for peace with France. During the 1550s the Mediterranean had become almost a Muslim lake. The first offensive expedition of Felipe's reign, against Tripoli in 1560, was badly led and ended in disaster with the loss of twenty galleys and more than six thousand men. It prompted a major naval construction campaign in Spain and Italy during the next four years, however, and Spanish forces conquered the Peñón de Vélez on the north Moroccan coast in 1564, then defeated a major Turkish attempt to seize Malta in the central Mediterranean the following year.

Felipe II had to face a series of new challenges between 1566 and 1568, starting with the Protestant revolt in the Low Countries in 1566. Though this was completely crushed in less than a year, Felipe decided in 1567 that he could no longer trust the affairs of that area to semi-autonomous local administration supervised by a viceroy, as in his father's reign. In 1567, he dispatched an Hispano-Italian army of occupation under his leading military commander, the duke of Alba. This marked a turning away from the ecumenical, federal policy of his father toward a more centralized and authoritarian Spanish Counter-Reformation policy. The decision to adopt an intransigent line against heresy in the Low Countries, involving the execution even of recanters, was primarily that of the king himself. His theological advisers did not themselves agree on such draconian measures. During the next six years, the "Council of Troubles" (also called the Council of Blood) in Brussels executed more than one thousand rebels and heretics, exceeding the peninsular Inquisition in its harshness.

The great crisis year of Felipe's reign was 1568. Muslims were still a major threat in the Mediterranean, where Spanish forces had not yet made good the losses of the 1540s and 1550s. The English and rebel Dutch navies in the North Atlantic were an incipient menace to the sea route to Flanders and communications with the Indies. Then there occurred simultaneously the beginning of French Huguenot military activity on the Catalan border and the momentary fear of rebellion and heresy in Catalonia (see chapter 9), a royal domestic tragedy resulting from the attempted flight and death of Felipe's apparently schizophrenic heir, D. Carlos, and, most perilous of all, the great Morisco rebellion in the Alpujarra mountains around Granada, involving nearly all the Muslims of southeastern Castile. The royal forces were unprepared—most of the trained units had been dispatched to the Low Countries—and the bloody struggle went on for nearly two years. What made the situation particularly dangerous was the Morisco appeal to Turkey and the threat of Turkish intervention which, however, never materialized. The Morisco revolt was finally crushed (see chapter 14).

As soon as this grave question of internal security was solved, the crown had to face a renewed Turkish threat in the Mediterranean. In 1570, the Turks launched a major expedition of conquest against the Venetian-held island of Cyprus. The papacy helped organize a Holy League bringing together the navies of the Spanish crown, Genoa, and Venice. Cyprus fell in 1571, but a few months later the Christian forces engaged the main Turkish fleet at the great battle of Lepanto in the Gulf of Corinth, the largest engagement in the history of naval warfare to that time. Thanks to superior naval technology, strong leadership, and tenacious combat, the Christian armada, under Carlos V's bastard D. Juan de Austria, won a smashing victory. More than one-third of the Turkish fleet was destroyed, with great loss of life, and the triumph inspired Christian confidence throughout the Mediterranean. Though the Christian forces did not follow up their triumph with any lasting conquests, the Turks were stopped. The Ottoman regime became increasingly preoccupied with affairs on its eastern border and drew away from Europe. A truce was signed with the Spanish crown in 1578 and renewed periodically for the rest of the century.

Yet achieving this balance in the Mediterranean did not completely restore the initiative to the crown, for the revolt in the Netherlands grew broader and more costly. In 1572, the Dutch "Sea Beggars" seized the port of Brill, giving them a permanent naval base in the

Low Countries. The Spanish forces were threatened by French invasion from the south, as well, an initiative that was choked off by the great massacre of French Protestant leaders by their Catholic rivals in Paris on St. Bartholomew's Day in August 1572. This French slaughter killed about as many people within twenty-four hours as did the Spanish Inquisition in three hundred years. Though Spain had no hand in the mass murder, it greatly benefitted the Spanish position by eliminating French support for the Flemish and Dutch rebels. The duke of Alba began a major counteroffensive in Flanders in 1572-1573, marked by some of the worst planned atrocities of sixteenth-century west European wars. By official policy whole populations of towns were slaughtered, and thousands of civilians perished. The growing savagery and ruthlessness of the reign of Felipe II reflected the intransigent religious position of the Spanish leaders and contrasted sharply with the temperate military policies of an earlier period in Spanish history. Yet it should be kept in mind that the Spanish outrages were no greater than those committed in certain other parts of continental Europe.

The duke of Alba's terror was also counterproductive, for it probably did even more than foreign political control and increased taxation to solidify opinion in the Low Countries, of both Catholic and Protestant, against Spanish rule. In 1573, the soldier Alba was replaced by the diplomat Luis de Requesens as viceroy in Brussels, but by that time the revolt was out of hand. Spanish resources were no longer sufficient to meet gigantic and prolonged military strains, and the result was a declaration of bankruptcy in 1575. Lack of pay eventually led to a mutiny by the main Spanish force at Antwerp—the so-called Spanish fury (though most of the troops were non-Spanish mercenaries) in which the city was sacked and at least seven thousand people slaughtered. Don Juan of Austria, the hero of Lepanto, who had been sent as the new viceroy, was forced to agree to withdraw the Spanish tercios. A decade after it began, the revolt in the Low Countries was settling into a draw, with little prospect of Spanish victory.

The king's outlook was made gloomier by the discovery that his chief personal secretary, Antonio Pérez, had been playing a double game in his relation to the crown and high officials and had maintained secret contacts with the rebels. Pérez was removed and arrested in 1579, and the elderly Cardinal Granvelle, who had served Felipe II at the beginning of his reign, was installed as imperial chancellor.

The years 1573-1579 were relatively static because of the crown's multiple burdens, financial shortages, and erratic policy in the Low Countries, but new opportunities presented themselves in 1580. Incorporation of the Portuguese monarchy increased the naval resources of the empire,* and by that time the flow of bullion from Spanish America had begun to increase markedly. By 1582, the Spanish forces in the Low Countries had been expanded once more to nearly sixty thousand, including the return of the tercios,† and Alessandro Farnese, viceroy since 1578, was able to launch a general offensive. Farnese was undoubtedly the most able lieutenant to serve the Spanish crown during the later sixteenth century, combining outstanding qualities of military and diplomatic leadership. From about 1579 he was assisted by a growing reaction among the Catholic aristocracy of Flanders and Brabant against radical urban middle- and lower-class Calvinists. Spanish strength had always been centered in the southern Low Countries, and after a social and ideological split developed in the rebel camp, Farnese was able to solidify much of the population of Flanders and Brabant behind the restoration of a Catholic regime which, though part of the Spanish empire, would be respectful of local rights. By 1585, he had conquered Antwerp. The entire southern half of the Low Countries—the predecessor of modern Belgium—lay under Spanish control and was being restored to Catholicism.

This threatened to return full Spanish domination to the Low Countries, which in turn would menace the political and religious independence of England. Elizabeth and her advisors could not afford to see the Dutch cause go under completely, while to the Spanish crown England stood as its principal maritime rival, after Holland, and the only encouragement for continued Dutch resistance. Hence the key to complete victory in the Low Countries and secure hegemony for the empire in western Europe seemed to be the subjection of England. The execution of Mary Queen of Scots by the English crown in 1587 finally removed the danger of a French succession to the English throne if Elizabeth were overthrown and thus left Felipe II free to act.

The Armada of 1588 was a much more complex enterprise than the expedition to Lepanto seventeen years earlier had been. It was the most massive high seas fleet that Europe had ever seen, but it was also part of an amphibious operation that planned to ferry much of the Spanish forces in the Low Countries to a land invasion of England. There were some one hundred thirty ships in the Armada. The English mustered a larger fleet, though their tonnage was considerably smaller. Spanish naval strategy relied on heavy short-range artillery to

* According to the best available estimate, after 1581 the combined Spanish and Portuguese fleets totaled 250,000-300,000 tons, that of Holland about 230,000, those of the German states 110,000, France 80,000, and England 42,000.

† Of the Spanish forces in the Low Countries after 1577, only 10 to 20 percent were actually soldiers from Spain itself.

close with the enemy vessels, wreck their rigging, and hold them still in the water to be boarded. The English relied on long-range artillery. Their ships were sufficiently maneuverable to frustrate Spanish strategy, but their long-range artillery was too weak to do great damage. The worst Spanish problem was lack of a deep-water port in which to pick up Farnese's troops, making the junction of forces almost impossible. After English fireships forced the Armada from Calais harbor in disarray, heavy winds cut it off from contact with Farnese. A storm blew the remnants of the Armada all the way around the British Isles. Only one-third of the vessels were completely wrecked, and most of these were merchantmen, but damage was heavy and there was great loss of life among skilled Spanish seamen.

Perhaps the greatest effect of the Armada was its psychological impact on the Spanish people. The struggles and triumphs of the century had built up a complex of Counter-Reformation messianism and imperialism among many Spaniards. The empire was associated with a sense of divine mission, and the Armada had been preached from many village pulpits. Its defeat for the first time began to raise doubts as to whether God would bless further imperial enterprise, whether the great physical burdens of taxation and military recruitment were really worthwhile for Castile.

Yet the losses of the Armada were made good within a year or two. Taxes could still be raised and bullion imports from America remained high. The Spanish fleet was still the strongest in the Atlantic, and in some respects Felipe II stood at the height of his power in 1590-1592. The crown was determined to combat the conquest of the French throne by the Protestant Henri IV, and in this connection Felipe II pressed the claim of his daughter, Isabel Clara Eugenia, whose mother had been a French princess. During 1590-1591, the Spanish invaded France from the northeast, northwest, and southwest. The Spanish crown also pressed the Austrian Habsburgs to pursue a more militant Counter-Reformation policy, provided Vienna with a subsidy in the struggle against the Turks, and even contemplated sending a Spanish force to campaign in the Balkans.

The new struggle in France distracted Spanish strength from the Low Countries, however, where the Dutch won important victories. It also encouraged a Franco-English-Dutch alliance against Spain in 1596. The English naval raid of that year against Cádiz was a smashing success. Two new Spanish efforts to send major expeditions to Ireland were blown back by storms in 1596 and 1597. In 1595, the crown was forced to declare bankruptcy for the third time in less than four decades. By the last year of his life, Felipe II was a chastened and disillusioned ruler who realized that dominance of western Europe and the repression of heresy abroad had escaped him. His last major act was to conclude peace with France before dying in 1598 at the age of 71.

The wisdom and prudence of Felipe II are open to doubt. He was stubborn and persevering in strategy, but his tactics were sometimes erratic. He occasionally followed long periods of caution by overreaching himself in grandiose enterprises, such as the Armada, which had the odds against it from the start. His drastic policy in the Low Countries proved partially counterproductive.

There is no questioning his devotion to duty and his sense of personal responsibility; he was the hardest working ruler of his time. Though he distinguished between Spanish political and Catholic religious interests in general European affairs (at one point in 1584 he was willing to subsidize French Protestantism to weaken the French crown), his religious ardor was genuine and complete, and he did far more than reason of state required to combat heresy. Thus the supreme moment of his reign was indeed 1588, when imperial interest and religious zeal were ideally combined in the great Armada. It is possible that he made his reign unnecessarily difficult by taking so much responsibility upon himself. At any rate, he had a great distrust of strong personalities and powerful advisers, and was even preparing to replace the brilliant Farnese at the moment of the latter's death in 1592.

With the passing of Felipe II, the Spanish politico-military hegemony did not by any means come to an end but would last half a century more. The Spanish sense of providential mission, however, of being the sword arm of Catholic Christendom, of expanding a divinely guided empire, was indeed beginning to wane. Multiple strains—economic, spiritual and psychological—compounded by the frustrations of the unrewarding final decade of 1588–1598, were leaving their effect.

Imperial Affairs under Felipe III (1598–1621)

Felipe III was a prince of pleasant, negative personality, with few vices and few virtues. He lacked the industry and driving sense of responsibility of his father and from the beginning left government to a personal favorite, the duke of Lerma. This set the style of Spanish government for most of the seventeenth century. Lerma had no long-range policy, but dealt with the vast problems confronting the empire on the basis of makeshift and procrastination.

There was clear reluctance to continue the aggressive policies of Felipe II. Peace had already been made with France (1598); it was followed by peace with England in 1604 and after another state bankruptcy in 1607 by a ten-year truce with Holland in 1609. The struggle to recover all of the Low Countries had turned into a hopeless drain of men and money. By the beginning of the seventeenth century, the seven northern provinces that made up rebel Holland were on their way to becoming economically and technologically the most dynamic part of western Europe, combining the maritime enterprise and daring of the Portuguese of an earlier period with the economic acumen of the Germans and north Italians. Holland presented an increasing contrast to Spain itself, which had developed an almost closed society during the sixteenth century and under the burden of war, taxes, and its own social values was no longer able to expand economically. Holland was becoming the freest, most open country in Europe, and for the next two generations the most socially and economically creative. The truce of 1609 recognized the apparent inability of Spain to reconquer it.

For most of the reign of Felipe III, the Spanish fleet remained the strongest in the western world, but its margin of superiority was dwindling. Sources of naval supplies in the peninsula were being exhausted and much had to be imported from the north. Spanish wages rose more rapidly than general prices in the early part of the seventeenth century, and costs of naval construction, outfitting, and maintenance were much higher—possibly two or three times higher— than in Holland, England, or even France. Moreover, the half century 1570-1620 was the heyday of west European piracy, and Spanish shipping was the main target. When the conflict with Holland began once more after expiration of the ten-year truce in 1619, the Dutch inflicted a crushing defeat upon the Spanish fleet and made it clear that the naval hegemony had passed from Spain.

The reign of Felipe III was a static period in most aspects of imperial affairs, but the loss of naval leadership was grave, for control of communications was vital to the integrity of the empire. Thus the apprehension and disillusion noticeable in the last years of the reign of Felipe II slowly increased during the period of his successor.

The Black Legend

The era of Spanish domination almost inevitably brought the enmity of most of western Europe against the Spanish crown and its subjects. This hostility was tinged with deference, as witnessed by the vogue of dark-hued Spanish clothing and the domination of Castilian literature and of Castilian as a literary language in western Europe. But among the chief foes of Spain and its royal policies there took shape a vague but sweeping denunciation, not merely of Spanish power but of almost all things Spanish. The conceptualization of this enmity defined as uniquely Spanish the vices of overweening pride, violence, intolerance, ethnocentrism, and obscurantism. By the beginning of the seventeenth century it was taking the form in which it would subsequently be known to Spaniards as the Black Legend.

The earliest roots of Black Legend theorizing lay in the anti-Aragonese feeling generated in the Italian peninsula during the fourteenth and fifteenth centuries. Denunciations of Aragonese expansion in the late Middle Ages were sometimes coupled with racial sneers referring to race-mixing in the Hispanic peninsula. By contrast, Italians preferred to consider themselves comparatively "pure" descendants of ancient Romans. In the 1490s, the Aragonese pope Alexander VI was called a *marrano* (Spanish Jew) by Italian enemies. Anti-Aragonese sentiment in Italy changed to general anti-Spanish and anti-Castilian feeling during the sixteenth century. By the middle of that century, with the tension between Carlos V and German Protestants and the first major Spanish campaigns in central Europe, German sources also began to launch general denunciations of things Spanish. Even more influential in building the image of brutal, violent, intolerant Spaniards were the long war with Holland and the struggle with Elizabethan England. The most important objective factor was the Spanish atrocities, particularly during the bloody epoch of the duke of Alba in the Low Countries, for this went beyond anything experienced in northwestern Europe in the sixteenth century. The French seem to have contributed rather less to the early formulation of the Black Legend, possibly because they usually equalled or surpassed the Spanish in their own atrocities, as in the case of the St. Bartholomew's Day massacre.

Paradoxically, the most important single document in establishing the Black Legend was written by a Spanish monk, Bartolomé de las Casas, in his effort to defend American Indians from the further depredations of Spanish colonists. His account of the destruction of the Indians of the West Indies, first published in 1552, was written in lurid, occasionally exaggerated tones, and later republished in foreign editions by Spain's detractors.* It should be kept in mind, however,

---

* The forged title page of the 1689 London edition of Las Casas' *Very Brief Recital of the Destruction of the Indies,* published as anti-Spanish propaganda, read, "Popery truly Displayed in its Bloody Colours: Or a Faithful Narrative of the Horrid and Unexampled Massacres, Butcheries, and all manner of Cruelties, that Hell and Malice could invent, committed by the Popish Spanish Party on the Inhabitants of West-India ... Composed first in Spanish by Bartholomew de las Casas, a Bishop there, and an Eye-Witness of most of these Barbarous Cruelties; afterwards translated by him into Latin, then by other hands into High-Dutch, Low-Dutch, French, and now Taught to speak modern English."

that Las Casas' campaign on behalf of the American Indians had been possible precisely because moral and political protest, as distinct from heterodox religious protest, had always been possible in Spain. For example, the Spanish crown of the Counter-Reformation period never committed an arbitrary act in domestic politics equivalent to the execution of Sir Walter Raleigh by the English crown.

The first full-blown statement of the Black Legend was the *Apology* of the Dutch leader William the Silent, prepared in 1580 and circulated throughout western Europe. It emphasized the fanaticism and cruelty of Spaniards, the horrors of the Inquisition, the suppression of Moriscos, destruction of "twenty million" Indians, the supposed tyranny of Spanish political institutions, and varied imagined iniquities of the personal life and reign of Felipe II. Some of this was invented and most of it was greatly exaggerated, yet it contained a certain kernel of truth, particularly for Dutchmen and Englishmen trying to preserve local freedoms, religious choice, and a more open society than that of militant, Counter-Reformation Castile.

14

Spanish Society and Economics
in the Imperial Age

The most notable quality of Spanish, especially Castilian, society in the early sixteenth century was its energy and self-confidence, which brought with it an expansive sense of power and new possibilities. The imperial age was not merely a period of outward movement; it was also one of steady population growth and of some economic development. The population of the lands of the united monarchy amounted to about 7,000,000 in 1500, increased to approximately 7,500,000 by 1540, and to around 8,500,000 in the 1590s, a level which was not surpassed for two hundred years. The peak of Spanish imperial power thus coincided with the greatest population density the peninsula had ever seen, without which the sixteenth-century empire might not have been possible. However, imperial responsibilities did not at first wear heavily on that population strength. Emigration to the Indies probably averaged no more than 2,000 people a year. The European wars were fought almost entirely outside Spanish soil, and the proportion of European mercenaries in the 50,000 to 70,000 troops maintained by the crown increased steadily, especially in the closing decades of the century.

Even so, most areas of the peninsula continued to be sparsely populated compared with the rest of western Europe. The demographic strength of Spain compared with potential rivals may be assessed from population estimates of 1600:

Spain and Portugal	9-9.5 million
The Germanies	20
France	16
Italy	13
Low Countries	3
England	4.5
Ottoman Empire	18-30

Only in the steppes of eastern Europe, outside the main orbit of European population, was density lower than in Spain. The population center of the peninsula throughout this period was Castile, with roughly four-fifths of all the people of the united monarchy. It was the size and vigor of Castilian society, its militant ethos, and its powerful system of monarchy on which the imperial system was based.

The social composition of the Spanish population at the beginning of the sixteenth century has been roughly estimated by Professor Santiago Sobrequés as shown in table 4. Compared with the social structure of the most productive areas of western Europe, that of Spain stands out for the higher proportion of peasants and the lower proportion of urban middle-class and artisan elements. The figures for the aristocracy do not include the tens of thousands of ordinary people in northern Castile able to claim petty hidalgo status and tax exemption from the sixteenth century onward because of local fueros.

Though the proportion of genuine aristocrats was not especially high compared with most of western Europe, the aristocracy in Spain, particularly in Castile, was conspicuous for its relative wealth and social prestige. The nobility dominated society in most parts of Europe during the sixteenth century, and in many areas it was their influence, not that of the middle classes, which increased during this period, but in no region was this so true as in Spain. Approximately half of the land in the peninsula was dominated by them, and most of the money spent ostentatiously flowed from grandes, not from capitalist or precapitalist elements. Economic developments of the sixteenth century accentuated, rather than diminished, the weight of these landholders in the society and economy.

Yet their dominance was not merely a matter of wealth. It derived above all from the acceptance of aristocratic norms and values by a large proportion of the population, a larger proportion than in any other west European country. As has been seen earlier, in Castile the common sense of identity had traditionally been predicated on a kind of caste superiority, in which a society of Christian warriors dominated the infidels. The military leader was or became an aristocrat ipso facto, and the lower classes often had access to that rank through military achievement. The other defining quality of the Christian

Table 4. *Social Composition of the Spanish Population at the Beginning of the Sixteenth Century*

Number	Class	Percentage of Population
	Aristocracy	
5,000	*Magnates* and ecclesiastical hierarchy	.07
50,000	Ordinary military or rural nobility	.72
60,000	Urban aristocracy (including many landowners)	.85
115,000		1.64
	Middle Classes	
70,000	Religious	1.00
160,000	Urban middle classes	2.30
25,000	Landowning peasants	.35
255,000		3.65
	Lower Classes	
850,000	Artisans and laborers, including at least 50,000 Muslims in Aragón and 100,000 Muslims in Castile	12.15
5,780,000	Peasants, including 200,000 Muslims in Aragón and 400,000 in Castile	82.50*
6,630,000		94.65

Source: Santiago Sobrequés, *Historia social y económica de España y América* (Barcelona, 1957), pp. 417-18.

* Slavery was somewhat less important in sixteenth-century Castile than in Portugal. The number of slaves, both black and Mediterranean Muslim, rose to an all-time high of about 100,000, or 1.2 percent of the population, around 1600. Half of them were concentrated in Andalusia, near the sources of supply. Other centers of slave population were the Levant, Galicia, and the central axis of Madrid-Valladolid.

warrior, beyond martial prowess, was his sense of honor, which distinguished him from the truly vulgar. In the expansion of Castilian arms through western Europe in the sixteenth century, people in other lands were frequently surprised by the gravity and exaggerated stress on status and honor demonstrated by even the common soldiers among the Spanish forces. In Castile, the lower classes too had imbibed aristocratic values.

Status, honor, and the dividends of fighting and conquest were prized, but mundane constructive labor was given a much lower priority. The idea of a major stratum of society in which people would be identified and judged by what they achieved through work was not taking hold to the extent that it was in some places elsewhere.

There did exist in Castile commercial-minded middle class elements, but they were proportionately fewer, less wealthy, and less influential. It is also true that in France and Italy, middle class people tended to use wealth as a means of lifting themselves to bureaucratic or neo-aristocratic status, by buying of land, offices, or titles, particularly during the seventeenth century. Only in England, Holland, and a few of the German and Italian towns was there any genuine bourgeois identification before late in the eighteenth century. The weakness of the Castilian middle classes was perhaps not so different in kind as in degree. But that degree of ambition and influence was decidedly less in Spain, and actually diminished during the sixteenth century, even though the size of the middle class did not. For ambitious elements in the lower classes, the empire and the military provided special opportunities for adventure, wealth, conquest, and ennoblement that were not easily found in other parts of western Europe.

The existing property structure of Castile was ratified by the Catholic Kings early in their reign. Their rulings of 1480-1481 and subsequent years were of extreme importance, because of the great changes of property that had occurred during the late-fourteenth and fifteenth centuries, with the broad extension of seigneurial domain and usurpation of town and crown lands. As explained in chapter 9, the united monarchy followed a dual policy toward the aristocracy: while reducing it to political obedience on the one hand, the crown fully ratified its social and economic predominance on the other. The aristocracy was required to return only half of the lands stolen from the royal domain during the reign of Enrique IV. Alienations before 1454 were thus officially confirmed. Moreover, after the conquest of Granada, all except the western part of the emirate was given to nobles in señorío, partly in compensation for the restitutions required earlier. The Cortes of 1504 specifically guaranteed the security of entailment (mayorazgos), providing permanent juridical protection for aristocratic domains. Such estates were further expanded in the early sixteenth century as a result of a new agrarian crisis occasioned by bad harvests, when a portion of the very small amount of land owned outright by peasants passed to the nobility.

Thus, by the beginning of the sixteenth century, there was established the system of seigneurial domain which would form the base of the Spanish social and juridical structure for the next three hundred years, down to the liberal reforms of the nineteenth century. Over half the land was held in señoríos, which grew even larger during the course of the century as some of the property of the crusading orders was sold to the nobility. The character of seigneurial domain remained heterogeneous in the extreme. There were basically three different kinds: territorial or *solariego*, based on the right to receive annual rents or dues from peasant tenants; jurisdictional, which held grants from the crown to administer justice and serve as local government; and vassalic, differing from the simple territorial in that peasant obligations took the form of personal services and special dues rather than annual rents. Many seigneuries, however, combined at least two of these privileges. Furthermore, in almost all, the local domains were either exempt from taxation or paid taxes through their own channels, at a lower rate, without the intervention of royal tax collectors. Most señoríos also brought the right of the *patronato particular*, or local church patronage.

The upper nobility was officially categorized by the government of Carlos V in 1520, when twenty-five houses of the highest rank of Castilian and Aragonese aristocracy were designated Grandes de España, with lesser noble families placed on a scale graduated downward. Though the grandes contributed little to economic expansion, those of Castile prospered mightily during the sixteenth century. The large landholders were the only social class thoroughly ensured against the effects of the sixteenth-century inflation, and as the population increased, land became all the more valuable. Landholders welcomed the elimination of the last vestiges of serfdom, for that freed them from certain obligations to the poorer peasants. Traditional relations were more and more transformed into simple rentals, which could be raised to meet increased demand or prices. Castilian aristocrats became immensely wealthy in an agrarian economy, proportionately more wealthy than any others in western Europe.

The dominance of the aristocracy, especially that of Castile, was not only social and economic. Increasingly, as the century wore on, most of the important positions in imperial administration were given to Castilian aristocrats and their sons, as were the principal posts in the army and all the best benefices in the church. By the end of the century, opportunities for social advancement for the middle and lower classes had become extremely limited, and the formerly open society which had identified with the aristocracy had become a largely closed society dominated by a nonproductive aristocratic caste.

The church controlled close to 20 percent of the land in the peninsula, including an even higher proportion in certain fertile areas. Church lands were also protected by their own form of entailment— the *mano muerta*. In northern Europe, church properties were thrown back on the market by the confiscations of the Reformation. Nothing of this sort occurred in Spain, where two-thirds of the land was dominated by church and aristocracy.

During the early sixteenth century there apparently arose, temporarily, a rural middle class—peasants renting large tracts of land and urban landowners or petty nobles of hidalgo status—who produced directly for the market and enjoyed considerable prosperity for a generation or two. This small minority of wealthier peasants and intermediate elements were able to take advantage of the same growing and inflated market exploited by the aristocrats who were raising rents and lowering shares for peasant clients.

The vestiges of serfdom that restricted freedom of movement for a small minority of the peasantry in Castile were struck down by the Cortes of 1481. After that date, and for the most part before it, the peasants of Castile were juridically as free if not freer than the peasantry of any other kingdom of Europe. Yet juridical freedom did not bring prosperity. Little more than 1 percent of the Castilian peasants actually owned their land or had any prospect of acquiring capital. In Old Castile and León, much of the peasantry did enjoy stable emphyteutical rental relations, but the increase in population, spread of aristocratic domain, relative sterility of soil, and backwardness of technique placed increasingly greater pressure on Castilian agriculture as the century advanced. The underlying malaise was revealed by the bad harvests and agrarian crisis of the years 1502–1509. In the kingdom of Aragón the situation was of course worse, for the legal status of the Aragonese peasantry actually declined during the reign of Fernando. In parts of Andalusia, there was a conversion to latifundist farming, with an ever-increasing class of hired laborers.

The saving grace for much of the peasantry was the peculiar psychology of Spanish society. Being free, and nominal members of the dominant Catholic warrior society of the peninsula, even poor peasants had a sense of honor and status, of identity and worth. During the first half of the sixteenth century they also had the opportunity for social advancement in the empire. Hence the Castilian lower classes were not psychologically downtrodden, and certainly not humble.

By the sixteenth century, Spain was divided, roughly, into four economic regions: the north, centered in Old Castile, León, and the Cantabrian ports, its chief towns being Valladolid, Burgos, and Bilbao, drawing some trade from the central plateau; the southwest, centered in the Atlantic and the Indies route, through the ports of Seville, Cádiz, and Málaga, and also drawing on the central plateau; the Castilian southeast, whence wool and other goods from Toledo and Cuenca moved to Italy through Murcia and through Aragonese Alicante; and finally, the Aragonese Mediterranean east, led by Valencia more than by Barcelona.

The Catholic Kings encouraged the corporatization of the urban economy of Castile, and merchant consulates were formed on the Catalan pattern in Burgos, Bilbao, and later Seville. Throughout the

Middle Ages, Castilian towns had resisted the formation of guilds, their lower level of production requiring less organization, but the Catholic Kings favored guilds in order to regulate the urban population more precisely. The Castilian towns of the sixteenth century thus developed an archaic guild system at the very time that such a pattern was beginning to die out and be replaced by more open and flexible relations in the most economically progressive regions of Europe.

Though it is an exaggeration to call royal economic policy in Spain truly mercantilist at any time before the eighteenth century, the commercial and monetary policies of the Catholic Kings were in some respects premercantilist. The monarchy tried by regulation to achieve a balanced (though not necessarily favorable) ratio of foreign trade, decreed navigation laws to foster Spanish shipping, instituted minor measures to protect domestic manufactures, and established strict control over precious metals from America, including a royal monopoly of the disposition of gold and silver, forbidding their export without prior approval. Though agriculture was ignored, a strong effort was thus made to advance commerce and protect the monetary resources of the united monarchy.

There was a definite increase in Spanish commerce during the reign of the Catholic Kings, thanks in part to their encouragement through protective maritime legislation and the fostering of wool exports. At first, northern Castile benefited as much or more than the south; the Flanders wool trade probably reached its height between 1480 and 1500, before increased competition from England and diversion of part of Castilian production to other markets. The late-fifteenth and sixteenth centuries were a time of undeniable prosperity for the Castilian mercantile class, and thus the exodus of the Jews was felt not quite so much as it would otherwise have been. In wealth, skill, or extent of their operations, the merchants of northern Spain or Seville were not equal to those of Italy, Germany, or Flanders, but at the end of the fifteenth century the scope of their activity exceeded those of France, England, and Scandinavia, or for that matter, Catalonia. Castilian had become the commercial lingua franca of the Bay of Biscay. There is evidence that it was Castilian merchants who first taught the drawing up of bills of exchange to their counterparts in western France, and double-entry bookkeeping to the English. Yet they did not have an expanding middle-class, prosperous peasantry, or rising domestic production behind them. They were dependent largely on raw material exports and luxury imports. Once the Flemish and French markets were reduced by war and the main trade swung to the Indies, the merchants of northern Castile fell into irreversible decline, in the second half of the sixteenth century, under the pressure of heavy taxes and reduced volume of trade.

The most important overseas commerce for Spain in the sixteenth century was with America. This was also the only commerce which attracted investment from the aristocracy (save for certain activities in Catalonia and the Basque country). American trade was first set up on a regular basis with the establishment of the Casa de Contratación (Board of Trade) in Cádiz in 1503, modeled on the Portuguese Casa da India. It attempted rigid control of trade with America, but terms were liberalized in 1510, and after 1529 nine ports on both the northern and southern coasts were permitted to trade with the Spanish Indies. Expansion of trade after about 1505 provided a new outlet for Spanish manufactures and stimulated market agriculture in the south, particularly in the Guadalquivir valley. Spanish towns, however, were not manufacturing enough to satisfy the needs of an expanding colonial society, and colonial production itself had to be stimulated. Readjustment of the colonial economy at mid-century toward production in the colonies, along with a temporary decline in purchasing power for imports, brought a serious slump to the Spanish American trade between 1550 and 1562, a recession made all the worse by effects of the war with the French in the Atlantic and the Muslims in the Mediterranean.

A marked upswing in the American trade began in 1562 and continued almost without interruption until the end of the century. The major commodity was silver. Large-scale production in Mexico and Peru was finally made possible in the 1560s by the development of a process of extracting silver from ore with the use of mercury. Hispanic silver production reached its height in the 1580s and remained at a fairly high level until about 1630. Royal shares of bullion production were indispensable to financing the ambitious enterprises of the last two decades of the reign of Felipe II and to sustaining a tenuous Spanish military hegemony during the more difficult reign of Felipe III. Registered Spanish bullion imports for the period 1531–1660 were divided as follows:

1531–1580	2,628,000 kilos
1581–1630	11,461,000
1631–1660	2,896,000
	16,985,000 kilos

From the 1560s on, the trade of the southern coast, and especially Seville, increased greatly. Though native Spanish merchants handled a significant part of the trade, the most important mercantile group was the Genoese merchants and financiers who lived in Seville. They provided capital, know-how, and initiative for large-scale commercial and financial transactions, and increasingly during the reign of Felipe II served as the bankers of the Spanish crown. They, in turn, received all manner of special grants, concessions, and monopolies, so that the commerce and finance of Seville could almost be called Hispano-Genoese. Genoese economic interests were important in establishing an absolute monopoly for Spanish manufactures in the markets of the Indies (1569), to the detriment of colonial and foreign products. They were also influential in giving the port of Seville a complete monopoly over the peninsula's colonial trade, as decreed by the crown in 1573.

The Catalan Economy during the Imperial Age

The economy of Catalonia remained a regional economy under the united monarchy, but it did enjoy a modest restoration of prosperity from the time of the reforms of Fernando II in the 1480s. The *redreç* of 1481 restored confiscated property and straightened out most of the tangled property disputes of the fifteenth century, and it was followed by the settlement of the agrarian problem in 1483. Catalan textile producers were subsequently given a market monopoly in the Mediterranean possessions of the Hispanic crown, so that Sicily became for the Catalan economy of the sixteenth century what Cuba later was for that of the nineteenth. A restrictive tariff against competitive imports was restored to the principality, the plague of piracy was controlled (at least during the late fifteenth and early sixteenth centuries), and by 1495, Catalan merchants were able to reopen their consulate in Alexandria. The early sixteenth century was a time of modest but general commercial expansion for Catalonia, as trade grew with both North Africa and northern Europe. After about 1516, however, Portuguese competition had a depressant effect on Catalan commerce in the Mediterranean, and the Spanish treaty with Genoa in 1528, opening Habsburg Italy to Genoese goods, was a severe blow to Catalan exports. In addition, as warfare spread with Muslim powers in the Mediterranean, the Catalans relinquished most of their trade with North Africa for fear of falling under papal interdict.

Most frustrating of all was Catalonia's exclusion from direct participation in the rich Indies trade, an exclusion which had a severe retardative effect for two centuries. There were four reasons for the barring of the Aragonese principalities from American commerce: a) the legal jurisdiction under which the American empire had been carved out as the patrimony of the Castilian crown; b) the concern of the crown to preserve the major commercial opportunities for the Castilian economy, which was paying most of the taxes; c) monopolistic pressures from the merchants of Seville, especially from the Genoese group; and d) the lack of aggressiveness of the Catalans themselves, who during the sixteenth century never recovered the vigor and dynamism of an earlier period. Catalan merchants made minor efforts to win a place for themselves in the American trade, but these were excluded by statute, especially after 1573. Thus throughout the Habsburg period the lands of the united monarchy for the most part retained their traditional regional economies. Catalan exports òverland to Castile, for example, had to pay three separate excise or transit taxes (Catalan, Aragonese, and Castilian).

The only measure of economic integration carried out by the Catholic Kings, and preserved by their successors, was the purely monetary reform of standardizing coinage values in their peninsular realms. Catalonia did, however, benefit from one aspect of the American trade, when after 1578 shipments of American precious metals were switched eastward to the Mediterranean route, stimulating Catalan commerce with Italy. And it should be noted that after 1581 most offices in the empire were theoretically open to all the crown's peninsular subjects (including the Portuguese).

Catalan agriculture did not prosper to any great extent during the sixteenth century, because of poor climatic conditions and lack of specialization, markets, and technical improvement. The social malaise of much of the peasantry, however, had been cured by the reforms of Fernando. A Corts decision of 1511 prohibiting the passage of flocks through cultivated districts of Catalonia was another positive step: it defended agriculture from the sort of ravages inflicted by the Mesta in Castile. The attractiveness of the Catalan countryside compared with that of Castile or of southwest France is demonstrated by the fact that it was the only Iberian region to which immigrants came in any numbers during this period. By 1600, 20 percent of Catalan peasants were from poor, overpopulated Gascony and Languedoc.

The most disaffected class in Catalonia was the rural aristocracy, whose economic status had declined as a result of fifteenth-century social and political conflict. Though 71 percent of Catalonia was still *terra de barons,* emoluments from land were no longer enough to maintain the status of many nobles. Of approximately two hundred major aristocratic families in early fifteenth-century Catalonia, only ten or twelve retained the same high position in 1500. On the other hand, the petty aristocracy, or rural gentry, were proportionately more numerous in Catalonia than in almost any other part of the peninsula. Their resources were steadily reduced by social change, and they lacked the opportunities for employment in empire and army open to the aristocracy of Castile.

Impoverished and feeling a loss of prestige, many turned to brigandage and robber baronry in the more thinly settled mountain areas. Catalan *bandolerisme* terrorized the countryside during the second half of the sixteenth and the early seventeenth century. It was very much like the brigandage in Calabria and the Balkans in the same period, which was also linked to economic stagnation. It was encouraged by the proximity of French Huguenots, who were on the border and sometimes crossed over to rob Catalan churches. The proportion of clergy in the general population—6 percent—was higher in Catalonia than in any other part of Spain, and church properties made attractive targets for the thieving and resentful. In some cases, Catalan robber barons won over the poorer peasants to assist them, and they became especially active when, after 1578, much of the American silver was shifted for eastward passage across Catalonia to Italy. This endemic plague did not abate until the passing of the old Catalan politico-social system after the middle of the seventeenth century.

During the sixteenth century the center of finance in the east remained the city of Valencia, which expanded its commerce and could draw on a prosperous hinterland of Morisco cultivation. Under the Catholic Kings, Valencia served as the banking center of the peninsula, until the weight eventually shifted to Seville. It might also be noted that the principality of Áragon had benefitted from the decline of Catalonia in the fifteenth century, and by the early sixteenth century Zaragoza was enjoying a modest new prosperity as a commercial and textile center.

Expansion and Decline of Sixteenth-Century Agriculture

The growth in Spanish population and the demand for food exports to the Indies before 1550, and to some extent after 1562, brought increasing amounts of land under cultivation. The aristocracy in some areas let out more and more land from its señoríos for farming, and tended to convert shares and feudal dues and services to straight land-rental agreements. Moreover, land had become the principal object of investment in the kingdom, even for fluid capital from urban sources: there were limitations on domestic manufactures, overseas commerce was uncertain, and most moneyed elements in Castile were oriented against risk and toward status. *Censos al quitar*—short-term farm loans—which sometimes bore as much as 50 percent interest, became one of the two major avenues of investment in Castile, rivaled only by state bonds. In 1618, it was estimated that there were more than one hundred million ducats invested in such short-term loans.

Yet it is erroneous ever to think in terms of general prosperity for sixteenth-century Castilian agriculture. The landholding aristocracy

was prosperous, and peasant agriculture in some areas—in several of
the better-balanced or more fertile of the north, and in the Guadalquivir valley—enjoyed a degree of prosperity until the 1570s or 1580s,
but Castilian agriculture as a whole advanced only in the amount of
land brought under cultivation, not in productivity. In fact, the increase in cultivation could not altogether keep up with the rise in
population, so that after the first great hunger of 1502–1509 there
were periodic shortages throughout the century, bringing an intermittent need to rely on food imports. Since the united monarchy had no
agrarian policy at all, its only response to the latent food problem was
to try to keep food prices down by the *tasa de trigo* (grain price
regulation) while encouraging grain imports. After 1539, the tasa de
trigo became fixed policy.

The beginning of a long decline in Castilian agriculture was noticeable after 1550. Three factors involved were the steady price increases, the decline in opportunity to export for the American market
after it began to produce for itself, and the unregulated competition
of cheaper imports. The high price of credit and the growth of
production costs, together with the comparatively lower sales price of
food, made production relatively unprofitable. It was harder and
harder for peasants to meet their loans and pay taxes and by the last
decades of the century flight from the land had become general. This
only increased the amount of territory under aristocratic control,
while at the same time it continued to boost the numbers in towns
and cities who were demanding cheap bread and lower food prices,
thus further discouraging agriculture. The most fertile districts—in La
Mancha of New Castile and in western Andalusia—may have remained fairly prosperous until the 1620s, encouraged in some instances by broader commercial cultivation of vineyards and olives, at
least in Andalusia. The rice-growing region around Valencia continued to do well, but the general contraction of agriculture from at least
the 1580s, if not earlier, was undeniable. It has been estimated that by
1600 one-third of the land cultivated earlier in the century lay fallow.
The process spurred absenteeism, for the aristocracy, which in most
cases had maintained their residences in a fairly profitable, income-
producing countryside early in the century, began more and more to
take up permanent residence in the cities. Yet the decrease in agricultural profits did not diminish the economic weight of the large landholders; their domains were so extensive that they could still collect
great incomes at reduced rates per hectare.

After 1570, food prices began to rise more rapidly than industrial
prices, but this did not benefit most of the peasantry. A good deal of
the profit went into the hands of black marketeers, and the cost of
credit, land rent, and rural taxes rose even more rapidly.

More of an effort was made to increase productivity during the second half of the century, as less and less capital went into commerce and most was invested in land *censos*. Swamp drainage and some new irrigation were introduced around a number of larger cities, but this was controlled to a great extent by the urban market and urban capital. It had no effect upon the vast unirrigated rural areas. To add to the hardship, evidence indicates that there was an abnormally large number of dry years in the sixteenth century.

The biggest single rural industry—the wool-producing Mesta—actually began to decline slightly as early as the 1520s and fell off markedly in the late 1550s. This is reflected in the size of Mesta herds as shown in table 5. The decline was the result of a drop in wool

Table 5. *Size of Castilian Mesta Herds, 1512–1561*

Years	Number of head
1512–1521	2,838,351
1522–1531	2,793,823
1532–1541	2,540,635
1542–1551	2,605,633
1552–1556	2,693,170
1557–1561	1,998,845

Source: J. Vicens Vives, *Historia ecónomica de España* (Barcelona, 1959), p. 318.

prices in western Europe while the sixteenth-century Castilian price level was rising. In addition, pressure against the Mesta began to mount during the reign of Carlos V, both from agricultural interests, in an ineffective effort to reduce grazing rights, and from domestic cloth producers, who wanted to reduce exports so that they might satisfy a greater share of Spanish textile consumption.

The problem of deforestation, already severe, became even more serious. The peninsula had never been heavily wooded, and it had lost many of its forests in the Middle Ages. The process accelerated in the sixteenth century, however, with the growth in population, need for more agricultural land, felling of trees for large-scale shipbuilding, and in Catalonia, the burning of forests in the struggles with *bandolers*.

Growth and Decline of Castilian Commerce and Industry

During the height of Spanish power in Europe, from about 1540 to 1590, Castilian manufactures enjoyed a period of peak production and export. First in importance were woolens, produced mainly in

Segovia, Toledo, Cuenca, and Córdoba, and in the east at Valencia, Barcelona, Zaragoza, Huesca, and Perpinyà. Second were the silks of Valencia, Granada, and Toledo. The only metals of consequence continued to be the iron and steel of Vizcaya, some of which was exported to France and England. Principal markets, aside from the rapidly rising domestic market, were the Indies, Portugal, and Spanish-dominated Italy. Spanish woolens and all other textiles save silk, however, were totally unable to compete with the textiles of Flanders or other advanced regions in the general international market either with respect to price or quality.

The decline of textile production after about 1590 came for a variety of reasons: the rise in prices, heavily increased taxes, steeper production costs, including fairly high wages, and the failure to improve technology and the rate of productivity. Even among the urban oligarchs and merchants there was little of a production-oriented, protobourgeois attitude. Profits were usually invested in land or land loans rather than reinvested in business, and the Cortes of Castile sometimes urged the crown to restrict exports so as to keep domestic prices low. Moreover, the expansion and rigidification of the guild system discouraged new production relations and the use of new techniques.

There was a great expansion of naval construction, above all in Vizcaya, the shipbuilding center of the peninsula, but also periodically in Barcelona. The expansion of the Castilian navy and commerce diverted the majority of Basque fishermen into the carrying trade. The place once held by Basque fishing in the fifteenth century was never regained, and most of the peninsula relied increasingly on imported fish, especially from Brittany. The size of ships increased greatly, culminating in the huge Spanish and Portuguese galleons and carracks, designed for great overseas cargos and for defense. After 1588, the success of smaller north European vessels encouraged a return to smaller ships, making it easier also to reach smaller ports and inland waterways.

Expansion of the Indies trade after 1515 tended to divert shipping and capital from commerce with northern Europe. Thus the history of business and finance in sixteenth-century Castile in large measure is that of the decline of the north, especially in the last four decades of the century, and the growing prominence of the south, especially the key Seville-Cádiz area. The descent of Burgos began in the 1560s with plague and the beginning of the disruptions in the northern trade. Segovia, however, the main textile center, enjoyed two decades of prosperity, from 1570 to 1590, and did not enter into decline until the last years of the century. In general, the 1570s were a prosperous decade for Spanish commerce, but this only encouraged the crown's policy of taxing exports more heavily than imports. The Basque industrial decline began about 1580 but was delayed by heavy shipping and shipbuilding orders. During the 1580s, however, the percentage of shipping from the northern ports in the American trade through Seville decreased from 80 to 50 percent. The province of Vizcaya suffered more than any other part of Spain in losses of men and shipping from the Armada.

Another factor weighing heavily against Castilian commerce and industry was the broad and mountainous terrain, which presented severe obstacles to transportation and made a national market almost impossible. Goods in Castile were carried almost entirely by mule pack; one contemporary estimate placed the number of mules used in this way at 400,000. Yet the system was inadequate for a large exchange of goods. Hence the persistence of localism, small-scale local industries producing for their native districts, much duplication, failure to lower production costs or achieve volume, and inability to compete with the lower-priced and higher-quality foreign goods which they faced in the market by the end of the century.

The Price Rise

Between about 1500 and 1660, bullion from America increased the silver in circulation in Europe by some 300 percent and the gold by about 20 percent. Nearly 40 percent of all this was paid into the Spanish royal treasury in the form of regular taxes and the "royal fifth" exacted on all precious metals. American bullion and the general increase in population were the two main causes of the general price rise of the sixteenth century. By twentieth-century standards, however, the sixteenth-century inflation was mild. Between 1516 and 1562, prices in Spain rose an average of 2.8 percent a year. From 1562 to 1600 the average annual rate dropped to 1.3 percent. That the rate of increase was no higher with so much bullion coming into the country was due in part to a slight increase in productivity, at least up until the last two decades of the century. Moreover, since so much of the metal soon left Spain, it was not all pumped directly into the Spanish economy. During part of the century, prices actually rose more rapidly in France than in Spain. Real wages for Spanish wage earners did not keep up with the price rise during most of the century, falling by about 20 percent during the first half and by about 12 percent during the second half as the inflation eased. The wage/price scissors presumably aided Spanish manufactures, reducing production costs that often tended to be uncompetitive. At the same time, it should be remembered that grain price regulation kept grain prices, at least, lower in Spain than in France.

The Fiscal System

The key factor in the Spanish economy toward the end of the century was the tax system, which had reached ruinous dimensions. In Castile, the principal taxes were the alcabala, a general sales tax originally set at 5 percent of the price of goods but later raised; the *servicio,* a poll tax, paid only by commoners, that became a standard assessment after 1525; and customs. To these were added various special taxes, as well as income from royal domain (especially from lands of the former crusading orders). Contributions from the church were another major source of royal income, consisting of the *dos novenos,* a nominal two-ninths of the tithe collected by the church in most parts of Spain, the cruzada, drawn mainly from indulgences, the *subsidio,* a large annual tax on church income to maintain naval defenses against the Muslims, and the *excusado,* a sort of tax on income from church lands. Though the church grants normally yielded less revenue than the alcabala, the retention of great church properties in a traditional Catholic society did provide a significant source of income to the crown, probably more than if such properties had been secularized and divided among the upper classes, who controlled most of the rest of the land.

Aside from Castile, the major source of income for the Spanish crown before 1568 was the prosperous Low Countries, which sometimes provided as much as 3,500,000 ducats per year. Most of the other dominions paid lump sums, though there were also special taxes: Milan usually paid at least 300,000 ducats annually, plus a lucrative salt tax; Naples paid an average of 290,000 ducats annually between 1535 and 1552, plus excises; Aragón paid 200,000 ducats annually after 1533 but no excise or special taxes; and Sicily, 75,000 ducats annually, plus a wheat impost. By contrast, the income from America averaged only 350,000 to 400,000 ducats a year during the reign of Carlos V, and so was a minor factor in royal finance for that period.

This was an enormous royal income for the sixteenth century and remained the highest in Europe for over one hundred years, yet it never sufficed to meet the enormous expenses, mainly military, of the crown. During the reign of Carlos V the nominal value of taxes raised in Castile grew by approximately 50 percent, yet inflation lowered its real value by almost the same proportion. Under Carlos V the crown normally spent about twice as much as it took in. The government of Felipe II inherited a debt of 70,000,000 ducats, which was partially repudiated in 1557. During the next sixteen years the crown's income doubled, but expenses increased even more rapidly. The inhabitants of the Aragonese principalities were protected by their constitutional systems from major tax increases, leaving the burden to Castile. The alcabala was sometimes raised to as much as 20 percent, and other excises were increased. Offices were sold at home and in the empire, as were a variety of monopolies. Bullion imports from America did increase greatly under Felipe II, accounting for between 20 and 25 percent of all royal revenue during the last fifteen years of his reign. This surpassed the income received from the church, which provided about 15 percent of the crown's resources, but amounted to only slightly more than the former revenues of the Low Countries, now mostly lost to the crown.

From the very beginning of the reign of Carlos V, the crown was forced to negotiate large-scale loans, and by the 1580s, if not before, borrowing by the Spanish crown had become the largest single financial operation in Europe. State bonds were fairly attractive to Spanish investors, and ranked with land purchases and short-term agricultural loans as one of the three main avenues of investment in the sixteenth century. Yet there was not enough fluid capital in concentrated sums within the peninsula to respond to most of the loan requests, and from the start the crown formed the habit of placing the bulk of its loans with foreign bankers, at first German and Flemish, and then to an increasing extent Genoese. Terms of these *asientos* became complicated in the extreme. They customarily took the form of *juros de resguardo,* or security bonds, each of which was assigned to account against one of the major sources of state income (such as the alcabala or cruzada), and which also served as negotiable securities, becoming the principal object of credit speculation in sixteenth-century Spain. Only about 10 percent of the *juros,* however, were paid off on time, and the rates of interest and payment were periodically adjusted. Approximately every twenty years the financial pressure on the crown became so great that there was no alternative to a declaration of partial bankruptcy and forced reconversion of the royal debt. This occurred in 1557, 1575, 1596, 1607, 1627, and 1647.

The financial burden carried by Castile increased steadily, while the decline of the Castilian economy in the late sixteenth century made it all the more difficult to meet the level of obligations. This created a vicious circle of mounting debt and weakening economic base. All commentators are agreed that overtaxation was a major cause of the breakdown of the Castilian economy, yet detailed studies of the effect of specific taxes on individual economic sectors and social classes are lacking. The servicio was paid only by commoners, as was customary with such assessments in every part of Europe. By contrast, the alcabala, Castile's main excise duty, was paid by all classes in direct proportion to their involvement in the commercial economy. A new tax, the *millones,* introduced in Castile in the 1590s, was levied on basic foodstuffs and so fell primarily upon the poor.

Liability to a tax such as the servicio varied greatly with the social structure of the regions. In the north, which had a stronger tradition of local rights and common privilege, a much higher proportion of the population were nominally of hidalgo rank and exempt from most taxes. More than half the people in the regions of Santander and Asturias claimed this status, and one-fourth in the Burgos district, but in New Castile, Extremadura, and Andalusia only a tiny minority were so favored. Altogether some 15 percent of all Castilians may have been exempt, and the Basque country retained its own regional fiscal system, with lower rates and widespread exemptions. The result was to throw a great burden on those least able to pay.

It is customarily presumed that the Castilian tax structure reinforced inherent social and psychological obstacles to the development of an achievement-oriented society—that it discouraged commercial and industrial enterprise and helped to fix ambition on the goal of nonproductive aristocratic status and escape from taxation. In general, this seems true enough, though during the first half of the century the actual burden of taxes in terms of real value decreased considerably, for rates were not increased to compensate for inflation. An exact correlation between increasing taxes and declining economic activity has never been worked out, but probably existed from the late decades of the sixteenth century on, as the rise in taxes outstripped the rising inflation. This may have been most important in the economic decline of northern Castile, where per capita rates on commoners were probably heavier than in the south: in the southern areas only a tiny fraction were exempt and hence the per capita burden on commoners was probably lower. On the other hand, continued prosperity in Seville and some other southern regions was due above all to the wealth of the American trade, and differential per capita rates of taxation may at first have been altogether secondary.

Taxation alone cannot be blamed for the lack of capital investment in productive enterprise. Since the system was totally regressive, large concentrated incomes were not reduced, and even at the end of the century significant sums were available for investment in state bonds, or, more commonly, in short-term agricultural or personal loans. Lack of productive investment was due more to the psychology, customs, and social values of Castile than to the undeniably severe fiscal pressure.

Social Psychology

Even though the lines between the nobility and lower classes were drawn more sharply than ever in the sixteenth century by social exclusion, economic discrimination, and dwindling domestic opportunity, the sense of class antagonism felt at that time and since in other parts of Europe was not so common in Spain. Lower-class Castilians continued to identify themselves not as peasants or laborers but as Catholic Castilians, part of the superior caste, defined by their honor, an ineffable quality that adhered to them naturally regardless of scale of life or accomplishment. If anything, the determination to preserve honor, or caste identity, even among the poor and vulgar, increased. This explains the concern with "purity of blood," that sixteenth-century Castilian obsession which was almost stronger among the lower than the upper classes. Converso blood was more common, or at least more obvious, in the middle and upper classes than among the miserable. To be the descendent of poverty-stricken Castilian peasants or laborers meant that one was indubitably of "pure," "old-Christian" stock, for no Jew had had to live under those conditions. Economic wretchedness was a badge of inherent caste superiority. All pure Castilians were members of nature's, or God's, elite. Hence the sense of individual dignity among the most lowly so frequently commented on by foreigners. This had nothing to do with equality or democracy. "Purity of blood" became rather the compensation for absence of equality or democracy in Spanish society. It helped justify a certain degree of informality in relations between classes that smoothed the great social and economic divisions that existed.

During the reign of Carlos V the influential Conversos so much a part of the court under the Catholic Kings were no longer to be seen. In 1556 Felipe II ratified an earlier church decree of 1547 making "purity of blood" necessary for clerical appointments. Among the upper classes, where many families had in earlier generations made wealthy Converso marriage connections, the purity of blood controversies were the excuse for bitter factional fighting, especially in local politics and business. Elaborate *libros verdes* were published revealing the taint or purity of family backgrounds of leading noble clans, leading to great scandal and exaggeration. Although nobles were in some cases not so caught up in the purity of blood mania as were commoners, the extent of accusation and persecution on such grounds was great enough to lead to a reaction in the seventeenth century, when libros verdes were finally banned.

This sense of Spanish society was transmitted to other areas with which Spaniards were in frequent contact, especially Italy. The pride and gravity of the Spanish demeanor became proverbial. These qualities were accompanied by a tendency toward the emphatic and exaggerated in Spanish temperament and behavior, which may have laid the basis in manners for the baroque mood of the late-sixteenth and seventeenth centuries, but caused some wonderment in other societies with more modest and easy-going ways.

Suppression of the Moriscos

The increasing costs and pressures of empire, the beginning of economic decline, and the paranoid fear of heresy first began to produce strains in Spanish society during the 1560s. Those working for uniformity in religion demanded stronger measures against the only large non-Catholic social group, the Moriscos.

The number of Moriscos within the kingdom of Castile in the second half of the sixteenth century was probably greater than half a million, and nearly 10 percent of the population. Of these, several hundred thousand were scattered through New Castile, Extremadura, and western Andalusia. By far the most concentrated nucleus were the quarter million who lived in the region of Granada in eastern Andalusia.

Possibly as many as two hundred thousand Moriscos had fled to north Africa after the original decree of nominal conversion in 1502. For two generations, the majority who had remained bribed their way to immunity from the Inquisition. They clung stubbornly to their religion and way of life, and their industry and skills sustained them despite onerous taxation. Some Moriscos were of slightly darker complexion than most Spaniards, but what set them apart was their clothing and their customs, for there seem to have been no very marked differences in physical or facial appearance. Their diet emphasized rice, fruit, and vegetables much more than the Christian, which was basically bread, meat, and wine. A more temperate, disciplined, and industrious mode of life and an emphasis on the family showed up in a distinctly faster rate of population growth. This was noted with dismay by Christians, who observed that "all Moors marry."

Carlos V had accepted the diverse territories and social groups of his empire, but Felipe II demanded greater conformity. It is true that factional interests among the aristocracy and court cliques influenced him to reject the process of bribery and toleration followed by royal officials in the past, but this decision accorded with the general trend of Spanish society and government. A decree of 1567 required that Muslim dress and social customs be abandoned. The measure was apparently enforceable among the several hundred thousand Moriscos scattered in various parts of New Castile, Extremadura, and western Andalusia. On the other hand, it was difficult to impose among the large, compact all-Morisco population of the Granada region and of the Levantine countryside. Since the latter were partly shielded by their aristocratic Christian overlords, the brunt of the measure fell on the quarter-million Granadan Moriscos.

The Granada community was the only large remaining Morisco nucleus with significant internal cohesion and group identity. Its members were already disgruntled by new export regulations, and special taxes handicapped their silk industry. They had political contact with Morocco and more distantly and indirectly with the Ottoman empire and thus constituted a latent "Ottoman fifth column"* in Spain. The decree of 1567 was issued partly for reasons of national security, but the Granadan Moriscos were the more determined to ignore it because they realized that, for the first time in more than half a century, Spain was in a relatively insecure position. The great Morisco revolt began in the last week of 1568. Nearly a year was required for the crown to muster enough troops to deal with it, and the rebellion was not fully suppressed until 1571. The conflict was conducted with savagery by both sides. Approximately 60,000 Moriscos were killed and several thousand more were sold into slavery. Perhaps 50,000 fled to Africa, while twice that number were afterward dispersed over widely scattered parts of Castile. It is conjectured that no more than 40,000 were allowed to remain in the Granada region.

After the 1570s the several hundred thousand Moriscos remaining in various districts of Castile underwent a slow but steady process of social and cultural absorption. The only large bloc remaining were those of the Levant and lower Aragón. There the old refrain *Quien tiene moro tiene oro,* "Whoever has a Moor has money," still seemed to be true. The landholding Valencian and Aragonese nobility continued to treasure the rents and other obligations paid by Morisco peasants, and managed in large measure to shield their tenants from the assimilation decree for the remainder of the century.

Yet the security problem had not been altogether eliminated. There were still Muslim pirates attacking the east coast, and rumors of secret intelligence between Levantine Moriscos and the Berber states. As Spanish power came under increasing strain during the reign of Felipe III, it became more and more difficult to accept with equanimity the existence of a still largely Muslim minority in eastern Spain. The final solution of the Morisco problem came, however, not so much as a protective measure but as a gesture that Spain still had the

* The phrase is that of Andrew C. Hess, "The Moriscos: An Ottoman Fifth Column in Sixteenth-Century Spain," *American Historical Review* 74, no. 1 (Oct. 1968): 1-25.

strength to resolve a domestic quandary and complete the unity of Spanish Counter-Reformation society. The decision to expel the Moriscos once and for all was taken on the same day that the truce with Holland was signed in 1609, for that gave the crown a respite during which it could concentrate its military and naval strength in the Mediterranean, where Spanish forces had largely been on the offensive against Muslim sea power since about 1601. There were at that time fewer than 300,000 Moriscos left in Spain. Of these, about 135,000 were concentrated in the Valencia region, one-third of its inhabitants, and about 60,000 in Aragón, where they were one-fifth. About 80,000 to 90,000 were scattered around Castile among its some 6,500,000 inhabitants. The Moriscos of Valencia were moved out en masse in 1609-1610 under heavy military security, but the roundup of Castilian Moriscos was more difficult and continued until 1614. Altogether, approximately 275,000 were expelled from Spain, mostly shipped out.

Technically, the expulsion was an impressive feat of logistics that could scarcely have been equaled by any other power at that time. It depopulated wide stretches of Valencia and southern Aragón and led to a great drop in agrarian and artisan production in those regions. It also struck an indirect but severe blow at the previously fairly prosperous Valencian middle classes. Since the regional aristocracy had already mortgaged much of their property to middle-class financiers and now found themselves without the Morisco labor from which most of the income from their domains was derived, the crown sanctioned cancellation of these debts. Yet there were no signs of immediate and severe economic dislocation, and price and wage levels remained about the same. Expulsion of the Moriscos was the last great step in eradicating the religio-ethnic pluralism of medieval Hispania. By 1614, the unitary Catholic society had been achieved.

Conclusion

Though their structures had not changed greatly in the late Middle Ages, the peninsular economies entered a new period of prosperity that began around 1510. The agrarian crisis of 1502-1509 had been overcome, there were new commercial opportunities, and in particular, the first imports of gold from the West Indies had begun arriving after 1505. From 1506 to 1521 wages rose more rapidly than prices, but after 1521 the price level started to rise more steeply. The beginning of this sixteenth-century inflation was the result of the political and social disturbances of 1520-1521, the arrival of Mexican treasure, and the rising demand in both the domestic and Spanish American markets. The price rise became even more rapid after about 1535, then finally slowed down in the 1560s.

During the middle decades of the century there was general expansion in the Castilian economy. Population rose, food production increased almost as rapidly, at least for several decades, the textile, shipbuilding, and Basque iron industries expanded, currency remained fairly stable, and after a mid-century decline, the Mesta began to grow again. The Aragonese economies also participated in this expansion, which continued during most of the reign of Felipe II.

The general contraction of the Spanish economy began around 1590. The last period of prosperity for the Castilian fairs was the 1580s. By the last decade of the reign of Felipe II, Castilian commerce and manufactures were in decline. State expenses were the most important single factor in this process, but for the common people the main problem was food. Major food shortages had reappeared intermittently since the mid-1550s and were frequent after the 1570s. The price of food staples rose more rapidly than prices in general, for the population continued to grow until the end of the century, while production was falling. By the close of the century, however, the sense of defeat and disillusion felt by the imperial government was being reflected in Spanish society. Castilians had not been especially poor by west European standards during the sixteenth century, but by the 1590s, if not before, their living standards were declining. More important was the diminishing will to cope with such challenges. By the turn of the century the population, ravaged by new outbreaks of plague, was declining, and Castilian society, in reaction to the challenges of empire, heresy, and its own ethnocentrism, was turning inward.

15

The Seventeenth-Century Decline

Spain's seventeenth-century decline has received less study than any other major period of Spanish history. In part, this is because it is more remote than the modern phase that began in the eighteenth century, but it must also be explained by the painful reactions that comparisons with the glories of the late-fifteenth and sixteenth centuries evoke. By the end of the first quarter of the seventeenth century, perceptive Spaniards were clearly aware that they were living in an age of marked decline, and the sense of frustration and of waning accomplishment became steadily more conscious and general as the decades advanced. Subsequently, in the eighteenth and nineteenth centuries, historiographic opinion viewed the period as decadent, a description still commonly used. More recently, twentieth-century nationalist historiography has questioned the judgment of decadence, suggesting that the time was merely one of stagnation in which the country was unable to develop at a rate equal to more expansive powers, because of the weight of imperial responsibilities. While it is true that Spain would have had to run faster than she had in the sixteenth century in order not to lose ground in the seventeenth century—a period of greater competition and development among west European powers—she was unable to maintain even the pace of 1600. The seventeenth century was, in fact, more than a time of stagnation; it was a period of general decline. Moreover, the society and culture showed signs of decadence in the strict sense of the term. An actual decline was reflected, first of all, in population. At the end of the sixteenth century, the Spanish homeland (excluding Portugal) had nearly 8,500,000 people, but in 1700 only about 7,000,000. Epidemic disease was the major cause for this decline, especially the bubonic plague but also typhus, smallpox, and other maladies. They were particularly lethal because the growth of towns in the sixteenth century had crowded many tens of thousands of the poor together in filthy conditions, and because economic decline brought a drop in food production, higher prices, lower purchasing power, reduced imports, and widespread malnutrition, particularly after years of poor harvests. The great plague of 1596–1602 attacked widespread areas of Castile and claimed 600,000 to 700,000 lives, or about 10 percent of the population, a figure almost equal to the gain of the preceding century. A second plague of great magnitude struck the eastern and southern parts of the peninsula in 1647–1652, and other devastating outbreaks occurred during the trough of the economic decline, between 1676 and 1685. Lesser epidemics raged intermittently throughout the century. It appears that altogether more than 1,250,000 deaths resulted from the extreme incidence of plague in seventeenth-century Spain, the worst era of epidemics in recorded peninsular history save for the period of the Black Death.

The other principal causes of population loss were emigration to America, deaths from warfare, and the expulsion of the Moriscos. The official emigration statistics indicate little more than 40,000 "legal" emigrants, but most were not licensed and the true figure was probably several times that. Military campaigns in the seventeenth century became increasingly costly in lives, especially during the middle years when there was widespread fighting and destruction in Catalonia. Deaths from disease and malnutrition far outnumbered combat fatalities, and the number of lives lost from war during the heaviest period of fighting from 1635 to 1659 may have reached a quarter million. The expulsion of the Moriscos early in the century lost the peninsula approximately 275,000 people.

Castile was affected more severely than the eastern principalities. The population of Catalonia, Navarre, and the Basque provinces was about the same at the end of the century as in the beginning. That of Aragón declined slightly, but proportionately not as much as Castile's. By 1700 Valencia was able to make good only half the losses suffered by the expulsion of the Moriscos, and showed a net loss of about 50,000 to 75,000 people. Castile, which bore the main financial and military weight of empire and provided most of the emigrants, suffered a net loss of some 1,250,000. Its population, excluding the

Basque country, dropped from around 6,750,000 in 1600 to 5,500,000 in 1700.

The Economic Decline

Jaime Vicens Vives has suggested seven prime causes of the seventeenth-century economic decline: 1) continued increase in the size of entailed domains held by the aristocracy and the church, which had the effect of withdrawing land from use and of lowering production; 2) increasing social disruption and vagrancy; 3) deforestation; 4) an overabundance of clerics; 5) the status orientation of society; 6) the negative, charity-oriented religious attitudes toward poverty that precluded serious thought of reform and new enterprise; and most important of all, 7) government policy, which maintained prohibitive taxes in Castile, produced capricious waves of alternating inflation and deflation that led to monetary chaos, overregulated some aspects of the economy, and was incompetent in planning and execution.

The tax burden on Castile, already destructive during the reign of Felipe II, became unbearable during the course of the seventeenth century. The constitutional systems of the eastern principalities continued to protect them from all special levies save sporadic grants made grudgingly by their Cortes, which averaged out to a per capita annual rate considerably less than that paid by Castilians. The only institution in the east that paid anything approaching a proportionate share of taxes was the church. In fact, the eastern principalities paid much less than did the Italian territories of the crown—Sicily, Naples and Milan—which in some years by the end of the sixteenth century were paying over five million ducats and carrying much of the cost of imperial defense in the Mediterranean and in south-central Europe. But the main responsibility still fell on Castile, which from the 1590s on was called upon to pay two-thirds of the cost of government out of its ordinary taxes. The nominal tax rates were not in themselves exorbitant, but the power of the aristocracy to shove the weight of them onto the middle classes and the peasantry, together with the exactions of tax farmers and agents who raked off much of the proceeds, led to crushing imposts on production that drove tens of thousands of peasant families off the land and into emigration or poverty in the crowded cities.

This situation was aggravated by a capricious, irresponsible royal monetary policy. During the sixteenth century the Spanish monarchy had maintained a sound currency based on a fairly steady silver value, but by 1599, with the bulk of royal income already going for debt service, it was decided to debase the coinage by issuing copper money. This led to a two-year bout of inflation, and after a temporary end to monetary debasement, a slight price decline from 1601 to 1610. During the next decade prices were generally stable, but further debasement led to serious inflation in the 1620s and sporadic inflation from 1636 to 1638 and in the 1640s. Altogether, prices rose nearly 40 percent in the quarter-century 1625-1650. This in itself would not have been so serious had it not been for the pendular swings from inflation to deflation that discouraged production and commerce even further.

Capital and credit were increasingly scarce from the latter part of the sixteenth century. The bankruptcy of 1596 was the final blow that completed the ruin of Medina and the other financial centers of northern Castile. The problem was not the absence of capital, for it existed among the aristocracy; it was a problem of values and priorities. The upper classes and the church had already established a pattern of preferring the moderately high rate of interest from state bonds and short-term loans to long-term investments involving greater risk. In view of these preferences, the existence of more capital would not in itself have guaranteed more productive undertakings. At any rate, even the favored "safe" investments proved less and less lucrative with the eventual near collapse of the state financial system and the decline of agriculture, the source of income from many short-term loans. In turn, the crown came to rely almost exclusively on foreign sources of credit.

The most serious domestic aspect of the seventeenth-century economic decline was in the most fundamental area—food production. Agriculture declined fairly steadily, with brief moments of recovery due mainly to better weather, until it reached a secular trough in the 1680s. The principal factor was probably the enormous weight of taxation on peasant agriculture in Castile. In some regions, the peasant paid five or six different kinds of duties—a tithe to the church that in certain districts amounted to nearer a fifth than a tenth of his production, seigneurial dues to his lord, rent to the landlord who held immediate economic jurisdiction (usually a different and lesser personage than the former), taxes to the crown, and in many instances, interests and payments on short-term loans without which he could not have stayed in production. In parts of Castile these amounted to more than half of an income which was often only marginal at best, and thus made it impossible to maintain a family on the land. The pressure of sheepherding interests was lessening, for wool exports were also declining in a more competitive international market, and market price restrictions on the food producer could often be evaded, but in general, nonagrarian prices rose more rapidly than did those for food produced, trapping the peasantry in a price scissors. All the while, land rents increased with the general inflation of the period. There was no escape from taxation and dues, and even the weather grew worse during the second half of the century. The result was drastic rural depopulation in large areas, particularly in the Duero valley of León and Old Castile, and in the Toledo and Guadalajara districts of New Castile.

Domestic manufactures, which had begun to decline in the late sixteenth century, continued their decline during the seventeenth century. The chief textile-producing towns of New Castile suffered a disastrous drop in population. During the course of the century, Toledo fell from 50,000 to 20,000 inhabitants, Segovia from 25,000 to 8,000, and Cuenca from 15,000 to 5,000. Much of the Spanish clothing market was lost to foreign competition, especially to durable, light-weight English woolens. Again, the chief reasons were the absence of enterprise, the failure to adapt to new demands and possibilities, the lack of technological improvement in production, and the loss of skilled labor. Relative inefficiency coupled with comparatively high wages resulted in high production costs that priced many Spanish manufactures out of the market.

The other two domestic industries that had been important were Basque iron production and shipbuilding along the northern coasts. These also declined rather precipitously, for the same factors were at work. After the general volume of shipping and commerce started to contract in the 1620s, demand for new vessels naturally lessened, but even the boats that were bought and chartered were increasingly apt to be foreign, because of superior design and construction. The cost of naval stores had been disproportionately high in the peninsula for a long time. This, plus the failure to improve techniques or design, left the north Spanish shipbuilding industry in the doldrums throughout the century. Similarly, Basque iron production, which at times had exceeded 3,000 tons annually in the sixteenth century, dropped off markedly and was unable to supply the domestic market or sustain the needs of the Spanish military. There was, however, some revival in the last two decades of the century.

Regional light industries and local crafts were affected much less by the general downturn than were the three major industries that had been directed toward national and international markets. Simple household goods were still supplied by local artisans, and this relationship was in most instances little disturbed by the rise of imported manufactures.

The decline in food and textile production was met by a corresponding rise in imports from abroad. Spain was largely dependent on northern Europe for naval stores, and relied increasingly on countries in that region and on France for textiles, hardware, paper, and enough grain to try to make up food deficits. Such increasing need, coupled with the military failures of the second half of the reign of Felipe IV, led to a series of commercial treaties between 1648 and 1667 with Holland, France, and England, granting these powers broad commercial privileges and comparatively low tariff rates on their exports to Spain. Spanish exports steadily declined. Wool remained the staple export, and Spanish wool continued to be of comparatively high quality. However, the size of the Mesta's herds had been dwindling since the late sixteenth century as a result of soil erosion, lack of credit, high export taxes, and legal pressure against the Mesta that was finally reducing its grazing privileges. The volume of wool export remained respectably high through the first half of the seventeenth century, but then sagged irretrievably. The other basic exports—wine, olive oil, Basque iron, and American cochineal—also declined as a result of the depression in agriculture and domestic manufacture and the slump in the American trade. The only general exception to this pattern was the trade of Bilbao, which remained fairly constant as a belated increase in iron exports helped to make good much of the loss suffered in the decline of the wool trade. Overall, however, the balance of Spanish foreign trade during the second half of the century was overwhelmingly unfavorable, and was sustained only by the re-export of American bullion. Yet the decline in bullion production reduced the possibilities of importing enough to compensate for the failure of domestic production and resulted in poverty and hunger for much of Spanish society.

The foreign share in Spanish commerce grew throughout the century until, by the second half, it was dominant. Not only was the volume of imports extremely high, but foreign capital established its control of the intra-Hispanic trade from the Andalusian ports, while east coast shipping, at least during the middle years of the century, was dominated largely by French and Genoese financiers and merchants.

Spanish America and the Colonial Trade

The greatest single achievement of the Spanish economy during the sixteenth century had been the development of a prosperous colonial trade with the American empire. This had provided an outlet for Spanish textiles and food products and had brought a return in bullion that served to balance Spanish commerce with Europe. Indeed, the development of the Spanish American colonial economy in that period was by far the greatest overseas economic accomplishment of any European power. The height of the Hispanic colonial trade was reached during the last third of the sixteenth century, though the high for a single year came in 1608; colonial trade in general remained rather static during the thirty-year period from 1593 to 1622. From there it fell into serious decline, dropping to a low by mid-century. Between 1606-1610 and 1646-1650 the volume of the colonial trade declined by 60 percent, as indicated in table 6, and remained in that trough for nearly one hundred years, until the middle of the eighteenth century.

Table 6. *Annual Averages of the Trade with Spanish America in the Seventeenth Century*

Period	Departures		Arrivals	
	Ships	Toneladas* of goods	Ships	Toneladas of goods
1600-1604	55	19,800	56	21,600
1640-1650	25	8,500	29	9,850
1670-1680	17	4,650	19	5,600
1701-1710	8	2,640	7	2,310

Source: J. Larraz, *La época del mercantilismo en Castilla, 1500-1700* (Madrid, 1944).
* A tonelada was equal to about three cubic meters.

This brought a steady decline in the wealth and population of Seville, the second city of Spain, after the 1620s. Seville was plagued not only by the falling off of trade in general, however, but also by the silting of the Guadalquivir, which made its harbor increasingly difficult to use. Thus the great Andalusian city could not maintain its place of leadership even within a diminished commerce. More and more traffic moved to Cádiz, which grew from 2,000 to 40,000 inhabitants between 1600 and 1700, and in the eighteenth century replaced Seville altogether as the main entrepôt of the American trade.

Imports of American treasure followed a roughly similar pattern. They averaged approximately 7,000,000 pesos per year in the 1590s, then dropped to between 5,000,000 and 6,000,000 annually between 1600 and 1625. From that point they fell rapidly, dropping to little more than 2,000,000 annually between 1646 and 1650 and only 500,000 in the years 1656-1660. The crown's share of the American treasure began to fall both earlier and more rapidly. Royal treasure receipts of American bullion averaged somewhat more than 1,500,000 pesos from 1595 to 1615, dropped to less than 1,000,000 annually from 1616 to 1645, dwindled to less than 400,000 during the ten years after that, and averaged little more than 100,000 annually between 1656 and 1660. Other income from American taxes fell at approximately the same rate. The general decline in colonial trade not only crippled one of the two main sources of crown income but deepened the general depression of production in metropolitan Spain.

Colonial trade declined for a variety of reasons. By the seventeenth century, Spanish America had begun to develop its own domestic production, at least in food and simple goods, and no longer needed the products of Spanish agriculture that had formed the staples of Spanish trade in the sixteenth century. Its economy now required finished industrial goods which the Spanish homeland was increasingly ill-prepared to supply. This led the colonies to turn more and more to foreign producers, and contraband trade increased greatly. In turn, merchants engaged in the American trade tended more and more to invest in American commerce and production rather than return their capital to Spain. Coupled with these factors was the progressive exhaustion of the largest silver mines in northern Mexico and the southern Andes, while no technique was being developed that would have made working the marginal deposits profitable. Discovery of several new but smaller sources of silver did not offset these limitations. Yet another factor was the drastic depopulation of central Mexico in the late sixteenth and early seventeenth centuries as a result of epidemics of European diseases and of the social and economic exploitation of the Indians. To this was added the growing weight of competition from other imperial powers, competition which had been nearly nonexistent through most of the sixteenth century. An increasing proportion of the taxes of Spanish America remained there to build defenses against English, Dutch, and French intruders. In general, the resistance of Spanish America was quite effective, reflecting the stability and rootedness of the Hispanic society being formed there, but it used up funds that the Spanish crown would otherwise have had available for its expenses in Europe. Finally, the pressure of Spanish taxation and the decline in Spanish shipping further handicapped the colonial trade. As volume diminished, taxes and fees on shipping were proportionately increased to pay for mounting costs of insurance and defense. This led to widespread fraud in the registration of commerce and gave further encouragement to contraband.

The shift in the internal economic relations of the Hispanic world during the seventeenth century thus resulted from the decline of the peninsular economy coupled with the growth of the Spanish American economy. It revealed the beginning of what would be an increasingly separate and eventually independent Spanish America.

Spanish Society in the Seventeenth Century

The pattern of society during the seventeenth century merely accentuated the trend toward aristocratic dominance established long before.
During this period the traditional Spanish nobility reached its apogee.
Altogether, nearly 10 percent of the people of Spain were nobles, but
wealth was concentrated in the upper strata—the grandes, and just
below them, the títulos. With the economy stagnating, Spanish society remained desperately upwardly mobile. Concern was directed
almost exclusively toward winning aristocratic status and, if that were
already achieved, toward rising into the elite, whose ranks were thus
steadily expanded. There had been twenty-five families of grandes
when the rank was legally defined in 1520, but ten more were raised
to that category in the year 1640 alone. In addition to the grandes
there had been thirty-five títulos in Spain in 1520. Table 7 shows the
number of titles created in the late-sixteenth and seventeenth centuries.

Table 7.   Creation of New Titles in Spain, 1556-1700

Ruler	Number of Titles			
	Dukes	Marquises	Counts	Viscounts
Felipe II, 1556-98	18	38	43	
Felipe III, 1598-1621		20	25	
Felipe IV, 1621-65		67	25	
Carlos II, 1665-1700		209	78	5

Source: Antonio Domínguez Ortiz, La sociedad española en el siglo XVII, 2 vols.
(Madrid, 1963), 1:209-22.

Basically, what separated the grandes and títulos from the rest of
the nobility was wealth, mainly in landed domains under seigneurial
jurisdiction and protected by right of entail. The proportion of land
held in seigneuries continued to grow in the seventeenth century for
the same reason that it had in the sixteenth. Though the holders of
great seigneuries did not expand their real income from land at the
rate that prices were rising, their preferment at court increased, and
many special honors, posts, and gifts were bestowed on them from a
swollen royal treasury. More than ever before they were living paras-
tically off not only the land but the royal income as well. Thus, as the
overall production of wealth from towns and commerce declined, the
proportionate share of the national wealth held by the great landholding aristocracy actually increased.

The nobles of middle rank, the caballeros, did not normally hold seigneuries of importance, but controlled many positions in municipal government and dominated much of local administration. This provided them with lucrative posts as well as the control of local taxes and government finance.

The hidalgos continued to be numerically the great bulk of the nominal nobility. Though many were indeed poor and lacked land or other possessions of note, their status was nevertheless of great advantage. It freed them from payment of most taxes and provided legal privileges in criminal and civil suits, and for some it was the status derived from not having to pay taxes, more than the money involved, that was important. If there were those even worse off than their classic prototype, Don Quijote de la Mancha, others were well enough to do, and at the very least, the hidalgos were a stable upper-middle-class elite, between the nobility and the ordinary middle classes.

A government minister remarked that every Spaniard

> in his own position desires above all else honor and esteem, and everyone tries to advance himself, as can be seen by the fact that sons rarely follow the occupations of their fathers. The son of a shoemaker hates that occupation, the son of a merchant wants to be a gentleman, and so it is with the rest.*

Though this observation was somewhat exaggerated, throughout the seventeenth century, as in the preceding one, there was a movement of urban middle-class people into the ranks of *hidalguía*. The quarter century 1625-1650—the period of major economic decline—seems to have featured the elevation of an unusually large number. The crown's need for money spurred sale of titles, but such patents actually drew comparatively few buyers, for the purchase of admission to the nobility, rather than the mere arrogation of status, was logically held to admit that one was not by nature inherently noble.

The mania for *endonamiento*, or being made an aristocrat, was a counterpart of declining interest in work or achievement. In an interesting study of the number of achievement images per thousand words in Spanish literature over a five-hundred-year period, Juan B. Cortés, S.J., has found that in samples from the years 1200-1492 the mean was 10.74, declining for the years 1492-1610 to 6.07, and for 1610-1730 to only 2.67.

This obsession with honor and status had little to do with individu-

* Antonio Domínguez Ortiz, *La sociedad española en el siglo XVII*, 1:47.

alism as understood in the English-speaking world. Spanish society was not interested in individual opportunities or rights but in the assertion of personal status and subjective privilege. Julio Caro Baroja has put it well:

> The Spanish are not individualists, but personalists, which is quite different. The individualist in effect believes that society is constituted by individuals who have or ought to have more or less the same rights and duties. He asks that his be respected and agrees to respect those of others. The personalist sees each person as isolated (beginning with himself), with a series of distinct characteristics, and has no scruples about abusing some and favoring others, since he sees them all as inherently different, some of them sympathetic and attractive to him and others not. The personalist starts from a boundless, instinctive, and capricious ego to judge his neighbor and determine what he does or does not deserve.*

Hence the period of decline was a time of great pomp and display of luxury as aristocrats vied with one another for positions of splendor, particularly during the first four decades of the seventeenth century. As a result, most of the nobility were financially pressed, because despite their incomes, expenses always ran ahead. Aristocratic lands were usually mismanaged and produced only a portion of what they might have, but the landed nobles considered such concerns beneath them. On the one occasion during the century when a sector of the aristocracy was dealt a severe economic blow—the loss of income suffered by the Aragonese and Valencian nobility after expulsion of the Moriscos—they tried to recoup by raising already onerous seigneurial exactions on Christian peasants who remained or were brought in.

The seventeenth century was a time of economic, and to some extent social, decline for the Spanish middle classes, but it is not so clear that their numbers actually diminished proportionately. Rather, the middle classes retreated from enterprise and clung more and more to whatever status they had or could find, especially in government employment or holy orders. The result was an increasingly bureaucratized middle class in the larger towns, for whom fairly broad educational opportunities were a means not of training for creative new skills but of preparing for a static bureaucratic post. There were of course exceptions, but they stood in contrast to the norm. It was this overriding social emphasis on status and honor, rejecting the risks and pressures of productive enterprise, that led the *arbitrista* (reform writer) González de Cellorigo to remark that "it seems as if one had

---

* *Los judíos en la España moderna y contemporánea* (Madrid, 1961), 3:258-59.

wished to reduce these kingdoms to a republic of bewitched beings, living outside the natural order of things."*

The middle classes had largely lost control of municipal government to the caballeros and hidalgos. Though many Castilian towns practiced the system of *mitad de oficios* by which offices were divided between nobles and commoners, nearly all the important and lucrative positions were held by the nobles. In the south they were all-powerful, though in the towns of central Castile and in the north, the middle classes made some effort to contest their leadership. These local government offices were not service positions filled by a patriotic gentry, but money-making posts through which the local nobility diverted the income of local government, and particularly its tax-collection, to benefit their own purses. Thus the nobility not only shifted the taxes onto the middle and lower classes but actually made a profit from collecting them.

The hypertrophy of the aristocracy and the failure of the middle classes left the entrepreneurial role to elements entirely outside Spanish society. Italian merchants and financiers had already been active in the sixteenth century, and their numbers were increased by new aliens from Portugal, France, and Holland. The movement toward a closed Counter-Reformation society had never been complete, and in practice there was considerable toleration for foreigners who limited themselves to clearly defined activities that Spaniards themselves were ill-prepared to carry on. By 1650 there were approximately 150,000 foreigners in Spain—nearly 2 percent of the population, the main segment of the country's entrepreneurial middle class.

The social stagnation of seventeenth-century Spain was not unique in Europe during that epoch, for the first half of the century was a time of economic depression and expansion of aristocratic status within a relatively immobile society for much of western Europe. The social pathology of Spain was nonetheless more pronounced and enduring. One of its most destructive consequences was the absence of leadership, whether for intellectual affairs, religion, the economy, government administration, or the military. Without the leavening of new leadership by a creative elite, a change in attitudes, values, or policies was not to be expected. There were many critics and *arbitristas* who wrote numerous essays on the problems afflicting the country and offered a great many recipes for their remedy, but active example and direction by a capable elite were no longer to be found in any major branch of activity. The privileged in society had withdrawn

* Martín González de Cellorigo, *Memorial de la Política* (Madrid, 1600). This was one of the first and most incisive analyses of Spanish problems by the arbitristas of the period.

and turned inward on their status, and their orientation was shared by the common people as well.

Spanish people no longer identified themselves with the struggle of the empire in Europe. Once it had been thought something of an honor to serve in the army, and the ranks were filled by volunteers, save in emergencies. By the beginning of the reign of Felipe IV, however, the crown lacked the money to fill its units with professional soldiers and resorted more and more to forced drafts among the Castilian peasantry. Ordinary people had little sense of the meaning of seemingly endless campaigns of the crown, and religious motivation had dwindled as the division of western Christendom became an accepted fact. To be condemned to the miseries of military life in units that were unpaid and ill cared for was considered among the greatest of misfortunes. Since funds were saved by quartering units on the civilian population, the army in some regions became almost an object of hatred. Exemption from service was yet another reason to aspire to or cling to hidalgo rank.

The misery of the lower classes deepened, with no relief in sight. There may have been a rise in real income that accompanied the increase in wages for town workers during the first decades of the century, but that was wiped out by the depression, devaluation, and inflation of the 1620s, after which real wages declined. Throughout the first half of the century, the size of some of the larger cities increased as they filled with ruined peasants and unemployed workers. Madrid swelled to over 300,000. The towns were not centers of economic activity but parasites on a strained countryside. Since the masses of poor in Madrid, Seville, and other cities could not hope to live well, many turned to a psychology of pure lackeyism, winning some security and a measure of status as servants in the employ of conspicuous noblemen. Crime and the underworld flourished in the cities, and hordes of vagabonds plagued areas of the countryside. For the totally indigent, the only relief was the charity of the church, which gave handouts without much effort at rehabilitation.

Only rarely did the lower classes lash out in their misery. There were occasional acts of violence by the peasantry against their oppressors, and a few spectacular bread riots in times of famine in the big cities. The biggest of these—the *Pendón verde* turmoil at Seville in 1652—kept a lower-class district in a state of riot for twenty-one days. Such explosions were spontaneous, without stable leadership, organization, or goals, a boiling over of misery and hunger by the poor in times of scarcity.

One reason the lower classes accepted their lot, by and large, was that they lacked any alternative ideals or models in society. Even they accepted, to some extent, the aristocratic norm, once as an attainable goal, and then in the seventeenth-century as a mirage in whose shimmering reflection the wretched might take heart. Despite the desperate status-seeking, or partly because of it, lines between classes tended to blur at the extremes to a degree untrue of some other countries of the period. The poor participated more conspicuously in royal festivals at Madrid than they did at Versailles. The Castilian lower classes remained free, legally more free than in parts of France. Though many peasants were ruined by aristocratic inroads and by taxes, some of their traditional rights and accompanying security were retained. Above all, Castilian society retained a unity of ideals, sustained by the church, and growing impoverishment and strain did not lead to ideological cleavage in Spanish society as a whole.

Religion and Culture

Flight from reality and unwillingness to face new challenge were also evident in the church. It kept its enormous influence and wealth, nearly 20 percent of the land in the kingdom, and copious tithes and dues that gave it a huge share, perhaps nearly one-third, of the Spanish income, but it lost much of the spiritual and missionary zeal, intellectual achievement, and reformist drive of an earlier time. During the seventeenth century, the Spanish Catholic church became the institution of middle class bureaucracy. The great income of the church, contrasted with the general shrinking of the economy, made holy orders attractive as the chief opportunity for an "honorable" career for those with some education but few opportunities. A cadastre of 1656 revealed that the Castilian clergy held nine times the wealth of the ordinary Castilian population, and this was a powerful lure. The clergy as a whole were probably never more than 3 percent of the population, but they were as much as 10 percent of adult males. In Catalonia, where local church endowments were more common and the middle strata of society more developed, the clergy temporarily swelled to about 6 percent of the population. This padding of the ranks of clergy diluted its spiritual zeal and moral and intellectual quality. There remained a saving remnant of truly devout and dedicated priests, and impressive overseas missionary work was still done by several church orders, but nothing to compare with the preceding century.

The decadence of some of the clergy was simply one aspect of a change in the spirit of Spanish religiosity, which showed an increasing obsession with asceticism and the avoidance of sexual sin. The atmosphere was one of growing gloom and fixation on death and punishment. Mounting hostility to the world and to religious expression through normal, outgoing human affairs was probably a not unnatural spiritual-psychological counterpart to the general sense of failure and decline. Gross superstition, already common in the sixteenth century, increased, and was accompanied by further exaggeration of formalism and ritualism.

Religious sensibility was heightened by the expansion of the "mission" movement, particularly in the two Castiles and Andalusia. This was almost exclusively the work of some of the orders, and consisted of local evangelistic campaigns in villages and small cities by small groups of monks. They preached an intense and graphic brand of hellfire-and-damnation revivalism, illustrated by vivid paintings and sketches of the nether regions. The effect of these visits on the lower classes was often extreme, if rather temporary, and brought many people into formal confrontation with religion who otherwise paid relatively little attention to it.

All the while, moral irregularity abounded in the larger towns, and the stress on external orthodoxy often resulted in a heavy overlay of hypocrisy. As far as behavior patterns were concerned, the extreme "religiosity" of Spanish society was belied by the life styles of the highest and lowest in the social order, high aristocrats living in self-indulgence, a large lower-class underworld in the towns battening off crime and vice. A singular aspect of moral degeneration was the perverse fascination with the image of the nun in the romantic imagination of upper-class men. The *galán de monjas* (wooer of nuns) became a stock figure in the erotic typology of the period.

Ecclesiastically, the Spanish church became increasingly divided. Factional disputes within the clergy were pushed to the point of fanaticism. There were intense quarrels between orders and among various prelates, as well as disputes over control of parishes, descending even to vendettas over the style of clerical clothing.

As had been the rule before, the overweening formal piety of the crown did not prevent it from asserting a degree of authority over the church. It retained the *regium exequator,* dating from the fourteenth century, that enabled it to control all papal communications. The majority of church spokesmen in Spain sided with the authority of the crown, and during the first half of the seventeenth century, a considerable number of regalist treatises were written by both lay and clerical Spanish jurists. In 1617, Felipe III protested the fact that the papacy had placed several of these on the Index. There were lengthy conflicts between leading Spanish prelates and papal nuncios, though at the same time there was also an ultramontane party within the church. During the reign of Felipe IV some efforts, largely unsuccessful, were made to reform the clergy and limit the increase of entailed church estates.

After the first quarter of the seventeenth century, little was seen of the kind of theological, philosophical, and scientific study that had flourished among the intellectuals of the sixteenth-century church. Not only did this work decline, but the Hieronymites, Reformed Carmelites, and other orders which had stressed serious work and systematic spiritual meditation did not prosper. Their program was not attractive to most of those being drawn into religious orders.

The church did spend a significant amount of its great income on education and on charity for the poor, for whom it was the only source of relief, usually of the *sopa boba,* simple soup kitchen, variety. In addition, orphan asylums and homes for the wayward young were maintained.

By any comparison with other countries, basic educational facilities were extensive in Spain at the beginning of the seventeenth century, though in the years following they declined. According to one survey, there were 32 institutions of higher learning and at least 4,000 grammar schools, many of them founded in the sixteenth century and largely supported by the church. In 1590 there were 7,000 students attending the universities and 20,000 in higher education as a whole, proportionately the largest student body in Europe. The dynamics of seventeenth-century Spanish education, however, belie the notion that extensive nominal education is the main precondition to societal progress. The Spanish system was increasingly oriented toward the mere attainment and maintenance of status. The *colegios mayores,* originally endowed to finance education of students from the middle classes, were taken over as status symbols for aristocratic youth. Despite these and other limitations, there remained significant school opportunities for the middle classes, and the number of degrees or certificates earned was not inconsiderable. Yet such diplomas were basically licenses in formal letters that served as entrees to the bureaucracy whose ranks in church and state were swelled with diplomates. Such an educational system did not encourage a more critical or inquiring attitude or a more productive, efficient elite. Curricula sank into a routine that was backward even by contemporary European standards, but leading universities maintained a placement service for clerical and bureaucratic posts that, in terms of sustained pressure on behalf of graduates, might be judged to have outdone the efforts of twentieth-century American institutions. The educated were largely unconcerned with practical problems or with creative service. On their professional level, they aped the nonproductive status-security fixation of the nobility. The involution of Spanish society, general resistance to the analytic dimension, stress on the medieval intellectual disciplines in opposition to change, and prizing of personalism rather than objectivism and achievement, converged to block intellectual development.

The exception in this general trend of decline was the continued flowering of Hispanic esthetic culture during the first half of the seventeenth century, when Spain led Europe in the development of baroque art. The painting of Velázquez, the dramas of Calderón, and the extravagant poetry of Góngora were achievements of the highest level in the European culture of the period. Through the years of midcentury, the prestige of Spanish culture remained high, as attested by the use of Spanish art motifs and the vogue of certain writers, such as the Jesuit Baltasar de Gracián, in France and other countries. Hispanic literature reached its height in the writing of Miguel de Cervantes. His *Don Quijote* was on one level a satire of extravagant and unrealistic ambitions held by Spanish society of the imperial period and was the most profound expression of the mood of disillusionment that was setting in. On another, it was the most eloquent expression of those ideals, a universal work, and the first modern novel.

Church patronage was largely responsible for this paradox of brilliant literary achievement in an age of social and economic decline. Another important factor was the great wealth of the high aristocracy, whose elaborate tastes led them to patronize art at a time when society lacked resources for more mundane accomplishment. Yet the Spanish elite were unable to sustain even these values, leading more and more to what has been termed the paradox of the Spanish baroque: growing contrast between extravagant style and increasingly poor materials used to express it in architecture and art. During the second half of the century, the effects of depression, depopulation, disillusion, and flagging energy made it impossible to continue the level of esthetic activity, which also began to fall into decadence.

Government under Felipe III (1598-1621)

The Spanish system of government changed during the seventeenth century with the distinctly less competent monarchs and the rising magnitude of the problems facing royal administration. The institution of the valido, the favorite and surrogate of the king, became the norm for the weak monarchs of the time. There was a sense in which the valido was understood to be the chief minister for the crown, but he was more than that, becoming the substitute for rulers unable or unwilling to fulfill their responsibilities. He also represented the triumph of the high aristocracy, for their system of personal status relationships and dispensation of patronage then dominated the government as well.

The Duke of Lerma, valido of Felipe III, was above all interested in prestige and fortune. He had no special policy for Spanish affairs, but established his control over patronage to the aristocracy and became the wealthiest man in Spain. The king himself took great satisfaction in depleting royal resources by granting concessions to aristocratic favorites. From this time forward, the ascendancy of the aristocracy in government increased. Membership in the Council of State had always been restricted to the aristocracy, but its work had been to some extent administered and coordinated by professional secretaries drawn from the petty hidalgo class. In the seventeenth century, the Council of State was directed entirely by the high aristocracy.

The conciliar system of state administration was maintained, but there was a growing tendency to appoint subcommittees to deal with special problems and concentrate executive attention. This resulted in further dispersal of leadership and greater division in administrative organization. The numbers in state service continued to increase, but a rational, central bureaucratic system was never worked out. The Council of Castile, which served as a ministry of sorts for the kingdom of Castile, lacked an integrated system of administration which could enforce its laws and regulations. Though corregidores were still appointed for the towns, local areas were often administered as decentralized units by local notables, and what was true in Castile held for the empire as a whole.

The government system tended more and more to get out of control. Social and institutional pressure to hire university diplomates resulted in a fantastic degree of featherbedding. As the government bankrupted itself, every possible device for raising money was snatched at. Sale of offices in all branches of state affairs became a standard device for raising revenues, and in the Indies the practice was extended from fee-earning positions to more important salaried posts as well. Twice, seats on the Council of Indies were sold, and it was ruled that offices bought might in many instances be resold to secondary buyers. The treasury system itself was an enormous rat's nest. Nearly all tax collection was indirect, either farmed out to tax collectors, many of them Portuguese cristãos novos, or recruited secondhand from municipal officials. One estimate has calculated that nearly 150,000 full or part-time agents were involved in Spain and America, and that after so many local notables, tax farmers, and agents had siphoned off funds for themselves, little more than 20 percent of the sum originally collected reached the crown.

Financial stress, favoritism, and maladministration eventually led to protest even among the upper classes. By 1618, Lerma had to appoint a special reform junta to think of ways of remedying the government's ills. Rule by valido normally meant direction of affairs by a personal faction of the favorite. Lerma's greed and selfish use of patronage, which he controlled absolutely between 1612 and 1618, built up strong hostility among the majority of the nobility who were not favored. After twenty years even the indolent Felipe III grew restive, and before the close of 1618 he dismissed his veteran valido. Yet the change was slight. For the remaining three years of the reign a new favorite, Lerma's own son the Duke of Uceda, coordinated government affairs, though he never held the full authority once enjoyed by Lerma.

Felipe IV (1621-1665) and the Leadership of Olivares

Felipe IV succeeded his father in 1621 when only sixteen years old. Though he was more energetic, he was also more frivolous and little disposed to devote himself to public affairs. Since he was young, inexperienced, and not well educated, it was inevitable that he devolve direction of government on a favorite of his own. This personage was a thirty-three-year-old Andalusian noble, Gaspar de Guzmán, later known as the Conde-Duque de Olivares. The new head of affairs was altogether different from Lerma. Olivares was well trained and used to responsibility, a man of great vigor and energy as well as overweening ambition. He was not after personal gain, however, but sought power—the direction and vindication of the Spanish empire. The dark, heavy count-duke was by far the most forceful Spanish figure of the century—authoritarian, stubborn, but also hardworking, attentive to detail, persistent, and devoted to government rather than patronage. Unlike Lerma, he had a policy, which was to strengthen the Spanish empire and lead it to victory over its many foes despite the formidable obstacles that were mounting against it.

The predominant policy in the Council of State since the death of Felipe II had been conservative, devoted simply to preserving and defending the empire as it existed. In terms of international law as well as of actual circumstance in most of the empire, this was not unrealistic. The American empire was developing a unique, symbiotic society that was just beginning to achieve its own natural growth. The European possessions of the crown were in general satisfied with Spanish rule, conducted on the confederal Aragonese pattern and respectful of local rights and customs. None of its principalities at that time sought or were capable of surviving independently and no other major power had so good a legal claim to them as the Spanish crown. There were four major difficulties: a) the size and potential wealth of the overseas empire made it an almost irresistible target for European rivals; b) the extent of the empire's European territories placed it in a dominant position that was eventually intolerable to a revitalized France determined to cut Spain down to size; c) the geographic pattern of the European empire was awkward, for the Low Countries and the Franche Comté were isolated from the southern base and were difficult to defend; and d) the government refused to recognize the independence of the only dissident part of the empire, Holland, which had long since broken away and made its own place in the world. This led to endless, futile, wasteful warfare on land and sea with a new power that was the most modern and efficient in Europe in the early seventeenth century. Such conflict in turn made the defense of the southern Netherlands, which Spain retained, more difficult. During the first half of the seventeenth century, the Spanish crown enjoyed the services of the finest diplomats to be found in the employ of any power, but the skill of Spanish diplomats, great as it was, could not offset the enormous burdens imposed by a policy determined to retain an anachronistic dynastic claim that kept the empire perpetually at war.

When the Thirty Years War began in central Europe in 1618, the Spanish government plunged in to prevent the triumph of hostile Protestant forces that would side with Holland and threaten Spain's remaining position in the southern Netherlands. In addition to subsidizing the Austrian Habsburg cause, the main Spanish field army, stationed in the southern Netherlands under an outstanding general, Ambrosio Spinola, intervened to seize the Lower Palatinate in western Germany and safeguard direct land communications with Spanish Italy.

The ten-year truce with Holland expired in 1621, and hostilities were resumed on a naval and commercial front that was literally worldwide. By 1625, England had come into the struggle against Spain while France moved against the imperial position in northern Italy, but the years 1625-1626 were a time of success for Spanish arms. Dutch invaders were thrown out of Brazil by a large Hispano-Portuguese fleet, the offensive was resumed in the Low Countries where Breda was captured (1625), the French were once more forced out of Italy and peace was signed with them in 1626. To increase the pressure on the French crown, the Spanish government had even been negotiating terms of assistance to French Protestant rebels.

Yet there was a serious drop in American treasure shipments that same year, and the crown was unable to sustain its huge military expenses and was forced to another declaration of partial bankruptcy in 1627. The entire annual treasure fleet from New Spain was captured by a Dutch squadron along the Cuban coast in 1628. The struggle continued against both Holland and England, while income to finance it dropped, and Spain's Catholic allies in central Europe showed no inclination to assist in fighting the Dutch.

Military commitments were increased still further in 1628 when a dispute arose over the succession to the duchy of Mantua in northwest Italy. The strongest legal claimant was a French duke, but Olivares ordered Spanish forces to seize the stronghold of Montferrat to prevent a French succession and secure the Alpine communications to the other Spanish possessions farther north. This led to a disastrous three-year war with France in northwest Italy that Spain was no longer in a position to win. In 1629, the Spanish army lost ground on the border of the southern Netherlands, and in 1630, the Dutch resumed more forcefully their invasion of Brazil. Spain was finally able to reduce the pressure on herself by negotiating peace with England in 1630 and ending the three-year Mantuan War by dropping claims to the duchy, bringing peace with France in 1631.

The quarrel with Holland remained, though it was becoming clear that Spanish resources alone were not sufficient for victory. Thus a major feature of Spanish policy was the effort to win Austrian Habsburg support. Such a policy was counterproductive, for it required major Spanish assistance to the Catholic forces in the Thirty Years' War in Germany, particularly after Sweden entered that struggle and turned the tide in 1631-1632. A mutual assistance treaty was signed between the two Habsburg crowns at the beginning of 1632, and a strong Spanish army was later built up in northern Italy. Its commander was the king's younger brother, the Cardenal Infante D. Fernando, by far the most vigorous of seventeenth-century Spanish Habsburgs, who had been placed in holy orders but found his true calling on the field of battle. In conjunction with Austrian forces, his army reversed the momentum of the conflict in Germany by smashing the main Swedish army at Nördlingen in 1634. This involvement increased the strain on Spanish resources, but the Austrian crown never lent any notable assistance against Holland. Rather, the joint Habsburg alliance and its victories in Germany so alarmed the French government that it officially entered the war on the other side, attacking the Spanish Netherlands. In the main northern theater of operations, Spain's position had become more difficult.

What made prospects more and more discouraging in the 1630s was that government receipts were not recovering from the decline of the previous decade, payment of state obligations was now falling years behind, and no relief was in sight. New excise taxes were imposed and old ones were raised further. For the first time, wealthy nobles were required to make direct contributions, but it was difficult to raise more money from a declining economy. Olivares himself had never been oblivious to the need for basic fiscal and administrative reforms. In 1622-1623, soon after he rose to power, he had appointed a reform junta that tried to promote fundamental changes: the establishment of strict sumptuary laws in Castile, import restrictions, curbs on corruption, and a steep reduction in local government offices. Almost nothing had been accomplished, for the effort met with apathy among the aristocrats who dominated public affairs in Castile. Even before the fifth declaration of partial bankruptcy (1627), it had become increasingly difficult to raise state loans. A new source was found by encouraging the gravitation to Madrid of wealthy Portuguese cristão novo financiers, but this provided only limited assistance. Olivares also tried to promote formation of a sort of national bank to float the royal debt, but could not muster the resources. The crown could only ask more from the already nearly exhausted Castilian taxpayer.

Final Eclipse of the Castilian Cortes

During the seventeenth century the powers of the Cortes of Castile, already minimal, lapsed completely. There were still occasional assemblies. Cortes were summoned six times during the reign of Felipe III and eight times during that of Felipe IV. Currency devaluation was carried on in both reigns with scarcely any attempt to win the approval of the Cortes, and new taxes were forced through with declining opposition. Though the demands of the crown were greater, there was less resistance than during the sixteenth century. The main reason for this was the structure of Cortes representation. The eighteen towns of Castile that had retained the right of representation were dominated by aristocratic oligarchies, and so was the representation in Cortes. The procuradores were allowed a 1.5 percent commission on new taxes which they voted, and appearance in Cortes also helped to win patronage in the form of appointments, pensions or honors from the government. During the reign of Felipe IV, there were efforts by unrepresented towns to win a voice, and a vote was given to Palencia, as well as single collective votes to Galicia and Extremadura. The main motive here was not to resist taxation or fight for local rights against royal power, but rather to cut the governing aristocracies of these regions into the lucrative business of fiscal votes. The idea of representing any interest other than that of the aristocracy was dead, and in a civic sense the Cortes had become completely nonfunctional. After the Cortes of 1662, no regular assembly was summoned for the remainder of the century.

Spanish Imperial Defense and the Catalan Revolt of 1640-1652

Throughout the reign of Felipe III and the first part of that of Felipe IV, the crown had been unsuccessful in bringing the Aragonese principalities to submit to regular taxation or make systematic contributions to the crown for imperial defense. Only meager, irregular grants were made by the regional Cortes of the eastern principalities. In Catalonia, the urban oligarchs even resisted the payment of the town excises which were owed to the crown; instead, they pocketed the proceeds themselves. Throughout the early seventeenth century, the Catalan countryside continued to be plagued with bandits led by the rural gentry. This banditry, along with contrabandage and counterfeiting, was sheltered by the Catalan constitutional system. To make matters worse, commerce took a downturn after about 1600 and the Catalan elite were determined to resist any kind of change or concession to the crown.

As early as 1625, Olivares had conceived a long-range plan, called the Union of Arms, by which each region of the empire would pay its share toward imperial defense. Aragón and Valencia reluctantly agreed to partial cooperation in 1626, and Spanish America, already heavily taxed, assumed an even greater permanent contribution, fully attending to its own protection. The Catalans, however, were still refractory and made only token contributions. Olivares merely proposed to redistribute the burden of taxation and recruitment more equally; he did not intend to alter the constitutional systems of the eastern regions, though he did plan greater centralization of leadership. He hoped to make heavier contributions more palatable by providing new economic opportunities within the empire for the eastern principalities, though this was difficult in that period of depression. Unfortunately, he also shared a common belief that there were approximately a million Catalans, instead of the four hundred thousand who actually existed.

The financial problem became even more acute after outbreak of war with France in 1635. Taxes in Castile were raised arbitrarily, new loans made, the currency devalued, and offices sold more recklessly than ever, but by 1637, annual expenses were nearly twice the annual state income. The war itself went badly both in Germany and the Netherlands. In 1638, the French invaded the Spanish Basque country, besieging Fuenterrabia. The relief force that drove them out included contingents from all major regions save Catalonia, which refused to help the rest of Spain.

Desperate to get the Catalans to make some contribution to the war effort, Olivares and his advisers decided to route the campaign of

1639 directly through Catalonia. A counteroffensive was planned across the eastern Pyrenees through the Catalan counties of Rosselló and Cerdanya. It was poorly organized and led. The Catalans did participate in sizable numbers, however, and after the border fortress of Salcés was lost to the French through military incompetence, Catalan forces suffered heavy casualties in trying to retake it. Shortly afterward, disaster struck in northern waters as the last major Spanish fleet to sail against the Dutch was destroyed by Admiral van Tromp at the Battle of the Downs in October 1639. It was clearer than ever that the empire lacked the resources to deal with such manifold military commitments.

Having committed the principal home forces to the Catalan front, Olivares resolved to continue the offensive from that base in 1640. Strong measures were taken to force the Catalans to pay many of the expenses involved, and some 9,000 troops, many of them disorderly and obstreperous, were billeted on the civilian population, causing intense resentment. Hatred of the exactions of a "foreign" soldiery erupted in general revolt in the north Catalan countryside in May 1640, as peasants attacked Spanish troops throughout the district. By June, the rebels had moved into Barcelona, where they mobilized the *segadors,* or farm laborers, into a revolutionary mob that took over the city and murdered royal officials, including the viceroy. Catalan resistance to the crown had originally been the work of the privileged upper-class oligarchy determined to lose none of its financial or administrative prerogatives, but the revolt of 1640 swelled into something approaching a social revolution. Poor peasants rose against their overlords, the laborers and unemployed in the towns took over the streets, and bandit gangs reasserted themselves in many parts of the countryside. Catalonia was not merely in revolt against the crown but nearly beyond the control of its own oligarchy.

The principality could not defend itself alone against the Spanish state. On the one hand, it was simply too small and on the other, Catalans were no more willing to submit to organized authority for the purpose of self-defense than for any other. The only alternative seemed to be help from Spain's powerful enemy, the crown of France. The Diputació of the Catalan Corts had begun secret negotiations in April 1640, one month before the revolt. In October, an agreement was concluded to supply French military assistance, largely at Catalan expense, and in January 1641, the Catalan leaders officially placed the principality under French protection. Meanwhile, a Spanish force of nearly 20,000 had been laboriously assembled during the summer and fall of 1640. It occupied Tortosa but was stopped outside Barcelona by the joint French and Catalan resistance. Its leadership was incompetent, and the killing of a number of Catalan prisoners only increased the will to resist. For the time being, the crown had to give up any hope of holding a military position in central Catalonia.

The Spanish were thus driven out, but only at the cost of turning Catalonia into a French protectorate. A French viceroy was appointed for Barcelona and his administration was packed with French supporters, while steep payments were exacted for the support of French troops. In 1642, French units occupied the north Catalan regions of Rosselló and Cerdanya and seized the westernmost city of the region, Lérida. Meanwhile, the French exploited Catalonia economically much more than had the Spanish crown. The depressed wartime Catalan economy had little opportunity to sell to France, but French exports poured into Catalonia. Food production declined drastically, taxes skyrocketed, inflation and monetary devaluation wracked the economy, and famine among the poor set the stage for the great plague of 1650-1654, which halved the population of Barcelona and decimated the population in many parts of the principality. As the years passed, many of the rebels began to feel that the yoke of France was heavier than that of Spain.

The forces of Felipe IV rewon Lérida and western Catalonia in 1643-1644 and blocked any further French advance. In 1644, the king took a formal oath to uphold the Catalan constitutional laws. After a slow but steady weakening of the French and Catalan position, a considerable Spanish army moved in to besiege Barcelona in mid-1651, and the city surrendered a year later. The Spanish crown pledged a general amnesty and preservation of the laws of Catalonia, ending the revolt on the terms of the pre-war status quo. Catalonia gained nothing from the revolt but years of misery and death. Conversely, the Catalan uprising further weakened the Spanish crown at a time when it was struggling desperately against great odds, and the Pyrenean districts of Rosselló and Cerdanya were never regained.

The Secession of Portugal

The Catalan revolt was paralleled by the secession of Portugal from the Spanish crown in the same year, 1640. Portuguese separation was a response to the crisis of the Spanish empire, the frustration of its leadership, the burden of its defense, and above all, the decline of its economy. The Spanish crown could no longer offer Portugal either the protection or the opportunities of a generation or two earlier. Rather, it would involve Portugal further in the suffering of its wars and their heavy cost. The Catalan revolt provided Portuguese leaders with a model which they were able to imitate more successfully.

Unlike the Spanish trade in the Atlantic, that of the Portuguese was in a phase of moderate expansion and helped to provide Portugal with an economic base for independence. After 1640, the Spanish crown was in no position to build a new army for the subjugation of Portugal.

The Resignation of Olivares and the Balance of the Reign of Felipe IV, 1643-1665

The ambitious policy of Olivares broke down completely after 1640. The American trade had taken yet another drastic downturn and showed no prospects of recovery, leaving the crown even more desperate financially. The withdrawal of the Castilian population from involvement had become marked. Even the military aristocracy tried to avoid volunteering, and new levies could scarcely be assembled. Failure of leadership was profound, and those forces that were organized failed through incompetent command. Even the Castilian grandes withdrew from the crown. The powerful and wealthy duke of Medina Sidonia, a cousin of Olivares and brother-in-law of the new king of Portugal, headed a short-lived conspiracy to oust the count-duke and turn Andalusia into an independent kingdom. The high aristocracy were bitterly opposed to Olivares and determined to break his power. They abandoned the court en masse and pressed the king for his dismissal.

Olivares recognized the failure of state policy and resigned at the beginning of 1643, leaving Felipe IV resolved to serve as his own chief minister, encouraged by his correspondence with the noted mystic Sor María de Agreda. He had a quick enough mind but was simply too self-indulgent and undisciplined, given to a lechery remarkable even among seventeenth-century kings, and by mid-1643, Olivares had been replaced with a new valido, his own nephew (and enemy), the Conde de Haro. Haro was more discreet and prudent than Olivares and never enjoyed the same overarching authority, for Felipe IV devoted more personal attention to state affairs in the second half of his reign than during the rule of Olivares. After the death of Haro in 1661, the king directed the government himself for the remaining four years of his life.

The resignation of Olivares brought no real change in policy or problems. The financial burden continued to mount. By 1644, the crown's income was pledged four years in advance, bringing further exactions on the shriveled Castilian economy. Still, there was no compromise in the objectives of royal policy. In 1643, an underequipped Spanish army was destroyed with great loss at Rocroi near the northern French border, the first disastrous field defeat suffered by

Spanish infantry since the union of the crowns. Though the southern Netherlands held fast, Dunkirk was lost in 1646. In 1647-1648, there was a major revolt in Naples and Sicily, where taxes had recently been raised, that was somewhat like the Catalan rebellion. This led to yet another suspension of payments and a new forced debt conversion by the crown. When the Thirty Years' War was finally brought to an end in Germany in 1648, the Spanish crown was forced after enormous expense and losses to recognize the obvious. It signed a separate peace conceding the independence of Holland, bringing seventy years of warfare against that power to an end.

Yet the war with France remained. The French crown was itself seriously weakened by the outbreak of a major civil war (the Fronde), but Spain lacked the strength to exploit this opportunity beyond regaining Dunkirk and ending the Catalan revolt. A new round of devaluation and attendant inflation was resorted to which, together with a major crop failure, resulted in some of the worst suffering of the century, and it was at this time that the *Pendón verde* riot broke out in Seville. Another partial bankruptcy was declared in 1652. The only fiscal reform of the 1650's was the extension of taxation to pensions and honors that had been granted to the upper classes by the crown, but before long it was common practice to evade this impost.

With the Franco-Spanish conflict stalemated, England entered the struggle aggressively in 1654 by seizing Jamaica and preparing a full-scale naval offensive against Spain. In 1656 and 1657, major portions of the American treasure fleets were seized by the English, who put the peninsula under a partial blockade for nearly two years. Nevertheless, in 1656 Spanish troops won an important victory at Valenciennes—the last they would ever win in northern Europe—and Felipe IV had an opportunity to make a compromise peace with a France that was also weary of the long contest. This he spurned, still hoping for a decisive victory, though his advisers urged him to accept a graceful withdrawal from the war.

By this time Spanish resources, both financial and human, were almost exhausted. In June 1658, the combined French and English forces defeated the Spanish army on the northern French front, recapturing Dunkirk. The Portuguese, emboldened by Spanish weakness, seized the offensive, invaded Extremadura, and besieged Badajoz. Bled white by a quarter-century of warfare, Spain possessed scarcely enough men to defend her own frontiers. Galicia, the most heavily populated region of Castile, had already been heavily recruited. The Portuguese front was left largely to the amateur militia of the Extremaduran towns, who were untrained, ineffective, and reported in increasingly short numbers. The siege of Badajoz was finally lifted in October by a force of 15,000 sent from Madrid. This army then pursued the retreating Portuguese across the border and itself laid siege to the Portuguese town of Elvas. About 20 percent of its effectives promptly deserted, and a new Portuguese army routed the Spanish, who left 4,000 casualties behind. In the Spanish Netherlands, the enemy front had advanced almost to the gates of Brussels. There were no reinforcements to send, and not enough naval strength to transport them had they existed. Even within Spain, new military units were filled mainly with recruits from Spanish Italy and with German and Irish mercenaries. The militarily skilled, valiant, and patriotic elements of the aristocracy had themselves been thinnned by casualties. They no longer provided leadership, and most of the nobility simply dodged the call of duty.

Felipe IV had no real alternative to signing the compromise Peace of the Pyrenees with France in 1659. Its terms were lenient. France retained Rosselló and Cerdanya, now a center of diehard anti-Habsburg Catalan emigres, and picked up the Artois district on its northeastern frontier, as well as minor border concessions in the Spanish Netherlands. The main consideration for the French crown was winning the hand of Felipe IV's daughter, Maria Teresa, for the heir to the French throne, Louis XIV, a valued match in view of the fact that the Spanish king had no male heir at that time.

In his last years Felipe IV was extremely depressed and full of remorse, certain as he was that God had punished his economically ruined kingdom for its monarch's sins. Indeed, Felipe IV had never held any concept of Spanish interests, but had relentlessly subordinated other considerations to regaining the dynastic territories of the Habsburg crown, an enterprise in which he failed completely. In the north, the crown retained the Franche Comté and the southern Netherlands, which remained staunchly loyal to their Habsburg sovereign largely because he allowed them almost complete autonomy. These territories remained with the crown, however, not because of the strength of imperial defense, which was now negligible, but because other European powers were also eager to thwart French expansion. The crown's original goals—complete control over the Low Countries and Habsburg hegemony in the Germanies, along with secure land communications from Spanish Italy to the north—were all frustrated. Felipe IV's last consolation had been that peace with France and England would leave him free to reconquer Portugal, but even that was not to be. The border district of Extremadura was being depopulated by the war, and Portugal gained new assistance from England. The king's last years were a time of unrelieved defeat, and three years after his death the independence of Portugal had to be officially recognized.

Government during the Minority of
Carlos II, 1665-1675

A male heir, the future Carlos II (1665-1700), was born to the royal
family in 1661. When his father died in 1665, Carlos II was only four
years old, and, moreover, a sickly, retarded child of less than average
intelligence who suffered from rickets. In his will, Felipe IV appointed
his Austrian queen to be regent for the minority of the new king, and
also created a Junta de Gobierno to serve as executive council for the
crown. Doña Mariana, the regent, was herself in a difficult situation
as a woman and foreigner, poorly educated, of only mediocre intelligence, and distrusted by the powerful Spanish aristocracy. While at
first cooperating with the Junta, composed of nobles, church hierarchs, and leading state officials, she looked for a personal adviser on
whom she could rely and found one in the person of her Austrian
Jesuit confessor, Johann Nithard. He was made a naturalized Spaniard and appointed to the Junta de Gobierno. Though sincere and
pious, Nithard lacked talent or preparation for government. He was
strongly opposed by royal officials and the aristocracy, not so much
for his inability as for the fact that he was the foreign appointee of a
foreign queen.

In 1667, Louis XIV launched the first of his aggressive wars against
the Spanish Netherlands, basing his claim to the territory on fictitious
inheritance rights of his Spanish wife. The "War of Devolution"
lasted only a year, thanks not to the feeble Spanish defenses but to
the anti-French alliance formed by England, Holland, and Sweden.
In the settlement of 1668, Spain was forced to make more territorial
concessions to France in the southern Netherlands. This further
weakened the position of Nithard, who lacked any support in Spanish
opinion and was considered to be usurping the role of the aristocracy
and high royal officials, undercutting the succession arrangements
made by Felipe IV.

Nithard's chief rival was Felipe IV's most ambitious bastard, D.
Juan José de Austria. This dark, handsome prince was restless and
intermittently energetic, popular with the aristocracy and with Madrid opinion. He had fought on many fronts in his father's wars, was
indisputably Spanish, and cut the figure of gallant and seducer of
women that impressed society. Forced from Madrid, D. Juan José
gained a following in Aragón and Catalonia by posing as a defender
of regional fueros. Collecting local military forces, he moved on
Madrid at the beginning of 1669 and forced the queen regent to send
Nithard into exile.

This represented the triumph of the aristocracy in royal government, eliminating the supervision of a royal valido. Don Juan was satisfied with appointment as vicar-general of Aragón and Catalonia. From 1669 to 1673, the government was administered jointly by the queen regent and the Junta de Gobierno. A new favorite emerged in 1673 in the person of Fernando Valenzuela, a petty noble and adventurer, but Valenzuela served mainly as personal confidant and patronage boss. He was not a true valido in the sense of directing the government.

Carlos II was officially declared of age in 1675 when he reached fourteen. By that time, however, it was clearer than ever that this pathetic prince would never rule. The degenerate product of five generations of Spanish Habsburg inbreeding, he remained in a permanent state of decrepitude, sick more often than well, unable to lead a normal life or even to think clearly. His face was so long and his jaw so malformed that he could not even masticate food properly and he suffered continually from digestive disorders. He was neurotic and superstitious in the extreme and dominated by priests. Although later twice married he was unable to father children. The Junta would have to govern for him, and the king would never do more than sign papers, and even that but intermittently. His real adviser was the queen mother, and it was she who arranged the dissolution of the Junta in 1676 and the appointment of Valenzuela as full valido and head of state affairs. Valenzuela was given the tital of *primer ministro* of government, the first time that such a designation was ever made officially by the Spanish crown.

Final Triumph of the Aristocracy

Within a matter of weeks, the high aristocracy declared their united and unremitting opposition to this new valido. They were determined that royal government would not be exercised by a favorite who failed to reflect the interests of the nobility, and particularly not by an upstart of comparatively modest birth. A joint manifesto was signed by twenty-four high aristocrats, and at the beginning of 1677, D. Juan José crossed into Castilian territory from Aragón at the head of 15,000 troops. Supporters of the befuddled young king stood aside as the aristocratic faction, led by D. Juan José, took over the government. The queen mother was banished to Toledo, and Valenzuela was sent into colonial exile, where he later died.

For the first time in the history of the united Spanish crown, the nobility had taken control of the government from the king. Their leader, D. Juan José de Austria, was hailed by ecclesiastical leaders and by much of common opinion in Madrid, and directed the government for two and a half years. He operated simply as a dispenser of patronage to the victorious aristocracy and persecutor of the former appointees of Valenzuela.

Thus the aristocracy came into almost complete control of affairs during the reign of Carlos II, making a mockery of the strong monarchy of Fernando and Isabel, Carlos I (V), and Felipe II. During the minority of Carlos II and the first years of his formal reign, there was scarcely any attempt at central state regulation, even in Castile. The only major institution that might have matched the influence of the aristocracy, the church, was entirely unable to. Though ecclesiastical income was great, most of it was committed to specific church expenses, and the leaders of the Spanish hierarchy had at their disposal only a fraction of the wealth of the grandes. The wasteful style and attitudes of the high aristocracy made it impossible for most of them to foster, or in many cases even to preserve, the wealth derived from their estates, but new sources were always available from government, which nobles controlled; during the financially prostrate reign of Carlos II, the *mercedes* and honors taken from the royal treasury reached a new volume, perhaps three million ducats a year, draining from the government the last reserves with which it might have defended a tottering empire. The aristocrats had no pity for the lamentable state of the crown's affairs or the defense of the empire. The fact that their status was based essentially on wealth did not mean that the shrinking economy would bring a decline in their numbers. Instead, a quasi-monopoly of the sources of true wealth enabled more and more of the middle-rank to rise. The 41 families of grandes that were recognized in 1627 had been increased to 113 by 1707.

The apogee of the aristocracy coincided with the nadir of the kingdom and the empire. While the remains of Spain's government and economy were picked clean by the nobility, the empire suffered repeated assaults from the voracious French monarchy of Louis XIV. This aggressively expansionist state had nearly three times the population and four or five times the wealth of Spain. The only hope of resistance lay in the fact that the naked greed and aggression of Louis XIV roused the opposition of the other major states of western Europe. In 1672, the French king launched an invasion of both Holland and the Spanish Netherlands. Weak Spanish forces were swept aside, while Catalonia was also invaded and French forces intervened in Spanish Sicily, aided by another local rebellion. The northern powers nonetheless fought the French military machine to a standstill, but in the peace of 1678 Spain was forced to cede Franche Comté and a few minor territories on the border of the Netherlands.

These losses, humiliating but not actually important, came as the seventeenth-century economic depression in Castile reached its depth. The government of D. Juan José de Austria had neither a foreign nor a domestic policy but existed on the basis of patronage to its supporters among the aristocracy. Amid unrelieved defeat, general dissatisfaction, and political bankruptcy, it ended with D. Juan José's death in September, 1679.

The Trough of the Depression: Castile's Disaster Decade, 1677-1687

The depression hit bottom in the disastrous decade of 1677-1687, in which the unhappy people of Castile were struck by every kind of economic misfortune. The basic cause was the catastrophic weather. This was not altogether unusual, for the severity and extremes of the Spanish climate have always retarded agriculture, but the alternation of torrential rainfall and great floods with years of extreme drought during that decade reduced Castilian harvests to their lowest level in many generations. Andalusia was the hardest hit, but famine was widespread in other parts of the kingdom as well. Severe malnutrition encouraged another outbreak of plague, which claimed another quarter million lives in those years.

Economic disaster was intensified by the severest monetary crisis of the century. Inflation had continued, due mainly to the persistent depreciation of currency by the government to lighten its debts. Between 1660 and 1680, the price level in Castile increased nearly 65 percent and almost all the coinage in circulation was copper vellon. Madrid had become the most expensive city in Europe, and public complaints increased. Finally, in 1680, the new royal government imposed drastic revaluation. Prices fell nearly 50 percent in two years, but the new money supply was totally inadequate for commerce and finance, and much of the economy virtually ceased to function. Taxes and bills could not be paid, producers now received minimal prices for their goods, and the commercial economy went into a complete tailspin. Many local districts had to revert temporarily to a barter system, for lack of money. All this further depressed trade and production at a time when new goods, food, and imports were more desperately needed than ever. Particularly in the south, towns filled up with desperate, begging peasants looking for the smallest scrap of relief. It was a time of misery unparalleled even in seventeenth-century Castile.

Recovery in Catalonia

Since the thirteenth century, the social and economic development of Catalonia and that of Castile have moved according to markedly different rhythms. The creative phase of the medieval Catalan economy came at a time when Castile had just begun to build a modest base of urban manufactures and finished production. The fifteenth century, which saw the rise of Castile, was a time of decline in Catalonia, and during the sixteenth-century phase of Castilian expansion, Catalan society remained comparatively static and secluded.

Another reversal came again in the late seventeenth century, when Catalonia became the first region to recover from the great economic decline. After 1652, the eastern principalities had complete autonomy under their regional systems of law during what, as it turned out, was the last period of the Aragonese constitutions. Several factors were responsible for Catalonia's economic regeneration: a) the eastern principalities still enjoyed relative monetary autonomy, and after a currency adjustment in the 1650s Catalonia was not affected by the brusque swings of inflation and deflation that wracked the Castilian monetary system; b) nonetheless, during the years 1688-1699 Catalonia experienced a rather mild inflation, unaccompanied by a rise in wages, that permitted a somewhat more rapid capital accummulation; c) the Peace of the Pyrenees in 1659 stipulated freedom for French exports into Catalonia and vice versa, opening the Catalan textile market to modern competition that stimulated improvement in the region's own production techniques and the quality of its textiles; and d) population growth and lower taxes in the smaller towns stimulated a more rapid economic development in them and in parts of the countryside than in Barcelona. Wine and brandy exports increased markedly, and textile shops in some of the towns made greater technical advances than did those of Barcelona. The Catalan capital nevertheless remained the great commercial and financial center of the principality. Maritime activity entered an expansive phase beginning about 1675 and grew rapidly in the 1680s. During the final years of the century, traffic in the port of Barcelona was almost twice as great as in 1600. Some firms now dealt in extremely large volume, exporting Catalan goods to western Europe and dealing in the American market by way of Cádiz and Lisbon. Their growing interest in the commercial possibilities of a developing Spanish America was a sign of an historic change in Catalan interests and energies. After strong objections, the crown in 1674 removed Catalan merchants dealing through Cádiz from the category of foreigners, allowing them to trade on an

equal footing with Castilians. Another sign of change was the significant contribution that a more prosperous and cooperative Catalonia made to the crown during the second half of the century, whereas before 1640 it had contributed very little.

Aragón and Valencia

The situation in the other two eastern principalities was less promising. Throughout the century, Aragón stagnated under its regional fueros. Its population did not increase appreciably, and no significant change occurred in its society. The landed aristocracy retained its overwhelming predominance, though now more embarrassed than before by the responsibilities involved in the *derecho de maltratar* (the right to punish), and there were no signs of new economic development. As for manufactured goods, the principality became virtually a colony of France in the second half of the century.

Valencia was scarcely any better off, for it did not recover from the expulsion of the Moriscos, either in terms of population or agriculture, until the middle of the eighteenth century. The economy of the city of Valencia did begin to expand in the 1660s, but the countryside, under more stern seigneurial control than most of the rest of the peninsula, was slower to respond. Peasants settling on ex-Morisco land were subjected to steep feudalistic exactions. Resentment grew more intense toward the end of the century as population expanded. The aristocratic oligarchy and church leaders of Valencia were intensely jealous of regional rights, yet they refused reform or greater rights to peasants on seigneurial domain. A semiclandestine peasant league was founded in the Játiva region south of the city of Valencia and in 1693 its members refused to pay seigneurial dues. They chose a *síndic*, or leader, for their syndicate and were assisted by a few village notables. Their crudely organized force of 2,000 was labeled by its chief the Eixèrcit dels Agermanats, recalling the great revolt of 1520. This rebellion was put down rather easily, but bitter discord remained and flared once more during the Succession War that followed the turn of the century.

Government Reform, 1680–1691

The depth of the Castilian depression lasted from 1640 to 16__ during the 1660s and 1670s the quality of government decli__ ther. The point of reversal may, for convenience's sake, b__

about 1680. After that new efforts were made to improve government and stimulate the economy. Catalonia was already recovering, and though there was no similar revitalization in Castile, modest economic gains were made in the 1690s, lifting the Castilian economy out of the trough of the preceding decade.

The restoration of government began early in 1680, when young Carlos II appointed the duke of Medinaceli *primer ministro*. Medinaceli was one of the wealthiest and most important of the grandes, but he was neither vain nor overweeningly ambitious. Though lacking original ideas, he was genuinely interested in commercial, financial, and colonial reform. His government held fast to the drastic currency revaluation imposed by the finance council, devastating though its short-term consequences were. After this reform, and a corrective devaluation of silver in 1686, the Spanish monetary system held steady for the remainder of the century and beyond. Though there was some slight inflation after the mid-1680s, the general price level stayed comparatively stable for the next fifty years. Medinaceli also appointed a capable general secretary to assist the primer ministro and prepare plans to increase colonial trade and revenue. The government tried to stimulate commerce and discussed the reform of taxes, though nothing was accomplished during Medinaceli's tenure, which coincided with the trough of the Castilian depression.

The Medinaceli government, like its predecessors, was soon impaled on the horns of French imperialism. After reports of the severe want in Castile, Louis XIV deemed the moment propitious for another assault, invading Catalonia and the Spanish Netherlands in 1683–1684. This aggression was soon ended, but only after France received another pound of flesh from the northern possessions, in this case the duchy of Luxemburg.

Economic and imperial misfortune forced Medinaceli to share power with a new figure, the Conde de Oropesa, who became president of the Council of Castile in 1684 and replaced Medinaceli altogether as primer ministro in 1685. Like his predecessor, he had won office in large measure through skill in personal intrigue and factional maneuver. Dynamic, able, and innovative, Oropesa became the outstanding reformist head of government in seventeenth-century Spain. Plans for tax reform were pressed. The government reduced expenditures, cut the budget for the royal household, eliminated superfluous offices, canceled some of the mercedes to the aristocracy, and drew up plans to shift more of the fiscal burden from the lower to the upper classes, though these plans were largely blocked. A general effort was made to reduce the bureaucracy and the number of seats in state councils, as well as to control the sale of offices. Oropesa also tried to arrest the parasitical growth of the clergy, and in 1689 the hierarchy was asked to suspend temporarily the ordination of new

priests. Oropesa thus met head on the key problems of state finance and taxation and the waste of resources by the three chief institutions of Spain—aristocracy, church, and state bureaucracy. His government also upheld earlier reform measures of 1679 and 1682 that encouraged immigration of skilled foreign craftsmen, reduced taxes for manufacturers, and specifically affirmed that commercial and industrial activity were compatible with aristocratic status. A Junta General de Comercio was later set up to stimulate commerce and finance.

Oropesa made many powerful enemies, but his administration was a domestic success and would not have ended when it did (1691) but for the latest round of French aggression. This stemmed from the anger of Louis XIV over the arrangement of Carlos II's second marriage (after the early death of his first queen, a French princess) to Mariana of Neuburg, a German princess related to the Austrian Habsburgs. The new invasion prompted the usual anti-French coalition in western Europe, and the resulting War of the League of Augsburg lasted from 1689 to 1697. It placed still greater pressure on Spanish finance, and brought a new invasion of Catalonia as well as defeats in the Netherlands and northern Italy.

During the 1690s, royal government relapsed into weakness, confusion, and disunity. The new queen dominated appointments, and there was another scramble for lucrative positions as the state suffered through the remainder of the decade without effective leadership. The only bright spot was the peace treaty of 1697 ending the latest French war without territorial loss to the Spanish crown.

The Dynastic Succession

The feeble and degenerate Carlos II survived until the age of thirty-nine, which was longer than many had expected. In his last years it became clearer than ever that, second marriage or not, he would never produce an heir to the throne. Since he had no younger brother, the succession would have to pass through his sisters or a collateral line. One of his sisters, María Teresa, was queen of France, and another had married Leopold I, the Austrian Habsburg emperor. The issue thus resolved itself into the question of a French Bourbon versus an Austrian Habsburg succession. After 1696, with the king more and more decrepit and likely to die at any time, the contest became acute. Though Louis XIV had invested much of the wealth and energy of his realm in efforts to conquer Spanish domains on the eastern border of France, he realized that any attempt to secure the entire inheritance for a French prince would upset the balance of power and bring forth a powerful international alliance against France. Similarly, he was

determined to frustrate the development of a great, new pan-Habsburg empire in western and central Europe, reminiscent of the territorial hegemony of Carlos V, that would result if the two branches of
the Habsburg crown were reunited by an Austrian inheritance of the
Spanish domains. Consequently, at various times during the reign of
Carlos II he negotiated three different partition treaties with other
European powers that attempted to provide for a balanced division of
the Spanish empire in Europe.

Such proposals infuriated the Spanish crown, for the only clear
goal that the miserable Carlos II retained was to transmit the entire
inheritance of the Spanish empire undivided to a capable successor.
French and Austrian diplomacy employed extreme pressure at the
Spanish court, rallying factions to each side, and this pulling and
hauling completed the prostration of government administration in
the last years of the century. French interests had the better of it for
four reasons: a) the prestige of the Bourbon dynasty, ruler of what
was now the strongest state in Europe, compared with which the
Austrian Habsburgs were distinctly less impressive; b) general distrust among most Spanish opinion, provoked by the intrigues and
manipulations of the German queen, Mariana of Neuburg, and of her
German-Austrian favorites and appointees at court; c) an increasingly strong desire for some kind of renovation and new leadership,
which it was felt that a successor from the powerful new Bourbon
state in France would more likely provide; and d) the fact that the
prime French candidate, Philippe, duke of Anjou, was a younger
grandson of Louis XIV and María Teresa, and hence removed from
the direct line of French succession. This would enable him to establish himself as a separate and independent Spanish king, whereas the
Habsburg candidate, Archduke Karl, was a younger son of the reigning Leopold, and the succession to his elder brother, Josef, was
somewhat uncertain, raising the possibility that a Habsburg heir
might treat the Spanish domains as a mere appendage to his central
European empire. In October 1700, one month before his death,
Carlos II made his final will, leaving the Spanish crown and all its
empire to Philippe of Anjou on condition that he preserve it undivided under a Spanish Bourbon monarchy.

Signs of Regeneration

The last years of the seventeenth century revealed certain signs of
recovery. The reforms of Oropesa, after about 1687, strengthened
royal finance and permitted a modest expansion of the fleet and the

formation of several new military units to bolster Spanish resistance in the War of the League of Augsburg. The economic resurgence of Catalonia was fully apparent, and Valencian textile production and commerce were also advancing. Levantine agriculture finally began to expand, for the first time since expulsion of the Moriscos. Even in Aragón, a new group of reformers had emerged who were trying to revive industry and commerce. In 1684 they had finally managed to eliminate local toll duties within Aragón. The commerce of the north Castilian ports was increasing slowly, Basque iron production was expanding, and there was also a slight growth in Andalusian wine exports. Some efforts were now being made to encourage Castilian agriculture, and some of the secondary cities that had formerly been productive centers and fallen into decline were now growing once more in population.

There were also signs of new intellectual stimulation. The principal foreign influences came from the University of Montpelier just across the French border and from scientists in Italy. The most important intellectual center in Spain by the 1690s was the University of Valencia, which proved receptive to new currents of learning from France and Italy. A new society for the study of modern philosophy had also been formed in Seville, and the basic problems of developing science in Spain were clearly analyzed by Juan de Cabriada's *Carta filosófico-médico-chýmica,* published in 1687.

The overseas empire had held firm despite numerous assaults from a variety of enemies. From among these vast territories, only the island of Jamaica had been lost, while Spanish American society was beginning to develop on the basis of its own strength. The Spanish colonial administration had demonstrated surprising vigor. Despite venality and widespread sale of offices, the Council of the Indies continued to function with a certain amount of efficiency, and the colonial bureaucracy proved more able than might have been expected.

Nevertheless, Castile in the 1690s remained socially and economically depressed. Seville, whose population had declined greatly, was handling only one-tenth the commercial traffic that it had registered at the beginning of the century. Agriculture and manufacture in Castile, in general, remained scarcely at the subsistence level. After further bad harvests in 1698-1699, riots broke out in Madrid and several other cities. At that moment there was promise of renewal and future achievement in Spain, but the country had lost much ground compared to the advanced regions of northwest Europe during the second half of the century, and the Spanish resurgence would not be fully affirmed for half a century more.

Spain in Seventeenth-Century Europe

The seeming paradox in the degeneration from the power and glory of sixteenth-century Spain to the misery of the late seventeenth-century have fascinated historical commentators for more than two hundred years. Since the seventeenth century was the first great age of modernization for the countries of northwestern Europe who became prototypes of modernism and subsequently the leaders of European civilization, the contrast has usually been drawn in terms of differences in economic function and moral values between the societies of those lands and of Spain. Spanish society stood in opposition, both figuratively and literally, to them. As for the reasons for Spain's growing social and economic weakness, these have been understood in their basic lines for more than a century, and recent scholarship has only added details and sharpened comprehension of certain points.

Yet the Spanish experience appears much less anomalous when compared with countries other than Holland, England, France, and Sweden. Only a corner of Europe was actually "modernizing" in the seventeenth century, and it might be argued that this region was out of step with the greater part of Europe rather than vice versa. The Spanish pattern was very close to that of all southern and eastern Europe and much of the center of the continent as well. A refeudalization resulting in the expansion of the numbers and power of the aristocracy, the decline of cities and the middle classes, the deterioration of the situation of the peasantry, severe regional and social revolts, economic stagnation, and the weakening of the state or public power—these were common phenomena throughout half of Europe in the seventeenth century. Even the advanced regions of Germany, among the best developed in Europe in the early sixteenth century, had lapsed into a kind of stagnation by the end of that century, and then were dealt a further serious blow by the Thirty Years' War. The decline of the rural economy of central and southern Italy in the seventeenth century was very much like that of Spain, and the experience of the broad peripheral empires of Poland and Muscovy in the east also reveals some striking similarities.

Poland, like Castile, developed in the Middle Ages as the strongest bastion of Latin Christendom on one of the crucial frontiers of the continent. The eastward expansion of the kingdom of Poland from the fourteenth century paralleled the southward and transoceanic expansion of Castile, and the union of Poland-Lithuania played a dynastic and expansionist function similar to the union of the Castilian and Aragonese crowns and the Habsburg succession in Spain. Polish society was also dominated by a militant warrior aristocracy engaged in a broad geographic expansion that during the sixteenth century carried far eastward into the Ukraine. The Polish elite were quite conscious of the historical comparison between Polish expansion and imperial Spain: in the advance on Moscow in 1613 Polish aristocrats likened themselves to the conquerors of Mexico and Peru. This imperial, expansionist experience solidified the power of the aristocracy, which usurped economic dominion in Poland to a degree at least as great as in Spain. Indeed, in Poland, as in most of eastern Europe, the process developed even further, as state and aristocracy imposed a second era of serfdom, beginning in the sixteenth century, that progressively shackled peasants to aristocratic estates and placed them under steep exactions. The opportunities and importance of the towns and middle class correspondingly shrank. In the early seventeenth century, aristocrat-dominated Poland became involved in a series of major imperialist wars that wasted her resources, and was shaken by the great Ukrainian revolt of 1648. With her economy unbalanced and retarded, Poland then relapsed into a deepening stagnation in the second half of the seventeenth century. The power of the nobility only increased, eventually negating the sovereignty of the monarchy itself, destroying national unity, and leading to the dissolution of Poland.

Farther east, the sprawling, backward Muscovite empire also underwent an era of stagnation and decline in the late sixteenth and early seventeenth centuries. There, too, the situation of the peasantry greatly deteriorated with the steady development of neo-serfdom. Throughout the eastern 60 percent of the continent, the seventeenth century, in particular, was a time of general social regression.

Seen against this panorama of rural decline and growing caste oppression in most of Europe during the late-sixteenth and seventeenth centuries, the Spanish decline no longer seems so anomalous. Spanish society was at least spared the disaster of the mass enserfment that retarded east European development. By the end of the seventeenth century it could even display a few minor foci of development on the northwest European pattern. In general, the Spanish experience may be placed in a secondary category of stagnation, but not total regression, that embraced most of southwestern and central Europe.

The great differentiating factor in the case of Spain—and Portugal—was the American empire. This provided a unique source of wealth in the sixteenth and early seventeenth centuries that might be compared with the new imperial domains and serf labor of Poland and Russia in the same period. Though it would be incorrect to say that the Castilian peasantry were spared only because of the empire, it is nonetheless correct that the semiservile Indian society of Spanish and Portuguese America (or, perhaps more correctly in the case of Brazil, the African slaves) constituted to a lesser degree the Hispanic equivalent of the serf economy that provided the economic surplus for the Polish and Muscovite states and their aristocracies during this period. The divergence of Spain and Portugal from the pattern of modernization being developed in northwestern Europe was fully apparent. Compared with Europe as a whole, however, the Hispanic problems of backwardness were not anomalous but to a greater or lesser degree common to most of the continent.

*

REFERENCE MATTER

Bibliography

Chapter 1

There are four recent multivolume general histories of Spain. Ramón Menéndez Pidal, the dean of Spanish philologists and a leading medievalist, has edited an *Historia de España* composed of contributions from the leading specialists in each period. Publication was begun in 1935, and the most recent volume (26) extends the history through 1833 only. Parts of the six-volume *Historia de España* edited by Luis Pericot García (Barcelona, 1935-62) are of high quality, but this work is less full and more uneven. The older single-author work, Antonio Ballesteros y Beretta's *Historia de España y su influencia en la Historia Universal*, 12 vols. (Barcelona, 1918-41), is especially notable for its copious bibliographies. Ferran Soldevila's *Historia de España* 8 vols. (Barcelona, 1952-59), is the only multivolume general account written from a Catalan viewpoint. Luis García de Valdeavellano began a multivolume *Historia de España* (Madrid, 1955), but the two volumes completed extend only through the early Middle Ages. See also his *Curso de historia de las instituciones españolas: De los orígenes al final de la Edad Media* (Madrid, 1968). On social and economic history, see Jaime Vicens Vives, ed., *Historia social y económica de España y América*, 5 vols. (Barcelona, 1957-59), which is uneven but very useful, and Vicens's own *Historia económica de España*, rev. ed., 2 vols. (Barcelona, 1964), now available in an English translation published by Princeton University Press. Though somewhat out of date, the basic bibliographical reference to Spanish historiography is B. Sánchez Alonso, *Fuentes de la historia española e hispanoamericana*, 3d ed.,

3 vols. (Madrid, 1952). Sánchez Alonso has also written the principal account of early Spanish historiography, *Historia de la historiografía española*, 3 vols. (Madrid, 1947-50).

The dean of Spanish prehistorians and leader of the "African" school is Pedro Bosch Gimpera. His two most important general works are *Etnología de la Península Ibérica* (Barcelona, 1932), and *Los pueblos de España* (Barcelona, 1946). A somewhat similar interpretation is given by Luis Pericot García, *La España primitiva* (Barcelona, 1950). The best recent general synthesis of the history of ancient Hispania is Julio Caro Baroja's *España primitiva y romana* (Madrid, 1957). Martín Almagro, *Origen y formación del pueblo hispano* (Barcelona, 1958), is also useful. Concerning ancient Hispanic art history, see José Camón Aznar, *Las artes y los pueblos de la España primitiva* (Madrid, 1954), and Luis Pericot García and Eduardo Ripoll Perelló, eds., *Prehistoric Art of the Western Mediterranean and the Sahara* (Chicago, 1964).

There are a variety of monographs dealing with individual regions, cultures, or aspects of prehistoric Hispania. On Tartessos, see Adolph Schulten, *Tartessos*, rev. ed. (Madrid, 1950). Other significant works of Schulten are *Hispania* (Barcelona, 1920), and *Numantia*, 4 vols. (Munich, 1914-31). On Greeks, Phoenicians, and Carthaginians in the peninsula, see Antonio García y Bellido, *Fenicios y cartagineses en Occidente* (Madrid, 1942), and *Hispania graeca*, 3 vols. (Madrid, 1948). For the Iberians, see Antonio Arribas, *The Iberians* (New York, 1965). The two best works on the peoples of the northern mountain ranges are Julio Caro Baroja, *Los pueblos del norte de la Península Ibérica* (Madrid, 1943), and Julio González Echegaray, *Los cántabros* (Santander, 1966).

On Roman Hispania, see R. Thouvenot, *Essai sur la province romaine de Bétique* (Paris, 1940); J. de Serra Ráfols, *La vida en España en la época romana* (Barcelona, 1944); C. H. V. Sutherland, *The Romans in Spain 217 B.C.-A.D. 117* (London, 1939); and F. J. Wiseman's manual, *Roman Spain* (London, 1956). M. Tarradell, ed., *Estudios de economía antigua de la Península Ibérica* (Barcelona, 1968), is tedious but rewarding.

There is no satisfactory history of Visigothic Hispania. The best general account has been written by Manuel Torres as volume 3 of Menéndez Pidal's *Historia de España*. See also E. A. Thompson, *The Goths in Spain* (Oxford, 1969); Ramón de Abadal, *Del reino de Tolosa al reino de Toledo* (Madrid, 1960); and volumes 1 and 3 of J. Orlandis, ed., *Estudios visigóticos* (Madrid, 1964). There is a narrative of Visigothic history in Harold Livermore's *The Origins of Spain and Portugal* (London, 1971). The church under the Visigoths is treated in Z. García Villada, *Historia eclesiástica de España*, vol. 2 (Madrid, 1929); A. K. Ziegler, *Church and State in Visigothic Spain* (Washington, D.C., 1930); and Abadal, *La batalla del adopcionismo en la desintegración de la iglesia visigoda* (Barcelona, 1949). Two key monographs on institutional changes by Claudio Sánchez Albornoz are *Ruina y extinción del municipio romano en España* (Buenos Aires, 1943), and *El 'stipendium' hispano-godo y los orígenes del beneficio prefeudal* (Buenos Aires, 1947). The Germanic kingdom of the Suevi in the northwest corner of the peninsula is treated in Wilhelm Reinhard, *Historia general del reino hispánico de los suevos* (Madrid, 1952).

Chapter 2

The first critical comprehensive study of Al-Andalus was Reinhardt Dozy, *Histoire des musulmans d'Espagne, 711-1110* (Leiden, 1861; Eng. tr., London, 1913). Dozy's work has been extended and corrected by E. Lévi-Provençal, *Histoire de l'Espagne musulmane,* 2d ed., 3 vols. (Paris, 1950-53), which covers only the years through 1031. Lévi-Provençal has treated the apex of Al-Andalus in *L'Espagne musulmane au Xe siècle* (Paris, 1932). A useful brief survey in English has been provided by W. Montgomery Watt, *A History of Islamic Spain* (Edinburgh, 1965). On the events of the eighth century, see the last part of Harold Livermore's *The Origins of Spain and Portugal* (London, 1971).

James T. Monroe has written a stimulating analysis, *Islam and the Arabs in Spanish Scholarship* (Leiden, 1970). C. Sánchez Albornoz, ed., *La España musulmana,* 2 vols. (Buenos Aires, 1946), provides accounts of major aspects of the entire period. Cultural orientalization and its sources are examined in Mahmud Ali Makki, *Ensayo sobre las aportaciones orientales en la España musulmana* (Madrid, 1968). The most up-to-date general study of the Mozarabs is Isidro de las Cagigas, *Los mozárabes,* 2 vols. (Madrid, 1947-48). E. P. Colbert, *The Martyrs of Córdoba (850-859)* (Washington, D.C., 1962), presents a revised interpretation of the major incident of Mozarab history.

There are cogent insights on Andalusi culture in the work of the leading twentieth-century Spanish Arabist, Miguel Asín Palacios, *Obras escogidas,* 3 vols. (Madrid, 1946-48). Henri Terrasse, *Islam d'Espagne* (Paris, 1958), deals mainly with art and architecture. A general account of the remarkable development of science in Al-Andalus will be found in J. A. Sánchez Pérez, *La ciencia árabe en la Edad Media* (Madrid, 1954). Rodolfo Gil Benumeya, *Marruecos andaluz* (Madrid, 1942), discusses interaction between Al-Andalus and Morocco.

Chapter 3

The best general one-volume history of Spain in the Middle Ages is Luis Suárez Fernández's *Historia de España: Edad Media* (Madrid, 1970). The leading historian of the kingdom of Asturias-León is Claudio Sánchez Albornoz. His principal works dealing with early medieval Spain are *En torno a los orígenes del feudalismo,* 3 vols. (Mendoza, 1942); *Despoblación y repoblación del valle del Duero* (Buenos Aires, 1966); and a collection of brief studies, *Estudios sobre las instituciones medievales españoles* (Mexico City, 1965). Joaquín Arbeloa, *Los orígenes del reino de Navarra,* 3 vols. (San Sebastián, 1969), is an interesting new work. The most extensive history of tenth-century Castile, though somewhat misleading on Castilian origins, is Justo Pérez de Urbel's *Historia del Condado de Castilla,* 3 vols. (Madrid, 1945). Pérez de Urbel has also written a biography of the leading Hispanic ruler of the early eleventh century, *Sancho el Mayor de Navarra* (Madrid, 1950). A. Cotarelo Valledor, *Historia crítica y documentada de Alfonso III* (Madrid, 1933), is a political biography of one of the most important Asturian kings.

The fundamental study of the question of an Hispano-Christian identity is José Antonio Maravall, *El concepto de España en la Edad Media* (Madrid, 1954). See also Maravall's *Estudios de historia del pensamiento español* (Madrid, 1967). The idea of Hispanic empire is treated by Ramón Menéndez Pidal, *El imperio hispánico y los cinco reinos* (Madrid, 1950), and Alfonso Sánchez Candeira, *El "Regnum-Imperium" leonés hasta 1037* (Madrid, 1951). Useful studies of reconquest and repopulation are contained in J. M. Lacarra, ed., *La Reconquista española y la repoblación del país* (Zaragoza, 1951).

There is a detailed survey of early medieval Hispanic society by Alfonso García Gallo, "Las instituciones sociales de España en la Alta Edad Media (Siglos VIII-XII)," *Revista de Estudios Políticos*, Suplemento de Política Social (1945), vols. 1 and 2. See also Sánchez Albornoz's *Estampas de la vida en León durante el Siglo X* (Madrid, 1926, 1965). The principal work on medieval Hispanic slavery is Charles Verlinden, *L'Esclavage dans l'Europe médiévale. I. Peninsule Ibérique-France* (Bruges, 1955). For early medieval Hispanic culture, see Enrique Bagué, *Historia de la cultura española: La Alta Edad Media* (Barcelona, 1953); and Gonzalo Menéndez Pidal, "Mozárabes y asturianos en la cultura de la Alta Edad Media," *Boletín de la Real Academia de Historia* 134 (1954): 137-291.

Chapter 4

The classic study of the Cid, though nationalistically biased, is Ramón Menéndez Pidal's *La España del Cid* (Madrid, 1947). Perhaps the principal historian of twelfth-century León and Castile is Julio González. His major works are *Regesta de Fernando II* (Madrid, 1940); *Alfonso IX*, 2 vols. (Madrid, 1942); *Repartimiento de Sevilla*, 2 vols. (Madrid, 1951); and *El reino de Castilla en la época de Alfonso VIII*, 3 vols. (Madrid, 1960). For the period of Alfonso el Sabio, see Antonio Ballesteros y Beretta, *Alfonso el Sabio* and *Sevilla en el siglo XIII* (Madrid, 1913).

The key work on the crusade in Spain is José Goñi Gaztambide, *Historia de la bula de Cruzada en España* (Vitoria, 1958). Two of the principal military orders are treated in Derek W. Lomax, *La Orden de Santiago (1170-1275)* (Madrid, 1965), and Francis Gutton's somewhat less useful *L'Ordre de Calatrava* (Paris, 1955). On military affairs, see Ambrosio Huici Miranda, *Las grandes batallas de la reconquista durante las invasiones africanas* (Madrid, 1956). The background of military organization is well explained in Elena Lourie, "A Society Organized for War: Medieval Spain," *Past and Present*, no. 35 (Dec. 1966), pp. 54-76. French influence is treated in Marcel Defourneaux, *Les Français en Espagne aux XIe et XIIe siècles* (Paris, 1949). The best Spanish account of the Almoravids is Jacinto Bosch Vilá, *Los Almorávides* (Tetuan, 1956). The fundamental work on the medieval Castilian Cortes, though weak on the origins of the institution, is still the study by the fin de siècle Russian Hispanist, W. Piskorski, *Las Cortes de Castilla en el período de tránsito de la Edad Media a la Moderna (1188-1520)* (Barcelona, 1930). Demetrio Ramos, *Historia de las Cortes tradicionales de España* (Madrid, 1944), gives a brief description. Joseph F. O'Callaghan, "The Beginnings of the Cortes of León-Castile," *American Historical Review* 74, no. 5 (June 1969): 1503-37, is vital for understanding the origins of the Leonese-Castilian Cortes. The main work on Castilian towns and local self-government in this period is María del Carmen Carlé, *Del concejo medieval castellano-leonés* (Buenos Aires, 1968). Pedro Corominas, *El sentimiento de la riqueza en Castilla* (Madrid, 1917, 1951), presents an important hypothesis on Castilian social and economic values.

Chapter 5

The best one-volume history of Catalonia is Ferran Soldevila's *Història de Catalunya*, rev. ed. (Barcelona, 1962). Soldevila is also the editor of a new multivolume *Historia dels catalans* (Barcelona, 1966—), which is superbly illustrated. The series Biografies Catalanes, published in Barcelona, provides detailed accounts of political and institutional history: see Ramon d'Abadal, *Els primers comtes catalans* (1958); Santiago Sobrequés, *Els grans comtes de Barcelona* (1961); P. E. Schramm, J.-F. Cabestany, and E. Bagué, *Els primers comtes-reis* (1960); Ferran Soldevila, *Els grans reis del segle XIII* (1955); J.-E. Martínez Ferrando, S. Sobrequés, and E. Bagué, *Els descendents de Pere el Gran* (1954); and Rafael Tasis, *Pere el Ceremoniós i els seus fills* (1957). The most thorough study of Catalonia-Aragón in the period of the expansion is J. L. Shneidman's *The Rise of the Aragonese-Catalan Empire 1200-1350*, 2 vols. (New York, 1970), which is topical in organization.

The most extensive study of early medieval Catalonia, still uncompleted, is Ramón d'Abadal's *Catalunya carolingia*, 4 vols. (Barcelona, 1925-55). A. R. Lewis, *The Development of Southern French and Catalan Society, 718-1050* (Austin, 1965), provides new understanding of early Catalan society and institutions. See also Emile Cauvet, *Etude historique sur l'établissement des espagnols dans la Septimanie au VIIIme et IXme siècles* (Narbonne, 1877), and Josep M. Guilera, *Unitat històrica del Pirineu* (Barcelona, 1964). Jordi Ventura has written two useful biographies that deal also with transpyrenean expansion and the question of heterodoxy: *Alfons el Cast* (Barcelona, 1962), and *Pere el Catòlic i Simó de Montfort* (Barcelona, 1960). R. Dalmau's booklet, *L'heretgia albigesa i la batalla de Muret* (Barcelona, 1960), is also helpful. The principal biographies of the two leading thirteenth-century rulers are by Soldevila: *Vida de Jaume I el Conqueridor* (Barcelona, 1958), and *Pere el Gran*, 3 vols. (Barcelona, 1950-1956). Ramon d'Abadal has recently published a new biography, *Pere el Ceremoniós* (Barcelona, 1972). On the fourteenth-century kings of Mallorca, see J.-E. Martínez Ferrando, *La tràgica història dels reis de Mallorca* (Barcelona, 1960).

Aspects of foreign affairs and expansion are studied in Juan Reglá Campistol, *Francia, la Corona de Aragón y la frontera pirenaica*, 2 vols. (Madrid, 1951); Vicente Salavert y Roca, *Cerdeña y la expansión mediterránea de la Corona de Aragón 1297-1314*, 2 vols. (Madrid, 1956); Antonio Arribas Palau, *La conquista de Cerdeña por Jaime II de Aragón* (Madrid, 1952); Francesco Giunta, *Aragonesi e catalani nel Mediterraneo*, 2 vols. (Palermo, 1953); Ch.-E. Dufourcq, *L'Espagne catalane et le Maghrib aux XIIIe et XIVe siècles* (Paris, 1966); and Lluis Nicolau d'Olwer, *L'expansió de Catalunya en la Mediterrània oriental* (Barcelona, 1926). Two useful brief summaries are J. F. Cabestany, *Expansió catalana per la Mediterrànea* (Barcelona, 1967), and Rafael Tasis, *L'expedició dels almogàvers* (Barcelona, 1960). Political and scientific ideas are treated in Francisco Elías de Tejada, *Historia del pensamiento político catalán*, 3 vols. (Seville, 1963-65), and J. Millás Vallicrosa, *Assaig d'història de les idees físiques i matemàtiques a la Catalunya medieval* (Barcelona, 1931). Armand Llinares, *Ramon Llull* (Barcelona, 1968), presents an excellent analysis of the leading figure of medieval Catalan religion and culture. Commercial organization is studied in Jaime Carrera Pujal, *La Lonja de Mar y los cuerpos de comercio de Barcelona* (Barcelona, 1953).

The best brief history of medieval Aragón is José Ma. Lacarra, *Aragón en el pasado* (Zaragoza, 1960). On Valencia, see the multivolume *Història dels valencians* (Barcelona, 1965—), and the first chapters of Joan Fuster, *Nosotros los valencianos* (Madrid, 1967). Thomas F. Glick, *Irrigation and Society in Medieval Valencia* (Cambridge, 1970), is an important new work. The basic new reference on Mallorca is J. Mascaró Pasarius, *Història de Mallorca*, 4 vols. (Palma de Mallorca, 1970).

Chapter 6

The best succinct account of Portuguese history is A. H. de Oliveira Marques, *History of Portugal*, 2 vols. (New York, 1972-73). The principal multivolume histories are Damião Peres, ed., *História monumental de Portugal*, 8 vols. (Barcelos, 1928-35); Fortunato de Almeida, *História de Portugal*, 6 vols. (Coimbra, 1922-29); and Alexandre Herculano de Carvalho, *História de Portugal desde o começo da monarchia até o fim do reinado de Afonso III*, 8 vols. (Lisbon, n.d.); rev. ed., by L. Gonzaga de Azevedo and D. M. Gomes dos Santos, 6 vols. (Lisbon, 1940-44). There are several one-volume narratives in English: Harold Livermore, *A History of Portugal* (Cambridge, 1947) and *A New History of Portugal* (Cambridge, 1966), and Charles E. Nowell, *A History of Portugal* (Princeton, 1958). The principal history of the Catholic Church in Portugal is Almeida's *História da Igreja em Portugal*, 4 vols. (Coimbra, 1910-22). The classic work on medieval administrative system is H. de Gama Barros, *História da administração pública em Portugal nos séculos XII a XIV*, 3 vols. (Lisbon, 1895-1914).

On the origins of Portugal, see Dan Stanislawski, *The Individuality of Portugal* (Austin, 1959); T. de Sousa Soares, *Reflexões sobre a origem e fundação de Portugal* (Coimbra, 1962) and *Contribuição para o estudo das origens do povo português* (Sa da Bandiera, 1970); A. A. Mundes Correa, *Raizes de Portugal* (Lisbon, 1944); and, for a political interpretation, Damião Peres, *Como nasceu Portugal* (Porto, 1942). M. Blöcker-Walter, *Alfons I von Portugal* (Zurich, 1966), is a recent study of the first Portuguese king. A useful recent economic history is Armando Castro, *A evolução económica de Portugal dos séculos XII a XV*, 4 vols. (Porto, 1964). A.-H. de Oliveira Marques, *A sociedade medieval portuguesa* (Lisbon, 1964; Eng. tr., Madison, Wis., 1970) is a topical analysis. On the grain question and agriculture, see Oliveira Marques's *A questão cerealífera durante a Idade Media* (Lisbon,

1962), and Virgínia Rau, *Sesmarias medievais portuguesas* (Lisbon, 1946). The Minho region is the principal focus of Alberto Sampaio's *Estudos históricos e económicos*, 2 vols. (Porto, 1923). See also Pierre David, *Etudes historiques sur la Galice et Portugal* (Coimbra, 1947). The basic cultural histories of Portugal are J. P. de Oliveira Martins, *A History of Iberian Civilization* (New York, 1930), and Antonio José Saraiva, *História da cultura em Portugal*, 3 vols. (Lisbon, 1950). Hernâni Cidade and Carlos Selvagem are preparing a projected eight-volume history of *Cultura portuguesa* (Lisbon, 1969—). On the idea of the crusade in Portugal, see Carl Erdmann, "Der Kreuzzugsgedanke in Portugal," *Historische Zeitschrift* 141, no. 1 (1929), pp. 23–53, translated as *A idea de cruzada em Portugal* (Coimbra, 1940).

Important aspects of political and social development are treated in "Os factores democráticos na formação do Portugal," in the first volume of Jaime Cortesão's *Obras completas*, 6 vols. (Lisbon, 1964); Edgar Prestage, *Royal Power and the Cortes in Portugal* (Watford, 1927); and two somewhat differing accounts of the 1383 revolt, Joel Serrão, *O carácter social da revolução de 1383* (Lisbon, 1946), and António Borges Coelho, *A revolução de 1383* (Lisbon, 1965).

Bailey Diffie's *Prelude to Empire: Portugal Overseas Before Henry the Navegator* (Lincoln, 1960), presents a brief synthesis of the medieval foundations of Portuguese maritime expansion. Other useful studies include Antonio Sergio, *En torno da designação de "monarquia agrária" dada à primeira época da nossa história* (Lisbon, 1941); Marcelo Caetano, *A administração municipal de Lisboa durante a primeira dinastia, 1179-1383* (Lisbon, 1951), and *Subsídios para a história das Cortes medievais* (Lisbon, 1963); Salvador Dias Arnaut, *A crise nacional, I: A sucessão de D. Fernando* (Coimbra, 1960); Virgínia Rau, *A exploração do sal de Setúbal* (Lisbon, 1951); and Oliveira Marques, *Hansa e Portugal na Idade Média* (Lisbon, 1959).

A very useful tool for Portuguese history is Joel Serrão, ed., *Dicionário de História de Portugal*, 4 vols. (Lisbon, 1963-1970). Joaquim V. Serrão's *História breve da historiografia portuguesa* (Lisbon, 1962), provides an account of pre-twentieth-century Portuguese historiography. For those especially interested in medieval Portugal, Oliveira Marques, *Guia do estudante de história medieval portuguesa* (Lisbon, 1964), is an important aid.

Chapter 7

There exists a vast corpus of Hispanic hagiography and ecclesiastical chronicles, but the real history of religion in the peninsula has received little attention. There are two general church histories: Z. García Villada, S.I., *Historia eclesiástica de España*, 5 vols. in 3 (Madrid, 1936), which stops at the eleventh century, and the dated work of Vincente de la Fuente, *Historia eclesiástica de España*, 4 vols. (Barcelona, 1855-59). Peter Linehan, *The Spanish Church and the Papacy in the Thirteenth Century* (Cambridge, 1971), is broader in scope than the title suggests. Aspects of the medieval church-state struggle are treated in Johannes Vincke, *Staat und Kirche in Katalonien und Aragon während des Mittelalters*, 2 vols. (Münster, 1931), and D. Mansilla Reoyo, *Iglesia castellano-leonesa y Curia romana en los tiempos del Rey San Fernando* (Madrid, 1945). The standard work on the pilgrimages to Santiago is L. Vázquez de Parga, J. M. Lacarra, and J. Uría Ríu, *Las peregrinaciones a Santiago de Compostela,* 3 vols. (Madrid, 1948). J. Pérez de Urbel, *Los monjes españoles en la Edad Media,* 2 vols. (Madrid, 1945), is of limited use; see also P. Maur Cocheril, *Etudes sur le monachisme en Espagne et au Portugal* (Paris, 1966). The establishment of church institutions in the Levant has been studied by R. I. Burns, S. J., *The Crusader Kingdom of Valencia,* 2 vols. (Cambridge, 1967). On the idea of the crusade, in addition to the work by José Goñi Gaztambide cited in bibliography 4, see Carl Erdmann, *Die Entstehung des Kreuzzuggedankens* (Stuttgart, 1935). An alternative strategy is the topic of Burns's "Christian-Islamic Confrontation in the West: The Thirteenth-Century Dream of Conversion," *American Historical Review* 76, no. 5 (Dec. 1971): 1386-1434.

The two leading rival interpretations of medieval Hispanic culture and society are Américo Castro's *The Spaniards* (Berkeley, 1971), rev. ed. of *The Structure of Spanish History*; and Sánchez Albornoz's *España: Un enigma histórico,* 2 vols. (Buenos Aires, 1956). Castro's *Aspectos del vivir hispánico* (Santiago de Chile, 1949, Madrid, 1970), is useful on late medieval Castilian religious currents.

The nineteenth-century polymath Marcelino Menéndez Pelayo produced a massive study of spiritual heterodoxy, *Historia de los heterodoxos españoles,* 8 vols. (Santander, 1946-48), but it is biased and out of date. Heresy in Catalonia has been studied by Jordi Ventura in "El Catarismo en Cataluña," *Boletín de la Real Academia de Buenas Letras* 28 (1959-60): 75-168, and "La Valdesía de Cataluña," 29 (1961-62): 275-317.

A classic history of Hispanic Jewry is José Amador de los Ríos's *Historia social, política y religiosa de los judíos de España y Portugal,* 2 vols. (Madrid, 1875-76). Two more recent accounts are A. A. Neuman, *The Jews in Spain,* 2 vols. (Philadelphia, 1942), and Yitzhak Baer, *A History of the Jews in Christian Spain,* 2 vols. (Philadelphia, 1961). Both concentrate on the Jewish communities in Catalonia-Aragon; Baer emphasizes political and interethnic relations, while Neuman gives more attention to internal Jewish history.

Chapter 8

The principal historian of the early Trastámara period in Castile is Luis Suárez Fernández. His most useful work is *Nobleza y monarquía. Puntos de vista sobre la historia castellana del siglo XV* (Valladolid, 1959), but see also *Intervención de Castilla en la Guerra de los Cien Años* (Valladolid, n.d.); *Navegación y comercio en el golfo de Vizcaya* (Madrid, 1959); *Juan I, rey de Castilla (1379-1390)* (Madrid, 1955); and *Castilla, El Cisma y la crisis conciliar (1378-1440)* (Madrid, 1960), a strictly narrative diplomatic study. The works of Suárez Fernández are complemented by P. E. Russell, *The English Intervention in Spain and Portugal in the time of Edward III and Richard II* (Oxford, 1955), which is written from an international point of view. Other significant studies of Castilian rulers of the period are Mercedes Gaibrois de Ballesteros, *Historia del reinado de Sancho IV de Castilla,* 3 vols. (Madrid, 1922-1928); Julio Valdeón Baruque, *Enrique II de Castilla* (Valladolid,

1966); and I. I. Macdonald, *Don Fernando de Antequera* (Oxford, 1948). There is further treatment of the nobility in E. Mitre Fernández, *Evolución de la nobleza en Castilla bajo Enrique III (1396-1406)* (Valladolid, 1968), and in "La Sociedad Castellana en la Baja Edad Media," *Cuadernos de Historia* (supplement to *Hispania*), 3 (Madrid, 1969). On the key institution of the *corregidor*, see B. González Alonso, *El corregidor castellano (1348-1808)* (Madrid, 1970). The best synthesis of fifteenth-century Catalonia is Vicens Vives's *Els Trastámares* (Barcelona, 1956). Pierre Vilar has written an excellent analysis of the Catalan decline, "El Declive catalán de la Baja Edad Media," published in his *Crecimiento y desarrollo* (Barcelona, 1965). Vicens Vives devoted much of his career to a nearly definitive series of studies of the political and social crisis of fifteenth-century Catalonia of which the principal are *Juan II de Aragon (1398-1479): Monarquía y revolución en la España del siglo XV* (Barcelona, 1953); *Historia de los remensas en el siglo XV* (Barcelona, 1945); and *El gran Sindicato Remensa (1488-1508)* (Barcelona, 1954); and *Política del Rey Católico en Cataluña* (Barcelona, 1940).

On Aragonese policy in Italy during the first half of the fifteenth century, see Alberto Boscolo, *La politica italiana di Ferdinando I d'Aragona* (Cagliari, 1954), and *I Parlamenti di Alfonso il Magnanimo* (Milan, 1953). The principal study of the Balearic peasant revolts is still José Ma. Quadrado, *Forenses y ciudadanos* (Palma de Mallorca, 1895). Valuable monographic studies of Catalonia, Aragon, and Mallorca during the fifteenth century will be found in the *IV Congreso de Historia de la Corona de Aragón* (Palma de Mallorca, 1955).

Aspects of social and economic conditions are treated in Julius Klein, *The Mesta* (Cambridge, 1920); Claude Carrère, *Barcelone, centre économique à l'époque des difficultés 1380-1462*, 2 vols. (Paris, 1967); Earl J. Hamilton, *Money, Prices and Wages in Valencia, Aragon and Navarre (1351-1500)* (Cambridge, 1936); Francisco Macho y Ortega, *Condición social de los mudéjares aragoneses (siglo XV)* (Zaragoza, 1923); an essay by Leopoldo Piles Ros, *La situación social de los moros de realengo en la Valencia del siglo XV* (Madrid, 1949); Jules Finot, *Rélations commerciales et maritimes entre la Flandre et l'Espagne au Moyen Age* (Paris, 1899); and María del Carmen Carlé, "Mercaderes en Castilla (1252-1512)," *Cuadernos de Historia de España* 21-22 (1954): 146-328.

A one-volume history of the Spanish navy has been written by Carlos Ibáñez de Ibero, *Historia de la Marina de guerra española desde el siglo XIII* (Madrid, 1943). A useful survey of Hispanic relations and activities in northwest Africa is provided by Tomás García Figueras, *Presencia de España en Berbería central y oriental* (Madrid, 1943). There is an excellent brief history of Nasrid Granada by M. A. Ladero Quesada, *Granada: Historia de un país islámico (1232-1571)* (Madrid, 1969).

Chapter 9

The best general accounts of Spain during the apex of its history are J. H. Elliott, *Imperial Spain 1469-1716* (New York, 1964), and A. Domínguez Ortiz, *The Golden Age of Spain 1516-1659* (New York, 1971). As a one-volume account of the sixteenth century, John Lynch, *Spain under the Habsburgs*, vol. 1, *Empire and Absolutism 1516-1598* (New York, 1964), supersedes R. Trevor Davies, *The Golden Century of Spain, 1501-1621* (London, 1937). The best synthesis of the period of the Catholic kings is J.-H. Mariéjol, *The Spain of Ferdinand and Isabella* (Rutgers, 1961). On Enrique IV there is Gregorio Marañón's *Ensayo biológico sobre Enrique IV y su tiempo* (Madrid, 1934). Orestes Ferrara, *L'Avènement d'Isabelle la Catholique* (Paris, 1958), is a revisionist study of the fateful contest between the two Castilian princesses. The principal biography of Isabel is Tarsicio de Azcona, *Isabel la Católica* (Madrid, 1964); see also Manuel Ballesteros Gaibrois, *La obra de Isabel la Católica* (Segovia, 1953). The key study of the early career of Fernando is Vicens Vives's *Historia crítica de la vida y reinado de Fernando II de Aragón* (Zaragoza, 1962). Luis Suárez Fernández, *Política internacional de Isabel la Catòlica*, 3 vols. (Valladolid, 1965-69), is not only the basic work on Spanish foreign policy in the late fifteenth century but is an important contribution to the study of the succession struggle. For the conquest of Granada, see M. A. Ladero Quesada, *Castilla y la conquista del Reino de Granada* (Valladolid, 1967).

Long controversy over the character of the revolt of the Castilian Comunidades has been largely resolved by the brilliant and exhaustive study of Joseph Pérez, *La Révolution des Comunidades de Castille 1520-21* (Bordeaux, 1970). Noteworthy works on the domestic social struggles of the period include J. A. Maravall, *Las Comunidades de Castilla* (Madrid, 1963); José Couselo Bouzas, *La guerra hermandina* (Santiago, 1926); Vicens Vives's *El gran Sindicato Remensa (1488-1508)* (Madrid, 1954); M. Danvila y Collado, *La Germanía de Valencia* (Madrid, 1884); and L. Piles Ros, "Aspectos sociales de la Germanía de Valencia," *Estudios de Historia Social de España* 2 (1952), pp. 431-78.

The most important books on internal politics and administration under Felipe II are A. González Palencia, *Gonzalo Pérez, secretario de Felipe II*, 2 vols. (Valencia, 1914); Gregorio Marañón, *Antonio Pérez*, 2 vols. (Madrid, 1958); Joan Reglá, *Felip II i Catalunya* (Barcelona, 1956); and the classic, if not fully useful, study by the Marqués de Pidal, *Historia de las alteraciones de Aragón*, 3 vols. (Madrid, 1862-63).

Chapter 10

The bibliography of the expansion is the most extensive of any segment of Hispanic historiography. Perhaps the best single volume on the expansion of Europe is John H. Parry, *The Age of Reconnaissance* (New York, 1963). Pierre Chaunu, *L'Expansion européenne du XIIIe au XVe siècle* (Paris, 1969), provides an excellent synthesis of the Hispanic expansion of the fifteenth century. The outstanding single-volume account of the Portuguese empire is Charles R. Boxer's *The Portuguese Seaborne Empire: 1415-1825* (New York, 1969), and Boxer has also written a useful brief survey, *Four Centuries of Portuguese Expansion, 1415-1825* (Johannesburg, 1965, Berkeley, 1969). There is more detail in the composite *História da expansão portuguesa no mundo*, 3 vols. (Lisbon, 1937-40).

Major works on the Portuguese discoveries include Luis Albuquerque, *Introdução à história dos descobrimentos* (Coimbra, 1962); Jaime Cortesão, *Descobrimentos portugueses,* 2 vols. (Lisbon, 1958, 1961); and Damião Peres, *História dos descobrimentos portugueses,* 2 vols. (Porto, 1943, 1946). The best study of the economics of the early phase is Vitorino de Magalhães Godinho, *A economia dos descobrimentos henriquinos* (Lisbon, 1962). On the socioeconomic background of fifteenth-century Portugal, see A. de Sousa Silva Costa Lobo, *História da sociedade em Portugal no século XV* (Lisbon, 1903); António Borges Coelho, *Raízes da expansão portuguesa* (Lisbon, 1964); Magalhães Godinho's *Os descobrimentos e a economia mundial,* 2 vols. (Lisbon, 1963-65); M. Nunes Dias, *O capitalismo monárquico português (1415-1549),* 2 vols. (Coimbra, 1963-64); and Veiga Simões, *Portugal, o ouro, as descobertas e a criação do Estado capitalista* (Lisbon, 1938).

The most important works dealing with Portuguese shipping and nautical science are Gago Coutinho, *A náutica dos descobrimentos,* 2 vols. (Lisbon, 1951-52); A. Fontoura da Costa, *A marinharia dos descobrimentos* (Lisbon, 1934, new ed., 1960); and Quirino da Fonseca, *A caravela portuguesa* (Coimbra, 1934).

On Portuguese expansion into the Atlantic islands, see Magalhães Godinho's *A economia das Canárias nos séculos XIV e XV* (Sao Paulo, 1952); Damião Peres, *A Madeira sob os donatários—séculos XV e XVI* (Funchal, 1914); and Jules Mee, *Histoire de la découverte des Iles Açores* (Ghent, 1901).

There is a succinct account of the Portuguese in Morocco by Brig. Gen. Vasco de Carvalho, *La Domination portugaise au Maroc* (Lisbon, 1942), which may be supplemented by David Lopes's article, "Les Portugais au Maroc, 1415-1769," in the *Revue d'Histoire Moderne* 14 (1939), pp. 337-68. Economic factors are studied in E. W. Bovill, *The Golden Trade of the Moors* (Oxford, 1958), and two works by Magalhães Godinho, *História económica e social da expansão: Marrocos* (Lisbon, 1947), and *O "Mediterráneo" saariano e as caravanas do ouro—séculos XI-XV* (Sao Paulo, 1955).

For Portuguese expansion into Africa see J. W. Blake, *European Beginnings in West Africa, 1454-1478* (London, 1937); T. G. McCall, *The Portuguese in South Africa, 1505-1795* (London, 1927); Eric Axelson, *South-East Africa, 1488-1530* (London, 1940); and C. F. Rey, *The Romance of the Portuguese in Abyssinia* (London, 1929).

There is a general introduction to the Portuguese in the East by M. de Faria e Sousa, *Asia portuguesa,* 3 vols. (Porto, 1945). On the long voyages, see Julio Gonçalves, *Os portugueses e o mar das Indias* (Lisbon, 1947), and S. E. Morison, *Portuguese Voyages to America in the Fifteenth Century* (Cambridge, 1940). Standard accounts of the Portuguese in south Asia include K. G. Jayne, *Vasco da Gama and His Successors* (London, 1910); R. S. Whiteway, *The Rise of the Portuguese Power in India* (Westminster, 1899); H. M. Stephens, *Albuquerque* (London, 1892); and Edgar Prestage, *Afonso de Albuquerque* (Watford, 1929). A. Martins Janeira, *O impacte português sobre a civilização japonesa* (Lisbon, 1970), studies Portuguese cultural influence.

The two best general accounts of the Spanish empire overseas are J. H. Parry, *The Spanish Seaborne Empire* (London, 1966), and Charles Gibson,

Spain in America (New York, 1966). An older account that emphasizes administrative history is C. H. Haring, *The Spanish Empire in America* (New York, 1947). The major study of Spanish navy and shipping is Cesáreo Fernández Duro, *Armada española desde la unión de los reinos,* 9 vols. (Madrid, 1895-1903). For Cantabrian shipping, see Antonio Ballesteros y Beretta, *La marina cántabra y Juan de la Cosa* (Santander, 1954). Ruth Pike, *Enterprise and Adventure: The Genoese in Seville and the Opening of the New World* (Ithaca, 1966), deals with the Genoese.

The best general Spanish account of the discovery and conquest of Spanish America is Francisco Morales Padrón, *Historia del descubrimiento y conquista de América* (Madrid, 1963). There are many books on Columbus. The best is S. E. Morison, *Admiral of the Ocean Sea,* 2 vols. (Boston, 1942). J. Pérez de Tudela Bueso, *Las armadas de Indias y los orígenes de la política de colonización* (Madrid, 1956), is also useful. F. A. Kirkpatrick, *The Spanish Conquistadores* (London, 1934), is still probably the best brief introduction to the conquerors. On the Spanish in Asia, see John L. Phelan, *The Hispanization of the Philippines* (Berkeley, 1959).

Chapter 11

The principal study of the reform of the Spanish episcopate is P. Tarsicio de Azcona, *La elección y reforma del episcopado español en tiempo de los reyes Católicos* (Madrid, 1960). On the reform of the Dominicans, see V. Beltrán de Heredia, *Historia de la reforma de la Provincia de España, 1450-1550* (Rome, 1939). Further material may be gleaned from the relevant sections of Vicente de la Fuente's *Historia eclesiástica de España,* 4 vols. (Madrid, 1855-59). Robert Ricard, *La Conquête spirituelle du Mexique* (Paris, 1933), is the best study of the main missionary enterprise of the Castilian Church during the sixteenth century. J. Bada, *Situació religiosa de Barcelona en el segle XVI* (Barcelona, 1970), is an excellent local religious study.

The fundamental study of the Inquisition remains Henry C. Lea's *The Spanish Inquisition,* 4 vols. (New York, 1906-1907). The best Spanish Catholic work is B. Llorca, S.J., *La Inquisición en España* (Madrid, 1936). Juan Antonio Llorente's classic work has recently appeared in an American edition as *A Critical History of the Inquisition of Spain* (Williamstown, Mass., 1971). Henry Kamen, *The Spanish Inquisition* (London, 1965), presents a lively monocausal interpretation. There are also useful works by Miguel de la Pinta Llorente, O.S.A.: *La Inquisición española* (Madrid, 1948); *La Inquisición española y los problemas de la cultura y de la intolerancia,* 2 vols. (Madrid, 1953, 1958); and *Aspectos históricos del sentimiento religioso en España* (Madrid, 1961).

The major account of Spanish Jews and Conversos after 1492 is Julio Caro Baroja, *Los judíos en la España moderna y contemporánea,* 3 vols. (Madrid, 1961), while the best brief treatment is A. Domínguez Ortiz, *Los Judeoconversos en España y América* (Madrid, 1971). B. Netanyahu, *The Marranos of Spain from the Late 14th to the Early 16th Century* (New York, 1966), provides material to refute the charge of crypto-Judaism.

General aspects of Christian heresy and heterodoxy are considered in Marcelino Menéndez Pelayo's *Historia de los heterodoxos españoles*, 8 vols. (Santander, 1946-48), and in E. Schäfer, *Beiträge zur Geschichte des spanischen Protestantismus*, 3 vols. (Gütersloh, 1902). The historian of Spanish Erasmianism is Marcel Bataillon, *Erasmo y España*, rev. ed., 2 vols. (Mexico City, 1950). J. E. Longhurst, *Luther's Ghost in Spain* (Lawrence, 1969), treats manifestations of Christian heterodoxy and their repression during this period. See also Domingo de Santa Teresa, *Juan de Valdés* (Rome, 1957).

Curiously enough, there are no major works on the Spanish Counter-Reformation. Among the more useful titles are R. Burgos, *España en Trento* (Madrid, 1941); C. Gutiérrez, *Españoles en Trento* (Valladolid, 1951); V. D. Carro, *Pedro de Soto y las controversias político-teológicas en el siglo XVI* (Salamanca, 1931); F. Cereceda, *Diego Laínez en la Europa religiosa de su tiempo, 1512-1565*, 2 vols. (Madrid, 1945-46); A. Astrain, *Historia de la Compañía de Jesús*, 7 vols. (Madrid, 1912-25); and J. Brodrick, S.J., *The Origin of the Jesuits* (London, 1948). The only study of censorship is A. Rumeu de Armas, *Historia de la censura literaria gubernativa en España* (Madrid, 1940).

There are two multivolume histories of higher education in Spain: C. Ma. Ajo G. y Sáinz de Zúñiga, *Historia de las universidades hispánicas* (1957-), whose five volumes to date reach to the eighteenth century, and Vicente de la Fuente, *Historia de las universidades, colegios y demás establecimientos de enseñanza en España*, 3 vols. (Madrid, 1884-85). See also G. Reynier, *La Vie universitaire dans l'ancienne Espagne* (Paris, 1902). On the concepts of progress and modernity in sixteenth-century Spain, there are two pioneering works by José Antonio Maravall, *Los factores de la idea de progreso en el renacimiento español* (Madrid, 1963), and *Antiguos y modernos: La idea de progreso en el desarrollo inicial de una sociedad* (Madrid, 1966). Very little exists in the way of critical, analytical study of sixteenth-century Spanish thought. One of the best books is Bernice Hamilton, *Spanish Political Thought of the Sixteenth Century* (Oxford, 1963). Two studies of Spanish scholasticism that might be consulted are José M. Gallegos Rocafull, *El hombre y el mundo de los teólogos españoles del Siglo de Oro* (Mexico City, 1946), and Marcial Solana's less imaginative *Los grandes escolásticos españoles de los siglos XVI y XVII* (Madrid, 1928). On two key figures, see Guenther Lewy, *Constitutionalism and Statecraft during the Golden Age of Spain: A Study of the Political Philosophy of Juan de Mariana, S.J.* (Geneva, 1960), and V. Beltrán de Heredia, *Francisco de Vitoria* (Madrid, 1939). Lewis Hanke's *The Spanish Struggle for Justice in the Conquest of America* (Philadelphia, 1949), is a classic study of the effort to apply enlightened moral and juridical norms to Spanish America.

For the development of Spanish science, the basic study is Marcelino Menéndez Pelayo's *La ciencia española*, 3 vols. (Madrid, 1887-89). See also the symposium of *Estudios sobre la ciencia española del siglo XVI* (Madrid, 1935); J. Rey Pastor, *Los matemáticos españoles: Siglo XVI* (Toledo, 1926); and, on economic thought, M. Grice-Hutchinson, *The School of Salamanca. Readings in Spanish Economic Theory, 1544-1605* (Oxford, 1952).

Chapter 12

There is no good general study of Portugal or its thalassocracy in the sixteenth century. João Lucio d'Azevedo, *Epocas de Portugal económico* (Lisbon, 1929), was a pioneering study of phases of Portuguese economic history. On the last Aviz rulers, see Alfredo Pimenta, *D. João III* (Porto, 1936), and J. M. de Queiroz Velloso, *D. Sebastião* (Lisbon, 1943), and *O reinado do Cardenal D. Henrique* (Lisbon, 1946). E. W. Bovill, *The Battle of Alcazar* (London, 1952), narrates the disaster of 1578. The principal student of the Spanish succession is A. Danvila, *Felipe II y el rey D. Sebastián* (Madrid, 1954), and *Felipe II y la sucesión de Portugal* (Madrid, 1956). On Sebastianism, see Lucio d'Azevedo, *A evoluçao do Sebastianismo* (Lisbon, 1916). For social and economic affairs, in addition to the works cited in bibliography 6, see Virgínia Rau, *Estudos de história económica* (Lisbon, 1961).

Sixteenth-century Portuguese Catholicism is treated in J. S. da Silva Dias, *Correntes de sentimento religioso em Portugal*, 2 vols. (Coimbra, 1960). The major account of the Portuguese Inquisition is by Alexandre Herculano de Carvalho; the American edition is entitled *History of the Origins and Establishment of the Portuguese Inquisition* (Stanford, 1926). See also A. J. Saraiva's *A Inquisição portuguesa*, rev. ed. (Lisbon, 1963). J. Mendes dos Remedios, *Os judeus em Portugal* (Coimbra, 1895), concentrates on the fifteenth and sixteenth centuries. The principal study of the *Cristãos novos* is Lucio d'Azevedo's *Historia dos Christãos novos portugueses* (Lisbon, 1921).

On Portuguese culture of this period, see Marcel Bataillon, *Etudes sur le Portugal au temps de l'humanisme* (Coimbra, 1952); Joaquim de Carvalho, *Estudos sobre a cultura portuguesa do século XVI*, 2 vols. (Coimbra, 1947-48); Cardinal Cerejeira, *O renascimento em Portugal* (Coimbra, 1949); and F. A. Costa Cabral, *D. João II e a renascença portuguesa* (Lisbon, 1914). Robert C. Smith, *The Art of Portugal, 1500-1800* (New York, 1968), is an excellent treatment of early modern Portuguese art.

James Duffy, *Shipwreck and Empire* (Cambridge, 1955), illuminates the *carreira da India*. Charles R. Boxer has written key works on the Portuguese in the East: *The Christian Century in Japan, 1549-1650* (Berkeley, 1951); *Fidalgos in the Far East, 1550-1770* (The Hague, 1948); and also *Race Relations in the Portuguese Colonial Empire 1415-1825* (Oxford, 1963). For the early establishment of Portuguese missions, see Antonio da Silva Rego, *História das Missões do Padroado português do Oriente*, vol. 1, *India, 1500-1542* (Lisbon, 1949). The use of Portuguese as lingua franca in the East is sporadically studied by David Lopes, *A expansão da Língua portuguesa no Oriente durante os séculos XVI, XVII e XVIII* (Barcelos, 1936).

Chapter 13

The best Spanish study of foreign affairs in the sixteenth century is Manuel Fernández Alvarez, *Política mundial de Carlos V y Felipe II* (Madrid, 1966). Fernand Braudel, *La Méditerranée et le monde méditerranéen à l'époque de*

Philippe II, rev. ed. (Paris, 1966), is a classic synthesis of comparative history. Aside from the work of Fernández Alvarez, the best biographies of Carlos V are Karl Brandi, *Charles V*, Eng. tr. (London, 1965), and Royall Tyler, *The Emperor Charles V* (London, 1956). On Felipe II, see C. Bratli, *Felipe II* (Madrid, 1940); Fernández Alvarez's *Felipe II* (Madrid, 1956); Rafael Altamira's *Ensayo sobre Felipe II* (Mexico City, 1950); and Henri Lapeyre's "Autour de Philippe II," *Bulletin Hispanique* 59 (1957): 152-75.

On Spanish policy in North Africa there is Giancarlo Sorgia, *La política nord-africana di Carlo V* (Padua, 1963). Bohdan Chudoba, *Spain and the Empire, 1519-1643* (Chicago, 1952), is useful on relations with the Austrian Habsburgs. Lucien Febvre, *Philippe II et la Franche Comté* (Paris, 1921), deals with the Spanish Habsburgs' French province. On the crown's Portuguese policy, see Alfonso Danvila, *Felipe II y la sucesión de Portugal* (Madrid, 1956), and J. M. Rubio, *Felipe II de España, rey de Portugal* (Madrid, 1939). Hans Koenigsberger, *The Government of Sicily under Philip II of Spain* (London, 1951), presents an interesting case study. Two biographies of key imperial figures are M. Van Durme, *El Cardenal Granvela* (Barcelona, 1957), and L. Van der Essen, *Alexandre Farnèse*, 5 vols. (Brussels, 1933-37). The finest narrative of any event in sixteenth-century Spanish history is Garrett Mattingly's *The Armada* (Boston, 1959).

Two works by J. A. Maravall are important on political theory: *Carlos V y el pensamiento político del Renacimiento* (Madrid, 1960), and *La teoría española del Estado en el siglo XVII* (Madrid, 1944). Spanish attitudes toward the imperial policies of Carlos V are treated in J. Sánchez Montes, *Franceses, protestantes, turcos: Los españoles ante la política internacional de Carlos V* (Madrid, 1951), and in J. M. Jover, *Carlos V y los españoles* (Madrid, 1960).

Genesis of the Black Legend has been studied by Sverker Arnoldsson, *La leyenda negra* (Göteborg, 1960). On its elaboration in England and later in the United States, see William S. Maltby, *The Black Legend in England* (Durham, N.C., 1971), and Philip W. Powell, *Tree of Hate* (New York, 1971).

Chapter 14

A general introduction to sixteenth-century Spanish society is provided by M. Fernández Alvarez, *La sociedad española del Renacimiento* (Salamanca, 1970). The key question of the sixteenth-century Spanish economy—the land—has received little attention. For an introductory essay, see Carmelo Viñas Mey, *El problema de la tierra en la España de los siglos XVI y XVII* (Madrid, 1941), supplemented by Noel Salomon's monograph, *La Campagne de Nouvelle Castile à la fin du XVIe siècle* (Paris, 1964).

The basic question of seigneurial domain, its extent and influence, has been examined in an important work: Alfonso Ma. Guilarte, *El régimen señorial en el siglo XVI* (Madrid, 1962). Though somewhat defective in analysis, the classic study of Spanish bullion and the inflation is Earl J. Hamilton, *American Treasure and the Price Revolution in Spain, 1501-1650* (Cambridge,

1934). On government finance and economic policy, see Ramón Carande, *Carlos V y sus banqueros*, 3 vols. (Madrid, 1943, 1949), a key work, and also J. Larraz, *La época del mercantilismo en España, 1500-1700* (Madrid, 1943). Some of the best work in Spanish social and economic history of the imperial period has been done by French scholars. The monumental piece of research from this group is Pierre and Huguette Chaunu's *Séville et l'Atlantique (1504-1650)*, 8 vols. (Paris, 1955-59). There are three important works by Henri Lapeyre: *Simón Ruiz et les Asientos de Philippe II* (Paris, 1953); *Une Famille de marchands: Les Ruiz* (Paris, 1955); and, especially, *Géographie de l'Espagne morisque* (Paris, 1959). On two of the most important cities of the century, there are Bartolomé Bennassar, *Valladolid au Siècle d'Or* (Paris, 1966); Domínguez Ortiz's brief *Orto y ocaso de Sevilla* (Seville, 1946); and Ruth Pike, *Aristocrats and Traders. Sevillian Society in the Sixteenth Century* (Ithaca, 1972).

Broader aspects of Spanish commerce and finance are treated in Jacob van Kleveren, *Europäische Wirtschaftsgeschichte Spaniens von 16. und 17. Jahrhunderts* (Stuttgart, 1960). There is one monograph on the grain problem, E. Ibarra y Rodríguez, *El problema cerealista en España durante el reinado de los Reyes Católicos (1475-1516)* (Madrid, 1942). Aspects of the Vizcayan economy have been studied by J. A. García de Cortázar, *Vizcaya en el siglo XV (Bilbao, 1966)*.

On the *limpieza de sangre* mania, see A. A. Sicroff, *Les Controverses des statuts de "Pureté de Sang" en Espagne du XVe au XVIe siècle* (Paris, 1960). The best study of Morisco society is Julio Caro Baroja, *Los moriscos del reino de Granada* (Madrid, 1957), and, on slavery, there is Domínguez Ortiz's "La esclavitud en Castilla durante la Edad Moderna," *Estudios de Historia Social de España* 2 (1952): 369-428.

Chapter 15

The best introduction to seventeenth-century Spain is volume 2 of John Lynch's *Spain under the Habsburgs*, entitled *Spain and America 1598-1700* (London, 1969). It should be supplemented with *La sociedad española en el siglo XVII*, 2 vols. (Madrid, 1964-70), an excellent social history by the chief Spanish specialist in that period, Antonio Domínguez Ortiz, who has also published an important volume of articles, *Crisis y decadencia de la España de los Austrias* (Barcelona, 1969). The classic studies by the great Spanish statesman, Antonio Cánovas del Castillo, still retain their usefulness. See his *Historia de la decadencia española* (Madrid, 1854, 1911), and *Estudios del reinado de Felipe IV*, 2 vols. (Madrid, 1888-89, 1927); and also Martin Hume's *The Court of Philip IV* (London, 1907). José Deleito y Piñuela has written a series of seven books on Spanish life during the era of Felipe IV. Perhaps the best of these is *La vida religiosa española bajo el cuarto Felipe* (Madrid, 1952), but see also his *El rey se divierte (1928), Sólo Madrid es corte (1942)*, and *El declinar de la monarquía española* (1947), all published in Madrid. The best history of court and government affairs under Carlos II is Gabriel Maura y Gamazo's *Vida y reinado de Carlos II*, 3 vols. (Madrid,

1942); there is a superficial biography by J. Langdon Davies, *Charles the Bewitched* (London, 1962). J. A. Maravall's *La teoría española del Estado en el siglo XVII* (Madrid, 1944), helps to explain political attitudes. The only biography of Olivares is Gregorio Marañón's *El Conde-Duque de Olivares* (Madrid, 1952), primarily a psychological study. There are also useful monographs on the issue of the *validos,* aristocratic conspiracy, the "Jewish problem," and financial problems: Francisco T. Valiente, *Los validos en la monarquía española del siglo XVII* (Madrid, 1963); R. Ezquerra Abadía, *La conspiración del Duque de Híjar, 1648* (Madrid, 1934); J. Caro Baroja, *La sociedad criptojudía en la corte de Felipe IV* (Madrid, 1963); Domínguez Ortiz, *Política y hacienda de Felipe IV* (Madrid, 1960); and J. L. Sureda Carrión, *La Hacienda castellana y los economistas del siglo XVII* (Madrid, n.d.).

The Catalan rebellion is the subject of one of the major studies in seventeenth-century Spain, John Elliott's *The Revolt of the Catalans* (Cambridge, 1963). See also José Sanabre, *La acción de Francia en Cataluña* (Barcelona, 1956); and Joan Reglà, *Els virreis de Catalunya* (Barcelona, 1962), and *El bandolerisme català del barroc* (Barcelona, 1966). Social problems in the Valencia region are treated in Reglà's *Aproximació a la història del País Valencià* (Valencia, 1968), and F. de P. Momblanch y Gonzálbez, *La segunda Germanía del reino de Valencia* (Alicante, 1957). S. García Martínez, *Els fonaments del País Valencià modern* (Valencia, 1968), is a key work that deals with the Valencian resurgence of the late seventeenth century.

Three basic studies in cultural history are Ludwig Pfandl's *Spanische Kultur und Sitte des 16. und 17. Jahrhunderts* (Kempten, 1924); R. Bouvier, *L'Espagne de Quevedo* (Paris, 1936); and Carl Justi's *Diego Velázquez und sein Jahrhundert* (Zurich, 1933). For science and the beginning of modern critical philosophy, see J. M. López Piñero, *La introducción de la ciencia moderna en España* (Barcelona, 1969), and O. V. Quiroz Martínez, *La introducción de la filosofía moderna en España* (Mexico City, 1949).

The classic comparison between Spain and Poland in this period was J. Lelewel's *Parallèle historique entre l'Espagne et la Pologne au XVI, XVII, XVIIIe siècles* (Paris, 1836). This thesis is updated by M. Malowist, "Europe de l'Est et les Pays Ibériques: Analogies et Contrastes," in the University of Barcelona's *Homenaje a Jaime Vicens Vives,* vol. 1 (Barcelona, 1965), pp. 85–93. Janusz Tazmir, *Szlachta i konkwistadorzy* (Warsaw, 1969), provides interesting examples of the attitude of the Polish elite toward Spain.

Index to Both Volumes

cline, 160-62; revolt of 1462, 166-68; compared with Castile, 168-69; under Catholic Kings, 176-78; early explorations, 189-90; dispute with Habsburgs, 186; measures against Jews, 207-8; economy in imperial age, 275-77; revolt of 1640-1652, 313-14; recovery of, 322; Bourbon subjugation of, 354-55; industrial growth, 386-87, 478, 501; compared with Portugal, 396-97; Carlism in, 438-39, 471; literary revival, 505-6; regionalism in, 496, 507-8, 579, 587, 605-6; autonomist revolt, 637; autonomy restored, 641; social revolution of 1936, 647-48; Nationalist conquest of, 657; mentioned, 28, 40, 51, 60, 64, 73, 77, 593

Cataluña en Espana, 507
Cataluña y los catalanes, 507
Catarina, queen of Portugal, 241
Catarina of Portugal, queen of England, 397
Cateau-Cambrésis, treaty of, 257
Cathari religion. *See* Albigensianism
Catholic Action, 604
Catholic Confederation (CEDA): political goals, 635; enters government, 636; unable to form ministry, 639; joins National Front, 640; mentioned, 637, 638
Catholicism: Visigothic conversion, 9; in medieval Portugal, 123-25; decline of Mozarab church, 131-32; medieval monasticism, 135; and crusading principle, 135-36; and Muslims, 136-37; medieval reform movements, 138-39; Hispanic variants, 140; reform under Catholic kings, 206-7; and Counter-Reformation, 216-20; intellectual activity, 215-16, 220-21; in sixteenth-century Spain, 222-23; in sixteenth-century Portugal, 228-31; Spanish clerical decline, 303-4, 377-78; Portuguese decline, 410; recognized as state religion, 427, 465; low point of, 441-42; and liberalism, 484-85; Portuguese revival, 524; Spanish revival, 604; mentioned, 489, 671. *See also* Church, the; Papacy
Catholic Kings. *See* Fernando the Catholic; Isabel the Catholic

Catholic peasants confederation (CONCA), 604
Catholic Union of Fribourg, 667
Catholic Union party, 494, 496
Cavaleiros vilãos, 121
Cavaller class, 101
Cazorla, treaty of, 72, 95
Celtiberians, 4, 6
Celtic tribes, 2, 4
Censalistes, 160
Censo mortages, 157, 277, 279, 377, 379
Central Commission, 444
Central Powers, 566
Centre Català, 507, 508
Centrist party, 556
Centro Académico da Democracia Cristã (CADC), 664
Cervantes, Miguel de, 306
Cervera, University of, 369
Cesantes, 472
Ceylon, 189, 233, 391, 392, 397
Chagas, João, 561, 562, 564
Chapí, 505
Charlemagne, 35, 86
Charles II, king of England, 398
Charles VIII, king of France, 248
Charter of 1826, 520, 528, 530, 546
China, 189, 200, 235, 392, 682
Chindaswinth, Visigothic king, 15
Christ, Order of, 194
Church, the: in Roman Hispania 7-8; in Visigothic Hispania, 11-12; in Muslim Hispania, 22; and neo-Gothic idea, 37; promotes crusades, 66-67; and state in Portugal, 124, 231, 409, 559-60; dispute over episcopal primacy, 132; medieval institutionalization, 132-33; wealth of, 138, 271; and reconquered areas, 137-38; taxes on, 282; reforms under Carlos III, 364; clerical decline, 377-78, 484-85; disamortized in Spain, 419, 441, 451, 476-77; disamortized in Portugal, 523-24; educational decline in Portugal, 546; and modern anticlericalism, 582; consequences of expropriation, 603; and Primo de Rivera dictatorship, 620; and Spanish Constitution of 1931, 631; and Franco, 653, 696; reinstated

TEXT DESIGNED
BY IRVING PERKINS
JACKET DESIGNED BY KAREN FOGET
MANUFACTURED BY THE GEORGE BANTA CO., INC., MENASHA, WISCONSIN
TEXT AND DISPLAY LINES ARE SET IN TIMES ROMAN, DISPLAY
FIGURES IN BODONI BOLD

Library of Congress Cataloging in Publication Data
Payne, Stanley G
A history of Spain and Portugal.
Bibliography: p. 333-349.
1. Spain—History.   2. Portugal—History.   I.   Title.
DP66.P382   946   72-7992   l
ISBN 0-299-06270-8   (v. 1)

The illustrations that follow have been made available through the generosity of the Spanish cultural relations office, the Casa de Portugal (New York), and Ruiz Vernacci of Madrid. Maps in this volume were prepared by the University of Wisconsin Cartographic Laboratory.

Roman theater at Mérida, capital of Roman Lusitania

The Roman aqueduct at Segovia

Palace of Ramiro I on Monte Naranco above Oviedo

Late medieval painting of
Alfonso III el Magno of Asturias

Interior of the Great Mosque at Córdoba

Alfonso X el Sabio of Castile

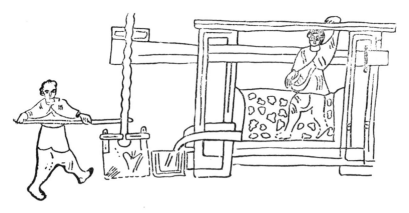

Scenes of medieval Spanish peasant life

Cathedral of Burgos

Castle of La Mota (Medina del Campo)

Castle of Belmonte (Cuenca)

The Alcázar of Segovia

*Auto de Fe Presided over
by Sto. Domingo de Guzmán,*
Pedro Berruguete (El Prado)

Cardinal Cisneros

Fernando and Isabel, the Catholic Kings

Carlos V

REGIMIENTO DE
NAVEGACION,
En que se côtienen las reglas, declaraciones
y auisos del libro del arte de nauegar. Fe-
cho por el maestro Pedro de Medina
vezino de Seuilla.
Con priuillegio real.

Title page of Pedro de Medina's
Regimiento de Navegación

Sixteenth-century galleons

Felipe II, by Sánchez Coello (El Prado)

Felipe IV

Carlos II

The Infante D. Henrique. Detail of
the polyptic by Nuno Gonçalves

Vasco da Gama. Portrait in the
collection of the Sociedade da Geografia

Afonso de Albuquerque, Viceroy of
the Indies

Royal cloister in the
great monastery at Batalha, Manueline style

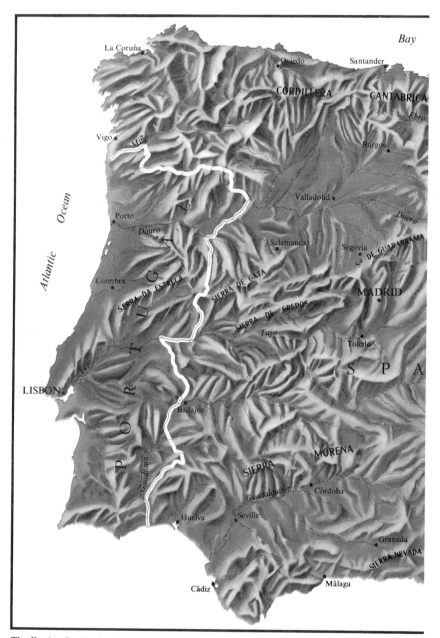

The Iberian Peninsula

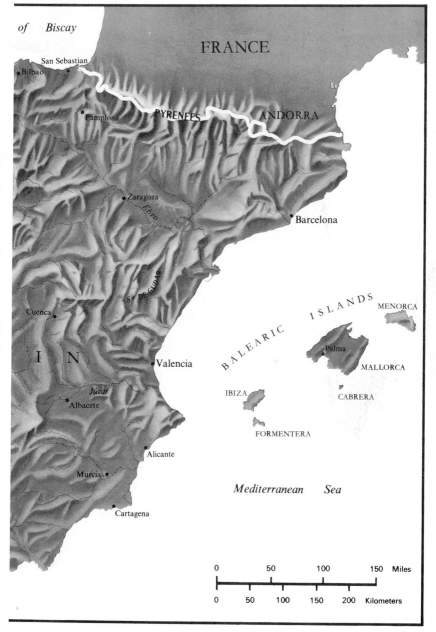

of Biscay

FRANCE

San Sebastian
Bilbao

PYRENEES

ANDORRA

Pamplona

Zaragoza

Ebro

Barcelona

Sa DE GUDAR

Cuenca

BALEARIC

ISLANDS

MENORCA

Palma

I N

Valencia

IBIZA

MALLORCA

CABRERA

Júcar

Albacete

FORMENTERA

Alicante

Murcia

Mediterranean   Sea

Cartagena

0	50	100	150 Miles
0	50	100	150	200 Kilometers

UWCL

Manueline exterior of the Mosteiro dos Jerónimos, Lisbon

Sebastião